HOPE IS NOT A STRATEGY

Be Deliberate About Alignment And Culture

SIRISHA AND HARISH BHAMIDIPATI

STARDOM BOOKS

www.StardomBooks.com

STARDOM BOOKS
A Division of Stardom Publishing
and infoYOGIS Technologies.
105-501 Silverside Road
Wilmington, DE 19809

Copyright © 2023 by Sirisha and Harish Bhamidipati

This book is copyright under the Berne Convention.
No reproduction without permission.
All rights reserved.

The right of Sirisha and Harish Bhamidipati
to be identified as the author of this work has been asserted by them in
accordance with sections 77 and 78 of the Copyright, Designs and
Patents Act, 1988.

FIRST EDITION DECEMBER 2023

STARDOM BOOKS

A Division of Stardom Alliance
105-501 Silverside Road Wilmington, DE 19809, USA

www.stardombooks.com

Stardom Books, United States
Stardom Books, India

The author and publishers have made all reasonable efforts to contact copyright-holders for permission, and apologize for any omissions or errors in the form of credits given. Corrections may be made to future editions.

HOPE IS NOT A STRATEGY

Sirisha and Harish Bhamidipati

p. 590
cm. 15.24 X 22.86

Category: Business and Economics - Organizational Development

ISBN: 978-1-957456-36-2

DEDICATION

To all founders and leaders who believed in us and applied the Dilemmas Resolution Framework to deliberately build alignment and culture in their teams.

In their illuminating book, "Hope is not a Strategy: Be Deliberate About Alignment and Culture," authors Sirisha and Harish unlock the transformative power of the Dilemmas Resolution Framework (DRF). Drawing from their expertise and partnership with Uplers, the authors shed light on the vital process of articulating and fostering a resonant company culture. Sirisha and Harish take us beyond mere definitions, unveiling a holistic approach to embedding values into daily operations. Their collaborative method empowers companies to cultivate culture playbooks that breathe life into their ideals. 'Hope Is Not A Strategy' presents an invaluable roadmap for businesses of all sizes, from startups to established enterprises, as they embark on the journey of cultural transformation. Dive into this enlightening guide and discover how strategic intentionality, thoughtful collaboration, and the DRF can shape a cohesive and thriving organizational culture.

Jaymin Bhuptani,
CEO – Uplers

Using the framework and guidance that Sirisha and Harish have codified in this book, we founders at Growsari were able to clarify better and codify our cultural values for wider dissemination. During the sessions facilitated by Sirisha, we realized how inconsistent and even unclear our previous articulation of values was, and from the wider team's perspective, difficult to use as a daily touchstone. At the same time, using the DRF, we vastly improved the value and purpose statements and got tips on how to socialize them within the organization. It's excellent to see that Sirisha and Harish have put their approach together into a very readable and actionable book - required reading for any founder who is looking to build a lasting company and understands the importance of deliberate culture building.

Siddhartha Kongara,
CTO, Growsari

Unlocking the boundless potential of organizational culture, the Dilemmas Resolution Framework is profound and strikes at the heart of a company's essence. In the spirit of revered texts across faiths, like Guru Granth Sahib in Sikhism, it helped us create a guide that presents the beacon for Pilgrim. With wisdom gleaned from navigating growth, the authors impart practical methodologies for culture articulation. The framework defines binaries, offering flexibility for unique growth paths. As organizations embark on scaling, "Hope is not a Strategy" will help leaders foster a culture that thrives and endures.

Anurag Kedia and Gagandeep M
Co-founders, Pilgrim

"Hope Is Not A Strategy" is an enthralling book that delivers a rational framework for developing organizational culture by laying a strong foundation of clear goals, reflecting on existing culture and realigning the values to reintroduce an ideal workplace culture. The methodology brings a fresh outlook on the existing challenges, which can prove to be an uphill climb for many enterprises. It breaks down the dilemmas and explains how all strategies, values, ethics, and goals can be artistically funneled to lead thriving businesses by providing a remedial model. It is an insightful and well-researched book and a must-read for all leaders.

Amit Gainda,
Managing Director and CEO, Avanse Financial Services

Building a business is a daunting task and demands a lot from the startup to survive and thrive. The path to success is treacherous, demanding a lot from those who embark on the journey, and not just the founders but also the rest of the members. At the end of the day, if the founder-level ownership doesn't propagate amongst the team, it is hard for the organization to take moonshots. Articulating the values and purpose not just justifies and alleviates the grind and the uncertainty, it even makes it pleasurable and desirable as a higher meaning is attached to it.

> *"He who knows why can bear any how."*
> - Nietsche

Culture is assumed to be a nebulous concept and often limits its definition to employee experience. But culture is how decisions are made in the org, what traits get rewarded, what it takes to thrive in the organization, who gets promoted, and what gets rewarded will be repeated.

The most difficult and critical part of articulated culture is making it part of the daily conversation and daily activities. It starts with ensuring the defined values are actionable and specific else no matter what, they will be just decorative words on the walls. Hence, the first step is to get that part right, which itself takes effort and time, it is a process, and you need to keep at it for a period of time till you get it right. This is where the Dilemmas Resolution Framework created by Sirisha and Harish was helpful in moving the conversation to the next realm.

The second part of it is creating rituals and processes for the articulated culture, the never-ending one for a growing organization.

Girish Shilamkar,
Co-founder and CEO, InfraCloud Technology Solutions

CONTENTS

Foreword — i
Acknowledgments — iii
Author's Note — v
How To Use This Book — vii

The Imperative of Deliberate Culture Building — 1

Step-By-Step Process of Building Culture

Step 1: Define the Purpose and the Desired Identity — 13

Step 2: Unearth the Existing Cultural Blueprint — 25

2.1	Foundation of the Organization	30
2.2	Employee Well-Being and Growth	39
2.3	Effective Communication and Transparency	50
2.4	Performance and Innovation	58
2.5	Stakeholder Relations and Responsibility	66
2.6	Adaptability and Learning	74
2.7	Decision-Making and Governance	82

Step 3: Deliberately Choose Your Identity Using the Dilemmas Resolution Framework (DRF) — 89

3.1	Organization Outlook Dilemmas	93
3.2	Organization Structure Dilemmas	165
3.3	Communication Dilemmas	194

3.4	Execution Dilemmas	236
3.5	Decision-Making Dilemmas	277
3.6	Collaboration Dilemmas	317
3.7	Innovation and Risk-Taking Dilemmas	356
3.8	People Dilemmas	393
3.9	Customer Dilemmas	428
3.10	Ethics and Social Responsibility Dilemmas	463
3.11	Leadership Dilemmas	498

Step 4: Discover Your Company's Core and Non-Negotiable Values — 533

Step 5: Bring It All Together — 537

Step 6: Bring Your Culture to Life — 541

Closing Note — 553

References — 555

About the Authors — 569

FOREWORD

In the wise words of Peter Drucker, "Culture eats strategy for breakfast." As a founder, I've wrestled with this truth on my journey, grappling with the elusive concept of culture and its indelible impact on the success of an organization. It's this wrestle, this struggle, which has led me to the realization that culture is not a by-product of success but, rather, a foundational element of it.

"Hope is Not a Strategy," a book penned by the seasoned business consultants Sirisha and Harish Kumar, resonates deeply with my experiences. It affirms that culture is not an accidental result of growth; instead, it's a deliberate choice demanding relentless commitment, focus, and action from the leadership.

Like many other founders, I was preoccupied with finding customers, hiring team members, and dealing with infrastructure challenges in the early days of my entrepreneurial journey. The concept of "culture" seemed like an abstract, distant idea to address once the company found its footing. However, I soon realized that culture is not a luxury of successful companies but a prerequisite. Echoing my experiences, Sirisha and Harish argue that the leaders of an organization need to invest time and energy in developing and nurturing their organizational culture. The metaphor of a gardener preparing the soil, planting the seeds, and diligently tending to the plants is apt. Indeed, the cultivation of a strong, healthy culture requires the same level of care, attention, and dedication.

The authors' six-step framework is a practical guide for leaders to make deliberate choices in building winning capacity. It starts by defining your purpose and auditing your existing culture. Navigating organizational culture's complex dynamics can feel like walking through a maze without a map. This is where the authors' Dilemmas Resolution Framework (DRF) comes into play. The DRF provides a systematic process to resolve 60 key organizational culture dilemmas, guiding leaders through the maze and providing a clear path forward.

As I have learned, an organization's values must be more than lofty ideals written on a wall. They should guide every decision and interaction within the organization. The authors' fourth step of discovering what the organization truly values resonates with this insight, offering practical guidance on ensuring these values are deeply ingrained in the organization.

Finally, Sirisha and Harish emphasize the importance of reinforcing these values consistently throughout the organization. I can attest that creating a strong culture is not a one-time event but an ongoing commitment, and this is where rituals play an important part in reinforcing culture. The processes, structures, and even the language used within the organization need to reflect and reinforce its value and purpose. In "Hope Is Not A Strategy," Sirisha and Harish argue the importance of organizational culture and offer a practical roadmap for achieving it.

To my fellow founders and leaders, this book is more than a guide; it's a companion on your journey to build a culture that drives long-term success. It's a call to action that encourages you to move from hoping for a strong organizational culture to making deliberate choices to create and sustain it. As you turn the pages, remember the words of Mahatma Gandhi: "Your beliefs become your thoughts, your thoughts become your words, your words become your actions, your actions become your habits, your habits become your values, and your values become your destiny." Here's to deliberately choosing our destiny.

Anand Deshpande
Founder and Chairman, Persistent Systems.
Pune, August 8, 2023

ACKNOWLEDGMENTS

We are grateful to many individuals whose support, feedback, and cooperation were invaluable in creating this book. We would like to express our profound appreciation to all who allowed us to complete this book.

Firstly, our heartfelt gratitude goes out to the courageous leaders with whom we have had the privilege to work closely. Girish Shilamkar, Vishal Biyani, Jaymin Bhuptani, Nital Shah, Amit Gainda, Anurag Kedia, Gagandeep Makker, Siddhartha Kongara, Anuraag Nallapati, Chad Monroe— your dedication, openness to new ideas, and willingness to question the status quo have been instrumental in shaping and refining the model we present in this book. You have helped us test our theories in the crucible of real-world business challenges, and your insights have been invaluable in refining our understanding. We cannot thank you enough for your time and feedback and for entrusting us with your organizational challenges.

Special thanks and heartfelt gratitude and appreciation to Ramanand J- you have been our sounding board. Your contribution to the idea's genesis and your unwavering commitment to refining it has shaped it into the framework it is today. Your collaborative efforts have been instrumental in shaping this book.

We also express our sincere thanks to all the business leaders, advisors, and investors who took the time to listen to our ideas and share their perspectives. Vishwanath Krishna, KS Prashant, Anand Deshpande, Monish Darda, and Ajay Hiraskar— your constructive feedback, practical insights, and wide-ranging experiences helped us see the gaps, possibilities, and real-world applicability of our framework. Our exchanges with you were enlightening, and we are grateful for your shared wisdom.

Our appreciation also extends to the dedicated interns and consultants who supported us throughout this journey. Special mention to Navya Bhamidipati, Shreya Shetty, Ravali Peddapudi, Dharmendra D, and the entire team at Choose To Thinq - the countless hours you invested in research, your attention to detail, and your relentless pursuit of knowledge contributed significantly to the strength of our framework. Your enthusiasm and commitment were contagious and energized us every step of the way. Thank you for your exceptional work and for sharing our passion for building healthier, more productive organizational cultures. Also, thanks to Agastya Bhamidipati for suggesting the title of the book.

Finally, we acknowledge all those who, directly or indirectly, contributed to the completion of this book. Thank you for your support, for believing in our ideas, and for being part of this enriching journey. We hope the insights and ideas in these pages will help create more purposeful and rewarding organizational cultures worldwide. Your invaluable contribution turned this book from an idea into a reality; we are forever grateful for that.

Thank you.
Deliberately,
Sirisha and Harish

AUTHORS' NOTE

In businesses, there's an often-overlooked challenge: alignment. While companies may have a vision, ensuring every cog in the machine moves in harmony towards that vision is a different ball game. Just as a tennis player needs every muscle to align for that perfect serve, companies need every team member to align with their core values and objectives.

We have worked with companies at different stages of growth - from a 10-member team spread across 3 continents to a 10-year-old company of 1100 people to a VC-funded business on growth steroids to bootstrapped companies to Series D-funded companies. Here are some myths about alignment that we have come across:

- We will do what Google/Cred/Netflix does, and we should be good.
- We don't really have to do anything special. We hire good people, and a good culture will happen on its own.
- Yes, it's important, but I have to focus on growth right now. We will sort out the culture later.
- We have a P&C (People and Culture) team with big budgets. Culture will get 'done.'
- I have been personally involved in hiring each of my senior leaders. We are fully aligned.

Our book, "Hope is not a Strategy: Be Deliberate About Alignment and Culture," is written to go beyond debunking these myths. We have provided a step-by-step process that you can use to articulate and build a culture that serves your business aspirations. Alignment and culture aren't byproducts of success; they are the foundation. Just as a tennis player doesn't merely rely on talent but hone skills, stamina, and strategy, companies must deliberately foster alignment.

Our journey, spanning startups to established organizations, has shown us that alignment isn't a one-size-fits-all concept. It's not about copying the giants. It's about understanding your unique organizational DNA and ensuring every part aligns with it. It's about recognizing that while strategy might get you on the playing field, alignment determines how the game is played.

While many books touch upon leadership, strategy, and confronting challenges, we felt a gap existed. Many leaders acknowledge the importance of alignment but often sideline it, leaving it to HR teams without fully grasping its essence. It's akin to a tennis coach focusing solely on forehands, neglecting the player's overall fitness and mindset.

This book is our attempt to bridge that gap. We aim to provide a hands-on guide for leaders to be deliberate about their organizational alignment. Think of it as a playbook, minus the jargon. We've distilled our insights into a step-by-step approach, hoping to make the intricate dance of culture and alignment accessible to all, from CEOs to fresh recruits.

In essence, we're offering an 'API' for organizational alignment. Just as an API ensures smooth communication between two software applications, our guide aims to facilitate seamless interactions within an organization, fostering an environment where everyone is in sync with the company's vision.

To all the readers, whether you're a seasoned leader or an aspiring entrepreneur, we hope this book serves as a compass, guiding you in cultivating alignment that not only defines your organization but also propels it forward.

As we present this guide, we acknowledge that our journey in articulating the steps of organizational alignment is not yet complete. Steps 4, 5, and 6, crucial for bringing the culture to life, are areas we plan to explore in depth in our next book. We believe it's essential to first lay a solid foundation with our framework, as getting this part right is critical. While many focus on implementation, the true value lies in understanding precisely what needs to be implemented. Without a clear grasp of this, even the best execution strategies can fall short. So, stay tuned as we delve deeper into these steps in our forthcoming work, aiming to provide even more comprehensive guidance for founders and leaders.

HOW TO READ THE BOOK?

Welcome to "Hope is not a Strategy." As you embark on this journey with us, here are some guidelines to help you navigate the book effectively:

- **A Comprehensive Guide:** This book is designed to be a comprehensive guide, a ready reckoner for leaders and founders. While we recommend reading it in its entirety to grasp the full depth of its content, we understand that time can be a constraint. For a quick overview, focus on the content within the boxes. These encapsulate the essence of each section and provide a high-level understanding.
- **Examples for Clarity:** Throughout the book, you'll find numerous examples to illustrate our points. These are presented in italics for easy identification. Please note that while these examples are based on real-world scenarios, they are sourced from publicly available data or company websites. To maintain confidentiality and integrity, we've refrained from using specific company names, especially when the information hasn't been validated directly.
- **Self-Reflection Questions:** We've included a series of questions aimed at prompting introspection. As a leader or founder, these questions will help you gauge where your company currently stands and where it needs to go.
- **Step-by-Step Guide:** Steps 2 and 3 are particularly detailed, guiding you through the processes of identifying your existing culture (Step 2) and articulating the desired culture (Step 3). While these sections are exhaustive, not everything may pertain to your specific situation. Choose areas that resonate with your company's unique challenges. In Step 3, you'll encounter 60 dilemmas. While comprehensive, not all may apply to you. Typically, when we work with companies, 13 to 15 dilemmas emerge as the most pertinent. Addressing these major dilemmas often resolves the minor ones as well.
- **Additional Resources:** We've curated a set of additional resources available at

https://www.alignbydesign.in/hopeisnotastrategy. Feel free to explore these resources and share them with others. If you have questions or need further guidance on applying this framework, don't hesitate to reach out to us at sirisha@alignbydesign.in or harish@alignbydesign.in.

We hope this book provides you with the insights and tools needed to deliberately shape your organization's culture and future.

Happy reading!

THE IMPERATIVE OF DELIBERATE CULTURE BUILDING

Culture is not just a buzzword in the world of business; it's the invisible yet influential force that shapes the identity and experience of an organization. Whether you think of it as the "smell of the place" or the "fabric of the organization," understanding and nurturing culture is crucial for creating a healthy and thriving workplace.

Think of culture as the fabric that weaves through every aspect of an organization. Just as a fabric defines the look, feel, and durability of a piece of clothing, culture defines the character and resilience of an organization. Every thread in the fabric represents an individual's actions, decisions, and behaviors. Over time, these threads weave together to form the culture of the organization. Whether it's how employees collaborate, the way they communicate, or the values they uphold, culture is the pattern that emerges from this intricate weaving. Just as the fabric's quality impacts the overall quality of a garment, an organization's culture has a direct impact on its success. A strong and well-aligned culture can lead to engaged employees, innovation, and a positive reputation. On the other hand, a frayed or misaligned culture can lead to disengagement, inefficiency, and challenges that can hinder growth.

What is Organizational culture, and why does it matter?

In the world of business, culture is like the shared personality of a company. It's the way everyone in the organization behaves, influenced by their values and habits. It's not about fancy office perks, but it's about how people work together every day. Culture matters because it can either help a company thrive or hold it back. A strong, positive culture boosts employee engagement, productivity, innovation, and customer satisfaction. It's the difference between a company that does well and one that struggles. Imagine culture as a guiding force that keeps everyone on the same track, working towards common goals. It's like a compass that helps a company stay true to its mission, even when things get tough.

In short, culture is like the personality of a company, and it can either help it succeed or hold it back. A positive culture boosts engagement, productivity, and innovation, making a company more successful. It's a powerful force that attracts talented people and helps a company adapt and thrive in a changing world.

Our Point of View (PoV) on Organizational Culture

There are multiple definitions of organizational culture that exist when you read through any literature. Through our years of consulting experience, we have built a strong point of view on organizational culture, which we are listing here:

- Culture is not about office perks like free snacks or fancy lounges. It's about how people treat each other, how they work together, and the values they uphold. Perks can be a nice addition, but they don't define the core of a culture.
- Culture is unique to each organization. It's deeply rooted in its history, values, and people. Trying to copy another company's culture is like wearing someone else's shoes – they won't fit, and they're uncomfortable.
- While hiring plays a role, culture is shaped by everyone's daily actions and behaviors. Even great hires won't make up for a culture that's toxic or misaligned with the organization's values.
- Building a strong culture takes time. It's a continuous process that requires consistent effort. You can't rush it or create it overnight.
- Culture is everyone's responsibility, not just HR's. Leaders, from top to bottom, influence culture through their actions, decisions, and the examples they set.
- Prioritizing growth over culture can lead to long-term problems. Neglecting culture can result in high turnover, low morale, and ethical issues that can harm the organization.
- Fancy HR budgets or extravagant team-building events don't automatically create a strong culture. Culture is about everyday practices and behaviors, not occasional spending.
- Just because senior leaders are aligned doesn't mean everyone else is. Culture should be nurtured at all levels of the organization to ensure alignment throughout.
- Culture may be intangible, but it has a real impact on an organization's success. It influences how engaged employees are, their productivity, and even the company's reputation.
- Culture can evolve and change, especially as organizations grow or face new challenges. It should adapt to remain healthy and effective.
- Culture is powerful but not a magic fix for all problems. It must align with the organization's strategy and be supported by effective leadership and processes.

- There's no universal culture template. What works for one organization may not work for another. Culture should reflect an organization's unique values and goals.
- Culture is essential for organizations of all sizes- not just big companies. Small startups can benefit from a strong culture just as much as large corporations.
- Culture directly affects an organization's financial performance. A positive culture can lead to higher employee engagement, customer satisfaction, and ultimately, increased profits.
- Ignoring culture is risky. Neglecting it can lead to disengaged employees, higher turnover, and even legal or ethical issues that can harm the organization.

Our attempt through this book is to help leaders and organizations prioritize and build a healthy culture that aligns with their purpose and values, creating a more productive and positive work environment.

What are the advantages of having a strong company culture?

A strong company culture offers many benefits:

- **Happy Employees**: People enjoy their work more when they feel part of a positive culture.
- **Top Talent**: It's easier to attract and keep great employees.
- **Creative Ideas**: A good culture encourages new and creative thinking.
- **Business Success**: Companies with a strong culture tend to make more money.
- **Happy Customers**: Satisfied employees provide better customer service.
- **Good Reputation**: A positive culture makes a company look good to the public.
- **Smart Decisions**: Culture helps employees make good choices.
- **Handling Challenges**: It helps the company adapt during tough times.
- **Less Employee Turnover**: Employees stay longer when they like the culture.

- **Healthy Workers**: A caring culture supports employee well-being.
- **Positive Vibes**: Employees feel more motivated and positive.
- **Teamwork**: People work together better in a good culture.
- **Long-Term Success**: A strong culture helps a company last a long time.

When is it the right time to build culture, and what happens when you delay being deliberate about culture building?

Culture begins right from the beginning, the very first day your initial employee joins your company. It's not something you can delay or consider at a later date. Instead, it's a living part of your organization that shapes your identity and future.

The Very First Domino: Day One

Think about this: your startup is just starting out. You have a small team, a fantastic product, and big dreams. It's easy to get caught up in the whirlwind of tasks, from developing your product to figuring out marketing strategies. During this rush, it might seem like culture can be put on the back burner. After all, you're a small team working closely together. But here's the truth: culture doesn't wait.

From the very moment your first employee walks through the door, culture starts to take shape. It's in the way you greet them, the way you collaborate, and the values you hold dear. Whether you realize it or not, culture is already forming. It's like planting a seed; it might start small, but it has the potential to grow into something powerful.

The Domino Effect: Unconscious Culture

Culture isn't just about big actions or official rules. It's the result of countless everyday interactions, choices, and attitudes. Your team members are watching, learning, and absorbing how things work. This subconscious culture affects how they do their work, how they treat each other, and how they represent your company to the world.

The Importance of Early Agreement

It's crucial to intentionally shape your culture right from the start.

- **Laying the Foundation**: Your initial team sets the foundation for future employees. Their actions and attitudes become the cultural norm, making it easier or harder to align new hires with your desired culture.
- **Matching Your Purpose**: When your culture lines up with your company's purpose and values from the beginning, everything your team does pushes you in the right direction.
- **Avoiding Culture Problems**: Ignoring culture in the beginning can lead to problems later on—issues that become harder to solve as your company grows.
- **Steering Clear of Culture Debt**: Culture Debt is the price you pay tomorrow for the compromises on company culture you make today. Just as financial debt accumulates, culture debt can accrue if you neglect your culture early on. This can lead to confusion, plummeting morale, and a dip in productivity.

What is the role of leaders in taking care of the culture and avoiding culture debt?

Consider forests and gardens: both beautiful in their own right but are crafted differently. A forest is nature's wild child, shaped by a myriad of factors, from rain dances to squirrel antics. It's diverse but can be a tad unruly. A garden, however, is nature on a leash. It's intentionally nurtured, and every plant is there for a reason. Similarly, company culture can either be a wild forest or a manicured garden. Left unchecked, it can grow into a tangled mess. But with care and intention, it can be a harmonious environment where every element has its place. Here's what we can learn if leaders swap their business suits for gardening gloves:

- **Alignment**: In a garden, every plant has to align with the layout. In a company, every employee should align with the company's mission. No rogue cacti in a bed of roses!
- **Engagement**: A thriving garden is a sight to behold. Similarly, a well-nurtured culture is a joy to be part of, leading to blooming productivity and rooted employees.

- **Performance**: A garden planned right promises a good harvest. Similarly, a robust culture can boost business metrics, from customer smiles to shareholder cheers.
- **Resilience**: Gardens built for all seasons can weather any storm. A strong culture, too, can help a company sail through challenges and bounce back from setbacks.

So, how can you nurture the right culture from the very beginning while avoiding culture debt? Continuing with our analogy of a garden, leaders are like the chief gardener. Here's how they can nurture their company culture:

- **Setting the Tone**: The leader's actions are like the watering can and sunlight, setting the stage for growth. If they're not embodying the culture they wish to see, they might as well be trying to grow roses in the desert.
- **Defining and Broadcasting the Culture**: Leaders need to be clear about the garden's theme. Tropical paradise or English cottage garden? Similarly, they must define and consistently broadcast the company's purpose, values, and norms.
- **Aligning Systems and Processes**: Just as a garden has pathways, trellises, and fences, a company's systems and processes should reflect and reinforce its culture.
- **Tending to the Culture**: As any good gardener knows, you can't plant seeds and forget about them. Culture needs regular attention, celebration of its blooms, and adjustments when weeds pop up.
- **Addressing Culture Weeds**: Just as weeds can overrun a garden, culture debt can choke an organization. Leaders must be vigilant weeders, ensuring nothing undermines the desired culture.

Why is it important for culture to align with the purpose and strategy of the organization?

Aligning the culture of an organization with its purpose and strategy is not just a nice-to-have; it's a strategic imperative for several compelling reasons.

- **Clarity of Direction**: When an organization's culture is aligned with its purpose and strategy, it provides a clear and unified direction for everyone involved. This clarity ensures that every employee understands why their work matters and how it contributes to the company's overarching goals.

    Example: Google's culture of innovation and collaboration aligns perfectly with its mission to organize the world's information and make it universally accessible and useful. This alignment has led to groundbreaking products and solutions.

- **Employee Engagement**: An aligned culture fosters a sense of purpose and belonging among employees. They see the meaningful impact of their work, which increases motivation, engagement, and overall job satisfaction.

    Example: Southwest Airlines has a culture centered around putting employees first, aligning with their purpose of providing affordable and reliable air travel. This alignment has resulted in a dedicated and passionate workforce.

- **Consistency in Actions**: Alignment ensures consistency in decision-making and behavior across the organization. This consistency builds trust internally and externally with customers, partners, and stakeholders.

    Example: Patagonia's culture of environmental responsibility is aligned with its mission to "build the best product, cause no unnecessary harm, use business to inspire and implement solutions to the environmental crisis." This alignment has helped them maintain trust and loyalty among eco-conscious consumers.

- **Resilience in Challenges**: During challenging times, a well-aligned culture and purpose act as a stabilizing force. They remind employees and leaders of the bigger picture, helping them stay focused on the long-term mission, even when facing adversity.

    Example: During the 2008 financial crisis, Johnson & Johnson's commitment to its "Credo," which emphasizes putting the needs and well-being of customers first, helped them make ethical decisions that protected their reputation and business.

- **Attraction and Retention of Talent**: Organizations with aligned culture and purpose tend to attract talent that shares their values.

These employees are more likely to stay with the company, reducing turnover and recruitment costs.

Example: The Bill and Melinda Gates Foundation's culture of philanthropy and social impact aligns with its mission to reduce poverty and improve global health. This alignment has helped them attract top talent passionate about making a difference.

- **Customer Loyalty**: An aligned culture often resonates with customers who share those values. This connection can lead to increased customer loyalty and brand advocacy.

  Example: The Body Shop's culture of ethical and sustainable practices aligns with its mission to "enrich people as well as our planet." This alignment has cultivated a loyal customer base that supports their values.

- **Ethical Behavior**: Purpose-driven cultures often prioritize ethical behavior. When culture and purpose align on principles of integrity and responsibility, it reduces the likelihood of unethical practices or misconduct.

  Example: Starbucks' culture of ethical sourcing and responsible practices aligns with its mission "to inspire and nurture the human spirit—one person, one cup, and one neighborhood at a time." This alignment has helped them maintain their ethical reputation.

- **Strategic Focus**: An aligned culture enables organizations to set and stick to strategic goals. The culture acts as a strategic enabler, guiding decisions and actions toward achieving those goals.

  Example: Apple's culture of innovation and design excellence aligns with its strategy of delivering innovative products. This alignment has allowed them to maintain a consistent brand identity and market leadership.

- **Long-Term Success**: Ultimately, aligning culture with purpose and strategy contributes to the long-term success and sustainability of the organization. It helps build a resilient, engaged workforce that is committed to achieving the company's mission.

  Example: The Walt Disney Company's culture of creativity and storytelling aligns with its mission to "entertain, inform, and inspire people around the globe." This alignment has made them a global entertainment giant.

In the chapters that follow, we'll dive deeper into the art of crafting your unique culture and purpose. We'll explore more real-life stories and practical insights that will help you navigate the exciting terrain of business while staying true to your organization's one-of-a-kind identity. Because in the world of business, it's not about fitting into a mold; it's about embracing your uniqueness and charting your path to success.

STEP-BY-STEP PROCESS OF BUILDING CULTURE

Step 1: Define the purpose and the desired identity.

Step 2: Unearth the existing cultural blueprint.

Step 3: Deliberately decide who you want to be - The Dilemmas Resolution Framework (DRF).

Step 4: Discover your company's core and non-negotiable values.

Step 5: Bring it all together.

Step 6: Bring you culture to life.

Step 1

DEFINE PURPOSE AND DESIRED IDENTITY

Why does one exist, and what do they want to be known for?

Purpose and desired identity are intertwined. The purpose is the 'why' - the reason the company exists. The desired identity, on the other hand, is the 'how' - the way the company manifests its purpose in the world. Both elements deeply influence company culture. A strong purpose offers stability and a sense of meaning, while a clear desired identity aligns behaviors, shaping interactions within the company and with the broader ecosystem.

Purpose

Purpose is the 'why' that fuels an organization's existence. It's the compass that guides every decision and action, transcending the pursuit of profits to define the difference a company aspires to make in the world. Imagine purpose as the North Star, providing unwavering direction amid the ever-shifting tides of the business landscape. Without a clear purpose, even the most successful organizations can lose their way, especially in times of growth or change.

So, why is purpose so vital? Firstly, it offers a distinct path forward. Like a lighthouse guiding ships to safety, a well-defined purpose ensures a company stays on course, even through turbulent waters. It serves as a steady anchor, grounding the organization amidst the relentless currents of competition and expansion. Furthermore, purpose kindles passion and commitment. It's the spark that ignites enthusiasm in every individual. When employees understand the greater impact of their work, they're more inclined to go beyond the call of duty. This passion extends not only to employees but also to customers and partners who share in the company's vision, forging a community of advocates.

Diving deeper into the essence of purpose, it transcends profit margins to focus on the lasting imprint a company leaves behind. For instance, an eyewear manufacturer may craft glasses, but its profound purpose could revolve around enhancing people's lives through improved vision. This profound insight can inspire innovation, propelling the company to explore new horizons beyond conventional boundaries.

A well-defined purpose serves as a powerful driver for organizational success, employee satisfaction, and societal impact. Some key advantages of a well-defined purpose statement include:

- **Clear Direction**: A defined purpose acts as a compass, providing a clear sense of direction for the organization. It helps leaders make informed decisions and set strategic priorities that align with the company's ultimate goal.
- **Inspired Workforce**: A compelling purpose inspires and motivates employees. When individuals understand how their

work contributes to a larger mission, they are more engaged, passionate, and committed to their roles.
- **Enhanced Innovation**: Purpose-driven organizations often foster a culture of innovation. Employees are encouraged to think creatively and find new ways to fulfill the company's mission, leading to breakthrough ideas and solutions.
- **Attracting Talent**: A well-defined purpose can attract top talent who are not just seeking a job but also a sense of meaning in their work. Purpose-driven organizations are often more successful in recruiting and retaining skilled employees.
- **Customer Loyalty**: Customers are drawn to companies that have a clear and meaningful purpose. They are more likely to support and remain loyal to brands that align with their own values and beliefs.
- **Stronger Brand Identity**: Purpose helps shape a distinct brand identity. It sets the organization apart from competitors and gives it a unique positioning in the market.
- **Resilience**: Purpose provides resilience during challenging times. When faced with adversity, purpose-driven organizations can rally around their mission and navigate crises more effectively.
- **Stakeholder Trust**: Purpose fosters trust among stakeholders, including investors, partners, and the community. When a company's purpose is transparent and authentic, it builds credibility and goodwill.
- **Social Impact**: Many purpose-driven organizations have a positive social impact. They contribute to social and environmental causes, making the world a better place while doing business.
- **Long-Term Sustainability**: A well-defined purpose contributes to the long-term sustainability of the organization. It helps leaders make decisions that prioritize the well-being of the company, its employees, and the broader community.
- **Adaptability**: Purpose can guide adaptability. In a rapidly changing business landscape, organizations can use their purpose as a constant, allowing them to pivot and evolve while staying true to their core values.

- **Measurable Goals**: A purpose often comes with measurable goals and objectives. This clarity helps organizations track their progress and evaluate their impact over time.
- **Higher Performance**: Purpose-driven organizations tend to outperform their competitors. Employees are more engaged, customers are more loyal, and innovation thrives—all of which contribute to better overall performance.

Step-By-Step Guide to Define Purpose

- **Soul-Searching**: Start by asking deep questions. Why does the company exist? What motivated you to start this organization? What issues or problems do you want to address? What kind of impact do you hope to have? Your purpose should reflect your passion and beliefs.
- **Engage Your Team**: Purpose isn't just a leadership decision; it's a collective effort. Involve your team in discussions about your organization's purpose. Their insights can be invaluable in shaping a purpose that resonates with everyone.
- **Define Impact:** Be specific about the impact you want to make. How will the world be different because your organization exists? What positive change do you want to see?
- **Test and Refine:** Your purpose may evolve over time. That's okay. Test it with stakeholders—employees, customers, partners—and be open to refining it based on feedback and changing circumstances.
- **Embed It:** Once you've defined your purpose, integrate it into every aspect of your organization. It should influence your culture, values, strategy, and day-to-day operations.
- **Communicate Authentically:** Share your purpose authentically with your team, customers, and the world. Transparency and sincerity build trust and credibility.

For example, take a hypothetical company, GreenTeas Inc. which is in the business of crafting healthier, organic beverages with a strong commitment to sustainable farming, ethical sourcing, and promoting health. Together with their team, they could craft a purpose statement that could read something like "Our purpose is to enrich lives and protect our planet by offering ethically sourced, sustainable teas. We champion farmer welfare, consumer health, and environmental sustainability."

Desired Identity

Desired identity, in the context of an organization, is the aspirational image or reputation that a company aims to establish in the minds of its stakeholders, including customers, employees, partners, and the broader community. It answers the fundamental question: "What do we want to be known for?" This identity goes beyond products or services; it encompasses the values, qualities, and characteristics that the organization seeks to embody. It is a strategic vision of the company's future image and how it wishes to be perceived in the marketplace.

Defining the desired identity is essential for several reasons. Firstly, it provides clarity and focus to the organization's branding and communication efforts. When everyone within the company understands the desired identity, they can align their actions and messaging accordingly, creating a consistent and compelling brand image. Secondly, a well-defined desired identity can help differentiate the company from competitors. In a crowded marketplace, a distinctive identity that resonates with customers can be a significant competitive advantage. It can attract like-minded customers who share the same values and beliefs. Moreover, the desired identity serves as a guiding star for decision-making. It influences the company's culture, product development, customer interactions, and social responsibility initiatives. When choices are aligned with the desired identity, they reinforce the company's authenticity and integrity.

Interplay Between Purpose and Desired Identity

Purpose and desired identity are intricately connected. The purpose represents the "why" of the organization, its deeper mission, and its reason for existence. The desired identity, on the other hand, represents the "how" – how the organization aims to be perceived as it fulfills its purpose. Together, they form the DNA of a company. Every decision, every strategy, every action should be a reflection of the company's purpose and identity. When these two are in sync, it creates a resonance that stakeholders can sense and appreciate. It's the difference between a company that merely exists and one that thrives.

Purpose and desired identity work hand in hand to shape an organization's character and reputation, making it a powerful combination for building a meaningful and enduring brand. The purpose provides the foundation for the desired identity. It informs the values, principles, and qualities that the organization wishes to project. For example, if an educational institution's purpose is to empower students with knowledge and critical thinking skills, its desired identity may be to be known as a trusted, innovative, and student-centric institution. Conversely, the desired identity reinforces the purpose. It helps convey the purpose to external audiences in a relatable and memorable way. When customers, employees, and partners see the organization consistently embodying its desired identity, they are more likely to connect with and support its purpose.

Take Patagonia, for instance. Their purpose is crystal clear: "We're in business to save our home planet." Their desired identity? A proactive leader in environmental sustainability. This identity has garnered Patagonia respect and loyalty from its customers. Apple, too, is a masterclass in intertwining purpose and desired identity. Steve Jobs envisioned Apple as a hub of innovation, challenging the status quo. Their tagline "Think Different" encapsulates this. From product design to customer service, Apple's identity is evident. They don't just sell gadgets; they sell an experience. Their stores, designed as community hubs, reflect this identity, making Apple not just a tech company but a lifestyle brand. Zappos, the online shoe retailer, is another example. With a purpose to "deliver happiness," their desired identity is clear: a company that prioritizes delightful customer experiences. This identity has positioned Zappos as a customer-centric brand par excellence.

These examples underline that a company's desired identity isn't a mere facade. It's a reflection of its core values and its promise to the world. Crafting this identity isn't just a strategic move; it's a commitment to a certain ethos.

In the quest to shape an organization's desired identity, certain techniques can be invaluable. Two such useful methods are -

- Destination Postcard Technique

- Writing Future Newspaper Headlines

The Destination Postcard Technique

Imagine receiving a postcard from the future of your organization. This isn't just a piece of paper; it's a vivid snapshot of your company's pinnacle of success, embodying the desired identity you've always aspired to achieve. This is the 'Destination Postcard' – a vision statement with a twist. Traditional vision statements can sometimes be vague or generic. A Destination Postcard, however, paints a detailed picture, making the future tangible and inspiring. It's not just about financial milestones but encompasses culture, impact, recognition, and more.

Step-By-Step Guide for Crafting Your Destination Postcard

- **Team Assembly:** Gather a diverse group from across the company, ensuring representation from various departments and leadership levels.

- **Current Identity Reflection:** Understand your company's present identity. What are your strengths and weaknesses, and how does the market perceive you?

- **Future Visualization:** Encourage team members to share their visions. What tangible and intangible achievements do you envision?

- **Postcard Drafting:** Collaboratively write a narrative capturing the company's envisioned future. Be vivid and inspiring.

- **Refinement:** Review and refine the draft, ensuring alignment with company objectives and aspirations.

- **Design & Visualization:** Collaborate with a graphic designer to create a visual representation of the postcard.

- **Share & Embed:** Disseminate the postcard throughout the organization. Use it as a guiding light and motivational tool.

- **Review & Update:** Regularly revisit the postcard. As the company evolves, so should its vision.

For example, by following the above-mentioned process, GreenLeaf Teas Inc. could come up with the following Destination Postcard:

23rd October 2027.

"Dear GreenLeaf Family,

Greetings from a thriving future! Here, GreenLeaf Teas is a globally recognized brand, not just for our exquisite organic tea but also for the values we steadfastly uphold.

We're celebrated worldwide for our unwavering commitment to sustainability, with our practices in the tea industry inspiring others to follow suit. Our GreenLeaf logo symbolizes our environmental stewardship, something we carry with immense pride.

Furthermore, we are a recognized leader in fostering social impact. Our work has revolutionized communities around our tea estates, bringing positive changes to lives, and it doesn't stop there.

We've also made significant strides in nurturing a culture of wellness. Our customers are no longer just consumers; they are a community that embraces and lives the healthy lifestyle we advocate. GreenLeaf is not just a tea but a lifestyle choice that enriches the daily routines of our customers.

Being a part of GreenLeaf in this future is an exhilarating experience, and we're continually working to ensure the years ahead are even more impactful.

Here's to a sustainable and healthy future,
GreenLeaf Teas"

Writing Future Newspaper Headlines

Visualizing success is a powerful motivator. One creative way to do this is by imagining the headlines you'd want to see about your company in the future. This exercise, termed 'Writing Future Newspaper Headlines', provides a snapshot of the organization's aspirations, helping to chart a clear path towards its desired identity.

Step-By-Step Guide for Writing Future Newspaper Headlines

- **Team Assembly**: Just like the Destination Postcard, gather a diverse group from various departments. This ensures a holistic perspective.
- **Current Standing Assessment**: Understand where the company stands today. This sets the foundation for where you want to go.
- **Future Envisioning**: Encourage open discussions about the company's future. What milestones and achievements would you like to see?
- **Headline Drafting**: Craft bold, specific headlines that encapsulate the company's future achievements. These should be both aspirational and inspiring.
- **Refinement**: Review and refine the headlines to ensure they align with the company's vision and resonate with the team.
- **Visualization**: Create graphic versions of these headlines. Display them prominently to serve as daily reminders of the company's goals.
- **Periodic Review**: As the company evolves, revisit these headlines. Adjust them to reflect new aspirations or celebrate achieved milestones.

For example, the team could work together and come up with the following future newspaper headlines:

"GreenLeaf Teas: The Global Gold Standard in Organic Tea"

"Leading the Green Revolution: GreenLeaf Teas' Sustainability Efforts Garner Global Acclaim"

"More than Just Tea: GreenLeaf Spearheads Global Wellness Movement"

Navigating the challenges of aligning the organization to the purpose and the desired identity

In the pursuit of defining and aligning purpose and desired identity, organizations inevitably encounter challenges. Whether it's lack of clarity, resistance from stakeholders, or difficulty in translating purpose into action, these obstacles can seem formidable. However, they are not insurmountable. By acknowledging these challenges and proactively devising strategies to overcome them, leaders can steer their organizations toward a robust and coherent culture.

The first hurdle is often the lack of clarity or consensus about the organization's purpose and desired identity. With diverse perspectives in the mix - from founders to employees to investors - arriving at a shared understanding can be daunting. Yet, it is vital for this foundational understanding to be inclusive and agreed upon. Overcoming this challenge requires active dialogue, effective communication, and a commitment to inclusivity. Leaders must ensure that everyone's voice is heard and respected during the process. Workshops, surveys, or brainstorming sessions can be utilized to invite input and foster a sense of ownership among stakeholders.

The second challenge lies in resistance or skepticism, particularly from employees. Change, even when positive, can be unsettling. Additionally, if the purpose and desired identity are seen as mere buzzwords or as a distraction from the 'real work,' it can hinder buy-in from the team. To counter this, leaders must demonstrate authenticity and consistency. The purpose and desired identity should not just be preached; they must be lived out in the company's policies, operations, and behaviors. Showcasing early wins, where alignment with purpose and identity has led to positive outcomes, can also help in winning over skeptics.

Translating the defined purpose and desired identity into tangible action forms the third challenge. It's one thing to articulate lofty ideals and another to embed them into the daily grind of business operations. To navigate this, leaders can use the purpose and desired identity as touchpoints to review and redesign processes, roles, and reward systems. For instance, if a company's desired identity involves being customer-centric, it should be reflected in the hiring process, performance metrics, and training programs.

The fourth challenge involves maintaining the relevance and resonance of the purpose and desired identity over time. As companies grow and evolve, there might be a need to revisit and recalibrate these elements. Leaders must ensure they stay connected with the pulse of their organization and their ecosystem to identify such needs timely. Regular surveys, feedback loops, and culture audits can be helpful in this regard.

Finally, the journey towards defining and aligning purpose and desired identity can feel overwhelming, especially for leaders who are already juggling multiple responsibilities. In such cases, bringing in external help like culture consultants or coaches can provide valuable support, objectivity, and expertise.

Step 2

UNEARTH THE EXISTING CULTURAL BLUEPRINT

A Deeper Dive into Organizational DNA

Understanding the current state of an organization's culture through a "Cultural Snapshot" is vital. It's not about finding faults but identifying existing elements, both positive and unique. It isn't judgmental; it's about comprehension. It helps recognize subcultures within teams and facilitates change. It involves listening, observing, and understanding from various angles because culture isn't separate from the business; it influences every aspect, from decisions to performance.

In this book, the goal is to set out to craft a culture that can power an organization forward. But before that, it's crucial to understand where the organization is right now. Think of this as taking a cultural snapshot of the organization. This isn't about identifying shortcomings or problems; it's about finding out what's already there. It's about identifying the good, the bad, and the unique elements of the existing culture.

Getting a clear picture of the organization's culture matters because culture isn't distinct from the rest of the business. It's intertwined with everything the organization does. It's part of every decision, every interaction, and every goal. It influences how employees work, how teams cooperate, and how an organization performs as a whole. By taking a cultural snapshot, the aim is to understand the existing values, practices, and patterns of behavior and to uncover the traits contributing to success. Leaders should build on these cultural strengths as they work towards their desired culture.

A Cultural Snapshot isn't about criticism or blame.

A cultural snapshot also helps to recognize the variety within an organization. Every team or department may have its subcultures; it's the organizational way of doing things. Understanding these different subcultures will help to create a broader culture that respects and makes use of these differences. It is the starting point and makes it easier to understand what needs to change and what should stay the same. It also helps to set a direction to decide where the desired destination is.

Taking a cultural snapshot involves looking at the organization from different angles. It's about listening to what people are saying, observing what they're doing, and understanding what they're thinking. It means looking at both formal systems and processes and informal norms and behaviors.

Taking a Cultural Snapshot isn't about judging; it's about understanding.

There are several areas that you need to explore in the functioning of the organization to get a true sense of the culture within. For convenience's sake, we grouped them into 7 areas:

Foundations of Organization:

- **Values and Ethics:** The core principles and moral standards that guide the behavior and decision-making of the organization and its employees. It defines what the organization stands for and the ethical framework it operates within.
- **Leadership and Management:** The styles, behaviors, and effectiveness of the leadership team and managers in shaping the organizational culture, setting the tone, and providing direction.
- **Organizational Structure:** The formal hierarchy, roles, and reporting relationships within the organization influence how work is organized, decisions are made, and information flows.

Employee Well-being and Growth:

- **Work-Life Balance and Well-being:** The organization's efforts to support employees in achieving a healthy work-life balance, managing stress, and ensuring overall well-being.
- **Employee Growth and Development:** The opportunities, programs, and initiatives in place to enhance employee skills, knowledge, and career growth, fostering a culture of continuous learning.
- **Team Dynamics:** How teams collaborate, communicate, and work together, impacting productivity, innovation, and employee satisfaction.
- **Diversity and Inclusion:** The organization's commitment to diversity, equity, and inclusion promotes a workplace that values and respects differences in backgrounds and perspectives.

Effective Communication and Transparency:

- **Communication and Transparency:** The clarity, openness, and frequency of communication within the organization, including the sharing of information, goals, and challenges.
- **Feedback Culture and Conflict Resolution:** The culture surrounding feedback, both positive and constructive, and the organization's approach to addressing and resolving conflicts.

- **Organizational Stories and Myths**: The narratives, stories, and cultural legends that shape the identity and values of the organization, influencing its culture and the behavior of employees.

Performance and Innovation:

- **Performance Management**: How the organization measures, evaluates, and rewards employee performance, including the setting of performance goals and the feedback process.
- **Innovation and Continuous Improvement**: The emphasis on creativity, idea generation, experimentation, and the processes in place for implementing innovations and driving ongoing improvements.
- **Technology and Innovation Adoption**: The organization's readiness and willingness to embrace technological advancements and innovative practices in its operations.

Stakeholder Relations and Responsibility:

- **Customer and Stakeholder Relations**: The organization's commitment to building strong relationships with customers and stakeholders, including how it handles feedback and complaints.
- **Corporate Social Responsibility (CSR)**: The initiatives and actions the organization takes to contribute positively to society and the environment, aligning its business practices with social and ethical responsibilities.
- **Compliance and Regulatory Adherence**: The organization's adherence to industry regulations, ethical standards, and legal requirements in its operations, governance, and business practices.

Adaptability and Learning:

- **Agility and Adaptability**: The organization's capacity to respond swiftly and effectively to changing circumstances, market dynamics, and emerging opportunities or threats.

- **Response to Failure and Learning**: How the organization deals with mistakes, setbacks, and failures, whether it promotes a culture of blame or embraces opportunities for learning and improvement.
- **Crisis Management and Resilience**: The organization's preparedness, response, and recovery strategies during crises, including its ability to adapt and maintain resilience in challenging times.

Decision-Making and Governance:

- **Decision-Making Process**: The methods and processes employed in making organizational decisions, including the level of transparency, involvement of employees, and alignment with the organization's values and goals.
- **Organizational Culture Metrics**: The metrics and key performance indicators used to measure and assess the effectiveness of the organization's culture, providing insights into its impact on various aspects of the business.

We will delve deeper into each of these areas and provide you with a few questions to probe and understand the nuances of how things actually work in the organization. Remember, the goal is not to have a perfect score on every data point but to understand where the organization stands today. This assessment can provide valuable insights, highlighting strengths to build upon and areas that may need more focus.

| 2.1 |
FOUNDATION OF THE ORGANIZATION

In this category, we examine the fundamental pillars that underpin an organization's culture. These foundations form the bedrock upon which the organization's values, behaviors, and identity are built. We will explore the organization's core values and ethical standards, the style and effectiveness of leadership and management, as well as the formal structure that defines roles, responsibilities, and the flow of information. By understanding these foundational elements, we gain insights into how the organization operates at its core and how it shapes the overall culture and direction.

Values and Ethics

In any organization, values and ethics serve as the compass guiding its actions and decisions. These principles form the moral foundation that shapes how employees interact, make choices, and conduct themselves within the workplace. Understanding and nurturing these values is essential not only for fostering a positive workplace culture but also for building trust with employees, customers, and stakeholders. Let's explore how an organization's commitment to ethical standards, alignment with shared values, and transparent communication of its moral framework impact its overall health and effectiveness.

Some warning signs that indicate that values and ethics in the organization are broken or are not uniform include:

- Increased reports of unethical behavior or violations.
- Declining employee trust in leadership or the organization's ethical commitment.
- A rise in ethical dilemmas without clear resolution.
- High employee turnover, especially among those who cite ethical concerns.

If you notice any of these in your organization, it's important you take cognizance of it and deliberately dig deeper into all aspects of values and ethics to identify the root cause of dissonance.

Values and Ethics covers

- **Ethical Standards**: The organization's commitment to upholding ethical principles and moral values in its actions and decisions.
- **Value Alignment**: The extent to which employees and the organization align with shared values, beliefs, and a common ethical framework.
- **Code of Conduct**: The presence and adherence to a clear code of conduct that defines expected behaviors and ethical guidelines.
- **Transparency**: The degree to which the organization is transparent about its values, ethics, and decision-making processes.
- **Whistleblower Protection**: Measures in place to protect employees who report unethical behavior or violations.
- **Ethical Dilemma Handling**: How the organization addresses and resolves ethical dilemmas and challenges.
- **Ethical Training and Education**: The effectiveness of ethics training programs and educational initiatives provided to employees.
- **Ethical Decision-Making Processes**: The presence of established processes or frameworks for employees to make ethical decisions.
- **Ethical Leadership**: The behavior and actions of leadership in promoting and modeling ethical conduct.
- **Ethical Sourcing and Supply Chain**: If applicable, the organization's commitment to ethical sourcing and supply chain practices.
- **Community Engagement**: How the organization engages with and supports the local community, considering ethical considerations in doing so.
- **Inclusivity**: Efforts to prevent discrimination and promote inclusivity as part of its ethical values.

Some sample questions you could ask employees across the organization to get some open, thoughtful responses to understand more about ethics and values in the company:

- Tell me about an instance where you felt proud of the organization's commitment to ethical standards. What happened, and why did it make you proud?
- Can you describe a situation where you had to make a challenging ethical decision at work? How did you approach it, and what was the outcome?
- In your opinion, what are the most important values that should guide our organization? Why do you think these values are crucial for our success?
- How would you rate the level of transparency within the organization when it comes to communicating our values, ethics, and decision-making processes? Can you provide an example of a transparent communication effort?
- Have you ever witnessed or heard of someone reporting unethical behavior? How was the situation handled, and did it lead to a resolution?
- What suggestions do you have for improving ethics training and education within the organization? How can we make it more effective and engaging for employees?
- In your view, how well does our leadership demonstrate ethical behavior and set an example for others? Can you share any specific instances or behaviors that stood out to you?
- How do you think our organization can better engage with the local community while upholding ethical values and principles? Are there specific initiatives or approaches you believe would be effective?
- Can you share your thoughts on how we can further promote inclusivity and prevent discrimination within our workplace? Do you have any ideas or experiences related to this?

> When you think about our organization's ethical standards, what words or phrases come to mind? What do you believe sets us apart in terms of our values and ethics?

There could be several associated implications because of broken values and ethics loop, such as:

- Erosion of trust and credibility with employees, customers, and stakeholders.
- Risk of legal and regulatory issues, potentially leading to fines or lawsuits.
- Decline in employee morale, engagement, and overall job satisfaction.
- Damage to the organization's reputation and brand.
- Negative impact on customer and stakeholder relations.

Potential loss of key talent and difficulty in attracting new talent. Apart from these qualitative responses, there can also be some measures or indicators that reflect the values and ethics of health in the organization like:

- Number of reported ethical violations and resolutions.
- Employee surveys measure perception of ethical behavior and alignment with values.
- Employee turnover rates.
- Customer and stakeholder satisfaction and feedback related to ethics and values.

Leadership and Management

Leadership and management are the cornerstones of effective organizational performance. They encompass the behaviors, practices, and strategies that guide teams, shape workplace culture, and drive success. Understanding the various aspects of leadership styles and managerial practices and their impact on employees is essential to building a resilient and productive workforce. In this context, we explore how leadership and management influence employee engagement, communication, decision-making, and overall organizational health.

Some direct and indirect warning signs that indicate poor leadership and management in the organization include:

- Increased employee complaints
- High turnover among high-potential employees
- Ineffective performance management
- Lack of employee development
- Decline in team productivity
- Increased employee absenteeism
- Decreased employee engagement
- Silos and lack of cross-functional collaboration
- Decline in innovation and creativity
- Decreased customer satisfaction
- Eroding organizational culture

If you notice any of these in your organization, it's important to deliberately focus effort on your leadership and management capability in the organization.

Leadership and Management includes

- **Leadership Styles**: Assess the different leadership styles present within the organization, such as transformational, transactional, autocratic, or servant leadership.
- **Managerial Practices**: Examine how managers organize work, set expectations, provide feedback, and support employee development.
- **Employee Engagement**: Evaluate the extent to which leadership and management foster employee engagement, motivation, and a sense of belonging.
- **Communication**: Explore the effectiveness of communication between leadership, management, and employees at all levels.
- **Decision-Making**: Understand how decisions are made within the organization, including the involvement of employees in decision-making processes.

- **Conflict Resolution**: Assess how conflicts are managed and resolved within teams and between leadership and employees.
- **Coaching and Mentorship**: Investigate the availability and impact of coaching and mentorship programs for employees.
- **Leadership Development**: Determine if the organization invests in leadership development programs and their impact on leadership skills and effectiveness.

Some sample questions you could ask employees across the organization to get some open, thoughtful responses to understand more about Leadership and Management in the company and how it is impacting them:

- Can you describe a specific instance where a leader or manager positively impacted your work experience? What did they do?
- What type of leadership style do you think is most prevalent within our organization, and how does it affect our work environment?
- How would you describe the communication between leadership, management, and employees? Are there areas where it could be improved?
- Can you share an example of a time when conflict arose in your team or department and how it was resolved?
- What support or resources do you believe would help managers better support your professional growth and development?
- In your opinion, what makes a great leader or manager? Are these qualities present in our current leadership?
- How involved do you feel in decision-making processes within your team or department? Can you provide an example?

Have you participated in any coaching or mentorship programs at the organization? What was your experience like, and did it impact your growth?

There could be several associated implications because of poor leadership and management in the organization like:

- Decreased employee morale, engagement, and productivity.
- Higher turnover and difficulty attracting top talent.
- Decreased team cohesion and collaboration.
- Increased absenteeism and stress among employees.
- Negative impact on organizational culture and reputation.

There are also some quantitative measures that directly or indirectly reflect Leadership and Management efficiency in the organization:

- Employee engagement scores and feedback.
- Manager effectiveness ratings in employee performance reviews.
- Leadership development program participation and outcomes.
- Employee turnover rates and exit interview data.
- Employee satisfaction and well-being surveys.
- Frequency and nature of conflict resolution processes.

Organization structure

Organization structure serves as the architectural framework defining how an organization operates and organizes its workforce. It encompasses the hierarchy, departmentalization, decision-making processes, and the overall design that shapes the flow of work and communication. In this context, we delve into the various aspects of organization structure, how it influences collaboration, decision-making, and adaptability, and the potential impact it has on an organization's efficiency and effectiveness.

Some warning signs that indicate a poor organization structure include:

- Increased reports of unethical behavior or violations.
- Declining employee trust in leadership or the organization's ethical commitment.
- A rise in ethical dilemmas without clear resolution.
- High employee turnover, especially among those who cite ethical concerns.

If you notice any of these in your organization, you should probe further and take corrective actions

Organization structure covers

- **Hierarchy and Reporting Lines**: The formal structure of the organization, including the hierarchy, roles, and reporting relationships.
- **Departmentalization**: How the organization groups employees into departments or teams based on functions, products, or regions.
- **Span of Control**: The number of employees directly supervised by a manager, which can affect decision-making and communication.
- **Centralization vs. Decentralization**: The distribution of decision-making authority between top management and lower levels of the organization.
- **Matrix Structures**: If applicable, explore the presence and effectiveness of matrix or hybrid organizational structures.
- **Cross-Functional Teams**: Assess how cross-functional teams are formed and operate within the organization.
- **Flexibility and Adaptability**: The organization's capacity to adjust its structure in response to changing circumstances or market dynamics.

There could be several associated implications because of poor organization structure like:

- Decreased efficiency and productivity.
- High turnover and difficulty retaining talent.
- Communication breakdowns and errors.
- Difficulty in responding to market changes or customer demands.
- Increased operational costs and delays.

> Some sample questions you could ask employees across the organization to get some open, thoughtful responses to understand more about the effectiveness of organization structure in the company:

- How does our organizational structure impact your ability to collaborate and communicate with colleagues from different departments?
- Can you describe a situation where the organizational structure either facilitated or hindered a project's success? What were the effects?
- What do you believe are the strengths and weaknesses of our current organizational hierarchy and reporting lines?
- How flexible do you perceive our organization's structure to be in responding to new challenges or opportunities?
- In your experience, how well do cross-functional teams function within the organization, and what improvements could be made?
- Do you think decision-making authority is appropriately distributed between upper management and lower levels of the organization? Can you provide an example?
- How does the departmentalization of our organization affect the flow of information and decision-making?
- What changes or adjustments to our organizational structure do you believe would enhance our overall performance and effectiveness?

Apart from these qualitative responses, certain other metrics could indicate the efficiency of the organization structure like:

- Employee satisfaction with their roles and responsibilities.
- Time-to-market metrics for new products or services.
- Cross-functional project success rates.
- Employee turnover rates by department or team.
- Customer feedback related to the organization's responsiveness and adaptability.

| 2.2 |

EMPLOYEE WELL-BEING AND GROWTH

Employee well-being and growth are vital pillars of a thriving workplace. It encompasses the pursuit of a balanced work-life environment, fostering continuous growth and development opportunities, nurturing effective team dynamics, and championing diversity and inclusion. This multifaceted approach ensures that employees not only find fulfillment and support within their roles but also contribute to a harmonious and forward-moving organizational culture. In this context, we explore how these elements contribute to the overall health and success of the workforce and the organization as a whole.

Work-life balance and well-being

Work-life balance and well-being are the cornerstones of a healthy and productive workforce. They encompass the management of workload and stress levels and the promotion of a supportive and flexible work environment. Employee well-being extends beyond physical health to mental and emotional health, nurturing a workplace culture that values individuals' overall quality of life. In this context, we delve into how these aspects contribute to employee satisfaction, productivity, and the overall success of both employees and the organization

Some warning signs that indicate poor work-life balance in the organization and reduced focus on employee well-being include:

- Increased absenteeism or sick leave requests.
- Declining employee satisfaction and engagement scores.
- A surge in reported stress-related health issues.
- High turnover rates in key positions.
- Frequent conflicts or strained team dynamics.
- Employee feedback indicating work-life imbalance or burnout.

If you notice any or all of these, even in pockets in the organization, sit up and act.

Work-life balance and well-being covers:

- **Workload and Stress Levels**: Assess employee workload and the stress levels it generates.
- **Flexibility and Remote Work**: Evaluate the organization's flexibility regarding work hours and remote work options.
- **Mental Health Support**: Explore the availability of mental health resources and support.
- **Physical Health**: Consider the promotion of physical health and wellness initiatives.
- **Workplace Culture**: Examine how workplace culture affects well-being and work-life balance.
- **Employee Recognition**: Assess the recognition and rewards system for contributions.
- **Burnout**: Investigate signs of employee burnout and its causes.

Some sample questions you could ask employees across the organization to get some open, thoughtful responses to understand more about work-life balance and focus on well-being in the company:

- How do you manage your work responsibilities while maintaining a healthy work-life balance?
- Are there challenges you face in terms of balancing work and personal life? What could be done to address them?
- How does your work environment impact your well-being, both positively and negatively?
- What kind of support or resources do you believe would enhance your well-being at work?
- Can you share any personal strategies you use to cope with stress and maintain a sense of balance?
- How effective do you find our organization's approach to promoting mental health and well-being?

- Have you ever experienced symptoms of burnout, and if so, how did you address them?
- In your opinion, what steps can the organization take to improve work-life balance for employees?
- Are there specific initiatives or practices from other organizations that you believe could benefit us in terms of well-being?

There could be several associated implications because of a poor work-life balance and focus on employee well-being:

- Reduced productivity and efficiency.
- Decreased employee morale and job satisfaction.
- Increased absenteeism and presenteeism.
- Higher turnover rates and difficulty in retaining talent.
- Impact on overall organizational culture and reputation.
- Potential legal and compliance issues related to employee health and well-being.

Apart from these qualitative responses, there can also be some other metrics that reflect on the work-life balance and focus on well-being in the organization like:

- Employee engagement and satisfaction survey results.
- Absenteeism rates and patterns.
- Turnover rates, especially in high-stress roles.
- Utilization of mental health resources and programs.
- Health and wellness program participation and outcomes.
- Feedback from performance evaluations and 360-degree assessments related to stress and work-life balance.

Employee growth and development

Employee growth and development form the bedrock of a thriving workforce. It encompasses the opportunities for learning, skill enhancement, and career advancement that an organization offers to its employees. This facet of the workplace is a critical driver of employee engagement, satisfaction, and long-term commitment. In this context, we delve into how employee growth and development initiatives contribute to building a skilled, motivated, and future-ready workforce, benefitting both individuals and the organization as a whole.

Some warning signs that indicate insufficient employee growth and development in the organization include:

- A high rate of employee turnover, especially among high-potential individuals.
- Low participation in training and development programs.
- Frequent complaints or dissatisfaction regarding performance evaluations.
- A lack of visible career advancement opportunities.
- Employee feedback indicating a disconnect between personal growth goals and organizational support.
- A decline in skill proficiency or competencies within critical roles.

If you notice any of these in your organization, it's important you take cognizance of it and deliberately dig deeper into all aspects of employee growth and development to identify the root cause of dissonance.

Employee growth and development covers

- **Training and Education**: Assess the availability and effectiveness of training and development programs.
- **Career Advancement**: Explore opportunities for career progression and growth within the organization.
- **Feedback and Performance Reviews**: Evaluate the feedback and performance review processes.
- **Skill Enhancement**: Consider initiatives that promote skill enhancement and continuous learning.
- **Mentorship and Coaching**: Investigate the availability and impact of mentorship and coaching programs.
- **Leadership Development**: Examine leadership development programs and their outcomes.

- **Feedback Culture**: Assess the organization's culture of providing constructive feedback.
- **Alignment with Personal Goals**: Explore how employee growth aligns with personal career goals.

> **Some sample questions you could ask employees across the organization to get some open, thoughtful responses to understand more about growth and development opportunities in the company:**
>
> - How satisfied are you with the opportunities for professional growth and development within our organization?
> - Can you share examples of training or development programs you found particularly beneficial for your career growth?
> - How do you perceive the feedback and performance review process? Are there ways it could be improved?
> - What role does mentorship or coaching play in your professional development, and how has it impacted your growth?
> - In your opinion, what steps could the organization take to further support your skill enhancement and learning needs?
> - Have you experienced career advancement within the organization? If so, what contributed to your progression?
> - How would you describe the organization's approach to leadership development, and have you benefited from it?
> - Do you feel your personal career goals align with the growth opportunities provided by the organization?

There could be several associated implications because of poor employee growth and development like:

- Reduced employee motivation and engagement.
- Difficulty in retaining top talent.
- A lack of skilled and qualified employees for critical roles.
- Negative impact on overall productivity and innovation.
- Increased recruitment and onboarding costs.

- Risk of decreased organizational competitiveness and adaptability.

Apart from these qualitative responses, there can also be some measures or indicators that reflect employee growth and development opportunities in the organization like -

- Participation rates in training and development programs.
- Employee satisfaction scores regarding growth opportunities.
- Employee turnover rates among high-potential individuals.
- Leadership pipeline and succession planning outcomes.
- Skill proficiency and competency assessments.
- Performance review ratings and feedback effectiveness.

Team Dynamics

Team dynamics define how groups of individuals collaborate, communicate, and function collectively to achieve shared goals. It encompasses the way team members interact, make decisions, and resolve conflicts within the group. These dynamics play a pivotal role in shaping team morale, productivity, and the overall success of projects and initiatives. In this context, we explore the key factors that influence effective teamwork, the impact of diversity and inclusion, and how trust, communication, and leadership contribute to harmonious and high-performing teams.

Some warning signs that indicate that broken team dynamics in the organization include:

- Frequent unresolved conflicts or disputes within teams.
- A decline in team morale, satisfaction, or engagement.
- High turnover or absenteeism within specific teams.
- Decreased productivity or missed project deadlines.
- An increase in employee complaints related to team dynamics. (workplace politics)
- Decreased innovation or a lack of initiative within teams.

If you notice any of these in your organization, then understand that team dynamics needs some attention.

Team Dynamics Covers

- **Communication**: Assess how team members communicate, share information, and collaborate.
- **Roles and Responsibilities**: Examine how roles and responsibilities are defined within teams.
- **Conflict Resolution**: Evaluate how conflicts are managed and resolved within teams.
- **Leadership and Decision-Making**: Explore leadership dynamics and how decisions are made.
- **Team Morale**: Consider the overall morale, cohesion, and motivation of team members.
- **Diversity and Inclusion**: Investigate the presence and impact of diversity within teams.
- **Trust and Psychological Safety**: Assess the level of trust and comfort team members have in sharing ideas and concerns.
- **Feedback Culture**: Evaluate the culture of giving and receiving feedback within teams.

Some sample questions you could ask employees across the organization to get some open, thoughtful responses to understand more about team dynamics in the company:

- How would you describe the communication and collaboration within your team?
- Can you provide an example of a time when your team effectively resolved a conflict or disagreement?
- What role do team leaders or managers play in facilitating teamwork and decision-making?
- In your experience, how does the diversity of team members impact the team's performance and dynamics?
- Are there opportunities for team members to provide input, share ideas, and give feedback openly?

> - What factors, in your opinion, contribute to a positive or negative team morale?
> - How do you perceive the balance of roles and responsibilities within your team?
> - What steps or changes could enhance trust and psychological safety within the team?
> - Have you observed any challenges or issues within your team that may require attention or improvement?

There could be several associated implications because of broken team dynamics like -

- Decreased team performance and productivity.
- Difficulty in retaining and attracting talent.
- Increased stress and absenteeism among team members.
- Negative impact on overall organizational culture.
- Potential delays in project completion and client dissatisfaction.
- Reduced employee satisfaction and engagement.

Apart from these qualitative responses, there can also be some measures or indicators that reflect the team dynamics in the organization like -

- Employee satisfaction scores related to teamwork.
- Team productivity and project success rates.
- Employee turnover rates within specific teams.
- Employee feedback on team cohesion and collaboration.
- Time-to-deliver projects or meet deadlines.
- Employee perception of diversity and inclusion within teams.

Diversity and Inclusion

Diversity and inclusion lie at the heart of a progressive and equitable workplace. They encompass the presence of individuals from various backgrounds and perspectives and the organization's commitment to fostering a culture of fairness and respect. Inclusion is not only about demographics but also about creating an environment where every voice is heard and valued. In this context, we delve into how diversity and inclusion initiatives contribute to enriching the workforce, enhancing creativity, and ensuring equal opportunities for all, ultimately driving both individual and organizational success.

Some warning signs that indicate poor diversity and inclusion in the organization include -

- A lack of diversity or underrepresentation in leadership positions.
- An increase in discrimination or harassment complaints.
- Decreased employee engagement and satisfaction scores.
- A decline in diverse talent recruitment or retention rates.
- Unequal access to opportunities or promotions.
- Negative employee sentiment related to diversity and inclusion.

If you notice any of these, you know you got to act.

Diversity and Inclusion Covers

- **Demographic Diversity**: Assess the representation of various demographic groups within the organization.
- **Inclusive Culture**: Examine the extent to which the organization fosters an inclusive and welcoming culture.
- **Equity**: Evaluate the fairness and equal opportunities for all employees.
- **Bias and Discrimination**: Investigate the presence of bias or discriminatory practices and their impact.
- **Leadership Commitment**: Assess the commitment of leadership to diversity and inclusion initiatives.
- **Employee Resource Groups**: Explore the existence and impact of employee resource groups.
- **Training and Education**: Evaluate diversity and inclusion training programs.
- **Feedback Mechanisms**: Consider the availability of channels for employees to provide feedback on diversity and inclusion issues.

> **Some sample questions you could ask employees across the organization to get some open, thoughtful responses to understand more about diversity and inclusion in the company:**
>
> - How do you perceive the organization's commitment to fostering diversity and inclusion?
> - Can you share examples of inclusive practices or initiatives that you believe are effective?
> - Have you ever encountered situations where you felt that bias or discrimination may have influenced decisions or interactions? How was it addressed?
> - In your opinion, what can the organization do to further promote a diverse and inclusive workplace?
> - What role do employee resource groups play in fostering inclusion, and have you been involved in any?
> - How does diversity and inclusion training impact your awareness and behavior within the organization?
> - Do you believe that diverse voices and perspectives are genuinely valued and heard within the organization?
> - What suggestions do you have for improving feedback mechanisms related to diversity and inclusion?

There could be several associated implications because of poor diversity and inclusion like:

- Difficulty in attracting and retaining diverse talent.
- Negative impact on employee morale and well-being.
- Increased turnover, especially among underrepresented groups.
- Decreased innovation and creativity within the organization.
- Reputational damage and potential legal issues.
- Limited market competitiveness in a diverse customer base.

Other data based measures that would indicate diversity and inclusion health in the organization include:

- Demographic data on employee composition.

- Employee engagement and satisfaction scores related to diversity and inclusion.
- Employee turnover rates among underrepresented groups.
- Performance and career progression data for diverse employees.
- Diversity and inclusion training program participation and feedback.
- Employee feedback on the inclusiveness of the organizational culture.

| 2.3 |
EFFECTIVE COMMUNICATION AND TRANSPARENCY

Effective communication and transparency serve as the pillars of a well-functioning organization. They encompass the open exchange of information, feedback culture, and the resolution of conflicts in a constructive manner. Additionally, organizational stories and myths contribute to the shared narrative and culture of the workplace. This multifaceted approach ensures that information flows seamlessly, conflicts are managed effectively, and employees connect with the organization's history and values. In this context, we explore how these elements contribute to a cohesive and thriving organizational culture and its impact on overall success.

Communication and transparency

Communication and transparency form the foundation of a well-informed and engaged workforce. They encompass the clear and open exchange of information, fostering an environment where employees feel informed, heard, and valued. Within this context, we explore the organization's communication practices, the accessibility of information, and the degree of transparency in decision-making. These elements play a pivotal role in shaping organizational culture, trust, and employee satisfaction, ultimately influencing the overall success of the organization.

Some warning signs that indicate that communication and transparency are not up to the mark include:

- A decline in employee morale and engagement.
- Increased employee turnover or absenteeism.
- Frequent conflicts or unresolved issues.
- A lack of participation in feedback mechanisms.
- Negative comments regarding communication and transparency.
- Decreased trust and satisfaction among employees.

If you notice any of these in your organization, its important you take cognizance of it and deliberately dig deeper into all aspects of communication and transparency to identify the root cause of dissonance.

Communication and Transparency Covers:

- **Information Flow**: Assess how information is shared and disseminated within the organization.
- **Accessibility of Information**: Examine the ease of access to relevant information by employees.
- **Communication Channels**: Evaluate the effectiveness of various communication channels used.
- **Transparency in Decision-Making**: Explore how transparent the decision-making processes are.
- **Honesty and Integrity**: Consider the organization's commitment to honesty and integrity in communication.
- **Feedback Mechanisms**: Investigate the presence and efficacy of feedback mechanisms.
- **Organizational Storytelling**: Assess how stories and narratives are used to convey organizational culture.
- **Conflict Resolution**: Evaluate how conflicts are addressed and resolved.

Some sample questions you could ask employees across the organization to get some open, thoughtful responses to understand more about communication and transparency in the company:

- How would you describe the flow of information within our organization? Are there any areas where it can be improved?
- Can you provide an example of a situation where transparency in decision-making positively or negatively impacted your work?
- In your opinion, how does the organization effectively engage employees in providing feedback and suggestions?
- How would you rate the organization's commitment to honesty

> and integrity in its communication with employees?
> - Are there any stories or narratives within the organization that you believe represent our culture and values well?
> - How conflicts are typically resolved within your team, and do you believe it's effective?
> - What suggestions do you have to improve the accessibility of important information within the organization?
> - Have you ever felt that you lacked essential information for your role, and how did it affect your work?
> - How can the organization enhance its communication and transparency practices to better support employees?

There could be several associated implications because of broken communication and transparency like:

- Reduced employee morale and engagement.
- Difficulty in retaining and attracting talent.
- Increased conflicts and misunderstandings.
- Decreased organizational efficiency and productivity.
- Negative impact on overall organizational culture.
- Potential legal and compliance issues.

Other metrics that directly or indirectly reflect transparency and communication in the organization include:

- Employee satisfaction scores regarding communication.
- Employee engagement survey results related to transparency.
- Employee turnover rates and reasons for leaving.
- Feedback participation rates and trends.
- Time-to-deliver critical information or decisions.
- Employee perception of the accessibility of information.

Feedback Culture and Conflict Resolution

A healthy feedback culture and effective conflict resolution mechanisms are the cornerstones of a harmonious and productive workplace. They encompass the willingness to provide and receive feedback openly and constructively, as well as the ability to address and resolve conflicts in a fair and timely manner. In this context, we explore how the organization encourages feedback, manages conflicts, and supports employees in navigating challenging situations. These elements are vital in fostering collaboration, trust, and a positive work environment, ultimately contributing to the overall success of the organization.

Some warning signs that indicate that there is some breakdown in the feedback culture and conflict resolution process in the organization include:

- Increased employee turnover or absenteeism associated with conflicts.
- Frequent unresolved conflicts or disputes.
- Decreased employee engagement and satisfaction scores.
- A lack of participation in feedback mechanisms.
- Negative feedback or comments regarding conflict resolution.
- A decline in trust and communication among teams.

Do any of the above statements sound familiar? then it's time for you to act.

Feedback Culture and Conflict Resolution Covers

- **Feedback Channels**: Assess the variety and accessibility of feedback channels within the organization.
- **Feedback Receptivity**: Examine how open and receptive the organization is to employee feedback.
- **Conflict Resolution Mechanisms**: Evaluate the processes in place for addressing and resolving conflicts.
- **Conflict Prevention**: Explore strategies for preventing conflicts from escalating.
- **Mediation and Support**: Investigate the availability and effectiveness of conflict mediation and support.
- **Feedback Timing**: Consider the timeliness of feedback and conflict resolution efforts.

- **Training and Education**: Assess the presence and impact of training on conflict resolution and feedback giving/receiving.
- **Cultural Barriers**: Identify any cultural or systemic barriers to open feedback and conflict resolution.

Some sample questions you could ask employees across the organization to get some open, thoughtful responses to understand more about feedback culture and conflict resolution process in the company:

- How comfortable are you with providing feedback to your peers or supervisors within the organization?
- Can you share an example of a constructive feedback experience, and how it was received and acted upon?
- In your opinion, how does the organization effectively address and resolve conflicts among employees or teams?
- Have you encountered any challenges related to feedback culture or conflict resolution? How were they managed?
- What strategies do you believe could improve the prevention and early resolution of conflicts within our organization?
- How do you perceive the organization's commitment to providing support and mediation during conflicts?
- Are there any instances where timely feedback or conflict resolution could have improved outcomes?
- Have you received training or guidance on providing effective feedback or managing conflicts within your role?
- What steps can the organization take to overcome any cultural barriers to open feedback and conflict resolution?

There could be several associated implications because of poor feedback culture and conflict resolution process like:

- Decreased employee morale and engagement.
- Difficulty in retaining and attracting talent.
- Increased conflicts and misunderstandings.
- Negative impact on overall organizational culture.

- Potential legal and compliance issues.
- Reduced teamwork and collaboration.

A few other metrics that are a reflection of the feedback culture and conflict resolution process in the organization include:

- Employee satisfaction scores related to feedback and conflict resolution.
- Employee turnover rates and reasons for leaving.
- Participation rates in conflict mediation or resolution processes.
- Time-to-resolution for conflicts or feedback implementation.
- Employee perception of the organization's openness to feedback.
- Number of unresolved conflicts and their impact on operations.

Organizational Stories and Myths

Organizational stories and myths are the narratives that define an organization's history, values, and culture. They encompass the tales and legends that employees share, reflecting the collective identity and experiences within the workplace. These stories hold the power to inspire, shape values, and create a sense of belonging among employees. In this context, we explore the significance of these narratives, their influence on organizational culture, and the role they play in fostering engagement and a shared sense of purpose among employees.

Some warning signs that indicate that the organizational stories and myths are being misused or misinterpreted in the organization include:

- Misinterpretation or misuse of historical narratives.
- Negative impact on employee morale or identity.
- Lack of inclusivity or relevance in stories.
- Disconnect between historical narratives and present-day values.
- Widespread myths or misconceptions among employees.
- Decline in the recognition of important organizational stories.

Organizational Myths and Stories Covers

- **Historical Narratives**: Assess the stories and myths that are part of the organization's history.
- **Values and Culture**: Explore how these stories reflect the organization's values and culture.
- **Impact on Identity**: Investigate how these stories shape the collective identity of employees.
- **Storytelling Channels**: Examine the platforms or channels through which these stories are shared.
- **Accuracy and Consistency**: Evaluate the accuracy and consistency of these narratives.
- **Inclusivity**: Consider whether these stories are inclusive and resonate with all employees.
- **Myth-Busting**: Examine the presence of any myths or misconceptions that need debunking.
- **Contemporary Narratives**: Assess the relevance and currency of stories in the present context.

Some sample questions you could ask employees across the organization to get some open, thoughtful responses to understand more about the popular organizational myths and stories and the associated impact in the company:

- Can you share a memorable organizational story or myth that has influenced your perception of the company?
- How do you believe these stories and myths contribute to our organizational culture and values?
- Are there any historical narratives or myths that you find particularly inspiring or impactful?
- In your opinion, how can these stories be effectively shared and passed down to new employees?
- Have you ever encountered myths or misconceptions about the organization that needed clarification?
- How do these narratives align with the diversity and inclusivity goals of the organization?
- Are there any contemporary stories or narratives that you

> believe should be added to our organizational history?
> - How do these stories influence your sense of belonging and identity within the organization?

There could be several associated implications because of misuse or misinterpretation of organizational myths and stories like:

- Loss of organizational identity and culture.
- Decreased employee engagement and connection.
- Potential misunderstandings or misalignment with values.
- Risk of myths affecting decision-making and behavior.
- Reduced cohesion and shared purpose among employees.
- Challenges in attracting and retaining talent.
- A few other metrics reflecting the same would include:
- Employee satisfaction scores regarding organizational culture.
- Employee engagement survey results related to shared values.
- Tracking the recognition and understanding of historical narratives.
- Monitoring myths or misconceptions and their impact on employee behavior.
- Feedback on inclusivity and relevance of organizational stories.
- Assessing the alignment of stories with diversity and inclusion goals.

These comprehensive responses provide a thorough approach to exploring organizational stories and myths within the organization, covering various aspects, indicators, and potential implications.

| 2.4 |
PERFORMANCE AND INNOVATION

Performance and innovation are essential pillars of organizational success. They encompass the effective management of employee performance, a commitment to continuous improvement, and the adoption of technology and innovation to drive growth. Within this context, we explore how performance is measured and optimized, the strategies in place for fostering innovation, and the organization's readiness to embrace technological advancements. These elements collectively contribute to an agile, competitive, and forward-thinking workplace, ensuring that the organization thrives in an ever-evolving business landscape.

Performance Management

Performance management is the cornerstone of organizational effectiveness, focusing on how individuals and teams perform, develop, and contribute to overall success. It encompasses goal-setting, feedback, coaching, recognition, and alignment with organizational objectives. Within this context, we delve into the strategies and processes that drive employee performance, development, and engagement. An effective performance management system not only motivates employees but also enhances the organization's ability to achieve its goals and fulfill its mission.

Some warning signs that indicate that performance management process breakdown include:

- A decline in employee engagement and satisfaction scores.
- Increased turnover, especially among high-performing employees.
- Frequent performance-related grievances or disputes.
- Inconsistent application of performance standards.
- A lack of participation in performance improvement plans.
- Negative feedback or comments regarding performance

management.

If you notice any of these in your organization, it's important you take cognizance of it and deliberately dig deeper into all aspects of performance management to identify the root cause of dissonance.

Performance Management Covers:

- **Goal Setting**: Assess the process of setting clear and achievable performance goals.
- **Feedback and Coaching**: Examine how feedback and coaching are provided to employees.
- **Performance Reviews**: Evaluate the effectiveness of performance review processes.
- **Recognition and Rewards**: Explore the mechanisms in place for recognizing and rewarding high performance.
- **Development Plans**: Assess how individual development plans are created and executed.
- **Performance Improvement**: Investigate how underperformance is identified and managed.
- **Alignment with Organizational Goals**: Examine how individual performance aligns with organizational objectives.
- **Employee Input**: Consider the degree to which employees are involved in their own performance management.

> **Some sample questions you could ask employees across the organization to get some open, thoughtful responses to understand more about the performance management process and its implications in the company:**
>
> - How would you describe the process of setting performance goals within the organization?
> - Can you share an example of a performance review experience, including feedback and development discussions?
> - In your opinion, how effectively does the organization recognize and reward high performers?

> - Have you been involved in creating your own development plan, and how has it impacted your growth?
> - What strategies or support do you believe would improve the identification and management of underperformance?
> - How do you see the alignment between your individual performance goals and the organization's objectives?
> - Are there opportunities for employees to provide input or feedback on their own performance management?
> - How does performance management impact your motivation and job satisfaction within the organization?

There could be several associated implications because of a poor performance management process like:

- Decreased employee morale and motivation.
- Difficulty in retaining high-performing talent.
- Lower productivity and performance levels.
- Potential legal issues related to performance evaluation.
- Negative impact on team dynamics and collaboration.
- Reduced overall organizational effectiveness.

Apart from these qualitative responses, there can also be some measures or indicators that reflect the effectiveness of the performance management process in the organization like:

- Employee satisfaction scores related to performance management.
- Employee turnover rates and reasons for leaving.
- Tracking the completion of individual development plans.
- The percentage of employees meeting or exceeding performance goals.
- Time-to-fill vacancies for critical roles.
- Employee feedback on the fairness and effectiveness of performance reviews.

Innovation and Continuous Improvement

Innovation and continuous improvement are essential drivers of organizational success, facilitating growth, efficiency, and adaptability. They encompass a culture of creativity, the generation and implementation of new ideas, and the ongoing pursuit of better processes. Within this context, we explore how the organization encourages innovation, fosters a culture of improvement, and integrates these practices into its strategic objectives. Embracing innovation and continuous improvement enhances competitiveness and ensures the organization's long-term sustainability in a dynamic business landscape.

Some warning signs that indicate that innovation and continuous improvement in the organization is not up to the mark include:

- A lack of participation or interest in innovation initiatives.
- Repeated failure to implement innovative ideas.
- Employee disengagement or frustration related to innovation.
- A decrease in employee morale or motivation.
- A decline in the organization's competitive edge.
- Negative feedback or comments regarding innovation efforts.

Innovation and Continuous Improvement Covers

- **Innovation Culture**: Assess the organization's culture around innovation and creativity.
- **Idea Generation**: Examine how ideas for improvement and innovation are generated.
- **Implementation**: Evaluate the processes for implementing new ideas and improvements.
- **Feedback and Learning**: Explore how feedback is gathered and learning from innovations is shared.
- **Resource Allocation**: Assess how resources are allocated to support innovation.
- **Leadership and Support**: Investigate the role of leadership in fostering innovation and improvement.
- **Integration with Strategy**: Consider how innovation aligns with

the organization's strategic goals.
- **Monitoring and Measurement**: Examine how the impact of innovations and improvements is measured.

> **Some sample questions you could ask employees across the organization to get some open, thoughtful responses to understand more about innovation and continuous improvement in the company:**
>
> - How would you describe the organization's approach to fostering innovation and continuous improvement?
> - Can you share an example of an innovative idea or process improvement you've been a part of?
> - In your opinion, how effectively does the organization implement new ideas and improvements?
> - What mechanisms are in place for collecting feedback on innovations, and how is this feedback used?
> - How do you see the allocation of resources to support innovation and improvement efforts?
> - What role do leaders and managers play in encouraging innovation within your team or department?
> - Do you feel that the organization's innovation efforts are well-aligned with its strategic objectives?
> - Are there ways in which the impact of innovations and improvements could be better measured?

There could be several associated implications because of lack of or an ineffective innovation and continuous improvement process like:

- Missed opportunities for growth and efficiency.
- Reduced competitiveness and adaptability in the market.
- Employee disengagement and attrition.
- Stagnation and inability to respond to changing market conditions.
- Inefficiencies and operational bottlenecks.
- A negative impact on the organization's reputation.

Apart from these qualitative responses, there can also be some measures or indicators that reflect the extent of innovation and continuous improvement in the organization like:

- Tracking the number of innovative ideas generated and implemented.
- Employee engagement scores related to innovation.
- Time-to-market for new products or improvements.
- Customer satisfaction and loyalty metrics.
- Employee perception of leadership support for innovation.
- Cost savings or efficiency gains attributed to improvements.

Technology and Innovation Adoption

Technology and innovation adoption are key drivers of organizational growth and competitiveness. They encompass the strategic integration of new technologies and a culture that encourages innovation. Within this context, we explore how the organization approaches technology adoption, provides the necessary support and training, and fosters a culture of innovation. The ability to effectively adopt and leverage technology and innovation not only enhances operational efficiency but also positions the organization for success in an ever-evolving business landscape.

Some warning signs that indicate that Technology and innovation adoption are not on track include:

- Low adoption rates or resistance to using new technologies.
- Frequent technological disruptions or inefficiencies.
- Declining employee morale or engagement related to technology.
- An inability to keep up with industry standards or competitors.
- Ineffective use of technology resources.
- Negative feedback or comments regarding technology adoption.

If you see any of these in you organization, you need to act soon before it is too late.

Technology and Innovation Adoption Covers

- **Innovation Strategy**: Evaluate the organization's strategy for adopting new technologies and fostering innovation.
- **Technological Infrastructure**: Assess the availability and effectiveness of technological infrastructure.
- **Employee Training**: Examine the level of training and support provided for adopting new technologies.
- **Innovation Culture**: Investigate the organization's culture of embracing innovation and technology.
- **User Feedback**: Consider how user feedback is collected and integrated into technology adoption.
- **Change Management**: Evaluate the change management processes related to technology adoption.
- **Integration with Operations**: Assess how new technologies are integrated into day-to-day operations.
- **Competitive Advantage**: Explore how technology adoption contributes to a competitive edge.

Some sample questions you could ask employees across the organization to get some open, thoughtful responses to understand more about technology and innovation adoption in the company:

- How do you perceive the organization's approach to adopting new technologies and fostering innovation?
- Can you share an example of a recent technology adoption initiative and its impact on your work?
- In your opinion, how effective is the organization in providing training and support for using new technologies?
- How would you describe the organization's culture regarding the adoption of innovative technologies?
- Are there mechanisms in place for collecting user feedback on technology adoption, and how is this feedback used?
- Can you share insights into how the organization manages change during technology adoption processes?

> - How well do new technologies integrate into your daily work processes?
> - How do you believe technology adoption contributes to our organization's competitive advantage?

There could be several associated implications because of a broken technology and innovation adoption in the organization like:

- Reduced efficiency and productivity.
- Loss of competitiveness and market share.
- Employee frustration and potential attrition.
- Inability to meet customer expectations.
- Missed opportunities for growth and cost savings.
- Impact on overall organizational effectiveness.

Apart from these qualitative responses, there can also be some measures or indicators that reflect technology and innovation adoption in the organization like:

- Technology adoption rates among employees or teams.
- Employee satisfaction scores related to technology resources.
- Time-to-market for new products or services.
- Customer feedback on the organization's technological capabilities.
- Employee perception of the organization's commitment to innovation.
- Cost savings or revenue increases attributed to technology adoption.

| 2.5 |
STAKEHOLDER RELATIONS AND RESPONSIBILITY

Stakeholder relations and responsibilities are fundamental aspects of an organization's commitment to ethical, sustainable, and responsible business practices. This encompasses the management of relationships with customers and stakeholders, adherence to regulatory and compliance standards, and the pursuit of corporate social responsibility (CSR) initiatives. Within this context, we explore how the organization engages with its stakeholders, fulfills its regulatory obligations, and contributes positively to society and the environment. These elements collectively shape the organization's reputation, trustworthiness, and its ability to create lasting value for all stakeholders.

Customer and Stakeholder Relations

Customer and stakeholder relations are pivotal elements in an organization's quest for sustainability and growth. They encompass the methods and strategies used to engage with customers and stakeholders, gather feedback, and build enduring relationships. Within this context, we explore how the organization approaches these interactions, resolves conflicts, and maintains transparency. Effective customer and stakeholder relations not only enhance trust but also play a critical role in shaping the organization's reputation and success.

Some warning signs that indicate that customer and stakeholder relations in the organization are severely compromised include:

- Increasing customer complaints or negative feedback.
- Declining customer or stakeholder satisfaction scores.
- Escalating conflicts or disputes with stakeholders.
- A lack of transparency or trust among stakeholders.
- High turnover or attrition among customers or key stakeholders.
- Regulatory or compliance issues related to stakeholder relations.

If you notice any of these in your organization, it's important you take cognizance of it and deliberately dig deeper into all aspects of customer and stakeholder relations to identify the root cause of dissonance.

Customer and Stakeholder Relations Covers:

- **Customer Engagement**: Assess how the organization engages and communicates with customers.
- **Stakeholder Mapping**: Identify key stakeholders and their interests in the organization.
- **Feedback Mechanisms**: Evaluate processes for collecting and acting on customer and stakeholder feedback.
- **Conflict Resolution**: Examine strategies for resolving conflicts or issues with customers and stakeholders.
- **Transparency**: Explore how transparent the organization is in its dealings with stakeholders.
- **Communication Channels**: Assess the effectiveness of communication channels used with stakeholders.
- **Responsiveness**: Evaluate the organization's ability to respond promptly to stakeholder concerns.
- **Partnerships and Collaborations**: Investigate partnerships or collaborations with external stakeholders.

> Some sample questions you could ask employees across the organization to get some open, thoughtful responses to understand more about customer and stakeholder relations in the company:
>
> - How would you describe the organization's approach to engaging with customers and stakeholders?
> - Can you share an example of how customer or stakeholder feedback led to a positive change within the organization?
> - In your experience, how effectively does the organization resolve conflicts or issues with customers and stakeholders?
> - How would you rate the organization's level of transparency in its interactions with stakeholders?

> - What communication channels do you believe work best when engaging with customers and stakeholders?
> - How well does the organization respond to and address concerns raised by stakeholders?
> - Are there examples of successful partnerships or collaborations with external stakeholders that you can share?
> - In your opinion, what could be done to improve customer and stakeholder relations within the organization?

There could be several associated implications because of poor customer and stakeholder relations like:

- Damage to the organization's reputation and brand.
- Loss of customers, revenue, and market share.
- Legal or regulatory penalties.
- Difficulty in attracting and retaining key stakeholders.
- Disruption of business operations and partnerships.
- Impact on long-term sustainability and growth.

Some other measures would include:

- Customer satisfaction scores and feedback analysis.
- Net Promoter Score (NPS) and Customer Effort Score (CES).
- Stakeholder engagement and satisfaction surveys.
- Resolution time for customer/stakeholder issues.
- Number of successful partnerships or collaborations.
- Compliance with regulatory requirements related to stakeholder engagement.

Corporate Social Responsibility (CSR)

Corporate Social Responsibility (CSR) is the ethical cornerstone of an organization's commitment to making a positive impact on society and the environment. It encompasses a wide range of initiatives, from sustainable business practices to community engagement and philanthropic efforts. Within this context, we explore how the organization embraces CSR, aligns with ethical principles, and contributes to the well-being of society. Effective CSR not only enhances the organization's reputation but also plays a vital role in creating a more responsible and sustainable future.

Some warning signs that indicate that the CSR work is not aligned include:

- Decreased community trust or negative sentiment.
- Environmental violations or reputational damage.
- Ethical misconduct or compliance issues.
- Employee dissatisfaction related to CSR efforts.
- Declining stakeholder engagement or support.
- Decreased participation in CSR initiatives.

Corporate Social Responsibility (CSR) covers:

- **CSR Strategy**: Evaluate the organization's strategy for CSR initiatives.
- **Community Engagement**: Assess the organization's involvement in community activities.
- **Environmental Impact**: Examine efforts to reduce environmental impact and promote sustainability.
- **Ethical Practices**: Evaluate adherence to ethical standards and responsible business practices.
- **Employee Well-being**: Explore initiatives promoting employee well-being and workplace ethics.
- **Philanthropy**: Assess charitable contributions and social investments.
- **Stakeholder Engagement**: Investigate engagement with stakeholders regarding CSR efforts.
- **Transparency**: Evaluate transparency in reporting CSR activities.

> **Some sample questions you could ask employees across the organization to get some open, thoughtful responses to understand more about CSR activities in the company:**
>
> - How would you describe the organization's commitment to Corporate Social Responsibility (CSR)?
> - Can you share examples of CSR initiatives that you've been a part of or have observed?
> - In what ways do you believe the organization engages with the community and addresses social issues?
> - How does the organization promote sustainability and minimize its environmental impact?
> - What ethical practices and responsible business conduct do you perceive within the organization?
> - Are there initiatives that support employee well-being and workplace ethics that you find particularly effective?
> - Can you share insights into the organization's philanthropic efforts or social investments?
> - How transparent do you feel the organization is in reporting its CSR activities to stakeholders?

There could be several associated implications because of poorly executed CSR activities like:

- Damage to the organization's reputation and brand.
- Loss of community support and trust.
- Legal or regulatory penalties.
- Employee disengagement and attrition.
- Negative impact on stakeholder relations and partnerships.
- Missed opportunities for positive social impact.

Some other metrics that could share insights include:

- CSR performance indicators and reporting.
- Community and stakeholder feedback on CSR efforts.
- Environmental sustainability metrics.

- Employee satisfaction scores related to CSR initiatives.
- Impact measurement of philanthropic activities.
- Transparency in CSR reporting and communication.

Compliance and Regulatory Adherence

Compliance and regulatory adherence stand as the pillars of an organization's commitment to operating responsibly within the boundaries of the law and established guidelines. It encompasses a comprehensive framework that ensures the organization's actions, policies, and processes align with legal and regulatory requirements. Within this context, we explore how the organization approaches compliance, maintains internal policies, and engages with regulatory authorities. Effective compliance not only mitigates risk but also upholds the organization's reputation and integrity, fostering trust among stakeholders.

Some warning signs that indicate that the compliance and regulatory adherence in the organization is broken or is not uniform include:

- Frequent compliance violations or incidents.
- Increased regulatory scrutiny or penalties.
- Declining employee knowledge or engagement with compliance policies.
- Ineffective reporting mechanisms or whistleblower complaints.
- Inadequate documentation or record-keeping.
- Stakeholder or public concerns related to compliance.

If you notice any of these in your organization, it's important you take cognizance of it and deliberately dig deeper into all aspects of compliance and regulatory adherence to identify the root cause of dissonance.

Compliance and Regulatory Adherence Covers:

- **Regulatory Framework**: Understand the regulatory landscape in which the organization operates.
- **Internal Compliance Policies**: Evaluate the organization's

internal policies and procedures for compliance.
- **Training and Awareness**: Assess the level of training and awareness among employees regarding compliance.
- **Reporting Mechanisms**: Examine mechanisms for reporting compliance-related issues.
- **Monitoring and Auditing**: Explore how the organization monitors and audits compliance.
- **Documentation and Record-Keeping**: Evaluate processes for maintaining compliance-related records.
- **Stakeholder Engagement**: Investigate how the organization engages with regulatory authorities and stakeholders.
- **Ethical Conduct**: Assess the organization's commitment to ethical conduct beyond regulatory requirements.

Some sample questions you could ask employees across the organization to get some open, thoughtful responses to understand more about compliance and regulatory adherence in the company:

- How would you describe the organization's approach to compliance with regulations and internal policies?
- Can you share examples of how compliance-related training has been implemented in your department or team?
- In your experience, how accessible are reporting mechanisms for addressing compliance concerns?
- What insights can you provide about how the organization monitors and ensures compliance with regulations?
- How effective are the processes for documenting and maintaining compliance-related records?
- Are there instances where the organization has engaged with regulatory authorities or external stakeholders regarding compliance matters?
- In your opinion, how does the organization promote ethical conduct beyond what is legally required?

There could be several associated implications because of a broken compliance and regulatory adherence like:

- Legal and financial liabilities.
- Damage to reputation and brand.
- Risk of regulatory sanctions or fines.
- Employee distrust and disengagement.
- Erosion of stakeholder trust.
- Operational disruptions and inefficiencies.

Apart from these qualitative responses, there can also be some measures or indicators that reflect the compliance and regulatory adherence health in the organization like:

- Regulatory compliance audit results.
- Number of compliance-related incidents or violations.
- Employee compliance training completion rates.
- Timeliness and effectiveness of reporting mechanisms.
- Regulatory fines or penalties incurred.
- Stakeholder trust and confidence levels.
- Ethical conduct and corporate culture assessments.

| 2.6 |

ADAPTABILITY AND LEARNING

Adaptability and learning serve as the bedrock of an organization's ability to thrive in an ever-changing business landscape. This encompasses the organization's agility and adaptability in response to market shifts, its approach to learning from failure, and its capacity for effective crisis management and resilience. Within this context, we delve into how the organization fosters a culture of adaptability, encourages continuous learning, and handles challenges with resilience. The ability to adapt, learn, and navigate crises not only ensures survival but also positions the organization for sustained growth and success.

Agility and Adaptability

Agility and adaptability are the cornerstones of an organization's ability to thrive in a dynamic and ever-changing business environment. It encompasses the organization's capacity to embrace change, foster innovation, and respond swiftly to emerging opportunities and challenges. Within this context, we explore how the organization cultivates a culture of adaptability, empowers its workforce to embrace change, and continually evolves to stay competitive. The ability to adapt and be agile not only ensures resilience but also positions the organization for sustained growth and relevance in an evolving landscape.

Some warning signs that indicate that the organization is not agile or adaptable include:

- Resistance to change among employees.
- Decreased innovation or stagnation.
- Lengthy decision-making processes or bottlenecks.
- Inefficient resource allocation.
- High employee turnover or disengagement.
- Decline in market share or customer satisfaction.
- Challenges in project or product delivery timelines.

- Competitive disadvantages.

These warning signs need to be taken seriously and acted upon efficiently before it sets into the culture of the organization.

Agility and Adaptability Covers:

- **Change Management**: Assess how the organization manages and implements changes.
- **Innovation Culture**: Explore the organization's culture of innovation and willingness to adapt.
- **Decision-Making**: Examine the speed and flexibility of decision-making processes.
- **Resource Allocation**: Evaluate how resources are allocated to respond to changing needs.
- **Learning and Development**: Assess the organization's commitment to employee learning and development.
- **Market Response**: Investigate how the organization responds to market shifts and competition.
- **Agile Frameworks**: Explore the use of agile methodologies in projects and operations.
- **Customer-Centric Approach**: Evaluate the organization's focus on meeting customer demands.

Some sample questions you could ask employees across the organization to get some open, thoughtful responses to understand more about agility and adaptability in the company:

- How do you perceive the organization's ability to adapt to changing market conditions and customer needs?
- Can you share examples of recent changes or innovations that were successfully implemented within your team or department?
- In your experience, how flexible and responsive are decision-making processes within the organization?
- How does the organization allocate resources to support agility

> and adaptability in its operations?
> - What opportunities for learning and development have you encountered in your role?
> - How does the organization monitor and respond to shifts in the competitive landscape?
> - Are there agile frameworks or methodologies that you find particularly effective in your work?
> - How is the organization's approach to customer satisfaction and meeting customer demands evolving?

There could be several associated implications if the organization is not agile or adaptable like:

- Missed growth opportunities.
- Loss of market relevance.
- Decreased employee morale and productivity.
- Ineffective resource utilization.
- Increased operational costs.
- Customer attrition and revenue decline.
- Reputation damage.

Apart from these qualitative responses, there can also be some measures or indicators that reflect the agility and adaptability quotient in the organization like:

- Speed of change implementation.
- Rate of innovation and successful product launches.
- Decision-making cycle time.
- Resource utilization efficiency.
- Employee development and retention rates.
- Market share growth or loss.
- Project delivery timelines.
- Customer satisfaction and loyalty metrics.

Response to Failure and Learning

Response to failure and learning are fundamental aspects of an organization's journey toward growth and improvement. It entails the organization's ability to embrace failures as opportunities for growth, cultivate a culture of continuous learning, and apply insights from setbacks to drive positive change. Within this context, we explore how the organization encourages the open discussion of failures, supports knowledge sharing, and leverages lessons learned to foster resilience and innovation. Effective response to failure and learning not only mitigates risk but also fuels the organization's capacity for sustained progress and adaptation in a dynamic environment.

Some warning signs indicating poor response to failure and learning include:

- High employee fear of failure or risk aversion.
- Lack of mechanisms for sharing failure-related insights.
- Repeated or unresolved issues stemming from the same failures.
- Leadership resistance to acknowledging failures or learning from them.
- Stagnation or lack of innovation.
- Employee disengagement or demotivation.
- Ineffective use of resources without learning or improvement.

If you notice any of these in your organization, it's important you take cognizance of it and deliberately dig deeper into all aspects of failure processing and learning to identify the root cause of dissonance.

Response to Failure and Learning Covers:

- **Failure Acceptance**: Evaluate how the organization views and accepts failure as a part of the learning process.
- **Learning Culture**: Assess the organization's culture of continuous learning and improvement.
- **Feedback Mechanisms**: Examine the effectiveness of feedback mechanisms for employees and teams.
- **Knowledge Sharing**: Investigate how knowledge and lessons learned are shared across the organization.

- **Adaptive Strategies**: Explore the strategies employed to adapt and improve after failures.
- **Leadership Role**: Evaluate the role of leadership in promoting a culture of learning from failure.
- **Resource Allocation**: Assess how resources are allocated to support learning initiatives.
- **Performance Evaluation**: Understand how performance evaluations incorporate lessons learned.

> **Some sample questions you could ask employees across the organization to get some open, thoughtful responses to understand more about response to failure and learning in the company:**
>
> - How does the organization view and handle failure, particularly in the context of experimentation and innovation?
> - Can you provide examples of how the organization encourages and supports learning from mistakes and failures?
> - In your experience, how effective are feedback mechanisms in helping individuals and teams improve?
> - What initiatives or practices exist for sharing knowledge and lessons learned with colleagues?
> - How does the organization adapt and evolve its strategies after experiencing setbacks or failures?
> - What role do leaders play in fostering a culture of learning and resilience within teams?
> - Are resources allocated for training, skill development, or knowledge sharing within your department?
> - How do performance evaluations incorporate lessons learned and growth from experiences?

There could be several associated implications because of a poor response to failure or no inclination to learning, like:

- Repetition of costly mistakes.
- Stunted organizational growth and innovation.

- Employee frustration and disengagement.
- Reduced competitiveness and market relevance.
- Missed opportunities for improvement and efficiency.
- Declining customer satisfaction and trust.
- Negative impact on brand reputation.

Other metrics to consider would include:

- Rate of successful initiatives following lessons learned from previous failures.
- Employee feedback on the organization's approach to learning from failure.
- Time-to-resolution for identified issues or failures.
- Frequency of knowledge-sharing activities and participation.
- Employee engagement and morale metrics.
- Customer feedback and satisfaction scores.
- Innovation and new product development success rates.

Crisis Management and Resilience

Crisis management and resilience are critical components of an organization's ability to navigate unforeseen challenges and disruptions effectively. It involves the organization's preparedness to respond to crises, the strategies employed during critical situations, and its capacity to rebound and adapt in the aftermath. Within this context, we explore how the organization approaches crisis preparedness, its response mechanisms, and the role of leadership. Moreover, we examine how lessons from crises are integrated into future planning, employee well-being is prioritized, and resources are allocated. Effective crisis management and resilience not only safeguard the organization's reputation but also contribute to its long-term sustainability and adaptability in a volatile world.

Some warning signs that indicate poor crisis management ability and subdued resilience include:

- Lack of documented crisis response plans.
- Ineffective crisis communication.

- Repeated or escalating crisis.
- Employee disengagement during and after crises.
- Resource misallocation during crises.
- High turnover following crises.
- Diminished reputation or trust among stakeholders.

Any or all of the above requires immediate attention

Crisis Management and Resilience Covers:

- **Crisis Preparedness**: Evaluate how well the organization is prepared to handle crises.
- **Response Plans**: Examine the existence and effectiveness of crisis response plans.
- **Leadership during Crises**: Assess the role of leadership in managing crises.
- **Communication**: Explore communication strategies during crises.
- **Learning from Crises**: Investigate how the organization learns from past crises.
- **Employee Well-being**: Examine how the organization supports employees during crises.
- **Adaptive Strategies**: Evaluate strategies for adapting to the aftermath of crises.
- **Resource Allocation**: Assess resource allocation for crisis management.

Some sample questions you could ask employees across the organization to get some open, thoughtful responses to understand more about crisis management and resilience in the company:

- How confident are you in the organization's ability to respond effectively to unexpected crises?
- Can you share examples of how the organization has handled past crises, and what lessons were learned?

- What role do leaders play in guiding the organization through crises, and how effective have they been?
- How transparent and timely is the organization's communication during times of crisis?
- In your experience, how has the organization supported employee well-being during challenging periods?
- What strategies or adaptations have you observed in response to crises?
- Are there resources or support systems in place to help teams and individuals during crises?
- How does the organization incorporate lessons learned from crises into its future planning?

There could be several associated implications because of poor crisis management ability and resilience like:

- Reputation damage and loss of trust.
- Financial losses and increased operational costs.
- Employee disengagement and attrition.
- Decline in customer confidence and satisfaction.
- Prolonged recovery periods after crises.
- Legal and regulatory consequences.
- Competitive disadvantages.

Apart from these qualitative responses, there can also be some measures or indicators that reflect the crisis management ability and resilience in the organization like:

- Response time and effectiveness during crises.
- Employee feedback on crisis management and support.
- Rate of learning and adaptation following crises.
- Customer trust and satisfaction metrics.
- Financial impact assessment of crises.
- Compliance with legal and regulatory requirements.
- Competitive position in the market during and after crises.

| 2.7 |
DECISION-MAKING AND GOVERNANCE

Decision-making and governance are the foundational pillars that guide an organization's actions, policies, and strategic direction. It encompasses the processes by which decisions are made, the structures that support effective governance, and the metrics used to assess the alignment of organizational culture with these decisions. Within this context, we delve into the organization's decision-making mechanisms, their transparency, and the roles of stakeholders. We also explore how metrics are leveraged to evaluate the culture and governance effectiveness, ensuring that decisions align with the organization's values and goals. Effective decision-making and governance not only foster accountability but also pave the way for sound organizational growth and ethical conduct.

Decision-Making Process

The Decision-making process is the backbone of organizational governance, guiding how choices are made, resources are allocated, and strategies are crafted. It encompasses the roles, procedures, and principles that underpin effective decision-making within an organization. In this context, we explore the clarity and inclusivity of decision-making processes, the utilization of data and information, and the alignment of decisions with organizational values. We also delve into the transparency and timeliness of decision-making activities. A well-structured decision-making process not only promotes accountability but also fosters a culture of informed, values-driven choices that propel the organization forward.

Some warning signs that indicate that the decision-making process in the organization is broken or is not uniform include:

- Discontent or confusion among employees regarding decision-making roles.
- Repeated instances of decisions being made without adequate

information.
- Lack of inclusivity leading to unaddressed concerns or ideas.
- Slow or inefficient decision-making processes causing delays.
- Decision-related conflicts or disputes among teams or individuals.
- Decisions that deviate from the organization's stated values or goals.

If you notice any of these in your organization, it's important you take necessary action.

Decision-Making Process Covers

- **Decision Roles**: Evaluate who has decision-making authority and responsibility.
- **Process Clarity**: Assess the clarity of decision-making processes and procedures.
- **Inclusivity**: Examine how inclusive and diverse perspectives are in the decision-making process.
- **Data Utilization**: Evaluate the use of data and information in decision-making.
- **Decision Documentation**: Review how decisions are documented and communicated.
- **Timeliness**: Assess the speed and efficiency of decision-making.
- **Alignment with Values**: Ensure that decisions align with the organization's values and goals.
- **Transparency**: Evaluate how transparent decisions are to relevant stakeholders.

> **Some sample questions you could ask employees across the organization to get some open, thoughtful responses to understand more about decision-making process in the company:**
>
> - Can you describe the typical decision-making process within our organization?
> - How clear are the roles and responsibilities in decision-making?
> - Are there instances when you believe decisions should involve more diverse perspectives?
> - How often do data and insights play a role in the decisions made here?
> - How are decisions documented and communicated to relevant parties?
> - In your opinion, are decisions made in a timely manner?
> - Do you feel decisions align with our organization's stated values and goals?
> - Is there room for improvement in the transparency of our decision-making processes?

There could be several associated implications because of unclear decision-making process like:

- Decreased employee morale and engagement.
- Inefficient resource allocation.
- Increased risk of poor strategic choices.
- Potential legal or compliance issues.
- Negative impact on innovation and adaptability.
- Damage to organizational reputation and trust.

Other metrics that could also determine the effectiveness of the decision-making process in the organization could include:

- Average time taken for key decisions.
- Employee satisfaction with the decision-making process.
- Frequency of decisions aligned with organizational values.

- Rate of decision-related conflicts and resolutions.
- Compliance with decision documentation and communication standards.
- Alignment of decisions with long-term organizational goals.
- Inclusivity metrics related to diverse perspectives in decision-making.

Organizational Culture Metrics

Organizational Culture Metrics refer to the systematic measurement and assessment of an organization's culture. These metrics provide valuable insights into how employees perceive, experience, and contribute to the prevailing culture. By utilizing data-driven methods, organizations can gain a deeper understanding of cultural dynamics, values alignment, and areas for improvement. Culture metrics play a pivotal role in shaping decision-making, fostering transparency, and ensuring that an organization's culture remains in sync with its mission and objectives. In this context, we explore the essential role of culture metrics in promoting a healthy, values-driven workplace.

Some warning signs that indicate that the organizational culture metrics is poor include:

- High employee turnover or dissatisfaction.
- Erosion of trust or ethical lapses.
- Conflicting subcultures within the organization.
- Lack of alignment between stated values and actual behaviors.
- Resistance to cultural change initiatives.
- Employee disengagement or apathy regarding culture.

If you notice any of these in your organization, it's important you take cognizance of it and deliberately dig deeper into all aspects of organization culture to identify the root cause of dissonance.

Organizational Culture Metrics Covers:

- **Culture Assessment**: Evaluate how the organization measures

and assesses its culture.
- **Governance Structures**: Examine the formal systems and structures that oversee culture.
- **Alignment with Values**: Assess the alignment of culture with organizational values and mission.
- **Communication of Culture**: Explore how culture is communicated and reinforced.
- **Feedback Mechanisms**: Evaluate mechanisms for employees to provide feedback on culture.
- **Change Management**: Examine processes for managing cultural change initiatives.
- **Leadership Role**: Assess the role of leadership in shaping and promoting culture.
- **Training and Development**: Review programs aimed at building and maintaining culture.

Some sample questions you could ask employees across the organization to get some open, thoughtful responses to understand more about organizational culture in the company:

- How would you describe our organization's culture?
- Are there specific metrics or measurements you think we should use to assess our culture?
- How involved do you feel in contributing to and shaping our organizational culture?
- Can you provide examples of how our values are reflected in day-to-day operations?
- What avenues are available for employees to provide feedback or suggestions regarding our culture?
- Have you experienced any recent cultural changes in the organization? If so, how were they managed?
- How do you see our leadership influencing our organizational culture?
- Do you feel that training and development programs support our desired culture?

There could be several associated implications because of poor organizational culture like:

- Decreased employee morale and productivity.
- Difficulty in attracting and retaining top talent.
- Reputation damage and loss of stakeholder trust.
- Compliance and legal issues.
- Inefficient decision-making processes.
- Risk of ethical lapses and misconduct.

Other metrics that can indicate the organizational culture include:

- Employee satisfaction and engagement surveys.
- Turnover rates and exit interviews.
- Alignment of individual and team goals with organizational values.
- Number of ethics or compliance violations.
- Cultural alignment scores in performance evaluations.
- Progress toward cultural change initiatives.
- Leadership effectiveness in fostering culture.

Step 3

DELIBERATELY CHOOSE YOUR IDENTITY USING

THE DILEMMAS RESOLUTION FRAMEWORK (DRF)

Deliberate culture building involves navigating dilemmas, or choices about how the organization operates and interacts. The Dilemmas Resolution Framework helps to consciously shape this culture by aligning actions and decisions with strategic objectives, thereby acting as a growth catalyst.

Every organization, whether they recognize it or not, has a culture. It's like an undercurrent, unseen but profoundly influential. This culture, neither inherently good nor bad, merely exists. The distinction lies in whether an organization allows its culture to evolve passively or whether it chooses to shape it intentionally. The decision to deliberately build culture is akin to seizing the reins of one of the most influential aspects of an organization. It's the decision to align every action, interaction, and decision with the organization's strategic objectives. This alignment between culture and strategy can act as a turbocharger for growth, enhancing efficiency, innovation, employee engagement, and customer satisfaction.

But how does one go about building culture deliberately? How can you ensure that the culture you're crafting aligns with strategic objectives and remains flexible enough to adapt to the ever-changing business environment? When you examine the choices an organization and its employees make on a day-to-day basis, you'll find that there's no one-size-fits-all answer. Should the organization prioritize speed or accuracy? Should they recognize individual achievement or emphasize teamwork? What should be their focus - short-term gains or long-term sustainability? None of these options is inherently superior to the others. It's not about picking one over the other; each dilemma represents a spectrum, and organizations can choose where they stand - at one end, the other, or somewhere in between. The "right" choice depends on the organization's strategic objectives, market position, and other unique contextual factors.

This is where the Dilemmas Resolution Framework comes into play. It provides a structured approach to navigate these dilemmas. It helps organizations identify the choices they need to make and guides them in making these choices in a way that aligns with their strategic objectives. Essentially, it offers a roadmap for deliberate culture building, ensuring that the culture drives organizational growth rather than acting as a barrier. Yet, the framework isn't only about making choices; it's also about managing the tensions that these choices create. Every choice entails trade-offs. By identifying and managing these trade-offs, organizations can steer clear of the pitfalls that often accompany cultural change. They can create a culture that not only aligns with their strategy but is also resilient, adaptable, and conducive to the well-being of all stakeholders impacted by the culture.

In the upcoming sections, we'll delve deeper into the Dilemmas Resolution Framework, exploring its components, principles, and applications. We'll look at how this framework can be used to build a deliberate culture that propels the organization toward its strategic objectives.

It's important to remember that culture isn't a "soft" aspect of business that can be ignored or left to chance. It's a potent force that can drive the organization toward its strategic objectives or away from them. By choosing to build culture deliberately and by using the Dilemmas Resolution Framework to guide this process, organizations can harness the power of culture to turbocharge their growth. Deliberate culture building is not a one-off project or a mere checklist item. It's a continuous journey that demands commitment, courage, and curiosity. It involves making difficult choices, managing tensions, and continually aligning the culture with evolving strategic objectives. This journey can transform an organization, unleashing potential, unlocking innovation, and propelling it toward its strategic goals.

Dilemmas Resolution Framework (DRF):

The Dilemmas Resolution Framework is a comprehensive list of 60 dilemmas that leaders need to look at and make a choice. The collective set of these deliberate decisions together results in the organization's culture.

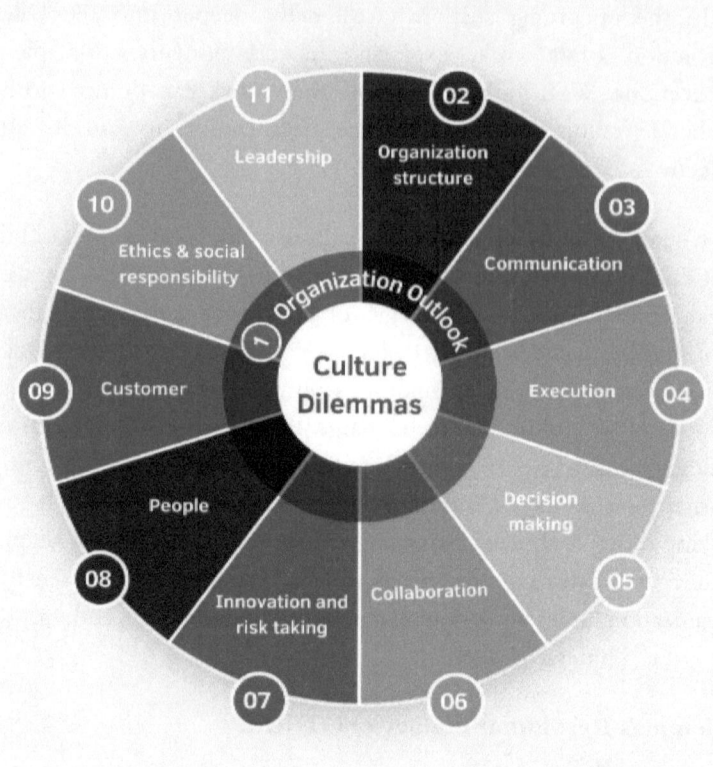

At the center are the **organization's outlook dilemmas**. Resolving these 10 dilemmas sets the tone for the rest of the dilemmas categorized under-

- **Organization structure dilemmas**
- **Communication dilemmas**
- **Execution dilemmas**
- **Decision-making dilemmas**
- **Collaboration dilemmas**
- **Innovation and risk-taking dilemmas**
- **People dilemmas**
- **Customer dilemmas**
- **Ethics & social responsibility dilemmas**
- **Leadership dilemmas**

| 3.1 |
ORGANIZATION OUTLOOK DILEMMAS

How Will You Use This Chapter of the Book?

If you are the founder or the CEO of a company and if you and your leadership team have a clear point of view (PoV) on the following questions and all of you are ALIGNED, then you can choose to move to the next chapter of the book. However, if you see a dissonance or have conflicting views, then we suggest digging deeper, going through this chapter and reflecting on different angles we bring in there.

Here are the questions for you to discuss and ponder-

- What's our big-picture plan for the organization, and how do we measure success?
- How do we see the organization changing in the next 5, 10, or 20 years?
- What values should shape our important decisions?
- How do we balance growth and stability right now?
- How does our money-making plan match our organization's purpose, and what should we think about?
- Should we focus on being local, global, or both? What affects these decisions and our identity?
- How can we continue being innovative, and why is it essential?
- What's our organization's culture, and how does it impact our overall success?
- What rules should we follow when making important decisions?
- How should we balance short-term success and long-term goals?
- Are there critical investments or strategies for our long-term success?
- How do we combine our purpose with being ethical and socially responsible?
- How do we make sure our products and services provide value to customers?

HOPE IS NOT A STRATEGY

In this chapter, we delve into what we term as "Organization Outlook Dilemmas," a set of complex and interconnected choices that stand at the heart of leadership's decision-making process. These dilemmas encompass critical aspects of an organization's identity, strategy, culture, and operations, forcing leaders to contemplate their organization's very essence.

The essence of these dilemmas lies not in just the black-and-white choices but in the shades of gray that exist in between too. They require leaders to carefully consider the trade-offs, the implications, and the repercussions of each path they choose. Every choice made has a ripple effect that touches every corner of the organization

For example, assume a CEO and her leadership team answered the questions mentioned above and are completely aligned on their organization outlook, this is what the output would look like-

"We aspire to be an organization that fosters controlled growth, recognizing that stability is the foundation upon which we build our future success. We want to be in the business for the long term and continue to deliver value to our customers. Being profitable is key and we believe that profit generation and our organizational purpose should be mutually reinforcing, where profitability sustains our ability to fulfill our core mission.

We want to cater to both the local and global markets - we aren't very sure, as of now, about where we will thrive, so want to be open to explore and be guided by the market and the customers.

Culturally, we are committed to creating an inclusive environment, diversity is important. We want to be a remote first workplace with flexibility to meet at offices. Defining the core fabric of the organization and nurturing it is key as, in the long term, we want to also have an identity for our workplace and what we value. We believe in empowering our employees with the right balance of autonomy and centralized control to drive innovation and efficiency.

Our decision-making process needs to be transparent - the criteria used to make a decision should be clearly known to everyone as we believe that is the only way for us to be able to empower people. Confidentiality will only be maintained around people and financial data.

HOPE IS NOT A STRATEGY

We recognize that short-term success is essential, but we also maintain a strong commitment to long-term sustainability, making strategic investments and decisions that preserve our integrity and long-term impact. Customer-centricity remains at the forefront of our product and service development and innovation will be driven by current and future needs of the customer

These decisions have significant ripple effects on subsequent decisions and various aspects of the organization like:

- The kind of people (diversity, location, skillset, attitude) to hire
- Financial decisions towards strategies that will strike a balance between profitability and alignment to the core mission
- Decisions related to market entry, localization efforts, and brand positioning.
- Actively exploring opportunities in diverse geographies and planning market-specific strategies and adaptations.
- HR policies, diversity initiatives, and employee empowerment programs, taking into account focus on diversity and remote work
- Fundamental transparency principles shape internal and external communication practices, influencing decision-sharing and trust-building efforts.
- Embed customer centricity as a key organizational value for it to be influencing product development, marketing, and customer service practices.

Let us look at ten critical dilemmas on the overall organization outlook that business leaders commonly face, exploring their impact on organizational culture.

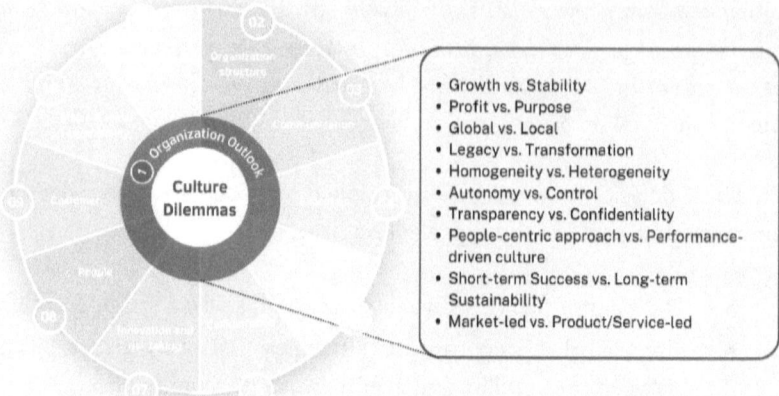

- Growth vs. Stability
- Profit vs. Purpose
- Global vs. Local
- Legacy vs. Transformation
- Heterogeneity vs. Homogeneity
- Autonomy vs. Control
- Transparency vs. Confidentiality
- People-Centric Approach vs. Performance-Driven Culture (Family vs. Sports team)
- Short-Term Success vs. Long-Term Sustainability
- Market-Led vs. Product/Service Led

Growth vs. Stability

> Should the organization pursue aggressive growth and expansion at the risk of destabilizing current operations or maintain stability with a slower, steadier growth rate or strike a balance somewhere in between?

Opting for aggressive growth signifies a strong commitment to expanding market presence, increasing revenue, and capturing new opportunities swiftly. This approach often involves exploring new markets, launching innovative products or services, and pursuing mergers and acquisitions. While aggressive growth can lead to rapid financial gains and elevated market visibility, it comes with substantial risks. Organizations may overextend themselves, leading to financial instability, operational challenges, and strained resources. Maintaining quality and customer satisfaction during rapid expansion can also be a significant challenge.

Choosing stability involves a more conservative approach, emphasizing the preservation of current operations, customer relationships, and financial health. Stability-focused organizations prioritize consistency and reliability over rapid expansion. They may focus on optimizing existing products or services, streamlining operations, and nurturing long-term customer loyalty. This approach minimizes the risks associated with rapid growth but can result in missed opportunities and a gradual decline in market competitiveness. Over time, a too-stable strategy can lead to stagnation, making it challenging to adapt to evolving market dynamics. This works best in the context of companies maintaining their niche.

Choosing one of the extremes has its own pros and cons.

Choosing Growth Only	
Pros	**Cons**
Opportunities for increased revenue, market share, and competitiveness	Strain on resources, potentially leading to operational disruptions.
Potential for rapid expansion and capturing emerging markets.	Increased risk exposure and financial volatility.
Attraction for investors seeking high returns.	Greater pressure on management to deliver consistent growth.

Choosing Stability Only	
Pros	**Cons**
Strong foundation, minimized risks, and consistent performance.	Missed opportunities for growth and innovation.
Enhanced ability to weather economic downturns or industry disruptions.	Potential complacency and resistance to change.
Focus on optimizing existing operations and maximizing efficiency	Limited appeal to investors seeking high-growth opportunities.

 Zoom, the video conferencing platform, represents a company with a growth-centric strategy. In response to the sudden surge in remote work and virtual meetings during the COVID-19 pandemic, Zoom rapidly expanded its user base and market share. This aggressive growth led to substantial revenue increases and global recognition as a go-to communication tool. However, the intense growth also brought challenges, including security and privacy concerns, scalability issues, and heightened competition from established tech giants. Zoom's growth-oriented approach allowed it to capitalize on immediate market needs but required constant innovation and adaptation to maintain its leadership position and address emerging challenges.

Campbell Soup, a well-established food company, embodies a stability-focused strategy. With a portfolio of enduring brands like Campbell's, Pepperidge Farm, and Prego, the company prioritizes consistent and reliable performance in the consumer goods sector. This stability-focused approach emphasizes product quality, customer loyalty, and risk mitigation. While it may not experience the rapid growth seen in tech startups, Campbell Soup benefits from a loyal customer base and enduring market presence. However, the stability-oriented strategy also means limited exposure to high-growth markets and potentially slower revenue growth compared to more aggressively expanding companies in the food industry.

Some questions for the leaders to reflect and answer to resolve the dilemma:

- How do you envision the organization's strategic direction in the short and long term?
- What does success look like for your organization in the context of growth and stability?
- Where does your organization stand in its life stage, and how does this influence your growth-stability balance?
- Are you in a phase of establishing a market presence, or are you focused on consolidating gains and market share?
- What is the current financial health of your organization, including cash reserves and debt levels?
- How does your financial situation impact your ability to pursue aggressive growth while maintaining stability?

There could be several factors that could influence this decision, like:

Industry Dynamics:

- How does the industry's pace of change affect your choice between growth and stability?
- Is your industry more conducive to rapid growth or steady stability, and why?

Market Opportunity:

- What opportunities exist in your market, and how do they align with your growth-stability strategy?
- Are there emerging markets or niches that warrant aggressive growth efforts?

Risk Tolerance:

- How comfortable is your organization with risk, and to what extent can you tolerate financial and operational uncertainties?
- Are there risk mitigation strategies in place for aggressive growth scenarios?

Competitive Landscape:

- How does the competitive landscape influence your choice between growth and stability?
- Are competitors pursuing aggressive growth, and how does that impact your market positioning?

Investor Expectations:

- What are the expectations of your investors, stakeholders, and shareholders regarding growth and stability?
- How do your financial backers view the trade-offs between these two objectives?

Resource Availability:

- Do you have the necessary resources, both in terms of capital and talent, to support aggressive growth plans?
- Can your organization effectively allocate resources to balance growth and stability?

There are other areas that get impacted because of a choice of this dilemma, like:

- Financial Health
- Market Position
- Operational Efficiency
- Workforce Management
- Product and Service Offerings

Striking a balance between growth and stability is a common approach, recognizing the need to capture new opportunities without jeopardizing current operations. Organizations adopting this strategy carefully assess expansion opportunities and their potential impact on existing resources and processes. They may invest in targeted growth areas while maintaining a strong focus on operational efficiency and customer satisfaction. This approach aims to combine the benefits of growth, such as increased revenue and market reach, with the stability necessary to sustain long-term success. However, achieving this balance can be complex, requiring precise planning and resource allocation. *Grubhub, an online food delivery and takeout platform, has demonstrated a knack for navigating the delicate balance between growth and stability. In the competitive and rapidly evolving food delivery industry, Grubhub has adopted a strategy that combines elements of both growth and stability. Grubhub has consistently pursued growth by expanding its market presence through partnerships with restaurants, universities, and corporate offices. The company has also invested in technological innovations to enhance its delivery and user experience. These efforts have allowed Grubhub to increase its customer base and revenue over the years. While focusing on growth, Grubhub has also shown a commitment to maintaining stability and profitability. The company has sought to optimize its operations, enhance cost management, and establish long-term partnerships with restaurants. This stability-oriented approach helps Grubhub maintain profitability and withstand the competitive pressures in the food delivery industry. Grubhub's success lies in its ability to strike a balance between aggressive growth and maintaining a stable operational foundation. By continually innovating and expanding its services while simultaneously ensuring operational efficiency and cost control, Grubhub has remained a prominent player in the food delivery space. This balanced approach has enabled the company to capture growth opportunities while mitigating the risks associated with rapid expansion.*

The decision of whether to prioritize growth or stability in a business is influenced by a multitude of factors, and these factors can vary depending on the organization's specific circumstances, industry, and market conditions. Here are some key factors that influence this decision:

- **Market Conditions**: The current state of the market plays a pivotal role. A growing market with ample opportunities may encourage a focus on growth, while a saturated or volatile market may lead to a more stability-oriented approach.
- **Financial Health**: The financial position of the organization is crucial. Companies with strong financial stability may have the resources to invest in growth initiatives, while those with financial constraints may prioritize stability to ensure sustainability.
- **Industry Dynamics**: Different industries have varying growth potentials and competitive landscapes. High-growth industries like technology may favor aggressive growth strategies, while mature industries may prioritize stability.
- **Competitive Landscape**: The level of competition and the presence of disruptive forces in the industry can impact the decision. Fierce competition may necessitate growth strategies, while stability may be chosen to consolidate a dominant position.
- **Leadership Vision**: The leadership's vision and strategic goals are instrumental. Leaders may have a preference for aggressive expansion or a focus on maintaining a steady course, which influences the overall direction.
- **Customer Demands**: Customer preferences and demands play a significant role. Rapidly changing customer needs may necessitate growth to meet those demands, while stable markets may require maintaining existing customer relationships.
- **Resource Availability**: The availability of resources, both human and capital, affects the feasibility of growth initiatives. Limited resources may push an organization towards stability until more resources become available.
- **Regulatory Environment**: The regulatory landscape can impact growth decisions. Stringent regulations may require compliance efforts that shift focus towards stability, while regulatory incentives may promote growth.
- **Risk Tolerance**: The organization's risk tolerance level is critical.

Some companies are more willing to take calculated risks associated with growth, while others prefer a conservative approach to minimize risks.
- **Existing Portfolio**: The composition of the organization's existing product or service portfolio can influence the decision. A diversified portfolio may allow for different strategies for individual offerings.
- **Investor Expectations**: Publicly traded companies may face pressure from shareholders for short-term growth. The expectations of investors and stakeholders can heavily influence strategic decisions.
- **Global Economic Conditions**: Broader economic conditions, such as recessions or economic booms, can impact the decision. During economic downturns, stability may be prioritized, whereas growth may be more viable in robust economies.
- **Technological Advancements**: The availability of new technologies and digital transformation opportunities can sway the decision towards growth strategies to capitalize on technological innovations.
- **Social and Environmental Responsibility**: Organizations with a strong commitment to corporate social responsibility may integrate sustainability goals into their growth or stability strategies.
- **Mergers and Acquisitions**: Growth can also be achieved through mergers and acquisitions. The availability of attractive acquisition targets can influence the decision.
- **Exit Strategy**: The organization's long-term goals and exit strategy, such as going public, being acquired, or remaining privately held, can impact whether growth or stability is prioritized.
- **Customer Base**: The organization's existing customer base may dictate the need for expansion or a focus on retaining and serving current customers.

In conclusion, the dilemma of growth versus stability is a fundamental strategic decision that permeates every facet of an organization. It determines the organization's trajectory, risk profile, and approach to innovation. Ultimately, the choice should align with the organization's vision, values, and capacity for adaptation, recognizing that there is no one-size-fits-all answer and that the ideal strategy may evolve over time.

Profit vs. Purpose

> Should the organization prioritize profit maximization and shareholder returns, or should it focus more on its purpose and the impact it can create to the community at large or figure a way of striking a balance between the two?

Opting for profit maximization underscores the organization's commitment to financial growth and shareholder value. Such organizations often prioritize revenue generation, cost optimization, and competitive market positioning. The pursuit of profits can lead to enhanced financial stability, increased market share, and a strong appeal to investors. However, this approach can potentially generate ethical concerns, as a relentless focus on profits may entail cost-cutting measures that negatively impact employees, communities, or the environment. This single-minded pursuit may also undermine employee morale and long-term sustainability.

Organizations that place a higher emphasis on purpose and societal impact aim to contribute positively to communities and the world at large. They may integrate environmental sustainability, social responsibility, and ethical practices into their core values and operations. While this approach resonates with a growing segment of socially conscious consumers and can enhance brand reputation, it may require allocating resources and profits toward initiatives that do not yield immediate financial returns. The challenge lies in balancing the desire to create a positive societal impact with the need for financial viability.

Making a choice between profit and purpose isn't straightforward.

Choosing Profit Only	
Pros	**Cons**
Focus on profit helps the organization stay financially secure	An exclusive focus on profit can harm the organization's reputation
Prioritizing profit can result in better profits for shareholders	Employees looking for a sense of purpose may leave
Profit-oriented companies often have more resources for growth and investment	Profit-only focus can turn away socially-conscious customers
A profit-driven approach can make the organization more competitive in the market	Short-term profit may lead to neglect of long-term sustainability efforts

Choosing Purpose only	
Pros	**Cons**
Prioritizing purpose can enhance the organization's reputation	Overemphasizing purpose may pose financial challenges
A clear purpose can boost employee motivation and retention	Investors seeking high returns may be less interested
Purpose-driven companies often build stronger customer loyalty	In highly competitive markets, a sole focus on purpose may not maintain competitiveness
Organizations with a purpose can make meaningful contributions to society	Achieving the right balance between purpose and profit can be challenging

HOPE IS NOT A STRATEGY

Ryanair, a low-cost airline based in Ireland, is renowned for its profit-driven strategy in the competitive airline industry. The company places a primary emphasis on cost minimization, operational efficiency, and revenue generation. While this approach has enabled Ryanair to become one of the largest and most profitable airlines in Europe, it has also garnered criticism for its frugal approach to customer service, including extra fees and minimal amenities. The profit-focused strategy has allowed the airline to consistently deliver financial gains to shareholders but has occasionally resulted in challenges related to customer satisfaction and reputation.

Toms, a footwear and lifestyle brand, exemplifies a purpose-driven approach centered on the "One for One" giving model. For every pair of shoes sold, Toms pledges to donate a pair to a person in need. This philanthropic mission is at the core of Toms' identity, attracting socially conscious consumers and fostering a sense of purpose among employees. While this purpose-driven strategy has garnered positive attention and consumer loyalty, it has also presented financial challenges. Toms' commitment to giving requires substantial resource allocation, impacting profitability and financial sustainability. However, the brand's dedication to making a positive societal impact aligns with its core values and resonates with customers who appreciate its philanthropic efforts.

Some questions for the leaders to reflect and answer to resolve the dilemma:

- What is the organization's strategic vision concerning profit and purpose alignment?
- What does success look like for your organization, striking the right balance between monetary returns and social impact?
- How are evolving customer expectations influencing your choice between profit and purpose?
- What role does a clear sense of purpose play in motivating and retaining employees?
- How do short-term profit-maximization strategies align with long-term reputational considerations?
- Can purpose-driven strategies contribute to long-term profitability through trust and loyalty building?

There could be several factors that could influence this decision in the context of your organization, like:

Customer-Centricity:

- How does a customer-centric approach influence your choice between profit and purpose?
- Are customer values and expectations guiding your strategic decisions?

Employee Motivation:

- To what extent does employee motivation and productivity depend on a well-defined organizational purpose?
- How does purpose impact employee retention and attraction?

Market Dynamics:

- How are market dynamics, including competitive forces and industry trends, shaping the profit vs. purpose landscape?
- Are there emerging opportunities or challenges that warrant a shift in focus?

Reputation Management:

- What role does company reputation management play in your decision-making, and how does it relate to profit and purpose alignment?
- Are there examples of your competitors that have faced reputational challenges due to a lack of purpose-driven initiatives?

Sustainability and Accountability:

- How can a balanced approach between profit and purpose contribute to sustainability and accountability?
- Are there frameworks, like B Corporation certification, that align with your organization's values and goals?

Stakeholder Impact:

- How does your decision impact all stakeholders, including employees, customers, shareholders, and the broader community?
- Are there potential conflicts of interest among these stakeholders that need to be addressed?

There are other areas that get impacted because of a choice of this dilemma, like:

- Financial Sustainability
- Organizational Culture
- Customer and Stakeholder Relations
- Employee Morale and Engagement
- Ethical Practices

Many organizations recognize the importance of balancing profit and purpose. This approach acknowledges that financial success is not inherently at odds with social responsibility. Organizations can seek innovative ways to align profit-making with purpose-driven initiatives, such as through corporate social responsibility (CSR) programs, ethical supply chain management, and sustainable business practices. Striking this balance requires a clear articulation of the organization's values, transparent communication with stakeholders, and a long-term perspective that considers the broader implications of business decisions. *Seventh Generation, a Vermont-based company specializing in environmentally friendly household and personal care products, exemplifies a balanced approach between profit and purpose. The company has a strong commitment to sustainability, transparency, and social responsibility, which are deeply ingrained in its brand identity. While Seventh Generation is purpose-driven, it recognizes the importance of profitability to sustain its mission. The company has made strategic decisions to ensure its products remain competitive in the market. For example, it has invested in research and development to create eco-friendly cleaning products that are not only better for the environment but also meet consumers' performance expectations. This approach aligns with its purpose while ensuring financial viability. Seventh Generation's commitment to purpose goes beyond product offerings. The company has championed causes related to environmental sustainability, including advocating for improved ingredient transparency and supporting legislative efforts to reduce the use of harmful chemicals in household products. These initiatives demonstrate the company's dedication to making a positive impact on society and the planet. Seventh Generation's ability to strike a balance between profit and purpose is reflected in its ongoing commitment to sustainability, ethical sourcing, and community engagement. While it maintains a clear focus on its mission to create products that are better for people and the planet, it also recognizes the need for financial sustainability to support its long-term goals.*

The decision of whether to prioritize profit or purpose in a business is influenced by a variety of factors, and it can depend on the organization's values, objectives, industry, and market conditions. Here are some key factors that influence this decision:

- **Organizational Values**: The core values and mission of the organization play a fundamental role. Companies with a strong commitment to social or environmental causes may prioritize purpose, while others may place a greater emphasis on profitability.
- **Industry and Market**: The industry in which the organization operates can significantly influence the choice. For example, consumer-facing brands may prioritize the purpose to appeal to socially conscious consumers, while highly competitive industries may focus more on profit.
- **Market Demand**: Customer preferences and market demand can steer the decision. If consumers increasingly favor purpose-driven brands, organizations may invest in purpose-aligned initiatives to gain a competitive edge.
- **Stakeholder Expectations**: The expectations of various stakeholders, including customers, investors, employees, and the broader community, can influence the decision. Meeting these expectations may require a balance between profit and purpose.
- **Competitive Position**: The organization's competitive position within its industry can impact the decision. Market leaders may have more leeway to invest in purpose-driven initiatives, while challengers may focus on profitability to gain market share.
- **Regulatory Environment**: Regulatory requirements related to

social and environmental responsibility can shape the decision. Compliance with environmental regulations or adherence to ethical standards may be mandated by law.

- **Investor Pressure**: For publicly traded companies, investor pressure can be a driving factor. Shareholders, including socially responsible investors, may push for a greater emphasis on purpose.
- **Consumer Trends**: Evolving consumer trends and preferences can sway the decision. If consumers increasingly support businesses that align with their values, organizations may invest in purpose-driven strategies.
- **Long-Term Sustainability**: Considerations of long-term sustainability and reputation can influence the decision. Purpose-driven initiatives can enhance brand reputation and customer loyalty over time.
- **Cost-Benefit Analysis**: Organizations may conduct cost-benefit analyses to assess the financial impact of purpose-driven initiatives. Demonstrating that purpose aligns with profitability can influence the choice.
- **Employee Engagement**: Employee engagement and retention can be a factor. A strong purpose can attract and retain talent, while a purely profit-driven approach may lead to high turnover.
- **Innovation and Differentiation**: Purpose-driven organizations may view purpose as a source of innovation and differentiation, enabling them to stand out in the market.
- **Global Trends**: Global trends related to sustainability, social responsibility, and ethical business practices can influence the decision, especially for multinational companies.
- **Ethical Leadership**: The leadership's personal values and ethical stance can shape the organizational culture and the emphasis on purpose.
- **Strategic Objectives**: The organization's strategic objectives and long-term goals can guide the decision. Balancing profit and purpose to achieve these objectives may be necessary.
- **Community Impact**: Organizations with a strong presence in local communities may prioritize purpose in order to make a positive impact on the areas where they operate.

- **Crisis or Reputation Management**: Businesses facing reputation challenges or crises may choose to emphasize purpose to rebuild trust and goodwill.
- **Ethical Supply Chain**: The ethics and sustainability of the supply chain can also influence the decision to prioritize purpose, especially in industries where supply chain transparency is critical.
- **Economic Conditions**: Economic conditions, including economic downturns or periods of growth, can impact the emphasis on profit or purpose.

The profit versus purpose dilemma permeates the organization's culture, strategy, and decision-making processes. It influences talent acquisition and retention, customer loyalty, investor relations, and overall reputation. Ultimately, the choice between profit and purpose should align with the organization's identity, values, and long-term vision. As societal expectations evolve, organizations often find that integrating purpose into their core mission not only aligns with ethical principles but also enhances financial resilience and competitive advantage. In an ever-changing business landscape, the profit versus purpose debate remains a central challenge for organizations seeking to thrive while contributing positively to the world.

Global vs. Local

> Should the organization aim to expand globally, facing cultural, regulatory, and logistical complexities, or focus on strengthening its position in the local market or use other criteria to deliberately strike a balance between the two?

Global expansion signifies a commitment to broadening the organization's presence beyond its local market. While this can unlock new revenue streams, access to diverse consumer bases, and opportunities for growth, it comes with a host of challenges. Cultural differences, regulatory complexities, and logistical hurdles must be navigated adeptly. Managing a global operation demands significant resources, including investments in market research, localization, international partnerships, and compliance with a myriad of laws and regulations. Additionally, global expansion may require adapting to varying consumer preferences, market conditions, and competitive landscapes in each region, necessitating flexibility and cultural sensitivity.

Conversely, a local market focus prioritizes consolidation and strength within a specific geographic area. Organizations that choose this path often concentrate their efforts on deepening their market penetration, enhancing customer relationships, and fortifying their position as a dominant local player. This approach allows for a more concentrated allocation of resources and simplifies operational management. However, it may limit opportunities for diversification and growth, particularly in an era when global markets offer vast potential.

The decision of choosing where you stand on the spectrum is extremely important

Choosing Global Only	
Pros	**Cons**
Access to new markets and customers	Managing diverse regulatory environments.
Increased scale and diversification	Handling cultural nuances and logistical challenges.

Choosing Local Only	
Pros	**Cons**
Deeper customer relationships.	Limited growth potential.
Optimized offerings.	Exposure to local market risks.
Consolidated market position.	

Airbnb, a company that connects travelers with unique accommodations worldwide, has strategically pursued global expansion. With a presence in nearly every corner of the globe, Airbnb has become a household name and a dominant player in the sharing economy. By expanding globally, Airbnb tapped into diverse markets, offering travelers a wide range of lodging options and hosts opportunities to generate income. However, this global approach has also exposed the company to regulatory challenges and cultural nuances. Compliance with varying local regulations, ensuring safety and security standards, and addressing concerns related to housing affordability have been ongoing challenges for Airbnb. Nevertheless, global expansion has positioned Airbnb as a leading player in the travel and hospitality industry.

Tim Hortons, a Canadian fast-food restaurant chain known for its coffee and quick-service menu, has primarily focused on its local Canadian market. While Tim Hortons has expanded into select international markets, it maintains a strong emphasis on its core Canadian operations. This local market focus has allowed the company to establish a deep and enduring connection with Canadian consumers, who view Tim Hortons as a beloved national brand. The company's strategy centers on consistently delivering quality products and a sense of community, resonating with Canadian values. By prioritizing the local market, Tim Hortons has cultivated a loyal customer base and maintained control over its operations and supply chain, ensuring product quality and consistency.

Some questions for the leaders to reflect and answer to resolve the dilemma:

- What are our core competencies, and how do they fit into global and local contexts?
- Are we more like a global company operating locally or a local company with global operations?
- How well do we understand our local and global customers?
- What are the unique risks and rewards of each choice, and how do they align with our goals?
- Can we balance the allure of new markets with the comfort of the familiar?

There could be several factors that could influence this decision in the context of your organization like:

Market Demand:

- Where is the demand for our products or services higher: in global markets or locally?
- How does market demand vary between regions, and what opportunities does this present?

Customer Understanding:

- Do we have a comprehensive understanding of our local customers' preferences and needs?
- How well do we comprehend the preferences and behaviors of our global customer base?
- Are there significant differences between local and global customer segments that we need to consider?

Strategic Objectives:

- What are our long-term strategic objectives, and how does global or local expansion fit into them?
- Does our vision prioritize global reach, or is local dominance more in line with our goals?
- How does our choice align with our broader strategic direction?

Risk-Reward Analysis:

- What are the unique risks associated with expanding globally, and what rewards can we expect?
- What are the potential risks and rewards of focusing solely on the local market?
- How does the risk-reward balance compare between the two options, and which aligns better with our risk tolerance and objectives?

There are other areas that get impacted because of a choice of this dilemma, like:

- Market Strategy
- Supply Chain Management
- Employee Talent Management
- Marketing and Branding
- Customer Relationships

Many organizations opt for a middle ground, strategically balancing global and local initiatives. This approach seeks to capture the advantages of both expansion and consolidation. It involves assessing market-specific opportunities and tailoring strategies accordingly. For instance, a company might identify certain regions with high growth potential and allocate resources for global expansion while maintaining a strong local presence in core markets. Striking this balance requires a deep understanding of market dynamics, a flexible organizational structure, and the ability to adapt swiftly to changing conditions.

HOPE IS NOT A STRATEGY

Nando's, a South African restaurant chain specializing in peri-peri chicken dishes, provides a compelling illustration of striking a balance between global and local approaches. While Nando's has expanded its presence globally, including in countries like the United Kingdom, Australia, and the United States, it has also maintained a strong commitment to adapting its menu and ambiance to suit local tastes and preferences. Nando's global strategy involves expanding its footprint into various countries and regions. The company aims to introduce its peri-peri chicken concept to a diverse range of markets, capitalizing on the popularity of its signature dish. This global expansion has allowed Nando's to tap into a broader customer base, gain international recognition, and achieve revenue growth. Simultaneously, Nando's places a strong emphasis on local adaptation. The company tailors its menu offerings to cater to local culinary preferences and dietary restrictions. For instance, Nando's menu in the UK includes options like chicken wraps and salads to align with local tastes. Additionally, the restaurant decor often features elements that reflect the local culture and art of the region. This approach ensures that Nando's retains a local charm and resonates with the cultural sensibilities of its diverse customer base. Nando's ability to strike a balance between global expansion and local adaptation is a key factor in its success. It combines the advantages of a global brand presence with the flexibility to cater to specific market nuances. This approach has allowed Nando's to establish a strong global footprint while maintaining a unique and appealing local character in each market it enters.

The decision of whether to prioritize a global or local approach in business operations is influenced by a wide range of factors like:

- **Market Demand and Size**: The size and growth potential of target markets play a crucial role. If there is significant demand in global markets, expanding globally may be the preferred choice. Conversely, if local markets offer substantial opportunities, a local focus may make more sense.
- **Market Saturation**: The level of market saturation in local and global markets can affect the decision. A saturated local market may drive a desire to explore global opportunities, while intense competition in global markets may lead to a focus on local niches.
- **Competitive Landscape**: The competitive landscape in both local and global markets is a key consideration. Entering highly competitive global markets may require substantial resources and differentiation strategies, while local markets may offer a chance to establish dominance more easily.

- **Regulatory Environment**: Regulatory requirements and compliance considerations can differ significantly between local and global markets. Organizations must assess the impact of regulations on their operations and compliance costs.
- **Cultural and Consumer Preferences**: Understanding cultural differences and consumer preferences is essential. Products, services, and marketing strategies may need to be adapted to align with local tastes and values in global markets.
- **Supply Chain and Logistics**: The efficiency and complexity of supply chains and logistics are important factors. Managing global supply chains can be complex and costly, while local operations may have simpler logistical needs.
- **Cost Structure**: Cost considerations, including labor costs, taxes, and overhead, can influence the decision. Some regions may offer cost advantages for specific operations.
- **Risk Management**: Risk assessment is crucial. Expanding globally may expose the organization to geopolitical, currency, and market risks, while a local approach may offer greater stability.
- **Resource Availability**: The availability of resources, such as skilled labor, technology, and capital, can influence the decision. Access to local talent pools and resources may drive a local focus.
- **Economies of Scale**: Economies of scale can be achieved through global operations, enabling cost efficiencies. Organizations must evaluate whether these efficiencies outweigh the costs of global expansion.
- **Global Partnerships and Alliances**: Existing global partnerships and alliances may impact the decision. Collaboration with global partners can facilitate entry into new markets.
- **Brand Strategy**: Decisions related to brand strategy and positioning can guide the approach. Some brands may emphasize their global presence, while others may focus on local identity.
- **Sustainability Goals**: Organizations committed to sustainability may assess whether a global or local approach aligns better with their sustainability objectives, such as reducing carbon emissions or supporting local communities.
- **Customer Segmentation**: Customer segmentation can guide the

decision. Some businesses may find that a global approach allows them to cater to diverse customer segments, while others may prefer a local approach tailored to specific customer needs.

- **Technology Infrastructure**: The state of technology infrastructure in both local and global markets can influence the organization's ability to operate effectively and efficiently.
- **Political and Geopolitical Factors**: Consideration of political stability, trade agreements, and geopolitical factors is essential for global expansion decisions.
- **Financial Goals**: The organization's financial objectives, including revenue growth, profit margins, and return on investment, can impact the choice between global and local strategies.
- **Scalability**: Scalability considerations are critical. Organizations must assess whether their operations can easily scale up globally or if local markets offer more manageable scalability.
- **Customer Service and Support:** Assessing the level of customer service and support required in local and global markets can guide decision-making. Different markets may have varying expectations.
- **Long-Term Strategy**: The organization's long-term strategic goals and vision play a pivotal role. The chosen approach should align with the organization's broader strategic direction.

The global versus local dilemma reverberates across multiple facets of an organization, including market research, supply chain management, branding, and human resources. It impacts resource allocation, talent acquisition, risk management, and brand identity. Ultimately, the choice hinges on the organization's strategic objectives, risk appetite, and its capacity to navigate the complexities associated with global expansion. As markets continue to evolve, organizations must continually reassess their global and local strategies to remain agile and responsive to changing conditions.

Legacy vs Transformation

> Should the organization hold onto its traditional practices and values or embrace transformation and change, which might disrupt its established culture and operations or strike the fine balance between the two.

Choosing to adhere to legacy practices and values signifies a commitment to preserving the organization's historical identity and culture. It can provide a sense of stability and continuity, especially if the organization has a long and successful history. Legacy-focused organizations tend to rely on established processes, hierarchical structures, and traditional leadership models. This approach can foster a sense of loyalty among long-serving employees who appreciate the familiarity and stability it offers. However, there are potential downsides to prioritizing legacy. Over time, an excessive attachment to tradition can hinder adaptability and innovation. Legacy processes may become outdated, leading to inefficiencies and missed opportunities for improvement. Moreover, maintaining the status quo in a rapidly changing business environment can result in diminished competitiveness and relevance. While holding onto tradition can provide a strong foundation, it may also create resistance to change, hindering the organization's ability to evolve and meet evolving market demands.

Opting for transformation and change represents a commitment to evolving and staying ahead of the curve. It involves embracing new technologies, adopting agile methodologies, and fostering a culture of innovation and adaptability. Organizations that prioritize transformation often seek to disrupt the status quo, leverage digitalization, and stay agile in response to market shifts. This approach can lead to enhanced competitiveness, improved customer experiences, and increased operational efficiency. However, the pursuit of transformation is not without its challenges. Implementing change can be disruptive and may encounter resistance from employees accustomed to legacy practices. There can be a learning curve associated with new technologies and methodologies. Additionally, the rapid pace of change can introduce uncertainty and ambiguity, potentially impacting employee morale.

Organizations must carefully manage these challenges to ensure a successful transformation journey.

No one end of the spectrum is good or bad. Both have their pros and cons.

Choosing Legacy Only	
Pros	Cons
Brings in a lot of stability. Things stay the same, which can be comforting.	Stagnation could set in. You might fall behind in a changing world.
Keeps the organization's history and identity intact.	You could miss out on opportunities to explore new and better ways of doing things.

Choosing Transformation Only	
Pros	Cons
You will be highly adaptable to the changing needs by staying up-to-date with what the world needs.	It could result in disruption. Changes might be too much for the organization to handle.
Trying new things can lead to exciting discoveries.	There could be a loss of identity because of losing touch with the organization's history and values.
You could build lot of efficiency and effectiveness in the ways of doing things	

Company A is a family-owned furniture manufacturing business that has been in operation for over a century. It prides itself on traditional craftsmanship, using time-

tested woodworking techniques and materials. The organization places a strong emphasis on maintaining the legacy of its founder's vision and preserving its longstanding values. While this legacy-focused approach has garnered a loyal customer base appreciative of the company's heritage and quality, it has faced challenges in adapting to modern manufacturing technologies and market trends. The reliance on legacy methods limited production scalability and efficiency, impacting competitiveness. However, the company's commitment to tradition has created a niche market for artisanal, handcrafted furniture, attracting a specific segment of consumers who value heritage and craftsmanship.

Company B is a tech start-up that specializes in software development. It was founded with a vision to disrupt the traditional software industry by embracing cutting-edge technologies and agile development methodologies. The organization fosters a culture of innovation, encourages continuous learning, and values adaptability. This transformation-oriented approach has enabled Company B to rapidly develop and deploy software solutions, staying ahead of market trends and meeting evolving customer demands. While it has achieved rapid growth and success in a short period, the relentless pace of transformation has posed challenges in terms of employee burnout and maintaining work-life balance. Additionally, the organization must navigate the risks associated with a highly dynamic industry.

So, what should one consider when making a choice between legacy and transformation?

Some questions for the leaders to reflect and answer to resolve the dilemma:

- What's important to us - keeping things as they are or trying something new and different?
- Do our values and strengths match the changes we want to make?
- Is the world around us asking for changes, and will we be left behind if we don't change too?
- Can we handle the changes without causing confusion or resistance inside our organization?
- How can we find the right balance between old and new?

There could be several factors that could influence this decision

in the context of your organization, like:

- **Organization's Values**: Are the changes in line with what the organization believes in?
- **Market and Customers**: Is the market asking for something different, and will customers like it?
- **Impact on Operations and Culture**: Can the organization handle the changes without causing problems?

There are other areas that get impacted because of a choice of this dilemma, like:

- Technology Infrastructure
- Operational Efficiency
- Customer Experience
- Cost Management
- Innovation and Adaptability

Many organizations recognize the need to strike a balance between legacy and transformation. This approach allows them to harness the strengths of tradition while fostering a culture of innovation and adaptability. It often involves selectively modernizing certain aspects of the organization while preserving core values and practices that remain relevant. Striking this balance can be particularly effective in industries where stability and reliability are paramount, but innovation is also essential for long-term sustainability. *Company C is a family-owned retail chain with a history dating back several decades. It operates a network of traditional brick-and-mortar stores specializing in home goods and furniture. While the organization values its legacy and the loyalty of long-standing customers who appreciate the nostalgic shopping experience, it has also recognized the need for transformation in response to changing consumer preferences and market trends.*

Company C preserves its legacy by maintaining a warm and personalized in-store shopping experience. The stores are designed to evoke a sense of nostalgia, and the staff is trained to provide exceptional customer service, mirroring the practices from the organization's early days. This commitment to tradition resonates with a specific segment of loyal customers who prefer the traditional retail atmosphere.

Recognizing the significance of digitalization in retail, Company C embarked on a transformation journey by investing in an e-commerce platform and digital marketing strategies. It leverages modern technology to reach a broader customer base and offer online shopping options. This transformation has allowed the organization to tap into new markets and respond to the growing demand for online retail. Company C carefully balances its legacy values with modernization efforts. While preserving the traditional in-store experience, it strategically integrates digital solutions to enhance customer engagement and convenience. The organization maintains core values such as quality and reliability while adapting to evolving consumer expectations. This balance has enabled Company C to continue catering to its loyal customer base while attracting new customers who prefer online shopping.

Whether to focus on legacy practices or embrace transformation in business operations is influenced by a wide range of factors such as:

- **Market Dynamics**: The nature of the industry and market conditions is a significant factor. Rapidly evolving markets may require continuous transformation to stay competitive, while stable markets may allow for legacy practices.
- **Competitive Landscape**: The level of competition and the presence of disruptive forces in the industry can impact the decision. High competition may necessitate continuous transformation to gain an edge.
- **Technological Advancements**: The pace of technological advancements in the industry is critical. Industries driven by innovation may require ongoing transformation to leverage new technologies.
- **Customer Expectations**: Understanding and meeting customer expectations is paramount. Shifting customer preferences may drive the need for transformation to adapt to changing demands.
- **Regulatory Environment**: Regulatory requirements and compliance considerations can be a driving force. Evolving regulations may necessitate changes in business practices and technology.
- **Resource Availability**: The availability of resources, including talent and capital, can influence the decision. Transformation efforts often require investments in skilled personnel and

technology.
- **Legacy Systems and Infrastructure**: The organization's existing systems and infrastructure play a role. The complexity of legacy systems and their adaptability to new technologies may impact the decision.
- **Leadership Vision**: Leadership's vision and commitment to innovation and change can be influential. Leaders who prioritize transformation are more likely to drive it throughout the organization.
- **Risk Tolerance**: The organization's risk tolerance level is essential. Transformation often involves risk, and organizations must assess their appetite for change-related risks.
- **Cost-Benefit Analysis**: A thorough cost-benefit analysis is crucial. Organizations must evaluate the potential return on investment for transformation initiatives compared to maintaining legacy practices.
- **Customer Retention**: The impact on existing customer relationships is a consideration. Transitioning to new practices should not jeopardize customer loyalty.
- **Brand Image**: The impact on brand image and reputation is vital. A commitment to innovation and transformation can enhance brand perception.
- **Scalability**: Considerations of scalability and growth are essential. Transformation efforts should align with the organization's scalability goals.
- **Long-Term Strategy**: The organization's long-term strategic goals and vision are pivotal. The chosen approach should align with the organization's broader strategic direction.
- **Employee Buy-In**: The support and buy-in from employees are crucial for successful transformation. Resistance to change can impede transformation efforts.
- **Customer Feedback**: Customer feedback and input can guide the decision. Customer insights may reveal opportunities for transformation to improve products or services.
- **Economic Conditions**: Economic conditions, including economic downturns or periods of growth, can impact the emphasis on legacy or transformation.

- **Sustainability and Environmental Goals**: Organizations with sustainability objectives may consider transformation to adopt eco-friendly practices and technologies.
- **Time-to-Market Considerations**: Time-to-market pressures can influence the decision. Rapid product or service development may require transformation.

In summary, the Legacy vs. Transformation dilemma encapsulates the tension between preserving an organization's historical identity and embracing change for continued relevance and competitiveness. The choice made significantly impacts an organization's culture, adaptability, innovation capacity, and long-term viability. Consequently, organizations must carefully evaluate their specific context and objectives when navigating this critical dilemma.

Heterogeneity vs Homogeneity

> Should the organization prioritize heterogeneity or diversity to bring in a wide range of perspectives and experiences, or should it emphasize homogeneity to maintain a cohesive, similar bunch of people in the organization to blend seamlessly into the culture and the way of doing things or figure a middle path?

Emphasizing heterogeneity means valuing diversity in terms of perspectives, backgrounds, experiences, and skills within the organization. This approach encourages the recruitment and retention of individuals from different cultural, educational, and professional backgrounds. It fosters a broad spectrum of viewpoints and approaches to problem-solving. Prioritizing heterogeneity has several implications. For instance, heterogeneous teams often generate more innovative ideas and creative solutions. Diverse perspectives can lead to breakthrough innovations that may not have arisen in a homogenous environment. These teams tend to excel at complex problem-solving, approaching challenges from various angles and offering a range of potential solutions. Moreover, in an increasingly diverse and globalized world, having a diverse workforce can help organizations better understand and respond to diverse customer needs and market trends. It also makes organizations more appealing to candidates seeking inclusive and culturally diverse workplaces, broadening the talent pool.

On the other hand, prioritizing homogeneity involves maintaining a more uniform and cohesive workforce in terms of backgrounds, experiences, and perspectives. This approach often aims to create a harmonious and consistent organizational culture. Prioritizing homogeneity also has its implications. For example, a homogenous workforce may experience fewer cultural conflicts and may find it easier to align with the existing organizational culture and values. It may also be more efficient in decision-making and execution, as there may be less need to navigate diverse viewpoints. In some cases, homogeneous teams may exhibit greater consistency in approaches, processes, and outcomes, which can be important in industries requiring strict adherence to standards.

Both heterogeneous teams and homogenous teams have their pros and cons.

Choosing Heterogeneity only	
Pros	**Cons**
Diverse perspectives can lead to more creative problem-solving and innovative solutions.	Differences in communication styles and cultural norms can sometimes lead to misunderstandings and conflicts.
A diverse workforce may better understand and connect with a wider range of customers, potentially expanding the organization's market reach.	Managing a diverse workforce may require additional resources and efforts for training and integration.
Diverse teams can offer insights into international markets and cultural nuances, helping with global expansion.	Some employees may resist or struggle with adapting to a diverse environment, leading to cultural clashes.
A commitment to diversity can make the organization more attractive to a broader pool of talented individuals.	Diverse teams may take longer to reach consensus due to varying perspectives and opinions.

Choosing Homogeneity only	
Pros	**Cons**
A homogeneous workforce may have a more unified organizational culture, making it easier to communicate and share values.	A lack of diverse perspectives can lead to a stagnant environment with fewer innovative ideas.

Similar thinking and approaches can lead to faster decision-making and execution of tasks.	A homogeneous workforce may struggle to relate to a diverse customer base, potentially limiting market opportunities.
Fewer diverse perspectives may result in fewer disagreements and conflicts.	Similar thinking can lead to groupthink and echo chambers, where critical voices and alternative viewpoints are suppressed, potentially resulting in poor decisions.
A homogeneous workforce can provide consistency in processes and practices.	A homogeneous workforce may overlook valuable insights and opportunities stemming from a more diverse perspective.

Patagonia, the outdoor clothing and gear company, is known for its strong commitment to environmental sustainability and social responsibility. Patagonia embraces heterogeneity by encouraging diversity in its workforce and supply chain. The company actively promotes a diverse and inclusive culture, aiming to bring in a wide range of perspectives and experiences. This approach has positively impacted Patagonia by fostering a culture of innovation and environmental stewardship. The diverse team at Patagonia has been instrumental in driving sustainability initiatives, creating environmentally friendly products, and connecting with a broad customer base that shares their values. By embracing heterogeneity, Patagonia has not only achieved business success but also contributed positively to environmental and social causes.

In-N-Out Burger, a popular fast-food chain primarily based in the western United States, is known for its consistency and simplicity. The company adheres to a homogenous approach in its operations, maintaining a uniform menu and store design. While this approach has allowed In-N-Out Burger to deliver a consistent customer experience and maintain tight control over quality, it also limits innovation and diversity in its offerings. The company's focus on homogeneity has led to a loyal customer base that appreciates the familiar menu items, but it may restrict the company's ability to adapt to changing consumer preferences or expand into diverse markets. In-N-Out Burger's homogenous approach has both positive and negative impacts, offering stability and consistency but potentially limiting its ability to innovate and diversify its offerings compared to competitors who embrace heterogeneity.

Some questions for the leaders to reflect and answer to resolve the dilemma:

- What's more important to us - having different perspectives or everyone being similar?
- Does "being similar" mean we all think the same way, or can it mean sharing values and beliefs?
- Is diversity just about checking boxes for gender, race, or where people come from, or is it about getting fresh ideas and experiences?
- Can we have a diverse group of people and still share some common values and ways of doing things?
- Does focusing too much on being similar risk us all thinking alike and not questioning important things?

There could be several factors that could influence this decision in the context of your organization, like:

Organization's Goals: Do our current organizational goals and strategies favor one approach over the other? Which approach aligns better with our mission and objectives?

Market and Customer Diversity: Does our customer base and the markets we serve require a diverse workforce and a range of perspectives to better understand and meet their needs?

Industry and Competitive Landscape: What does our industry demand? Are there competitive advantages to be gained through innovation, which may be influenced by diverse perspectives?

Talent Availability: What is the talent pool like, in our industry and location? Can we easily find diverse candidates who also align with our culture and values?

Regulatory and Ethical Considerations: Are there legal or ethical considerations that require us to prioritize diversity and inclusion in our organization?

Employee Engagement and Retention: How does our workforce feel about our current approach to diversity and cultural fit? Does it impact employee morale, engagement, and retention?

Leadership and Communication: How will our leadership team communicate and lead in either scenario? What are the implications for building a shared vision and commitment among employees?

There are other areas that get impacted because of a choice of this dilemma, like:

- Organizational Culture
- Talent Diversity
- Product or Service Offerings
- Market Strategy
- Decision-Making Processes

Finding a middle path between heterogeneity and homogeneity is often the preferred approach. Organizations can aim to embrace diversity while promoting an inclusive culture that values and leverages differences. This approach allows organizations to harness the benefits of diverse perspectives while mitigating potential challenges. Striking a balance is essential because it fosters an environment where diverse teams collaborate effectively, leveraging their unique strengths. It promotes innovation by combining diverse viewpoints with a shared vision, and it enhances organizational resilience by being adaptable to change while maintaining cultural cohesion. *Consider the example of "Etsy," an online marketplace that specializes in handmade, vintage, and unique products. Etsy is known for striking a balance between heterogeneity and homogeneity in different scenarios. Etsy embraces heterogeneity in its seller base. It encourages individual artisans, crafters, and small businesses from diverse backgrounds and locations to sell their unique products on the platform. This approach allows for a wide range of products, styles, and artistic expressions, fostering creativity and innovation within the seller community. While Etsy promotes seller diversity, it maintains a level of homogeneity in the user experience for buyers. The website's user interface and features provide a consistent and user-friendly shopping experience, regardless of the diverse products available. This consistency ensures that customers can easily navigate the platform and find what they are looking for.*

Some key factors that influence the decision of choosing between heterogeneity and homogeneity include:

- **Industry and Market Dynamics**: The nature of the industry and the competitive landscape can influence the choice. In fast-changing and dynamic industries, heterogeneity may be favored to adapt to market shifts, while in stable industries, homogeneity might be preferred for maintaining a consistent market presence.
- **Customer Base and Preferences**: Understanding the customer base and their preferences is critical. Companies may choose heterogeneity to cater to diverse customer needs or opt for homogeneity to provide a standardized experience that aligns with customer expectations.
- **Innovation Goals**: Companies seeking continuous innovation and creativity often opt for heterogeneity to bring in diverse perspectives. Homogeneity may be chosen when innovation is more incremental and focused on refining existing products or services.
- **Risk Tolerance**: The level of risk tolerance within the organization can impact the decision. Heterogeneity can introduce more uncertainties, while homogeneity may reduce certain risks associated with standardization.
- **Talent Strategy**: Talent acquisition and retention strategies also come into play. Companies aiming to attract a broad talent pool from diverse backgrounds may prioritize heterogeneity. Conversely, those emphasizing cultural fit may lean towards homogeneity.
- **Market Expansion**: Companies looking to expand into new markets or regions may choose to adapt their approach based on local market dynamics. Heterogeneity can be valuable for understanding and addressing local needs.
- **Regulatory and Compliance Requirements**: Regulatory constraints and compliance requirements can influence the choice. Some industries may require standardized processes and products to meet legal and quality standards, favoring

homogeneity.
- **Technology and Systems**: The level of technological integration and available systems can impact the decision. Modern technologies may enable companies to manage heterogeneity more effectively, while legacy systems may favor homogeneity.
- **Leadership Vision and Competency:** The leadership's vision and competency in managing diverse teams can shape the approach. Leaders with experience in leveraging diverse teams may be more inclined towards heterogeneity.
- **Competitive Strategy**: The competitive strategy pursued by the company can be a determining factor. Companies aiming for differentiation and offering unique products or services may embrace heterogeneity, while those focused on cost leadership may prioritize homogeneity.

In conclusion, the choice between heterogeneity and homogeneity in an organization is not binary. It is a nuanced decision that requires careful consideration of the organization's goals, industry, and culture. Striking the right balance can lead to a dynamic and inclusive workplace that fosters innovation, creativity, and adaptability while maintaining cultural cohesion and efficiency. This approach aligns with the evolving demands of a diverse and interconnected world, where embracing differences often leads to greater success.

Autonomy vs. Control

> Should the organization encourage autonomy and empower employees to make decisions, or should it maintain tight control over operations to ensure alignment with its strategic goals or strike a balance somewhere in between?

When an organization leans towards promoting autonomy, it trusts its employees to take ownership of their work and make decisions independently. This can lead to several positive outcomes. For instance, it often results in a more engaged and motivated workforce, as employees feel a sense of ownership and responsibility. Autonomy fosters innovation, as employees are more likely to explore new ideas and take calculated risks. Furthermore, it can lead to faster decision-making, as employees do not need to constantly seek approvals or instructions from higher-ups. However, an overemphasis on autonomy can also pose challenges. Without proper guidelines or alignment with strategic goals, employees may make decisions that do not align with the organization's overall objectives. This can lead to fragmentation and a lack of cohesion in efforts across different teams or departments. In some cases, it may even result in a loss of control over critical processes or assets, potentially jeopardizing the organization's stability.

On the other hand, an organization that leans heavily towards control maintains a structured environment where decisions are centralized, often by higher management or a select few. This approach can provide clarity, consistency, and alignment with the organization's strategic vision. It helps ensure that decisions are in line with the established norms and guidelines, reducing the risk of deviations that could harm the organization. However, a control-oriented approach can also stifle creativity and innovation. Employees may feel micromanaged, leading to decreased job satisfaction and engagement. Moreover, decision-making processes can become slow and bureaucratic, hindering the organization's ability to adapt to rapidly changing market conditions. It may also discourage initiative and entrepreneurship among employees, as they become accustomed to waiting for instructions.

Both autonomy and control have their own advantages and disadvantages

Choosing Autonomy Only	
Pros	**Cons**
More freedom can lead to fresh and innovative ideas.	Too much freedom may result in errors or lack of alignment with goals.
Autonomy can make employees feel trusted and motivated.	With autonomy, it can be harder to pinpoint responsibility for decisions gone wrong
Autonomy can speed up the decision-making process.	With autonomy, it can be harder to pinpoint responsibility for decisions gone wrong

Choosing Control Only	
Pros	**Cons**
Control ensures that processes and decisions align with company goals.	Excessive control can hinder creativity and new ideas.
Tight control can minimize mistakes and risks.	Employees may feel micromanaged and less engaged.
Control provides clear lines of responsibility.	Control can slow down the decision-making process as decisions often require approval.

Valve Corporation, a prominent video game developer and distributor, is known for its unique approach to organizational structure. Valve's organizational philosophy is built on autonomy, where employees have a high degree of freedom and self-determination

in their work. There are no traditional managers or supervisors, and employees choose their projects based on their interests and expertise. This approach positively impacts Valve as it fosters innovation and creativity. Employees are highly motivated and engaged, leading to the creation of successful game titles like "Half-Life" and "Portal." However, this approach may also pose challenges in terms of coordination and decision-making in a rapidly growing organization, potentially leading to inefficiencies and resource allocation issues.

McDonald's Corporation, a global fast-food chain, is an example of a company that relies on control as a fundamental aspect of its business model. McDonald's maintains strict control over various aspects of its operations, including menu offerings, ingredients, store design, and operational procedures. This control enables McDonald's to provide a consistent customer experience across thousands of locations worldwide. The positive impact of this approach includes brand consistency, efficient processes, and predictable quality. However, it may also limit innovation and adaptability, making it challenging to cater to diverse regional preferences and respond quickly to changing market trends.

Some questions for the leaders to reflect and answer, to resolve the dilemma:

- How much freedom should we give our employees to make their own choices?
- Is too much freedom leading to mistakes, or is too much control stifling innovation?
- What are our company's strategic goals, and how does autonomy or control fit into them?
- Does our company culture value rules and precision, or does it encourage creativity and flexibility?
- Do our employees have the skills and experience to handle more independence?
- How can we strike a balance between control and autonomy that suits our unique situation?

There could be several factors that could influence this decision in the context of your organization, like:

Strategic Goals:

- How do our strategic goals impact autonomy vs. control?
- Are specific objectives better suited for a controlled approach?
- In which areas can autonomy align with our strategic goals?

Company Culture:

- Does our culture prioritize rules and control or encourage flexibility and innovation?
- How does culture shape our autonomy-control balance?
- Are there cultural norms influencing our decision-making?

Employee Capabilities:

- Do our employees possess the skills for more autonomy?
- Can training improve their ability to handle autonomy effectively?
- How do employee capabilities impact our control needs?

Risk Tolerance:

- What's our organization's risk tolerance, and how does it affect autonomy-control choices?
- How can we balance risk mitigation (control) and innovation potential (autonomy)?
- Are there areas where risk management is paramount?

Nature of the Business:

- How does our industry impact the autonomy-control requirement?
- Do regulations influence our decision?
- Do different parts of our organization need varying oversight levels?

Innovation Needs:

- Does our growth rely on innovation?
- How can autonomy boost innovation while controlling essential processes?
- Do innovation teams need more autonomy?

Market Dynamics:

- How do market dynamics and competition influence our choice?
- Are changing conditions demanding more adaptability (autonomy) or stability (control)?
- How can our approach give us a competitive edge?

There are other areas that get impacted because of a choice of this dilemma, like:

- Decision-Making Processes
- Employee Empowerment
- Organizational Structure
- Risk Management
- Innovation Culture

In practice, finding the right balance between autonomy and control is often the key to success. This involves defining clear boundaries and guidelines for decision-making, while also empowering employees to take initiative within those boundaries. Striking this balance can lead to a culture where employees feel both supported and accountable, fostering innovation and alignment with strategic goals. *HubSpot, a leading inbound marketing and sales software company, encourages autonomy and innovation among its product development teams. Engineers and product managers are given the freedom to explore new ideas and features. This approach fosters a culture of creativity, resulting in innovative marketing solutions that meet the evolving needs of customers. While promoting autonomy in product development, HubSpot maintains control and standardized processes in its sales and marketing operations. The company follows well-defined inbound marketing strategies and provides comprehensive training for its sales teams. This control ensures a consistent and efficient approach to customer engagement and lead generation.*

The decision of whether to choose autonomy or control in various aspects of running a business is influenced by several factors. These factors can vary based on the industry, organizational goals, leadership style, and other contextual considerations. Here are some key factors that influence this decision:

- **Nature of the Industry**: The industry's characteristics and competitive dynamics impact the choice. In rapidly changing industries, such as technology or fashion, autonomy may be favored to adapt quickly. In regulated industries like healthcare or finance, control is often necessary to meet compliance standards.
- **Leadership Style**: The leadership style of top executives can influence the approach. Leaders who trust their teams and promote empowerment are likely to opt for autonomy. Leaders who prefer a more centralized approach may lean towards control.
- **Innovation Goals**: The organization's innovation goals and strategies are a significant factor. Autonomy is often favored when fostering innovation and creativity is a top priority. Control may be chosen when standardization and risk mitigation are critical.
- **Risk Tolerance**: The level of risk tolerance within the organization plays a role. Autonomy can introduce more uncertainties and risks, whereas control provides a sense of security and predictability.
- **Customer-Centric Approach**: The focus on meeting customer needs can influence the decision. Companies prioritizing a customer-centric approach may opt for autonomy to respond to diverse customer preferences. Those emphasizing consistency may choose control to ensure a uniform customer experience.
- **Complexity of Operations**: The complexity of the organization's operations is a key consideration. Complex operations often require more control to ensure coordination and compliance, while simpler operations may allow for more

autonomy.

- **Regulatory Environment**: Regulatory requirements and compliance standards can dictate the level of control necessary. Industries with strict regulations may have limited flexibility, requiring a controlled approach.
- **Talent Strategy**: The organization's talent acquisition and retention strategies come into play. Attracting and retaining top talent may involve offering autonomy to employees who value creative freedom.
- **Market Expansion**: The choice may vary when expanding into new markets. A balance between autonomy and control can be essential to adapt to local market dynamics while maintaining a standardized approach in core operations.
- **Technological Infrastructure**: The availability and sophistication of technology solutions can impact the decision. Modern technologies can enable organizations to manage autonomy more effectively, while legacy systems may favor control.

The decision on where to position the organization on the autonomy-control spectrum has far-reaching consequences. It affects not only employee engagement, innovation, and decision-making speed but also the organization's adaptability, alignment with strategic goals, and overall stability. Therefore, leaders must carefully consider the specific needs of their organization and industry context when navigating this crucial dilemma.

Transparency vs. Confidentiality

> Should the organization emphasize openness and transparency, even when it might expose its vulnerabilities, or should it prioritize confidentiality to protect its strategic interests or be selective about situations in which to be transparent and where secrecy needs to be maintained?

Opting for a culture of transparency involves a commitment to open communication and the sharing of information with stakeholders, including employees, customers, investors, and the public. This approach can foster trust, accountability, and goodwill. When the organization is transparent about its operations, decision-making processes, and financial performance, it can strengthen relationships with stakeholders and build a positive reputation for honesty and integrity. Employees often feel more engaged and motivated in a transparent environment, as they understand the broader context of their work and the organization's goals. However, a purely transparent approach may also expose vulnerabilities, sensitive data, or strategic plans that competitors or adversaries could exploit. In some cases, excessive transparency may create confusion or anxiety among employees, especially when it comes to discussing difficult topics like financial challenges or layoffs. Furthermore, transparency may not always align with the need for confidentiality, such as when protecting intellectual property, trade secrets, or sensitive personal information.

On the other hand, prioritizing confidentiality means safeguarding sensitive information and maintaining discretion, especially in situations where exposure could harm the organization's strategic interests or stakeholders. Confidentiality is crucial for protecting proprietary technology, financial data, legal matters, and other sensitive areas. By maintaining confidentiality, the organization can reduce the risk of data breaches, leaks, or competitive disadvantages. However, an overly secretive approach can also have downsides. It may create a culture of mistrust or suspicion among employees and stakeholders if they perceive that information is being withheld unnecessarily. Lack of transparency can limit engagement and feedback, as employees and customers may feel left in the dark about the organization's decisions and actions. Additionally, regulatory requirements in certain industries may demand a certain level of transparency and disclosure, making it essential to strike a balance.

Neither transparency nor confidentiality are good or bad.

Choosing Transparency Only	
Pros	**Cons**
When organizations are open about their actions and decisions, it builds trust with employees and stakeholders.	It can expose weaknesses and failures, leading to reputation damage
It makes organizations accountable for their actions, leading to better ethical behavior.	Sometimes, too much transparency can slow down decision-making as everything needs approval.
It encourages innovative ideas and collaboration when everyone knows what's happening.	Sharing too much can give competitors insights into the organization's strategies.
Choosing Confidentiality Only	
Pros	**Cons**
Confidentiality keeps sensitive information safe from leaks. Keeping strategies secret can give organizations a competitive edge.	Too much secrecy can lead to distrust among employees and stakeholders.
It allows for fast decision-making when discussions can happen behind closed doors.	It can stifle creative ideas and collaboration when everything is hidden.

It allows for fast decision-making when discussions can happen behind closed doors.	Excessive confidentiality can lead to unethical behavior as there's no accountability.

Buffer, a social media management platform, is known for its commitment to transparency. The company shares detailed financial information, including revenue, salaries, and even equity distribution, with the public. This transparency positively impacts Buffer by building trust with its users and potential customers. Stakeholders appreciate the openness, which has resulted in loyal users and an active and engaged online community. However, this approach can also pose challenges, as competitors and other stakeholders gain insights into Buffer's operations, potentially affecting the competitive landscape.

Apple, one of the world's leading technology companies, maintains a strict policy of confidentiality regarding its product development and intellectual property. While Apple is known for its product announcements shrouded in secrecy, this approach has been beneficial for the company. Confidentiality allows Apple to build anticipation and generate massive media attention around product launches, positively impacting sales and market share. However, the downside is that this secrecy can create frustration among some customers and can limit the company's ability to gather feedback during the development process.

Some questions for the leaders to reflect and answer to resolve the dilemma:

- Do our transparency efforts align with our organization's strategic objectives, or do they potentially expose vulnerabilities that could hinder our goals?
- Does our emphasis on transparency or confidentiality align with our organizational culture, and does it contribute positively to fostering the desired work environment?
- What are the primary concerns and preferences of our key stakeholders, such as employees, investors, and customers, regarding the level of information disclosure?
- How do existing regulatory requirements and industry standards impact our approach to transparency and

- confidentiality, and how can we navigate these effectively?
- To what extent do our transparency or confidentiality practices impact our risk management strategies and our ability to foster innovation within the organization?
- How does our chosen stance on transparency and confidentiality align with our long-term vision and our commitment to building trust and safeguarding strategic interests over time?

There could be several factors that could influence this decision in the context of your organization, like:

Regulations and Industry Standards: Compliance requirements and industry-specific regulations influence the choice.

Stakeholder Preferences: The desires of customers, investors, and partners shape the decision.

Competition and Market Dynamics: The competitive landscape and the need to protect intellectual property impact the choice.

Risk Management: An organization's risk tolerance and efforts to safeguard sensitive data play a role.

Nature of Information: The type of information, whether financial or proprietary, determines the approach.

There are other areas that get impacted because of a choice of this dilemma, like:

- Organizational Communication
- Trust and Accountability
- Data Security and Privacy
- Employee Morale
- Legal and Ethical Compliance

Transparency sounds cool but that shouldn't be the reason why we choose it. Even worse is promising employee's transparency while in reality you cannot 'live' it. *In a culture audit and leadership alignment workshop we did for a financial services institution, when this dilemma was presented, the majority of the leaders instantly chose transparency. They also proudly claimed it to be a key highlight in their onboarding process. Specific objections surfaced when we began probing about different facets of the dilemma. They are regulated by the RBI (Reserve Bank of India), and so they cannot be completely transparent, even if they want to. As we delved deeper, they realized that they are closer to the confidentiality end of the spectrum than the transparency end. So they removed this aspect of promising transparency in their communication with employees and candidates. Within 6 months, the leaders realized that the employees started to trust the management more because they were saying what they were doing!*

Take the case of Patagonia, the American outdoor clothing company, which has managed to strike a commendable balance. Known for its environmental activism, Patagonia has been transparent about its supply chain, revealing both its triumphs and failures in environmental stewardship. Yet, it maintains confidentiality around its design and product development processes to keep its competitive edge.

The decision of whether to choose transparency or confidentiality in various aspects of running a business is influenced by several factors like:

- **Industry and Competitive Environment**: In highly regulated industries like healthcare or finance, confidentiality may be mandated by regulatory bodies. In contrast, technology startups may embrace transparency to differentiate themselves and build trust.
- **Legal and Regulatory Requirements**: Companies must comply with laws governing data privacy, financial reporting, and intellectual property protection. Failure to do so can result in legal and reputational risks.
- **Stakeholder Expectations**: Stakeholder expectations, including those of customers, investors, and employees, play a pivotal role. Investors may seek transparency in financial reporting, while customers may value confidentiality in data handling.
- **Brand Reputation**: Brands that promote transparency can build trust with customers, while those that prioritize confidentiality may be viewed as protective of sensitive information.
- **Competitive Advantage**: Some businesses use transparency as a

strategic tool to gain a competitive edge, while others consider confidentiality a means of safeguarding proprietary information.

- **Business Lifecycle**: Startups and early-stage companies often opt for transparency to establish credibility, while more mature organizations may adopt a balanced approach.
- **Risk Management**: Companies must evaluate the potential risks associated with both transparency (e.g., data breaches) and confidentiality (e.g., missed opportunities due to lack of information sharing).
- **Innovation and Collaboration**: Companies seeking innovation may lean towards transparency to foster collaboration and idea-sharing, while others may prioritize confidentiality to protect intellectual property.
- **Leadership Style**: Leaders who value transparency may set the tone for open communication, while leaders who value discretion may emphasize confidentiality.
- **Customer Data Handling**: For companies handling customer data, data privacy regulations and customer expectations may dictate the level of transparency or confidentiality required.
- **Crisis Management**: Transparency can be essential for managing crises related to product recalls or data breaches, while confidentiality may be maintained in other areas.

Therefore, in the balancing act of transparency vs. confidentiality, organizations must navigate a nuanced path. By carefully aligning their choices with strategic goals, stakeholder needs, and regulatory demands, they can forge a sustainable equilibrium that cultivates trust while safeguarding vital interests. The key is to recognize that, majority of the time, this is not a binary choice but a spectrum offering diverse shades of operational integrity.

People-Centric Approach vs. Performance-Driven Culture
(Sports Team vs. Happy Family)

> Should the organization focus on employee well-being and work-life balance, which might impact short-term productivity, or should it prioritize performance and productivity or strike a fine balance between the two?

Imagine how things work in a sports team vs a happy family. In a Sports team, it is very competitive and performance trumps everything else. Each person's place in the team is also uncertain. If someone doesn't perform, they are replaced. In the process, dedicating time and energy to excel in sports or a demanding career can lead to personal success and achievement. On the other hand, an excessive focus on individual accomplishments can strain relationships, potentially leading to feelings of disconnection among the people who spend the majority of the time together. On the other hand, in a family, people cover up for each other's gaps and shortcomings and together they thrive. No one, ever, gets dropped off for non-performance. Relationships trump everything.

Prioritizing a people-centric approach involves valuing employee well-being, job satisfaction, and work-life balance as top priorities. Companies embracing this approach often invest in employee development, health and wellness programs, and flexible work arrangements. This approach can foster a positive workplace culture where employees feel valued, leading to higher morale, better retention rates, and a sense of loyalty. However, focusing on employee well-being and work-life balance can potentially impact short-term productivity. Employees may be less inclined to work long hours or under intense pressure, which could affect immediate performance metrics. Additionally, the organization might need to allocate resources to support these programs, which can increase operational costs.

On the other hand, a performance-driven culture places a strong emphasis on achieving organizational goals and productivity. In such cultures, performance metrics, targets, and KPIs are central to decision-making. Employees are often encouraged to meet or exceed performance expectations, which can lead to increased output and efficiency. However, a relentless focus on performance can come at a cost. Employees might experience higher stress levels, burnout, and reduced job satisfaction. Over time, this can lead to higher turnover rates, increased absenteeism, and a less positive workplace environment. Moreover, organizations may become myopic, prioritizing short-term gains at the expense of long-term sustainability.

Both ends of the spectrum have their own pros and cons

Choosing People-Centric Approach Only	
Pros	Cons
Enhanced employee satisfaction and well-being	Potential short-term dips in performance
Higher retention rates and improved talent attraction	Adjustments needed in performance expectations and metrics
Positive impact on workplace culture and morale	Need for careful communication to manage expectations

Choosing Performance-Driven Culture Only	
Pros	Cons
Potential for short-term performance gains	Risk of employee burnout and turnover
Alignment with industries that prioritize productivity	Negative impact on employee morale and culture
Clear performance metrics and expectations	Potential long-term sustainability challenges

Zappos, an online retailer renowned for its unique company culture, places a strong emphasis on being people-centric. They prioritize employee happiness, personal development, and a positive work environment. This approach has yielded several positive outcomes. Zappos is often praised for its high employee satisfaction rates and low turnover, contributing to a motivated and committed workforce. The company's people-centric culture fosters creativity and innovation, leading to unique customer service initiatives like their famous "Wow Customer Service" approach. However, critics argue that this approach can be costly, as Zappos offers extensive employee benefits, and it may sometimes prioritize individual well-being over stringent performance metrics.

Salesforce, a leading customer relationship management (CRM) software company, is recognized for its strong performance-centric culture. They place a significant emphasis on achieving and exceeding performance targets, which aligns closely with their highly competitive industry. This approach has resulted in remarkable revenue growth and market dominance. Salesforce's culture encourages healthy competition, and their sales-driven performance metrics have led to consistent financial success. Nevertheless, critics argue that a relentless focus on performance can create a high-pressure work environment and may occasionally neglect employee well-being, potentially leading to burnout and turnover.

Some questions for the leaders to reflect and answer to resolve the dilemma:

- Does our organizational culture currently lean towards valuing long hours and unrelenting performance, or does it prioritize employee well-being and work-life balance?
- What do our employees expect and value more—work-life balance and well-being or high-performance expectations and outcomes resulting in higher bonus?
- Are our short-term and long-term business goals better served by emphasizing immediate performance, even if it compromises well-being, or by investing in employee welfare for sustainable success?
- Is our industry characterized by a culture of burnout, or does it promote sustainability, well-being, and a balanced approach to work?
- Can we create flexible work models that accommodate performance and well-being, allowing employees to thrive in their roles while maintaining a healthy work-life balance?
- How does our chosen approach impact employee morale,

retention, and overall engagement, and what ripple effects does it have within the organization?

There could be several factors that could influence this decision in the context of your organization, like

Culture Compatibility: Does our organizational culture align with the chosen approach, and how can we shape it to support our objectives?

Employee Well-being: What specific measures can we take to prioritize employee well-being without compromising our performance goals?

Performance Metrics: How can we redefine performance metrics to encompass both employee well-being and productivity effectively?

Leadership Commitment: Are our leaders committed to modeling the desired approach and advocating for employee welfare while achieving performance targets?

Workplace Flexibility: Can we introduce flexible work arrangements that accommodate both performance-driven expectations and employee well-being?

Communication Strategy: How can we communicate our chosen approach to employees transparently, ensuring they understand and align with our priorities?

There are other areas that get impacted because of a choice of this dilemma, like:

- Employee Engagement and Satisfaction
- Talent Recruitment and Retention
- Organizational Values and Culture
- Leadership Style and Behavior
- Performance Metrics and Evaluation

Striking a balance between a people-centric approach and a performance-driven culture is often the preferred route. This entails recognizing that employee well-being and performance are not mutually exclusive but can reinforce each other. When employees feel supported and valued, they are more likely to be engaged and motivated, ultimately contributing to better performance in the long run. Organizations can also manage their resources more efficiently, ensuring that investments in employee well-being align with strategic objectives. *An excellent example of this balance is the Danish pharmaceutical company Novo Nordisk. They introduced 'Aspirational Working Hours,' - where people could choose the number of hours to work, thereby encouraging employees to work smart, not long, and prioritize their well-being. This approach has improved not only employee satisfaction but also productivity and performance.*

Every company has certain industries, roles, and life stages where employees may need to prioritize performance. They may need to prioritize performance at the cost of employee well-being. In some cases, these situations may be seasonal/cyclical. Companies where leaders acknowledge these conditions and tell candidates upfront that they may have to be available on call outside of working hours, or they may need to come to work on a holiday because the client's welfare depends on it. In the case of a legal services firm, whether the client will go to jail or spend the night with their family depends on employees being ready to work on a Sunday evening! People understand such requirements and are ready to go beyond work hours or cancel their personal plans. What makes employees feel let down by their company is when this is done for unreasonable demands or artificial emergencies; when this happens all the time; when leaders think this is normal and expect everyone to do this all the time. Everyone understands that wartime is different from peacetime. What they're not ok with is the feeling of being at war all the time!

The decision of whether to choose a people-centric approach or a performance-driven culture in various aspects of running a business is influenced by several factors:

- **Industry and Competitive Environment**: In highly competitive sectors, organizations may lean towards a performance-driven culture to stay ahead, while others in less competitive sectors may prioritize employee satisfaction.
- **Leadership Style**: Leaders who value employee development and engagement are more likely to opt for a people-centric

approach, while results-focused leaders may emphasize performance.

- **Organizational Size and Stage**: Startups and smaller companies may prioritize performance-driven cultures to establish themselves, while larger, more mature organizations may shift towards a people-centric approach to retain talent.
- **Talent Market**: In industries with a shortage of skilled workers, companies may adopt a people-centric approach to attract and retain top talent.
- **Business Strategy**: Companies with a growth-oriented strategy may prioritize performance to achieve ambitious targets, while those focused on sustainability may emphasize employee well-being.
- **Regulatory Environment**: Industries with strict labor laws or safety regulations may be more inclined towards a people-centric approach to ensure compliance.
- **Employee Expectations**: Organizations need to align their approach with what their workforce values. If employees expect a supportive and flexible work environment, the company may opt for a people-centric approach.
- **Customer-Centricity**: Companies heavily focused on delivering exceptional customer experiences may prioritize a performance-driven culture to meet customer demands.
- **Crisis Management**: For instance, during economic downturns, companies may temporarily shift towards a performance-driven culture to ensure financial stability.
- **Long-Term vs. Short-Term Goals**: Companies with long-term sustainability as their primary objective may lean towards a people-centric approach, while those with short-term profit goals may prioritize performance.

In conclusion, the choice between a people-centric approach and a performance-driven culture is a complex decision with far-reaching implications. Organizations need to carefully assess their unique context, industry, and goals to strike the right balance that fosters a healthy work environment, sustains long-term performance, and meets the needs of their employees and stakeholders.

Short-Term Success vs. Long-Term Sustainability

> Should the organization focus on achieving short-term goals and quick wins, or should it prioritize long-term sustainability, even if that means slower progress in the short run or strike a balance to optimize?

Opting for short-term success typically involves focusing on achieving immediate goals and objectives. Organizations may prioritize strategies that generate rapid revenue growth, quick profits, or immediate market share gains. This approach can be appealing, especially in industries with high competition or when external pressures demand immediate results. Short-term success can boost investor confidence, provide quick returns, and satisfy stakeholders who expect instant gratification. However, there are potential drawbacks to this approach. Overemphasizing short-term gains may lead to a myopic focus on quarterly financial results, often at the expense of long-term sustainability. Companies might engage in practices such as cost-cutting, reducing R&D investments, or compromising on quality to meet immediate financial targets. This can erode the organization's competitive edge, damage its reputation, and limit its capacity to adapt to changing market dynamics in the long term.

Prioritizing long-term sustainability entails making strategic decisions that aim to secure the organization's future viability and success. It involves investments in research and development, talent development, environmental and social responsibility, and building strong relationships with customers and partners. While the results of these efforts may not yield immediate returns, they contribute to the organization's resilience and enduring competitive advantage. Long-term sustainability often aligns with responsible business practices and ethical considerations. It can enhance the organization's reputation, attract socially conscious investors, and foster strong customer loyalty. Companies committed to sustainability are more likely to weather economic downturns, adapt to industry disruptions, and remain relevant over time. However, the challenge with this approach is that it may require substantial resources and patience. It can be challenging to secure buy-in from stakeholders who prioritize short-term gains, such as shareholders looking for quick profits.

Additionally, measuring the impact of sustainability initiatives can be complex and may not yield immediate financial metrics that satisfy short-term expectations.

Choosing Short-Term Success Only	
Pros	Cons
Quick growth	Risk of long-term instability
Satisfying stakeholders	Loss of strategic direction
Flexibility to adapt	Sustainability challenges

Choosing Long-Term Sustainability Only	
Pros	Cons
Enduring success	Slower initial progress
Stable foundation	Possible short-term hurdles
Clear strategic vision	Greater long-term commitment

Zynga, known for popular mobile games like "FarmVille" and "Words With Friends," pursued a short-term success strategy by heavily focusing on churning out hit games to drive immediate revenue. While this approach led to rapid growth and substantial profits in the short term, it had its downsides. The company faced challenges related to player retention and quality, as some games were criticized for being repetitive and monetization-focused. The constant pressure to release new titles to maintain revenue growth led to burnout among employees. Over time, Zynga's reputation in the gaming community suffered, and the company had to pivot towards a more sustainable, player-centric approach to regain trust and ensure long-term viability.

Tesla, the electric vehicle (EV) and clean energy company founded by Elon Musk, is a prime example of a company that has prioritized long-term sustainability over short-

term gains. Tesla disrupted the automotive industry by focusing on the development and mass production of electric vehicles when the market was dominated by traditional gasoline-powered cars. Tesla's early years were marked by substantial financial challenges and skepticism from investors. However, the company remained committed to its mission of accelerating the world's transition to sustainable energy. It invested heavily in research and development, including battery technology and autonomous driving capabilities, which incurred significant costs. In the short term, this approach led to financial losses and production challenges. However, in the long run, Tesla's unwavering commitment to sustainability paid off. The company became a leader in the EV market, and its stock price soared as investors recognized the potential for electric vehicles and clean energy solutions.

Some questions for the leaders to reflect and answer to resolve the dilemma:

- How fast is our industry changing, and do we need immediate wins to keep up?
- Can we afford to invest in long-term sustainability without sacrificing short-term success?
- What do our stakeholders - shareholders, employees, and customers - expect from us?
- Are our competitors chasing short-term gains, or are they thinking long-term?
- Can we strike a balance between short-term success and long-term sustainability?
- What are the potential benefits and drawbacks of choosing one over the other?

There could be several factors that could influence this decision in the context of your organization like:

Market Dynamics:

- How fast is your industry changing?
- Do you need quick wins to keep up?
- Are competitors sprinting ahead or moving slowly?

> **Financial Health**: Can your organization invest in long-term sustainability without harming short-term success?
>
> **Stakeholder Expectations**: What do shareholders, employees, and customers expect? Immediate gains or sustainable growth?
>
> **Competitive Landscape**:
>
> - Are competitors focusing on short-term gains or long-term strategies?
> - What's the balance in your industry?
>
> **There are other areas that get impacted because of a choice of this dilemma, like:**
>
> - Strategic Planning and Goals
> - Financial Planning and Budgeting
> - Innovation and Research
> - Risk Management
> - Stakeholder Relations

Many organizations recognize the need to strike a balance between short-term success and long-term sustainability. This approach seeks to optimize immediate gains while ensuring that actions align with a broader, enduring vision. Striking a balance may involve setting realistic short-term goals that support long-term objectives, investing in innovation while maintaining core operations, and being agile enough to respond to changing circumstances without sacrificing long-term values. *Titan Company Limited, a subsidiary of the Tata Group, is an excellent example of an Indian organization that has managed to strike a balance between short-term goals and long-term sustainability in various scenarios. In the short term, Titan focuses on meeting consumer demand and achieving financial targets by introducing trendy and innovative products in its jewelry and watch segments. This approach allows the company to maintain profitability and market leadership. However, Titan's commitment to long-term sustainability is evident in several aspects of its operations.*

- ***Ethical Sourcing:*** *Titan has a strong focus on responsible sourcing of raw materials, especially in the jewelry segment, ensuring that its products adhere to ethical and environmental standards. This sustainability initiative not only aligns with long-term industry trends but also appeals to conscious consumers.*
- ***Employee Welfare:*** *Titan places significant emphasis on employee well-being and has implemented several employee-friendly policies and practices. This people-centric approach helps in retaining talent and fostering a positive work environment.*
- ***Innovation and R&D:*** *The Company invests in research and development to stay ahead of market trends and technological advancements, ensuring its long-term relevance and competitiveness.*
- ***Social Responsibility:*** *Titan is involved in various social initiatives, including community development and education programs. These efforts demonstrate the company's commitment to the long-term well-being of society.*

Several factors influence a company's decision to prioritize short-term goals or long-term sustainability:

- **Market Conditions**: In highly competitive markets, companies may prioritize short-term goals to maintain market share. In growing markets, companies may lean towards long-term sustainability to capture future opportunities.

- **Financial Health**: Companies with strong financial reserves may have more flexibility to invest in long-term sustainability initiatives. High short-term debt may force a company to focus on short-term goals to meet financial obligations.

- **Industry Dynamics**: Stringent regulations may require immediate compliance, impacting short-term goals. Industries facing rapid technological changes may prioritize long-term sustainability through innovation.

- **Stakeholder Expectations**: Investor demand for short-term returns vs. sustainable, long-term growth can influence decisions. Customer preferences for eco-friendly products may drive companies towards sustainability.

- **Leadership Vision**: The vision and values of top leadership often shape the company's priorities. Long-serving leaders may focus on long-term sustainability, while interim leaders may emphasize short-term results.

- **Risk Tolerance**: Risk-averse organizations may prioritize short-term stability, while risk-tolerant ones may invest in long-term sustainability.

- **Resource Availability**: Limited resources may necessitate focusing on short-term goals over long-term initiatives. Easier access to capital can support long-term sustainability investments.

- **Brand Reputation**: A strong brand may allow companies to emphasize sustainability to enhance reputation and customer loyalty. Companies with tarnished reputations may prioritize short-term image repair.

- **Global Economic Conditions**: Economic downturns may encourage short-term cost-cutting, while upturns can support long-term investments.

- **External Events**: Crises like pandemics or natural disasters can shift priorities towards short-term survival.

Short-term success focuses on quick wins, while long-term sustainability prioritizes lasting success. Balancing both means setting smart goals, investing wisely, adapting to change, and involving everyone. It's about thriving today and building for tomorrow. The choice between short-term success and long-term sustainability isn't black and white; it's a dynamic balance. Companies that find this equilibrium thrive in the present and secure their future. It's a strategic puzzle that, when solved well, can be the difference between surviving and thriving.

Market-Led vs. Product/Service-Led

> Should the organization adopt a market-centric approach, constantly listening to the market and adapting to meet customer needs, or should it remain inwardly focused with product/service-centric mindset, focusing on developing its products to the highest standards or could attempt to blend the two and reap greater benefits?

A Market-led organization places the customer at the heart of its operations and decision-making. It relentlessly seeks to understand customer preferences, respond to changing market trends, and tailor its products or services accordingly. Here, the customer's voice is crucial, feedback is valued, and adaptation is rapid. Market-led companies are adept at identifying emerging opportunities and swiftly aligning their strategies to capture them. This approach aims to achieve customer satisfaction, loyalty, and market share through an unwavering focus on customer needs and preferences.

In contrast, a Product/Service-led organization prioritizes excellence in its offerings. It invests heavily in research and development, striving to create top-quality products or services. Innovation, precision, and craftsmanship are the hallmarks of this approach. Such companies believe that by delivering the best-in-class products or services, they can lead the market, attract discerning customers, and maintain a competitive edge. They may consider customer feedback but often with the perspective of improving the product, rather than reshaping the entire business model.

Choosing To Be Market-Led Only	
Pros	Cons
Strong customer relationships.	Risk of losing focus on product quality.
Quick adaptation to changing market trends.	Potential resource strain from frequent adaptations.
High customer satisfaction.	Intense competition in meeting customer needs.

Choosing To Be Product/Service Led Only	
Pros	Cons
High product/service quality.	May miss shifts in customer preferences.
Competitive advantage through innovation.	Slower response to market changes.
Focused resource allocation.	Risk of product/service obsolescence.

Lenskart, a prominent Indian eyewear retailer, exemplifies a company that prioritizes market-led offerings. The company closely monitors consumer trends and preferences, allowing it to swiftly adapt its product portfolio and retail strategies. Lenskart's emphasis on understanding the market has helped it introduce innovative offerings like affordable, high-quality eyeglasses, home eye check-ups, and an expansive online presence. By aligning its offerings with market demands, Lenskart has experienced significant growth and established itself as a leader in the eyewear industry. However, this approach also means frequent adjustments and investments to keep up with evolving customer expectations, putting pressure on the company's resources.

HOPE IS NOT A STRATEGY

FabIndia, an Indian retail brand known for handcrafted products and traditional textiles, primarily follows a product/service-led approach. The company focuses on maintaining the authenticity and craftsmanship of its products, which often adhere to traditional techniques. While this approach has helped FabIndia build a strong brand associated with quality and cultural heritage, it can also limit the company's ability to swiftly adapt to market trends and changing consumer preferences. In some cases, FabIndia's commitment to preserving traditional methods may restrict its ability to expand into emerging product categories or address rapidly evolving market demands. Despite this, the company's dedication to its core values has attracted a loyal customer base appreciative of its unique offerings.

Some questions for the leaders to reflect and answer to resolve the dilemma:

- Does the industry focus on customer preferences or technological advancements?
- Does our organization thrive on customer feedback or technological innovation?
- Are our competitors emphasizing customer needs or product excellence?
- How actively are we gathering and acting upon customer feedback?
- Are we maintaining product/service quality while addressing customer needs?
- Are we continuously innovating to meet evolving customer demands?

There could be several factors that could influence this decision in the context of your organization like:

Financial Resources: Can the organization afford to invest in both customer-centricity and product excellence?

Talent and Expertise: Do we have the right skills and knowledge to excel in both areas?

Market Trends: Are current market trends favoring market-led strategies or product/service-led approaches?

> **Regulatory Environment**: Does industry regulation impact our choice between market-led or product-led strategies?
>
> **Customer Segmentation**: Can we identify distinct customer segments with varying needs?
>
> **Technology**: How does technological advancement affect our ability to balance these approaches?
>
> **There are other areas that get impacted because of a choice of this dilemma, like:**
>
> - Market Strategy and Customer Focus
> - Product or Service Development
> - Competitive Positioning
> - Marketing and Sales Approach
> - Innovation and Research Focus

Being market-led and being product/service led need not be mutually exclusive. *Zomato, a popular Indian food delivery and restaurant discovery platform, is an organization that effectively strikes a balance between being market-led and product/service-led in various scenarios. Zomato continuously monitors market trends, customer preferences, and competitive dynamics in the food delivery industry. It adapts to changing market conditions by offering promotions, discounts, and loyalty programs to attract and retain customers. Zomato's ability to respond swiftly to market demands has allowed it to expand its presence in multiple countries and gain a significant market share. At the same time, Zomato places a strong emphasis on the quality of its platform and services. It invests in user-friendly app features, restaurant partnerships, and food quality assurance. This product/service-led approach ensures that customers have a seamless and enjoyable experience when using the platform, which contributes to customer retention and positive word-of-mouth.*

Several factors influence a company's decision to prioritize a market-led approach or a product/service-led approach:

- **Customer-Centric Factors**: Companies may prioritize a market-led approach when customer preferences are rapidly evolving or when there is a diverse range of customer needs. Continuous customer feedback and market research can drive companies toward offering products/services that align with market demands.

- **Competitive Dynamics**: In highly competitive markets, a market-led approach may be essential to stay ahead and differentiate from rivals. Companies aiming to gain or maintain a dominant market share may prioritize market-led strategies to capture a broad customer base.
- **Industry Characteristics**: Industries heavily influenced by technology trends often require a market-led approach to stay relevant. Highly regulated industries may need to focus on product/service quality to meet legal requirements.
- **Brand Identity and Reputation**: Companies with a strong brand identity may emphasize product/service-led approaches to maintain consistency and quality. Brands looking to enhance their reputation may prioritize delivering exceptional products/services.
- **Innovation and Differentiation**: Organizations aiming to be industry leaders may prioritize a product/service-led approach to create unique offerings. Companies that thrive on product/service excellence may opt for this approach to stand out.
- **Resource Availability**: Limited resources may lead to a market-led approach that focuses on immediate revenue generation. Easier access to capital can support investments in product/service development and quality.
- **Market Growth and Maturity**: In early-stage markets, a market-led approach may be suitable for capturing opportunities, while mature markets may require more product/service differentiation. Niche markets often favor product/service-led approaches to cater to specific customer segments.
- **Long-Term vs. Short-Term Goals**: The company's strategic outlook, whether it's focused on short-term gains or long-term sustainability, can influence the chosen approach. Aligning with investor preferences for short-term profits or long-term growth

can be a determining factor.
- **Geographic Considerations**: Market-led or product/service-led strategies may vary based on regional market conditions and cultural preferences.
- **Management Philosophy and Leadership**: The leadership's philosophy and long-term vision often guide the approach a company takes.

Ultimately, the choice between a market-led and product/service-led approach should align with an organization's industry, competitive landscape, and customer base. It's essential for organizations to periodically assess and adapt their strategies as market conditions evolve, customer expectations change, and technological advancements reshape industries. The ability to flexibly adjust the balance between these two perspectives is a key driver of sustained success.

| 3.2 |

ORGANIZATION STRUCTURE DILEMMAS

> **How will you use this chapter of the book?**
>
> If you are the founder or the CEO of a company and if you and your leadership team have a clear point of view (PoV) on the following questions and all of you are ALIGNED, then you can choose to move to the next chapter of the book. However, if you see a dissonance or have conflicting views, then we suggest digging deeper, going through this chapter and reflecting on different angles we bring in there.
>
> Here are the questions for you to discuss and ponder-
>
> - How does our current organizational structure align with our long-term strategic objectives, and what changes might be necessary to better support these goals?
> - Are we structured in a way that allows us to effectively meet the evolving needs and expectations of our customers?
> - Is our current hierarchy conducive to rapid decision-making and adaptation? Should we be more agile in future?
> - Given the changing nature of work, are we optimizing the balance between in-office and remote work arrangements to support employee productivity and satisfaction?
> - How do we decide between global standardization and local adaptation to maximize market responsiveness and efficiency?
> - Do our leadership capabilities and talent development strategies align with our chosen organizational structure?
> - Are our communication channels and collaboration tools effective in facilitating information flow and teamwork across the organization?
> - How do we foster a positive work environment, employee engagement, and a healthy work-life balance?

> - Do we have well defined success and effectiveness measures for our chosen organizational structure?
>
> Do we have an adaptable structure that anticipates and responds to future market changes, technological advancements, and industry disruptions?

Organization structure is like the blueprint of how a company or group is organized to work together effectively. It shows who does what and who reports to whom. Business leaders face critical dilemmas surrounding organizational structure that hold immense power to shape culture and define the path to success.

When it comes to organization structure, leaders need to make decisions about various aspects, including:

- **Hierarchy**: Leaders decide how many levels of management the organization should have, like who's the boss of who, and how many people report to each manager.
- **Departmentalization**: They figure out how to group employees, like by functions (marketing, finance) or by products, regions, or customers.
- **Decision-Making**: Leaders decide who gets to make important decisions, whether it's a few top leaders or if it's spread out to different teams.
- **Communication**: They plan how people in the organization talk to each other. Do they need to follow strict rules, or is it more informal?
- **Roles and Responsibilities**: Leaders define what each person's job is and what they're responsible for. This helps avoid confusion and overlaps.
- **Flexibility**: They consider how much the organization can change and adapt. Too much structure can slow down change, while too little can lead to chaos.
- **Culture**: Leaders shape the way people work together and the values and attitudes in the organization. This can influence the structure too.
- **Global or Local**: If the organization works in different places around the world, leaders decide how much should be the same

everywhere and how much can be different to fit local needs
- **Technology**: Leaders need to use technology to help the organization work efficiently and communicate effectively. This can affect how the structure is set up.
- **Growth and Future Planning**: As the organization grows, leaders need to think about how the structure should change to keep up with the growth and the future goals.

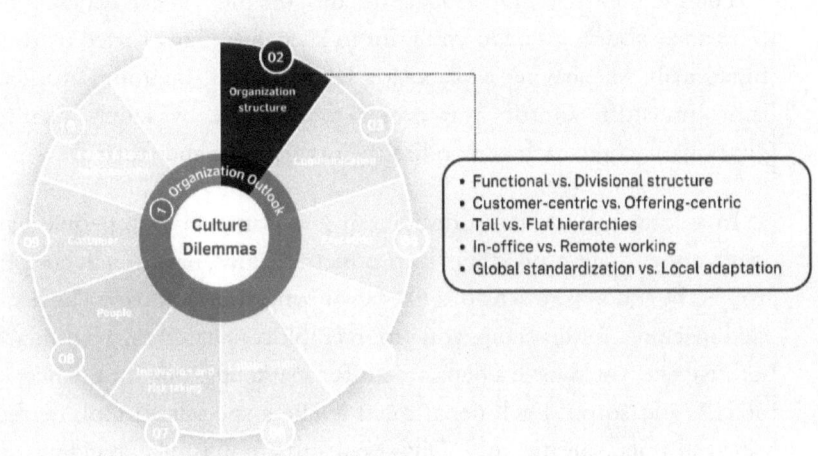

While there are countless dilemmas within the domain of organizational structure, one must focus their attention on five pivotal ones that often take center stage:

- **Functional vs. Divisional structure**
- **Customer centric vs. Offering centric**
- **Tall vs. Flat hierarchies**
- **In-office vs. Remote working**
- **Global standardization vs. Local adaptation**

Let's look at each of them in greater detail.

Functional vs. Divisional structure

> **This dilemma is all about balancing the choice between organizing the company by functions (e.g., marketing, finance, HR) or by divisions or business units (e.g., products, regions, customer segments) or a mix of the two.**

The Functional vs. Divisional structure dilemma is like deciding how to organize your house. Do you want to keep everything sorted by rooms (functional), like having a place for kitchen stuff, bedroom stuff, and bathroom stuff? Or do you prefer to organize by family members (divisional), where each person has their own space and stuff?

In a company, it's about deciding if you want to group people based on what they do or group them by products, regions, or different customer groups. Functional structure is like organizing your company like a well-oiled machine. In this setup, you group employees based on what they do. For instance, you'd have a department for marketing, one for finance, one for HR, and so on. Each department is like a specialized tool, perfectly honed for its specific job. Divisional structure is like building your company as a collection of smaller, more agile boats. Each boat (division) is responsible for a specific area, like a product line, a geographic region, or a customer segment. Each division operates almost like its own mini-company within the larger organization.

Choosing Functional Structure Only	
Pros	**Cons**
Clear expertise in each function.	Limited focus on products or regions.
Consistent processes and standards.	Slow to adapt to specific customer needs.
Easy to manage and control.	Can create silos and lack of collaboration.

Choosing Divisional Structure Only	
Pros	**Cons**
Tailored approach to products, regions, or customer segments.	Duplication of functions across divisions.
Faster response to local or market needs.	Coordination challenges between divisions.
Encourages innovation and creativity within divisions.	Potential for inconsistency in processes and standards.

The Coca-Cola Company, one of the world's largest beverage companies, has a predominantly functional structure. It organizes its operations into specialized functional areas, including marketing, finance, supply chain, research and development, and sales. Coca-Cola's success with its Functional structure is evident in its ability to create and market a wide range of beverages worldwide. The company's marketing function, for instance, focuses on developing and promoting brand strategies across various markets and demographics. The finance function handles financial planning and management, ensuring the company's profitability. The supply chain function manages the production and distribution of products efficiently. Coca-Cola's functional organization has allowed it to maintain consistency in product quality, branding, and market presence while adapting its strategies to meet the diverse preferences of consumers in different regions. This functional structure has contributed to Coca-Cola's enduring success as a global beverage leader.

In contrast, General Electric (GE) is a multinational conglomerate that follows a Divisional structure. The company is organized into various divisions, each focused on distinct industries, including aviation, healthcare, power, renewable energy, and more. GE's thriving with its Divisional structure is attributed to its divisions operating as autonomous business units. This structure fosters innovation, adaptability, and responsiveness to industry-specific demands. For instance, GE Aviation excels in aircraft engine manufacturing, while GE Healthcare specializes in cutting-edge medical imaging and diagnostics technology. The divisional approach allows GE to effectively navigate diverse markets, tailor strategies to unique industry requirements, and maintain a strong presence in various sectors.

On the other hand, Sears Holdings, once a retail giant in the United States, predominantly operated with a Functional structure. The company structured its operations into separate departments for retail operations, finance, marketing, and more. Sears' downfall was partly attributed to its Functional structure. The organization's siloed departments struggled to coordinate and collaborate effectively. This lack of synergy hindered Sears' ability to adapt to evolving consumer preferences and the growing presence of e-commerce competitors. The company's failure to innovate and respond swiftly to changing market dynamics ultimately led to its bankruptcy in 2018, marking the end of an iconic American retail brand.

Likewise, Sony Corporation, at various points in its history, implemented a Divisional structure, where different divisions operated with significant autonomy over their respective products and markets. Sony faced challenges when its divisions operated too independently within the Divisional structure. This approach led to duplicated efforts, a lack of cross-divisional synergy, and difficulties in integrating technologies across the company's diverse product lines. While each division had a strong track record of innovation, Sony struggled to create a cohesive ecosystem of products and services, which limited its ability to compete effectively in the evolving consumer electronics industry.

Some questions for the leaders to reflect and answer to resolve the dilemma:

- What makes more sense for our business: grouping people by what they do or by what they work on?
- How can we balance having experts in each function with having teams that focus on specific products or regions?
- Do we want to make decisions centrally for the whole company or let each division make some decisions on their own?
- What will help us communicate better: having separate groups for functions or closer teams working on specific areas?
- Can we have a mix of both structures in different parts of the company, or does it need to be all one way?
- How will our choice affect the way people work together and how quickly we can adapt to changes in the market?

There could be several factors that could influence this decision in the context of your organization like:

Size and Complexity: How big and complicated your company is can determine if one structure works better than the other.

Market Needs: If your customers vary a lot by region or product, divisional might be better. If they have similar needs, functional could work.

Leadership Style: How you want to lead – more centralized or decentralized – plays a role.

Technology: Sometimes, the tools and tech you use can make one structure easier to manage than the other.

Competitive Environment: What your competitors are doing might also impact your choice.

There are other areas that get impacted because of a choice of this dilemma, like:

- Decision-making autonomy.
- Resource allocation and efficiency.
- Communication flow and collaboration.
- Adaptability to market changes and customer needs.

Many companies strike a balance between Functional and Divisional structures to harness the benefits of both. This approach, often referred to as a matrix structure or a hybrid structure, allows organizations to tailor their structure to their specific needs and objectives. *For example, IBM employs a matrix structure that combines both functional and divisional elements. The company has specialized functional units, such as research and development, sales, and marketing. Simultaneously, it organizes its business into divisions dedicated to specific industries or sectors, such as cloud and cognitive software, global business services, and systems. IBM strikes a balance by allowing its divisions to have autonomy over industry-specific strategies while relying on functional expertise to support them. This structure enables IBM to offer tailored solutions to clients while leveraging core capabilities across divisions.*

When a company aims to strike a balance between Functional and Divisional structures, several factors should be considered:

- **Strategic Objectives**: Align the organizational structure with the company's strategic goals. Determine whether divisional autonomy or Functional specialization is more critical to achieving these objectives.
- **Market Complexity**: Assess the complexity of the markets in which the company operates. Highly diversified markets may benefit from Divisional structures, while more homogeneous markets may lean toward Functional structures.
- **Customer Needs**: Consider the diversity of customer needs and preferences. If customers in various segments require distinct products or services, a Divisional structure may be more appropriate.
- **Innovation and Agility**: Evaluate the importance of innovation and adaptability in the industry. Balancing structures can foster innovation within divisions while maintaining operational efficiency through functional expertise.
- **Resource Sharing**: Assess the potential for resource sharing and collaboration between divisions and functions. Determine how shared resources and knowledge can enhance overall performance.
- **Leadership and Culture**: Examine leadership capabilities and the organizational culture. Ensure that leaders can manage and facilitate collaboration in a matrix structure and that the culture supports cross-functional and cross-divisional cooperation.
- **Communication and Information Flow**: Establish effective communication channels to ensure information flows seamlessly between functions and divisions. Clear communication is essential to prevent conflicts and promote collaboration.
- **Performance Metrics**: Develop appropriate performance metrics to evaluate the success of the balanced structure. Monitor key performance indicators (KPIs) related to Divisional and Functional goals.
- **Flexibility**: Maintain the flexibility to adapt the structure as the business evolves or market conditions change. A balanced structure should allow for adjustments based on emerging needs.

In summary, the choice between a Functional structure and a Divisional structure involves trade-offs. Functional structures offer clarity and efficiency but may lack agility and adaptability. Divisional structures allow for customization and quick responses but can introduce coordination challenges and potential inconsistency. The decision should align with the organization's strategic goals, market conditions, and cultural preferences, and it may involve a mix of both structures in different parts of the organization.

Customer-Centric vs. Offering Centric

> This dilemma is all about deciding whether the organization's structure is centered around serving specific customer segments or focused on developing and delivering specific products or services or striking a balance somewhere to optimize performance.

Imagine you're steering a ship, and you have two compasses guiding you towards your destination. One compass points to your customers, and the other to your products or services. The dilemma lies in deciding which compass to follow more closely in organizing your company's structure. Customer-centric approach is like having a GPS that constantly tracks the preferences, needs, and behaviors of your passengers (customers). It involves organizing your company primarily around understanding and serving the distinct desires and expectations of different groups of customers. Offering-centric approach is like designing and perfecting a specific type of ship (product or service) and then steering your company towards delivering and promoting that ship as effectively as possible. It focuses on creating exceptional offerings.

Choosing Customer-Centric Only	
Pros	**Cons**
Deep customer loyalty and long-term relationships.	May require more resources for personalized service
Better adaptability to changing customer needs.	Potential complexity in managing diverse customer demands.
Potential for brand advocacy and positive word-of-mouth.	Risk of spreading efforts too thin across customer segments

Choosing Offering-Centric Only	
Pros	**Cons**
Streamlined operations and marketing.	May overlook specific customer needs.
Strong focus on product/service quality and innovation.	Vulnerable to changes in product demand or competition.
Clear branding and positioning.	Difficulty in building strong customer loyalty without a strong customer-centric component.

Amazon, one of the world's largest e-commerce and technology companies, is known for its customer-centric organizational structure. The company is organized around a customer-focused approach, where all departments, from product development to marketing and logistics, prioritize understanding and satisfying customer needs. Amazon's customer-centric structure has been instrumental in its success. The company's obsession with customer satisfaction has driven innovations like one-click shopping, personalized product recommendations, and Prime membership benefits. These strategies have led to high customer loyalty and repeat business, making Amazon a global e-commerce leader.

On the other hand, Apple Inc., the tech giant known for its iconic products like the iPhone, iPad, and MacBook, employs an offering-centric organizational structure. The company places a strong emphasis on product design, development, and excellence. Apple's offering-centric structure has propelled it to the forefront of the technology industry. The company's unwavering focus on creating groundbreaking products, each with a unique design and user experience, has cultivated a dedicated customer base and a strong brand identity. Apple's product-centric approach has consistently driven sales, making it one of the most valuable technology companies globally.

Some questions for the leaders to reflect and answer to resolve the dilemma:

- Should our organizational structure primarily revolve around understanding and serving the unique needs of distinct customer segments or around developing and delivering specific products or services?
- How do we define our core value proposition: through exceptional customer experiences or through the excellence of our products/services?
- Which approach aligns better with our strategic objectives and long-term vision: prioritizing customer-centricity or offering-centricity?
- Do we believe that standing out in the market is achieved by catering to diverse customer needs or by offering standout products or services?
- How do we intend to allocate our resources - towards deepening customer relationships and market insights, or towards refining and innovating our core offerings?
- Are we operating in markets with rapidly changing customer preferences and segments, or are we in markets where product excellence and uniqueness are paramount?

There could be several factors that could influence this decision in the context of your organization like:

Market Segmentation: The degree of market segmentation and the diversity of customer needs can impact the need for structural flexibility to accommodate different customer groups.

Product Portfolio Complexity: The complexity and variety within your product or service portfolio can determine whether your structure needs to be flexible enough to support diverse offerings.

Customer Engagement Model: The level of engagement required with customers can influence how customer-facing teams are structured within the organization, affecting the overall structure.

Resource Allocation: How you allocate resources, both financial and human, can impact the structure. For example, investing more in customer support might necessitate a specific customer-centric department.

Cross-Functional Collaboration: The extent to which different functions (e.g., marketing, sales, R&D) need to collaborate to meet customer needs can shape the need for cross-functional teams or divisions.

Technology Integration: The role of technology in personalizing customer experiences or optimizing product development can determine the level of technology integration required in the structure.

Leadership Philosophy: The leadership's philosophy and approach to business, whether customer-focused or product-focused, can set the tone for the organizational structure.

Market Responsiveness: How quickly and effectively your organization needs to respond to market changes and customer demands can impact the structure's adaptability and agility.

Competitive Landscape: The nature of competition in your industry may require a structure that enables rapid product innovation or superior customer service to gain a competitive edge.

Geographical Expansion: If your organization is expanding into new regions or markets with different customer behaviors, you may need to adapt the structure to accommodate local variations.

Cultural Considerations: Cultural factors, both within your organization and in the regions you operate, can influence how teams are structured and how customers are engaged.

Historical Legacy: Legacy structures and processes within your organization can also play a role in determining the ease of transitioning to a more customer-centric or offering-centric approach.

There are other areas that get impacted because of a choice of this dilemma like:

- Customer satisfaction and loyalty
- Product/service innovation and development
- Marketing and sales strategies
- Competitive advantage and market positioning

Many companies strike a balance between being customer-centric and offering-centric in their organizational structure to optimize their performance. *For example, Nike, the global sports apparel and footwear company, balances both approaches. While they have teams focused on product innovation and quality, they also have a strong customer-centric element in their structure, emphasizing customer feedback and personalization through the Nike app and online services. Also Tesla, the electric vehicle and clean energy company, emphasizes product excellence through innovative electric cars and energy solutions. Simultaneously, they maintain a customer-centric approach by continuously improving customer service and listening to customer feedback for product enhancements.*

Companies must consider factors such as market diversity, product portfolio complexity, competitive landscape, and technological capabilities when making this decision. While some organizations excel with a pure customer-centric or offering-centric approach, many find success by striking a balance between the two, embracing the benefits of both strategies. This balance enables innovation, customer satisfaction, and business growth.

Tall vs. Flat Hierarchies

> This dilemma deals with balancing the number of hierarchical levels within the organization (tall hierarchy with many levels vs. flat hierarchy with few levels).

The dilemma of choosing between tall and flat hierarchies in an organization transcends size and industry, impacting startups and established companies alike.

Choosing Tall Hierarchy Only	
Pros	**Cons**
Provides clear lines of supervision and defined roles, reducing ambiguity in decision-making.	Multiple layers can slow down decision-making, making it less responsive to immediate needs.
Allows for specialization within roles and career progression opportunities, which can foster expertise.	Complex hierarchies can hinder efficient communication flow, leading to misunderstandings and delays.
Effective allocation and management of resources due to centralized control.	May be less adaptable to change, making it challenging to respond to dynamic market conditions.
Enhanced control over processes and compliance with regulations, which can be crucial in certain industries.	

Choosing Flat Hierarchy Only	
Pros	**Cons**
Faster decision-making due to fewer layers, enabling agility in responding to changes and opportunities.	May lead to coordination and alignment difficulties across functions or teams.
Empowers employees to take ownership of their work and make decisions, leading to innovation.	Increased risk of fragmentation and inconsistent execution of strategies without clear oversight.
Can lead to resource and cost efficiency as decision-making is streamlined.	Resource allocation may become less centralized, potentially leading to inefficiencies if not managed well.

In the global business arena, Valve, a US-based software company, is known for its radical organizational structure, or rather, lack thereof. Valve operates without managers. Every employee is a contributor, fostering creativity and innovation. This unorthodox approach suits their disruptive nature in the gaming industry.

On the other side is the Japanese automobile giant Toyota, which uses a formal hierarchical structure. Their approach, famously known as the Toyota Production System, emphasizes clear roles and responsibilities, ensuring efficient operations and high-quality production. This disciplined structure is a critical factor behind their reliable, high-quality vehicles.

However, some companies have paid a hefty price for not choosing their tune carefully. Consider the case of Nokia. The Finnish tech company, at its peak, was the world's largest vendor of mobile phones. However, their rigid hierarchical structure stifled innovation, causing them to miss the smartphone revolution.

Some questions for the leaders to reflect and answer to resolve the dilemma:

- How can we structure our organization to optimize efficiency and productivity while ensuring clear roles and responsibilities?
- What hierarchy best supports our need for nimble and swift decision-making without compromising the quality of our choices?
- How do we design our hierarchy to facilitate effective communication and collaboration among team members at all levels?
- To what extent should we empower our employees to make decisions and contribute to the organization's growth while maintaining accountability?
- What structure allows us to provide career development opportunities and nurture leadership skills within the organization, regardless of its size?
- How can we structure our organization to remain adaptable and responsive to changing market conditions and growth phases?

There could be several factors that could influence this decision in the context of your organization like:

Organizational Size: Consider the size of the organization, whether a startup or a larger entity, and how the hierarchy aligns with its current and future needs.

Industry Dynamics: Evaluate industry-specific demands, as some sectors may require quicker decision-making and innovation, while others may prioritize stability and control.

Resource Constraints: Assess the availability of resources, both in terms of manpower and finances, and how the hierarchy can make the most of these resources.

Competitive Landscape: Examine the competitive environment to

> determine whether a more agile hierarchy is necessary to respond to market changes.
>
> **Growth Trajectory**: Consider the expected growth trajectory of the organization and how the chosen hierarchy can scale accordingly.
>
> **There are other areas that get impacted because of a choice of this dilemma like:**
>
> - Communication flow and speed
> - Decision-making efficiency
> - Employee empowerment and engagement
> - Organizational agility and adaptability

There are companies like Netflix that blend the two approaches. While they maintain a level of hierarchy, decision-making powers are distributed. This hybrid model allows them to reap the benefits of both systems – maintaining order and hierarchy while promoting innovation.

So, what's the best choice? Tall, Flat, or a blend of both? To answer this, consider the following factors:

- **Business Stage and Size**: Early-stage startups and small businesses may thrive in a flat organizational structure where everyone wears multiple hats and contributes to decision-making. As the company grows, however, a more formal hierarchy might be necessary to manage the increased complexity and specialization.
- **Industry Pace**: In fast-paced industries such as technology, a flat structure that encourages quick decision-making and innovation can be advantageous. More stable sectors might require a hierarchical approach where processes and protocols drive operations.
- **Strategic Focus**: Is the company's strategic goal oriented towards rapid innovation or operational efficiency? The former might benefit from a flat structure that encourages collaboration and creativity, while the latter might be better served by a

hierarchical setup that ensures consistent quality and efficiency.
- **Talent Management:** Consider the type of employees the organization wants to attract. A flat structure might appeal to self-starters and those who value autonomy, while a hierarchical structure might appeal to those who prefer clear leadership and defined career progression.
- **Organizational Culture:** An often-overlooked factor is the existing culture of the organization. A shift from a hierarchical to a flat structure, or vice versa, might require significant cultural changes. Are the employees ready for this shift, and how will it impact the overall morale?
- **Customer Expectations:** Depending on the customer base, they might have certain expectations from the organization. For instance, customers seeking innovative solutions might prefer companies with a reputation for being agile and creative, often associated with a flat structure. Conversely, those seeking reliable and consistent service might lean towards companies with a more formal, hierarchical structure.

In making this crucial decision, leaders must weigh these factors and carefully contemplate the questions to determine the hierarchy that best aligns with their organization's unique goals and circumstances.

In-office vs. Remote Working

> **This dilemma is all about deciding the extent to which employees work in a physical office versus remotely, and how communication is managed in each scenario.**

In the modern work landscape, organizations face a critical decision regarding where and how their employees perform their tasks. This decision revolves around whether employees primarily work in a physical office space or remotely from different locations, such as their homes or satellite offices. This dilemma also extends to defining how communication and collaboration occur within the organization.

Employees in a traditional office environment benefit from structured routines, face-to-face interactions, and access to resources. However, commuting and rigid schedules may reduce work-life balance. On the other hand, remote employees enjoy flexibility, potentially saving time and money on commuting. However, isolation, blurred boundaries between work and personal life, and reliance on technology can be challenges.

Choosing In-Office Style Only	
Pros	Cons
Enhanced focus and productivity in a controlled office setting.	Reduces work-life balance and flexibility for employees.
Easier collaboration and spontaneous interactions among employees.	Limits access to talent based on geographic location.
Facilitates a strong, in-person organizational culture.	Incurs higher operational costs for maintaining physical office spaces.

Choosing Remote-Working Only	
Pros	**Cons**
Enhances work-life balance and flexibility for employees.	Requires robust technology and strategies to maintain effective communication.
Widens the talent pool by allowing remote recruitment.	Potential reduction in spontaneous collaboration and face-to-face interactions.
Reduces operational costs related to physical office spaces.	Risk of weakening organizational culture and employee engagement.

GitLab has been a fully remote company since its inception in 2011, with employees spread across more than 65 countries. The decision aligns perfectly with their strategy of tapping into global talent and maintaining operational efficiency. They've designed systems and practices that foster communication, ensuring no one feels isolated. GitLab stands as an exemplar of a thriving remote-first culture.

On the other side, Apple has remained committed to an in-person office culture, considering it crucial for fostering innovation and collaboration. The Apple Park, a testament to this belief, was designed to facilitate chance encounters and interactions, fostering a creative cauldron that Apple is renowned for.

Some questions for the leaders to reflect and answer to resolve the dilemma:

- Is the nature of our work inherently tied to a physical location, or can it be effectively performed from various locations?
- What are the preferences and needs of our employees regarding their work environment, and how do these preferences align with organizational goals?
- Are there any operational constraints, dependencies, or regulatory requirements that necessitate a specific work

arrangement?
- How does our choice of work arrangement impact our ability to attract and retain top talent, considering evolving workforce expectations?
- Do we have the necessary technology and infrastructure to support remote work effectively, or are there limitations that require an in-office presence?
- What role does physical presence play in nurturing our organizational culture and fostering collaboration, and how does this align with our strategic objectives?

There could be several factors that could influence this decision in the context of your organization like:

Nature of Work: Assess the type of work performed by employees, considering whether it necessitates physical presence or can be conducted remotely.

Employee Preferences: Take into account employee preferences for remote or in-office work, considering their role in shaping the company's culture.

Technological Infrastructure: Evaluate the organization's technology capabilities and investments needed to enable remote work effectively.

Industry Standards: Consider industry norms and competitive standards regarding remote work and office presence.

Legal and Regulatory Compliance: Ensure compliance with labor laws, regulations, and tax implications associated with remote work.

Market Dynamics: Think about how remote work affects market responsiveness and competitiveness within your industry.

There are other areas that get impacted because of a choice of this dilemma like:

- Employee productivity and satisfaction

- Collaboration and team dynamics
- Real estate costs and resource allocation
- Technology infrastructure and cyber security

Some organizations choose a hybrid model, combining in-office and remote work. This allows employees to balance the advantages of both approaches. However, it requires careful planning to maintain collaboration and communication. Some criteria worth considering include:

- **Nature of Work**: Creative work that requires intense collaboration might benefit from an in-person culture, while tasks that require deep, uninterrupted focus might be better suited for remote work.
- **Workforce Demographics**: The preferences of millennials and Gen Z'ers might differ from those of older generations. Balancing these expectations is key.
- **Talent Acquisition and Retention**: Remote work could broaden the talent pool, including those who prefer not to relocate.
- **Company Culture and Values**: Some companies thrive on in-person interactions and serendipitous collaborations. Others might prefer the quiet focus that remote work can provide.
- **Technological Infrastructure**: A successful remote work policy requires robust digital tools for collaboration and communication.
- **Cost Implications**: Remote work can reduce the cost of maintaining physical office spaces. However, it could also involve investing in digital infrastructure and ensuring employees have suitable workspaces at home.

The choice between in-office, remote, or hybrid work arrangements is a critical organizational decision. It impacts productivity, employee satisfaction, talent acquisition and retention, and the overall structure and culture of the organization. Leaders must understand that there's no one-size-fits-all answer. Deciding where to land on this spectrum depends on an insightful understanding of the company's strategic goals, work nature, and employee preferences. Whatever choice is made, it's essential to communicate the reasons behind it to the team. Clarity of purpose, after all, can turn a potentially divisive decision into a unifying one.

Global Standardization vs. Local Adaptation

> This dilemma involves deciding whether to maintain a consistent organizational structure across all locations and markets, regardless of local difference or alternatively choosing to adapt the organization's structure to local market conditions and cultural preferences.

The dilemma of Global standardization vs. Local adaptation in organization structure is of paramount importance due to its far-reaching implications. It arises from the need to decide whether to maintain a uniform organizational structure across all locations and markets, irrespective of local differences, or to tailor the organization's structure to align with local market conditions and cultural preferences.

This dilemma is critical because it directly impacts an organization's market relevance and competitiveness. Failing to adapt to local market dynamics and cultural nuances can lead to products, services, or strategies that are out of touch with local needs, potentially resulting in decreased market share and effectiveness.

Moreover, the decision has operational, cultural, and brand-related dimensions. It affects operational efficiency, as global standardization can streamline processes but may overlook local regulations and practices. It also demands cultural sensitivity to ensure that the organization does not inadvertently offend or alienate local customers. Furthermore, it raises questions about brand consistency, talent management practices, and the balance between global strategy and regional autonomy.

Choosing Global Standardization Only	
Pros	**Cons**
Cost Efficiency	Potential Market Relevance Loss
Consistent Branding	Cultural Insensitivity
Streamlined Operations	Reduced Decision-Making Autonomy

Choosing Local Adaptation Only	
Pros	**Cons**
Enhanced Market Relevance	Operational Complexity
Cultural Sensitivity	Branding Challenges
Empowered Regional Teams	Potential Inconsistencies

Toyota is known for its global standardization of organizational structure. The company has established consistent management practices, hierarchies, and reporting structures across its worldwide operations. This uniformity allows Toyota to maintain high-quality manufacturing processes and product standards while efficiently coordinating its global supply chain. On the other hand, IBM is an example of a company that has practiced local adaptation in its organization structure. IBM operates in numerous countries with diverse market conditions and customer needs. To adapt to local variations, IBM allows its regional offices a degree of autonomy in decision-making and organizational design. This approach enables IBM to tailor its sales, marketing, and service strategies to suit local markets while benefiting from its global brand and expertise.

Some questions for the leaders to reflect and answer to resolve the dilemma:

- How critical is local market relevance in our business strategy, and to what extent should we adapt our structure to meet local needs?
- What aspects of our organization's operations can benefit from global standardization, and where might local adaptation be more advantageous?
- Are there cultural considerations or market-specific regulations that necessitate local adaptation, and how can we strike a balance with global consistency?
- What role should regional teams play in decision-making, and how can we maintain alignment with a global strategy?
- How important is brand consistency across markets, and what flexibility can we afford in local brand representation?
- What talent management practices should be standardized, and where can we allow local HR team's autonomy to cater to unique workforce needs?

There could be several factors that could influence this decision in the context of your organization like:

Market Diversity: The extent of diversity across markets and the significance of local preferences.

Regulatory Environment: The impact of local regulations on business operations and structure.

Brand Strategy: The importance of maintaining a consistent global brand image.

Operational Complexity: The level of complexity in managing standardized vs. adaptable operations.

Competitive Landscape: How competitors approach this dilemma in the industry.

> **There are other areas that get impacted because of a choice of this dilemma like:**
>
> - Operational Efficiency
> - Decision-Making Autonomy
> - Brand Consistency
> - Talent Management

The key to striking a balance in organization structure between global standardization and local adaptation lies in careful consideration of market conditions, operational efficiency, and decision-making processes to ensure that the organization remains agile and responsive to local needs while maintaining a global presence and identity. *For example, Nestlé, a global food and beverage company, follows a balanced approach. While it has global functional units for areas like research and development and quality control to maintain consistent product quality, it grants its regional branches autonomy in marketing and product portfolios to cater to local tastes. General Electric (GE): GE, a multinational conglomerate, combines global coordination with local flexibility. It centralizes certain functions like finance and HR for efficiency while allowing its business units to tailor their strategies to local market conditions.*

Some aspects to consider to determine the balance -

- **Market Dynamics**: Assess the degree of variation in market conditions and customer preferences across regions. A more diverse market may require greater local adaptation.
- **Operational Efficiency**: Identify processes and functions that can be standardized globally to achieve operational efficiency, while allowing flexibility in areas where local adaptation is necessary.
- **Decision-Making Authority**: Define the boundaries of decision-making authority between global headquarters and regional or local branches to ensure effective coordination.
- **Resource Allocation**: Allocate resources efficiently to support both standardized processes and local adaptations, considering factors like talent and technology availability.

- **Communication Framework:** Establish clear communication channels between global and local teams to facilitate information flow, knowledge sharing, and collaboration.
- **Talent Localization:** Determine the extent to which talent and leadership roles should be localized to support local adaptation efforts.

Ultimately, the choice between global standardization and local adaptation in organization structure should align with an organization's strategic objectives, market conditions, and the need to maintain a global brand identity while catering to local market variations. By carefully considering these factors and applying a balanced approach, companies can navigate this dilemma effectively and thrive in a globalized business landscape.

| 3.3 |

COMMUNICATION DILEMMAS

How will you use this chapter of the book?

If you are the founder or the CEO of a company and if you and your leadership team have a clear point of view (PoV) on the following questions and all of you are ALIGNED, then you can choose to move to the next chapter of the book. However, if you see a dissonance or have conflicting views, then we suggest digging deeper, going through this chapter and reflecting on different angles we bring in there.

Here are the questions for you to discuss and ponder-

- What is our organization's overall communication strategy, and how does it align with our mission, vision, and strategic goals?
- How can we foster a culture of open, transparent, and effective communication throughout the organization?
- What methods and channels should we use to ensure that important information reaches all levels of the organization in a timely manner?
- How can we strike a balance between centralized control over communication for consistency and decentralized autonomy to adapt to specific needs?
- Are we effectively using technology and tools to facilitate communication and collaboration within our organization?
- What measures do we have in place to proactively identify and address communication challenges and opportunities?
- How do we assess the impact and effectiveness of our communication efforts, both internally and externally?
- What guidelines or approval processes should be in place to manage potential risks associated with communication?
- How do we handle sensitive information and balance the need for transparency with the need for confidentiality?

In times of crisis or change, how do we ensure that our communication strategy supports our ability to manage risk and maintain stakeholder trust?

Communication plays a crucial role in any organization, serving as the lifeblood that facilitates the flow of information, ideas, and feedback among employees, departments, and leadership. Effective communication is essential for several reasons:

- **Information Sharing**: Communication ensures that important information, such as company policies, objectives, goals, and updates, is disseminated to all members of the organization. It helps employees stay informed about what's happening within the company.
- **Coordination**: Communication helps different departments and teams coordinate their efforts. It ensures that everyone is on the same page and working towards common goals. Without effective communication, departments may work in silos, leading to inefficiencies.
- **Decision-Making**: Leaders rely on communication to gather data, insights, and feedback to make informed decisions. Effective communication channels enable leaders to collect input from various stakeholders, fostering better decision-making processes.
- **Conflict Resolution**: Misunderstandings and conflicts are common in any organization. Effective communication can help identify and address these issues promptly, reducing the negative impact on productivity and morale.
- **Employee Engagement**: Open and transparent communication fosters employee engagement. When employees feel heard and included, they are more likely to be motivated, satisfied, and committed to their work.
- **Feedback Mechanism**: Communication provides a platform for employees to provide feedback to leadership. Leaders can use this feedback to make improvements, address concerns, and adapt to changing circumstances.
- **Crisis Management**: In times of crisis, effective communication is vital. Leaders must convey critical information to employees, stakeholders, and the public in a clear, timely, and empathetic manner to manage the situation effectively.

Leaders need to make decisions about various areas of communication within the organization, including:

- **Communication Channels**: Leaders must choose appropriate communication channels, such as meetings, emails, messaging apps, intranet, or social media, based on the nature of the message and the audience.
- **Communication Culture**: Leaders set the tone for the organization's communication culture. They must decide whether the culture will be open, transparent, and inclusive or more hierarchical and controlled.
- **Content and Messaging**: Leaders need to ensure that the content and messaging align with the organization's values, goals, and objectives. They should also decide how to tailor messages for different audiences.
- **Feedback Mechanisms**: Establishing feedback mechanisms, such as surveys, suggestion boxes, or regular one-on-one meetings, is essential for leaders to gather insights from employees and stakeholders.
- **Crisis Communication Plans**: Leaders must develop clear crisis communication plans to respond effectively to unforeseen challenges or crises, outlining who communicates what and when.
- **Training and Development**: Decisions regarding communication training and development programs are crucial. Leaders need to invest in enhancing the communication skills of their team members.
- **Technology and Tools**: Leaders should decide on the adoption of communication technologies and tools that facilitate collaboration, information sharing, and remote work if applicable.
- **Diversity and Inclusion**: Leaders need to promote diversity and inclusion in communication by ensuring that all voices are heard and that communication is accessible to all members of the organization.
- **Legal and Ethical Considerations**: Leaders must make decisions that ensure compliance with legal requirements and ethical standards in communication.

While there are countless dilemmas within the domain of communication, we will focus on the following five dilemmas.

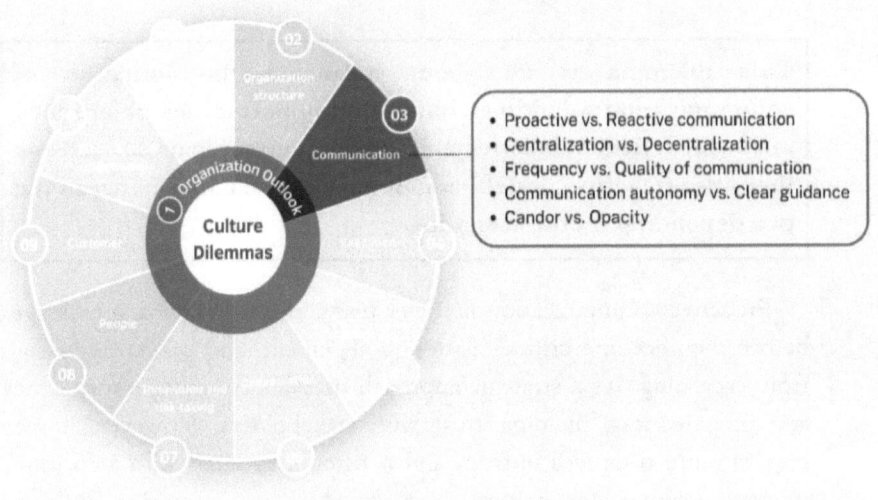

- **Proactive vs. Reactive communication**
- **Centralization vs. Decentralization**
- **Frequency vs. Quality of communication**
- **Communication autonomy vs. Clear guidance**
- **Candor vs. Opacity**

    Let's look at each of them in greater detail.

Proactive vs. Reactive Communication

> This dilemma is all about balancing the initiation of communication to address issues and opportunities before they arise (proactive) versus responding to communication needs as they arise (reactive) or deliberately striking a balance between the two depending on the scenarios.

Proactive communication involves planning and conveying messages before they become critical, fostering alignment, and preventing issues from escalating. It's a strategic approach that demonstrates transparency and preparedness, building trust with stakeholders. However, it may require more resources upfront and is often associated with a forward-thinking organizational culture.

Conversely, reactive communication is response-driven and addresses immediate needs, making it useful for managing issues as they arise. It can be more flexible and resource-efficient in crisis situations, as it focuses on addressing immediate challenges. Reactive communication can also be effective in handling unforeseen events and disruptions.

Choosing Proactive communication only	
Pros	Cons
Prevents problems before they become big issues.	Can be time-consuming if overused.
Keeps everyone informed and aligned.	May lead to information overload.
Enhances organizational stability.	Some issues are hard to predict.

Choosing Reactive communication only	
Pros	**Cons**
Quick response to urgent matters.	May result in missed opportunities.
Less time and effort spent on planning.	Can lead to a culture of firefighting.
Flexibility in handling unexpected situations.	Could harm long-term planning and stability if overused.

The communication style you choose has a lot of downstream repercussions on different aspects of the business. *For example, Apple is known for its proactive communication approach. The company regularly hosts product launch events, providing detailed information about new products and software updates before they are released. These events generate anticipation and excitement among consumers and the media. Apple's proactive communication strategy ensures that its customers are well-informed about upcoming products and innovations, contributing to strong brand loyalty and a culture of anticipation among its customer base. On the other hand, BP's style of communication and how it manifested during the Deepwater Horizon oil spill in 2010 is noteworthy. BP's communication response was largely reactive. The company faced severe criticism for its delayed and often insufficient communication efforts. BP struggled to provide timely and accurate information about the extent of the disaster, the measures being taken to contain it, and the environmental impact. This reactive communication approach resulted in a loss of trust among stakeholders, extensive damage to its reputation, and significant financial and legal consequences. Similarly, in 2017, United Airlines faced a significant communication failure in the aftermath of a passenger, Dr. David Dao, being forcibly removed from an overbooked flight. United's initial response was perceived as reactive and insensitive. The company's CEO issued a statement that did not adequately address the incident, which went viral on social media. United's reactive communication approach, coupled with a lack of empathy in their response, led to a severe backlash, damage to its reputation, and a public relations crisis.*

Some questions for the leaders to reflect and answer to resolve the dilemma:

- What are the key factors or triggers that would prompt us to use proactive communication in our organization?
- In what situations or contexts would we prioritize reactive communication to address immediate needs or issues?
- How do we ensure that our communication strategy aligns with the unique needs and challenges of our organization?
- Are there historical examples within our organization where a lack of proactive communication or an overreliance on reactive communication had notable impacts?
- How do we intend to incorporate feedback from stakeholders and employees into our communication strategy to strike the right balance?
- What resources and capabilities do we currently possess, or need to develop, to effectively implement both proactive and reactive communication strategies, as the situation demands?

There could be several factors that could influence this decision in the context of your organization like:

Nature of the Business:

- What type of industry are you in, and how does it impact the need for proactive or reactive communication? (e.g., technology companies may require more proactive communication due to rapid changes)

Organizational Culture:

- What is your organization's preferred approach to communication, and how does it align with your culture and values?

Stakeholder Expectations:

- What do your stakeholders (employees, customers, investors, etc.) expect in terms of communication style? Do they prefer regular updates or a more hands-off approach?

Risk Assessment:

- What are the potential risks and crises that your organization could face, and how likely are they to occur?
- Are there critical areas where proactive communication is necessary to prevent major problems?

Resource Availability:

- Do you have the necessary resources, such as time, staff, and technology, to support proactive communication efforts effectively?

Market Dynamics:

- How fast-paced and unpredictable is your industry, and how does this impact your need for reactive communication readiness?

Feedback Mechanisms:

- Do you have mechanisms in place to gather feedback from employees and stakeholders regarding your communication approach?
- Are you actively listening and making adjustments based on this feedback?

Historical Data:

- What can you learn from past experiences? Have there been instances where a lack of proactive communication led to problems, or where reactive communication was more appropriate?

> **Competitive Landscape:**
>
> - How do your competitors handle communication? Are there best practices or lessons you can draw from their approaches?
>
> **Strategic Goals:**
>
> - How does your communication strategy align with your overall strategic goals and objectives?
> - Are there specific areas where proactive communication is essential to achieving those goals?
>
> **There are other areas that get impacted because of a choice of this dilemma like:**
>
> - Crisis management and risk mitigation
> - Innovation and continuous improvement
> - Resource allocation and prioritization
> - Stakeholder trust and perception

Organizations often strike a balance between proactive and reactive communication by considering various factors to strike an equilibrium. *For example, Google proactively communicates about its new products, features, and innovations through events like Google I/O. They provide detailed information in advance, generating anticipation and excitement. But when issues arise, Google reacts swiftly. For example, in response to privacy concerns, they adjusted their privacy settings and communicated the changes to users. Google balances innovation (proactive) with responsiveness (reactive) by evaluating the importance of being first to market with new products while maintaining trust and addressing concerns promptly. Factors include market dynamics, user feedback, and competitive landscape.*

Take the example of Starbucks. Starbucks proactively communicates its commitment to sustainability and social responsibility through initiatives like its ethical sourcing practices and community programs. In response to crises, such as controversies involving employee behavior or store incidents, Starbucks takes reactive measures by issuing public apologies, implementing new policies, and engaging in dialogue with stakeholders. Starbucks balances its brand image (proactive) with crisis management (reactive) by considering its values, customer expectations, and the need to address incidents swiftly. They aim to ensure their brand's positive associations are not undermined by negative events.

Pfizer proactively communicates about its research, drug development, and healthcare advancements through press releases and scientific publications. But in response to health crises, such as recalls or safety concerns related to its products, Pfizer takes reactive measures by swiftly addressing issues, issuing recalls, and collaborating with healthcare authorities. Pfizer balances research and development (proactive) with crisis response (reactive) by considering patient safety, regulatory requirements, and maintaining trust in the healthcare industry.

The factors influencing the choice of proactive or reactive communication include:

- **Risk Assessment**: The level of risk associated with a situation is a primary factor. High-risk situations often require reactive communication, whereas proactive communication is preferred in lower-risk scenarios.
- **Speed of Change**: The speed at which a situation is unfolding impacts the choice. Rapid developments may necessitate reactive communication, while gradual changes may allow for a proactive approach.
- **Stakeholder Impact**: Consider the potential impact on stakeholders, including customers, employees, investors, and the public. Reactive communication is employed when stakeholders are directly affected or concerned.
- **Legal and Ethical Obligations**: Compliance with legal and ethical obligations is critical. Companies must ensure that their communication aligns with regulations and ethical standards, especially in reactive communication during crises.
- **Resource Availability**: Resource constraints, including personnel, time, and technology, play a role in deciding whether proactive or reactive communication is feasible and effective.
- **Communication Channels**: The choice of communication channels (e.g., social media, press releases, internal memos) also affects the decision. Some channels are better suited for proactive efforts, while others facilitate rapid reaction.

- **Organizational Culture**: The organization's culture, values, and communication norms influence the choice. Some organizations inherently favor one approach over the other based on cultural norms.
- **Historical Data**: Past experiences and lessons learned from previous situations can guide the decision. If proactive or reactive communication has been more effective in similar past situations, it can inform the strategy.

By carefully evaluating these aspects, organizations can make informed decisions about when to employ proactive or reactive communication strategies to effectively manage specific situations.

Centralization vs. Decentralization in Communication

> This dilemma is all about deciding the level of control and authority regarding communication, whether it should be centralized under a single authority or distributed across various units or individuals.

The centralization vs. decentralization dilemma in communication is a fundamental question that organizations grapple with. At its core, it involves deciding whether communication within the organization should be tightly controlled and managed from a single central authority or distributed across various units, teams, or individuals. This dilemma carries significant weight because it shapes how information flows, decisions are made, and the organizational culture is nurtured.

Centralization in Communication involves consolidating communication processes and decision-making under a central authority or department. This approach has several impacts on various areas within the organization. Firstly, it promotes consistency in messaging. Centralized communication ensures that messages are uniform, aligned with the organization's core values, mission, and strategic objectives. This consistency can reinforce the organization's brand identity and provide a clear and cohesive image to stakeholders.

Moreover, centralization provides a high degree of control and oversight over communication efforts. It enables leadership to monitor and manage messaging to ensure it remains in alignment with the organization's goals and values. This centralized control can be essential in maintaining brand reputation and mitigating risks associated with inconsistent messaging. Additionally, centralization can lead to greater efficiency in decision-making. With a single authority responsible for planning, executing, and monitoring communication activities, resource allocation becomes more straightforward, and processes tend to be more streamlined.

However, centralization also comes with its set of challenges. One of the most significant challenges is rigidity. A centralized approach can be inflexible and slow to adapt to local or specific needs. It may not respond quickly to emerging issues or opportunities. Furthermore, there is a risk of misalignment. Decisions made at the central level may not always align with the unique realities and requirements of different departments, regions, or units. Lastly, there is the potential for overload as the central communication team may become overwhelmed with the volume of communication tasks, especially in large organizations, leading to bottlenecks in the process.

On the other hand, Decentralization in Communication involves distributing communication responsibilities across various units, teams, or individuals within the organization. This approach also has significant impacts on various facets of the organization. Firstly, it offers greater adaptability. Different units or departments can tailor their communication to local contexts and audience preferences, allowing for more personalized messaging.

Decentralization also facilitates faster response times. In situations requiring quick decisions or responses to local issues, decentralization allows local teams to make decisions independently, without waiting for centralized approval. Moreover, decentralization promotes empowerment. It grants autonomy to employees and teams, enabling them to have more control over communication efforts in their respective areas. This empowerment can lead to increased engagement and ownership.

However, decentralization comes with its own set of challenges. One significant challenge is inconsistency. Decentralized communication may result in messaging variations across different units or regions, potentially diluting the organization's brand identity. There is also the risk of fragmentation. Information may become siloed, making it challenging to ensure that critical information reaches all relevant parties within the organization. Additionally, decentralization can lead to a lack of centralized control and oversight, potentially resulting in communication efforts that do not align with the organization's overall objectives.

Choosing Centralized Communication Only	
Pros	Cons
Messages are consistent and aligned with organizational goals.	It can lead to rigidity and slow response to local needs.
Centralized oversight allows for better control of communication.	Centralized decisions may not always align with local realities.
Decision-making can be streamlined	Centralized teams may become overwhelmed with communication tasks.

Choosing Decentralized Communication Only	
Pros	Cons
Communication can be tailored to local contexts.	Messaging may vary across different units.
Faster response to local issues and opportunities.	Information may become siloed and fragmented
Promotes autonomy and employee empowerment.	Less centralized control can lead to misalignment with organizational goals.

Apple is known for its centralized communication structure. Apple's communication strategies and messaging are tightly controlled and managed from its Cupertino headquarters. Apple's centralized approach ensures unparalleled consistency in messaging and branding. Messages are carefully crafted to align with Apple's core values and product design philosophy. This consistency has contributed to Apple's strong and iconic brand image. Centralized communication allows Apple to maintain a high level of secrecy around product launches and innovations. This secrecy generates anticipation and excitement among customers, enhancing product launches' impact.

However, Apple's centralized structure can limit regional teams' autonomy and responsiveness to local market dynamics. Decisions related to product launches and marketing strategies are made centrally, potentially missing out on local insights.

On the other hand, Airbnb, a global online marketplace for lodging and travel experiences, follows a decentralized communication structure. Airbnb empowers its hosts and local teams to manage communication and marketing strategies tailored to their regions. This decentralization enables hosts to provide localized experiences. Hosts can create unique listings and communicate with guests in ways that cater to their specific region or property. Decentralization allows Airbnb to respond quickly to local market dynamics, regulatory changes, and cultural differences, ensuring that its platform remains relevant and adaptable. While decentralization offers localization benefits, it can pose challenges in maintaining consistent branding and messaging across diverse markets. Airbnb spends a lot of time and energy to strike a balance between allowing host's creative freedom and ensuring a consistent and high-quality guest experience.

Some questions for the leaders to reflect and answer to resolve the dilemma:

- How critical is speed in our decision-making process, and how does centralization or decentralization impact it?
- Do we value uniform messaging across the organization, or is it more important to adapt messages to local contexts?
- What type of organizational culture do we aim to foster, one that is highly centralized, or one that values autonomy and local decision-making?
- How do we balance the need for transparency with the risk of information becoming fragmented in a decentralized structure?
- Are there specific functions or departments where centralization or decentralization would be more beneficial?
- How do we ensure that our chosen approach aligns with our strategic goals and the expectations of our stakeholders?

There could be several factors that could influence this decision in the context of your organization like:

Organizational Size: The size of the organization plays a pivotal role.

Larger organizations may lean toward centralization to maintain consistency, while smaller ones may prefer decentralization for flexibility.

Industry and Regulations: The specific industry and regulatory environment impact the decision. Industries with strict regulations often favor centralization to ensure compliance, while others may have more flexibility.

Technology Infrastructure: The availability and capability of communication tools and technology are influential. Advanced technology can facilitate decentralized collaboration and information sharing.

Stakeholder Expectations: Understanding and meeting stakeholder expectations, including customers, employees, investors, and regulators, is paramount. Their preferences for communication style and consistency guide the decision.

Resource Allocation: The allocation of resources, including budget, personnel, and technology, plays a significant role. Consider how centralization or decentralization aligns with resource allocation and utilization.

Market Dynamics: Rapidly changing markets may benefit from decentralization to respond quickly to shifts, while stable markets might lean towards centralization for consistency.

There are other areas that get impacted because of a choice of this dilemma like:

- Decision-making speed and agility
- Consistency in messaging
- Organizational culture and autonomy
- Information flow and transparency

Organizations often strike a balance of choosing between centralized and decentralized communication to make the most of it in different scenarios. *Marriott International, a leading global hospitality company, adeptly strikes a balance between centralized and decentralized communication strategies to maximize its global presence while catering to diverse local markets. Marriott ensures a consistent global brand image and core messaging through centralized communication efforts. The central corporate communications team is responsible for conveying the company's mission, values, and overarching brand message. Major marketing campaigns that promote Marriott's loyalty programs, new hotel openings, or sustainability initiatives are often executed on a global scale, ensuring a unified message reaches a broad audience. On the other hand, Marriott recognizes the importance of decentralization in a highly diverse and localized industry like hospitality. Individual Marriott hotel properties have the autonomy to tailor their services and communication to meet the unique preferences of their local guests. This includes adapting room service menus, offering cultural amenities, and personalizing guest interactions. Also, Marriott properties engage with their local communities through various decentralized initiatives, such as participating in local events, supporting local charities, or collaborating with nearby businesses. This fosters a strong sense of community and goodwill. Marriott also employs a decentralized approach in handling crisis situations. Local management teams are empowered to respond swiftly to emergencies or incidents that may occur within or near their properties. This ensures a rapid and appropriate local response.*

The choice of centralized or decentralized communication could depend on several factors:

- **Organizational Strategy and Goals**: The alignment of communication with the overall organizational strategy and goals is paramount. Consider whether centralization or decentralization better supports the strategic direction of the organization.
- **Communication Objectives**: Clearly define the objectives of communication. If the goal is to ensure uniform messaging and brand consistency, centralization may be favored. If it's about responding rapidly to local needs and fostering innovation, decentralization might be more suitable.
- **Risk Tolerance**: Assess the organization's risk tolerance. Centralization can provide more control and risk mitigation, while decentralization may introduce greater adaptability but also risks of inconsistency.
- **Resource Allocation**: Evaluate the available resources, including budget, personnel, and technology. Consider how centralization

or decentralization aligns with resource allocation and utilization.
- **Market Dynamics**: Analyze the dynamics of the markets in which the organization operates. Rapidly changing markets may benefit from decentralization to respond quickly to shifts, while stable markets might lean towards centralization for consistency.
- **Customer Preferences**: Understand the preferences of your customer base. Different customer segments may prefer centralized or localized communication approaches. Tailor communication to meet customer expectations.
- **Employee Skillsets and Empowerment**: Assess the skillsets of employees and their readiness for empowerment. Consider how centralization or decentralization can leverage employee strengths and engagement.
- **Technology Infrastructure**: The availability and capability of communication tools and technology play a crucial role. Modern technology may facilitate decentralized collaboration and information sharing.
- **Regulatory Environment**: Compliance with industry-specific regulations and standards is vital. Industries with stringent regulations may require a centralized approach to ensure compliance.
- **Crisis Preparedness**: Evaluate how centralization or decentralization impacts crisis preparedness. Centralization may ensure a coordinated response, while decentralization may enable rapid local crisis management.
- **Organizational Culture**: The existing organizational culture, values, and communication norms must be considered. Assess whether centralization or decentralization aligns with the prevailing culture or if it requires cultural shifts.
- **Feedback Loops**: Establish feedback mechanisms to gather input from employees, customers, and stakeholders. Continuously assess the effectiveness of the chosen communication approach and make adjustments as needed.
- **Geographic Diversity**: If the organization has a diverse geographic presence, assess whether centralization or decentralization best serves the needs of different regions and markets.
- **Competitive Landscape**: Consider how competitors approach

communication. Analyze whether centralization or decentralization provides a competitive advantage in the industry.

- **Stakeholder Expectations**: Understand the expectations of various stakeholders, including customers, employees, investors, and regulatory bodies. Ensure that the chosen approach aligns with these expectations.
- **Historical Data and Lessons Learned**: Reflect on past experiences and lessons learned from communication practices within the organization. Determine if historical data suggests the need for adjustments.

In essence, the decision between centralized and decentralized communication is not solely based on broad factors but involves a deep understanding of the organization's unique context, culture, industry, and stakeholder dynamics. These nuanced aspects must be considered to strike the right balance between centralization and decentralization, aligning communication strategies with the organization's goals and values.

Frequency vs. Quality of Communication

> This dilemma is all about balancing the frequency of communication (frequent updates) with the quality of communication (comprehensive, meaningful messages)

The Frequency vs. Quality of Communication dilemma is a fundamental challenge organizations face when determining how they communicate with stakeholders. At its core, this dilemma revolves around the balance between how often an organization communicates (frequency) and the depth and quality of that communication.

When an organization leans towards emphasizing communication frequency, it strives to keep stakeholders continually updated. This approach can have several implications across various areas. In terms of information dissemination and awareness, frequent communication ensures that stakeholders receive regular updates about the organization's activities, initiatives, and developments. This ongoing flow of information can help stakeholders stay informed and aware. However, there's a risk of information overload, where stakeholders are bombarded with so many messages that they become overwhelmed. In such cases, important messages might get lost in the noise, leading to reduced engagement and understanding.

In the context of employee engagement, frequent communication can be beneficial as it fosters a sense of involvement. Employees feel connected to the organization's day-to-day operations and decisions. However, excessive communication, especially if the information isn't relevant or meaningful, can disrupt workflow, reduce productivity, and even lead to employee disengagement. During crisis management, an organization that emphasizes communication frequency aims to provide rapid updates and reassurance to stakeholders during critical situations. Frequent communication can help manage crises effectively. However, if the crisis-related messages lack substantial content and appear insincere or repetitive, it can erode trust and credibility, leaving stakeholders skeptical about the organization's crisis response.

In contrast, organizations that prioritize communication quality focus on delivering comprehensive, accurate, and meaningful messages. This approach has its own set of implications. High-quality communication contributes to informed decision-making within the organization. Decision-makers have access to well-researched, relevant, and reliable information, which is crucial for making strategic and informed choices. However, a strict emphasis on quality may lead to delayed decisions, particularly in fast-paced environments where timely action is critical.

In terms of trust and reputation, high-quality communication enhances the organization's standing with stakeholders. It conveys transparency, reliability, and expertise, fostering trust and credibility. However, an overemphasis on quality may lead to a lack of visibility and engagement, causing stakeholders to perceive the organization as distant or unapproachable.

Choosing Frequent Communication Only	
Pros	Cons
Keeps stakeholders continuously informed.	May lead to information overload and decreased attention.
Enables rapid response to emerging issues.	Could dilute the importance of critical messages.
Fosters a sense of transparency and engagement.	May strain resources and become unsustainable.

Choosing Quality Communication Only	
Pros	**Cons**
Enhances trust and credibility with stakeholders.	May result in missed opportunities due to delayed communication.
Ensures well-informed decision-making.	Could leave stakeholders feeling uninformed or disconnected.
Conveys a sense of professionalism and expertise.	Requires significant time and effort to produce high-quality content.

Walmart, one of the world's largest retail chains, places a strong emphasis on frequent communication with its employees and stakeholders. This approach has both positive and negative impacts on the company. On the positive side, Walmart's frequent communication strategy aligns with its commitment to operational efficiency and real-time decision-making. The company communicates regularly with its employees regarding work schedules, safety protocols, and updates on store operations. This real-time communication helps in keeping employees informed and engaged in their day-to-day tasks. Moreover, Walmart frequently communicates with suppliers and partners to coordinate supply chain activities, ensuring products are readily available to customers. However, on the negative side, the high frequency of internal communication can sometimes lead to information overload for employees. Keeping up with constant updates and messages may become challenging, potentially impacting productivity. Additionally, the external messaging may be seen as overly promotional or impersonal due to its frequency.

On the other hand, Patagonia, an outdoor apparel and gear company, is known for its commitment to high-quality communication regarding environmental and sustainability initiatives. This approach has both positive and negative impacts on the company. On the positive side, Patagonia's high-quality communication aligns with its core values and mission to protect the environment. The company communicates in-depth information about its sustainability efforts, including details about sourcing eco-friendly materials, reducing carbon footprint, and supporting environmental causes. This high-quality communication resonates with environmentally conscious consumers, fostering *brand loyalty and trust. However, on the negative side, the focus on high-quality communication may limit the reach of Patagonia's message to a specific audience of environmentally conscious consumers. Some potential customers may prioritize other factors, such as price or convenience, over sustainability, which could affect market penetration.*

Some questions for the leaders to reflect and answer to resolve the dilemma:

- How does our organization's communication strategy align with our overall objectives and priorities?
- What do our stakeholders value more: frequent updates or comprehensive, meaningful messages?
- Are there critical phases or situations where we should prioritize one aspect of communication over the other?
- How do we strike a balance that prevents information overload while ensuring everyone receives essential information?
- What feedback mechanisms do we have in place to gauge the effectiveness of our communication strategy?
- How can technology and automation assist us in managing the Frequency vs. Quality dilemma more effectively?

There could be several factors that could influence this decision in the context of your organization like

Nature of Information: The type of information being communicated, whether routine updates, strategic plans, or crisis management, impacts the choice.

Stakeholder Expectations: Understanding the preferences and expectations of stakeholders, such as customers, employees, and investors, is crucial.

Industry Dynamics: The competitive landscape and industry norms play a role. Some industries may require frequent updates, while others prioritize in-depth analysis.

> **Resource Constraints**: The availability of resources, including time, budget, and personnel, can limit the extent to which both frequency and quality can be achieved.
>
> **Technological Tools**: The use of communication tools and technology can facilitate both frequency and quality, but it's important to leverage them effectively.
>
> **Organizational Culture**: The prevailing culture and values within the organization may lean toward one aspect of communication over the other
>
> **There are other areas that get impacted because of a choice of this dilemma like:**
>
> - Information overload and distraction
> - Engagement and understanding
> - Time and resource allocation for communication
> - Decision-making and alignment with strategic goals

Frequency and quality of communication can coexist in an organization by carefully segmenting communication efforts. Routine updates and operational matters may benefit from frequent communication, while critical decisions, strategic plans, and sensitive issues may require high-quality, well-thought-out messages. Effective segmentation ensures that each communication serves its purpose without overwhelming recipients. *For example, Southwest Airlines, a major U.S. airline known for its unique corporate culture and customer-centric approach, demonstrates a well-balanced communication strategy that adapts to various scenarios. In operational scenarios such as flight schedules, boarding procedures, and safety updates, Southwest Airlines prioritizes frequent and real-time communication with its passengers and employees. This approach aligns with the airline's commitment to efficiency and passenger convenience. Passengers receive regular updates on flight status, gate changes, and baggage information, enhancing their travel experience. Employees are also kept informed about operational changes to ensure smooth operations. When it comes to brand messaging, customer experience, and corporate social responsibility (CSR) initiatives, Southwest Airlines emphasizes high-*

quality communication. The airline is known for its engaging and customer-friendly branding, which includes humorous in-flight announcements and social media interactions. These high-quality communications align with the airline's goal to create a positive and memorable brand image. During crisis scenarios, such as weather-related disruptions, Southwest Airlines strikes a balance between frequency and quality of communication. The airline provides frequent updates to passengers about flight delays or cancellations due to adverse weather conditions, ensuring passenger safety. Simultaneously, it maintains high-quality communication by offering clear explanations, options for rebooking, and empathy in its messages. This balanced approach helps manage passenger expectations and maintain trust during challenging situations. Southwest Airlines also tailors its communication strategies to different stakeholders. For frequent travelers, it offers loyalty programs and frequent flyer updates, catering to their desire for regular engagement. On the other hand, for investors and industry stakeholders, the airline emphasizes high-quality financial reporting and corporate governance.

There could be several factors that influence the decision of Frequency vs. Quality of Communication across various scenarios:

- **Nature and Criticality of Information**: The type of information being conveyed plays a significant role. Critical, sensitive, or complex topics may lean toward high-quality communication, while routine updates or non-critical information may allow for more frequent, concise communication.

- **Stakeholder Preferences and Expectations**: Understanding the preferences and expectations of different stakeholder groups is crucial. Some stakeholders may value frequent updates, while others prioritize in-depth, well-researched content. Tailoring communication to these preferences is essential.

- **Urgency and Timeliness**: Consider the urgency of the information. In situations where immediate action is required, such as crisis management, frequent updates with essential information should be prioritized. However, high-quality communication is still crucial to ensure accuracy and clarity during crises.

- **Complexity of Subject Matter**: Complex topics often require high-quality communication to ensure stakeholders fully grasp the details.

Simpler matters may allow for more frequent communication, but the messages should remain clear and concise.

- **Resource Availability**: The availability of resources, including time, budget, and skilled personnel, can significantly impact the decision. High-quality communication often requires more resources, so organizations must assess what they can realistically allocate.

- **Organizational Culture and Values**: An organization's culture and values play a role in this decision. Organizations that prioritize transparency and accuracy may lean toward high-quality communication, while those emphasizing agility and rapid response may favor frequent updates.

- **Regulatory and Compliance Requirements**: In regulated industries, compliance with specific communication standards may necessitate high-quality communication. Understanding industry-specific regulations is critical.

- **Competitive Landscape**: The competitive environment and industry norms also influence the decision. In some industries, frequent updates are expected, while others prioritize in-depth analysis and high-quality content.

- **Feedback Mechanisms**: Organizations should establish feedback mechanisms to gauge the effectiveness of their communication strategy. Regular feedback from stakeholders can help adjust the balance between frequency and quality as needed.

- **Technology and Tools**: Leveraging technology and communication tools can assist in managing the balance. Automation can handle routine updates, allowing resources to be directed towards high-quality content creation.

- **Scalability and Scalable Communication**: Consider how communication strategies can scale as the organization grows. Balancing frequency and quality should remain sustainable as the organization expands.

- **Crisis vs. Routine Communication**: Recognize that the balance may shift during different scenarios. Crisis communication may require a higher frequency of updates but still demands high-quality information delivery.

- **Organizational Goals**: Align the communication approach with the organization's overarching goals. Whether it's reputation management, stakeholder engagement, or timely decision-making, the communication strategy should serve these goals effectively.

To strike a balance between frequency and quality of communication, organizations can adopt a segmented approach. Routine updates, which may not require in-depth content, can be communicated frequently to keep stakeholders informed. In contrast, strategic communications, major announcements, and critical issues necessitate high-quality communication to ensure stakeholders have the information they need to make informed decisions. Establishing feedback mechanisms and leveraging technology can assist in achieving this balance while considering organizational objectives, stakeholder expectations, and available resources.

Communication Autonomy vs. Clear Guidance

> This dilemma is all about deciding whether employees have the autonomy to communicate (decide on when, what, how and how much) independently or whether they require clear guidance and approval for communication or there could be a fine balance struck between the two.

The Communication autonomy vs. Clear guidance dilemma is a critical consideration for organizations, as it revolves around how much freedom employees should have in making communication decisions. On one end of the spectrum lies communication autonomy, where employees are empowered to decide when, what, how, and how much to communicate independently. On the other end is clear guidance, where communication is structured, controlled, and subject to approval or oversight.

Choosing one over the other can significantly impact various facets of an organization's functioning. When an organization leans towards communication autonomy, it often fosters a sense of trust and empowerment among employees. They feel free to express their creativity, innovation, and individuality in their communication efforts. Autonomy can enhance engagement, motivation, and a sense of ownership among employees, as they feel valued and responsible for shaping the organization's messages.

However, the pursuit of communication autonomy can have its drawbacks. The potential for inconsistency in messaging arises when employees have varying interpretations of the organization's goals or values. Miscommunication or errors may occur, particularly when employees lack the necessary skills, experience, or training. Moreover, in industries subject to strict regulations or compliance requirements, excessive autonomy may lead to legal risks or non-compliance with industry standards.

On the other hand, opting for clear guidance provides the organization with more control over its messaging. It ensures that communication aligns with strategic goals, brand image, and legal requirements. Clear guidelines can also help in risk management by minimizing the chances of communication errors, misinformation, or misalignment with organizational values.

However, a communication strategy heavily reliant on clear guidance may risk stifling creativity and innovation. Employees might feel micromanaged or limited in their ability to adapt messages to specific situations or audiences. This could potentially lead to disengagement, as employees may perceive communication as rigid and uninspiring. Moreover, the approval process for every communication piece may slow down response times in fast-paced or urgent situations.

Choosing Communication Autonomy Only	
Pros	Cons
Empowers employees, fostering creativity and innovation.	May lead to inconsistent messaging.
Speeds up communication processes.	Can introduce communication risks.
Demonstrates trust in employees' abilities.	Potential for misalignment with organizational goals.

Choosing Clear Guidance In Communication Only	
Pros	Cons
Ensures alignment with organizational objectives.	Slows down communication processes.
Reduces communication risks.	May stifle creativity and employee empowerment.
Maintains message consistency and brand integrity.	Could lead to a perception of micromanagement.

HOPE IS NOT A STRATEGY

HubSpot, a prominent player in the inbound marketing and sales software industry, stands out for its strong emphasis on communication autonomy. This approach has distinct impacts on the company. On the positive side, HubSpot's culture of communication autonomy encourages creativity and innovation among its employees. Teams have the freedom to devise unique marketing strategies and messaging that resonate with their target audiences. This autonomy has proven beneficial, as it has helped the company maintain a competitive edge in the fiercely competitive marketing technology sector. Moreover, this emphasis on autonomy has a direct impact on employee engagement. It fosters an organizational culture built on trust, ownership, and empowerment. HubSpot's employees are motivated to take responsibility for their communication initiatives, leading to higher levels of engagement and job satisfaction. Furthermore, the autonomy-driven approach lends itself to adaptability. In a rapidly evolving industry, HubSpot's teams can respond swiftly to emerging opportunities or challenges without the hindrance of extensive approval processes. This agility allows them to capitalize on market trends and customer needs efficiently. However, there are also challenges associated with this approach. The primary concern is messaging consistency. With significant autonomy granted to various teams or individuals, there's a risk of inconsistency in branding and messaging. Different interpretations of the company's goals or values can lead to confusion among customers or partners. Ensuring quality control and accuracy in communication materials can be challenging when autonomy is prevalent. Errors or misinformation in messaging can compromise the company's reputation and credibility, particularly in a field where accuracy is paramount. Lastly, in industries marked by stringent regulations, such as data privacy or financial services, too much autonomy can lead to compliance issues and legal risks if employees are not well-informed about the regulatory landscape.

On the other hand, Johnson & Johnson, a global healthcare and pharmaceutical giant, places a strong emphasis on clear guidance in its communication strategy. This approach has notable impacts on the company's operations. On the positive side, the emphasis on clear guidance at Johnson & Johnson ensures messaging consistency across its diverse business units and adheres to strict regulatory requirements. This consistency fosters trust among stakeholders, including healthcare professionals, patients, and investors. Moreover, in the highly regulated pharmaceutical industry, clear guidance plays a pivotal role in risk mitigation. It minimizes the risk of compliance violations, legal issues, and reputation damage. Employees understand the boundaries and responsibilities associated with communication, reducing the likelihood of costly errors. Additionally, clear guidance reinforces the company's commitment to brand integrity. In the healthcare sector, where trust and credibility are paramount, adherence to guidelines helps maintain a positive public image. However, this approach also has its challenges. One potential drawback is its impact on innovation. A strong focus on clear guidance may sometimes hinder creativity and innovation. Employees may feel constrained in their ability to explore unconventional communication strategies, which could limit the company's ability to adapt to changing market dynamics. In addition, in situations demanding rapid responses, such as crisis management or seizing market opportunities, the need for approval and adherence to guidelines may slow down decision-making and communication processes. This reduced agility can be a significant drawback in fast-moving industries. Lastly, a culture of clear guidance may affect employee autonomy and empowerment. Employees might perceive micromanagement and may become less engaged in their communication roles, potentially impacting overall organizational morale.

Some questions for the leaders to reflect and answer to resolve the dilemma:

- Do we prioritize creative freedom and autonomy or consistency and clear direction in our communication?
- Are we comfortable with communication risks, and to what extent?
- What are our primary communication goals: innovation and empowerment or consistency and risk management?
- Who are our key stakeholders, and what communication style do they prefer?
- Is our communication primarily routine and operational, or does it often involve sensitive or crisis-related topics?
- Do our employees lean towards having the freedom to shape messages, or do they prefer clear guidelines and structure in their communication?

There could be several factors that could influence this decision in the context of your organization like:

Regulatory Environment: The industry-specific regulations and legal requirements significantly impact the decision. Highly regulated industries, such as healthcare and finance, often demand clear guidance to ensure compliance and mitigate legal risks.

Communication Complexity: The complexity of communication initiatives is a key factor. More complex communication efforts, such as crisis management or financial reporting, may require clear guidance to ensure accuracy and consistency.

Risk Sensitivity: The organization's sensitivity to risk plays a crucial role. Risk-averse organizations may prefer clear guidance to minimize the potential for communication errors or misalignment that could lead to reputational or legal risks.

Stakeholder Diversity: The diversity of stakeholders, including customers, investors, employees, and suppliers, can influence the decision. Stakeholders with varying expectations may require a more structured approach to communication to ensure their needs are met.

Communication Goals: The specific goals of communication initiatives are vital. If the goal is to maintain a consistent brand image or ensure legal compliance, clear guidance may be necessary. In contrast, goals focused on innovation or employee empowerment may favor autonomy.

Communication Urgency: The urgency of communication needs can impact the decision. Rapid responses to immediate communication needs may require autonomy, while less time-sensitive communication can allow for clearer guidance and oversight.

There are other areas that get impacted because of a choice of this dilemma like:

- Consistency in messaging and brand image
- Employee empowerment and satisfaction
- Risk management and compliance
- Speed of response to market changes and opportunities

Most organizations strike a balance between communication autonomy and clear guidance in different scenarios. *Take the example of the Red Cross. The International Federation of Red Cross and Red Crescent Societies (IFRC), a humanitarian organization, adeptly balances communication autonomy and clear guidance in its operations. In times of disaster response and relief efforts, the IFRC relies heavily on clear guidance. When responding to natural disasters, health crises, or conflicts, there's a paramount need for standardized communication to ensure efficient coordination and timely assistance. The organization has well-established protocols and guidelines that are strictly followed in such situations. Clear guidance ensures that communication is consistent, accurate, and aligned with the organization's mission to provide humanitarian aid. However, the IFRC also recognizes that humanitarian work often involves diverse and dynamic local contexts. In fundraising and community engagement efforts, the organization encourages a degree of communication autonomy at the local level. Local Red Cross and Red Crescent chapters have the flexibility to tailor their messaging and engagement strategies to resonate with the specific needs and cultures of their communities. This autonomy allows for a more personalized and effective approach to fundraising and community building. Moreover, in advocacy and awareness campaigns, the IFRC takes a balanced approach. While it provides overarching messaging guidelines to ensure alignment with the organization's core values, it empowers its members to adapt these messages to the unique challenges and opportunities they face in their respective regions. This approach allows the IFRC to address global issues while acknowledging the nuances of local contexts.*

There are several factors that influence the decision between communication autonomy and clear guidance within an organization:

- **Organizational Culture**: The prevailing culture within the organization plays a significant role. Cultures that value innovation, employee empowerment, and open communication may lean toward providing more autonomy. In contrast, organizations with a hierarchical or risk-averse culture may prefer clearer guidance and oversight.
- **Industry Regulations**: Industries with strict regulations, such as healthcare or finance, often require clear guidance and compliance with legal standards. In highly regulated sectors, deviation from established guidelines can result in severe consequences, making clear guidance essential.
- **Nature of Communication**: The type of communication being undertaken can influence the decision. Routine, everyday communications may allow for more autonomy, while sensitive or crisis communications may require stricter guidance to manage

risks effectively.

- **Employee Skill Levels**: The skill levels and experience of employees matter. Experienced and trained communicators may handle autonomy well, while less-experienced staff may benefit from clear guidelines and mentorship.
- **Stakeholder Expectations**: Understanding the expectations of stakeholders is crucial. If stakeholders, such as customers or investors, expect consistent and professional communication, it may necessitate clear guidance to meet those expectations.
- **Organizational Risk Tolerance**: The organization's risk tolerance is a critical factor. Some organizations are more risk-averse and may choose clear guidance to minimize risks associated with communication errors or misalignment. Others with higher risk tolerance may allow for more autonomy.
- **Communication Goals**: The specific goals of communication initiatives can influence the decision. If the goal is to maintain a consistent brand image and messaging, clear guidance may be preferred. Conversely, if the goal is to encourage innovation and creativity, autonomy might be prioritized.
- **Technology and Tools**: The availability and use of technology and communication tools can affect the decision. Advanced tools may enable employees to communicate effectively while adhering to clear guidelines, striking a balance between autonomy and guidance.
- **Organizational Size and Complexity**: The size and complexity of the organization also matter. Larger and more complex organizations may require a more structured approach to communication due to the sheer volume of messaging and the potential for misalignment.
- **Crisis Management Preparedness**: Organizations with a proactive crisis management approach may provide clearer guidance for crisis communication, ensuring a rapid and coordinated response during emergencies.
- **Employee Feedback**: Soliciting feedback from employees on their communication needs and preferences can inform the decision. If employees express a desire for more autonomy, leadership can consider adjusting communication policies accordingly.

- **Competitive Landscape**: Assessing how competitors handle communication can provide insights. In some industries, adopting a communication strategy similar to successful competitors may be advantageous.
- **Evolution of Communication Trends**: Staying abreast of evolving communication trends, including shifts toward more personalized and interactive communication, can influence the decision. These trends may necessitate a more autonomous approach.
- **Organizational Values**: The core values and principles of the organization also play a role. Organizations that prioritize transparency and employee empowerment may lean toward autonomy, while those valuing precision and consistency may favor clear guidance.
- **Feedback Mechanisms**: Establishing feedback mechanisms for communication effectiveness can help fine-tune the balance. Regular feedback from stakeholders can highlight areas where adjustments are needed.

In essence, the decision between communication autonomy and clear guidance is a multifaceted dilemma. It extends its influence beyond the realm of communication and touches upon broader aspects of organizational culture, employee engagement, risk management, and the organization's ability to adapt to various communication needs. Organizations must carefully consider their unique values, goals, industry regulations, and risk tolerance when navigating this dilemma. Striking the right balance between autonomy and guidance is essential, and it may vary from one organization to another, depending on their specific circumstances and objectives. A well-informed decision ensures that an organization's communication strategy aligns with its overarching mission and optimally supports its functions.

Candor vs. Opacity

> This dilemma is all about balancing transparency and honesty (candor) in communication with the need to withhold sensitive information (opacity) to protect the organization or stakeholders.

The Candor vs. Opacity dilemma is a critical aspect of organizational communication, requiring a nuanced approach that balances the values of transparency and honesty (candor) with the necessity of discretion and sensitivity (opacity). In this dilemma, leaders grapple with determining when to be forthright and when to exercise diplomacy or withholding certain information to safeguard the interests of the organization or its stakeholders. This dilemma is inherently complex because it necessitates a thoughtful weighing of competing values and interests. While candor promotes openness and trust, opacity may at times be essential to protect sensitive information, maintain diplomatic relationships, or uphold legal and ethical obligations.

The decision between candor and opacity carries profound implications that ripple through various facets of an organization's functioning. First and foremost, the choice significantly shapes stakeholder trust. Candor, characterized by transparent and honest communication, serves as a cornerstone for building trust among stakeholders. When organizations communicate openly, they enhance their credibility and foster confidence among customers, investors, employees, and the public at large. However, there are scenarios where discretion and opacity play a crucial role. Diplomacy and prudent communication are often necessary, especially in sensitive negotiations, mergers, or situations involving confidential information. In such cases, organizations may need to withhold certain details to protect their interests or maintain productive relationships. Striking the right balance is vital, as excessive candor in such contexts can lead to misunderstandings or damage relationships.

Choosing Candor Only	
Pros	**Cons**
Enhanced trust and reputation	Increased vulnerability
Stakeholder confidence	Potential legal challenges
Ethical alignment.	Greater pressure for transparency.

Choosing Opacity Only	
Pros	**Cons**
Protection of sensitive information	Erosion of trust
Legal compliance	Reputational damage
Risk mitigation	Ethical concerns

Patagonia, the renowned outdoor clothing and gear retailer, has established itself as a shining example of candor and transparency in its communication practices. The company's core ethos revolves around environmental sustainability and social responsibility, and this commitment is reflected in its open and authentic communication strategy. One of the most significant positive impacts of Patagonia's candor is the unwavering trust it has cultivated among its customer base. By candidly sharing its efforts to minimize its environmental footprint and its dedication to ethical manufacturing practices, the company has created a strong and loyal customer following. Patagonia's transparency has become a hallmark of its brand, resonating with environmentally conscious consumers who value authenticity and ethical business practices. Beyond just transparency, Patagonia has leveraged its platform for activism and advocacy. The company openly champions environmental causes, encouraging its customers to take action and be part of the solution. This transparent and active engagement with social and environmental issues has further solidified the brand's reputation as a responsible corporate citizen.

HOPE IS NOT A STRATEGY

Internally, Patagonia's culture of candor has had a profound impact on employee engagement and satisfaction. The organization actively encourages its employees to voice their concerns, share ideas, and contribute to the company's mission. This open and inclusive atmosphere has led to a collaborative and innovative work environment, where employees feel valued and empowered. However, there are some challenges associated with Patagonia's candor approach. While it resonates strongly with its core audience, it can also polarize consumers with different views, potentially limiting the brand's appeal. Additionally, competitors may gain insights into Patagonia's sustainability practices and strategies through its transparent communications.

In stark contrast to Patagonia's candor approach, Apple Inc., the technology giant, is known for its strategic use of opacity in communication, particularly concerning product launches and proprietary technology. One of the most evident positive impacts of Apple's opacity approach is the extraordinary excitement and anticipation it generates among consumers leading up to product launches. The company's secretive nature creates a sense of mystery and suspense that keeps consumers eagerly awaiting new product releases. This strategy has consistently translated into strong market presence and a high demand for Apple's products. Moreover, Apple's strategic opacity provides the company with a distinct competitive advantage. By closely guarding its product innovations until the actual launch, Apple remains a trailblazer in the industry. Competitors have limited time to react and imitate its new features, contributing to Apple's continued market dominance. From an investor's perspective, Apple's discretion in financial matters, such as its approach to new markets or acquisitions, often instills confidence. Shareholders view this strategic opacity as a sign of the company's ability to make calculated and impactful decisions.

However, there are some negative impacts associated with Apple's opacity approach. The secrecy surrounding product launches can sometimes lead to rampant speculation and the proliferation of rumors. While this generates buzz and excitement, it can also result in unrealistic expectations or disappointment among consumers when products are finally unveiled. Additionally, the limited transparency regarding product development means that consumers have relatively little input into the design process. While Apple's design prowess is widely acclaimed, there have been instances where consumer preferences have not aligned with the final product offerings. Lastly, Apple has faced criticism for not being as transparent about its environmental impact as some of its competitors. This opacity has led to concerns from environmentally conscious consumers and advocacy groups.

Some questions for the leaders to reflect and answer to resolve the dilemma:

- Do our core values emphasize unwavering transparency, or do they acknowledge the strategic use of discretion and opacity in certain situations?
- To what extent are we prepared to embrace potential risks, including damage to our reputation and stakeholder perceptions, when we opt for opacity over candor?
- How well do we understand the unique expectations for candor among our various stakeholder groups, and are we prepared to adapt our communication approach accordingly?
- What ethical principles and legal obligations guide our decisions regarding candor and opacity, and how do we navigate situations where these principles may conflict?
- What strategies and mechanisms have we established for crisis management, and how do they strike a balance between candor and opacity to ensure effective crisis resolution and reputation protection?
- In the long term, how do our choices regarding candor and opacity influence our organizational culture, employee trust, and the sustainability of our relationships with stakeholders?

There could be several factors that could influence this decision in the context of your organization like:

Legal Requirements: Laws and regulations may dictate the level of transparency required in certain industries or situations.

Ethical Values: The organization's ethical principles and commitment to honesty play a crucial role.

Stakeholder Expectations: Understanding what stakeholders expect in terms of transparency guides the decision.

Nature of Information: The sensitivity of the information in question is a key factor.

Risk Assessment: Evaluating the potential risks and consequences of candor or opacity informs the decision.

> **Industry Standards**: Industry-specific norms and practices can influence the approach.
>
> **There are other areas that get impacted because of a choice of this dilemma like:**
>
> - Trust and credibility with stakeholders
> - Reputation management and crisis communication
> - Employee morale and loyalty
> - Legal and ethical considerations

Candor and opacity can coexist when transparency is upheld as a general principle, but exceptions are made when sensitive information is involved. In such cases, clear guidelines and ethical frameworks can delineate boundaries. Different scenarios call for different choices:

- **Nature of Information**: The type and sensitivity of the information in question are paramount. Leaders must assess whether the information is routine, strategic, sensitive, or confidential and tailor their communication approach accordingly.
- **Stakeholder Expectations**: Understanding the expectations of different stakeholder groups is crucial. Investors, employees, customers, regulators, and the public may have varying degrees of expectation for candor or understanding of the need for opacity.
- **Contextual Relevance**: Decision-makers should consider the context in which communication occurs. Candor might be more suitable in routine updates or positive news, while opacity may be necessary during negotiations, mergers, or legal matters.
- **Legal and Regulatory Obligations**: Compliance with legal and regulatory requirements plays a significant role. Organizations must adhere to laws governing disclosure, data protection, and transparency, which can affect the choice between candor and opacity.
- **Reputation and Trust History**: An organization's past track record of candor or opacity can influence its current choices.

Consistently transparent organizations may benefit from trust built over time, while those with a history of opacity may face skepticism.
- **Ethical Framework**: Aligning communication choices with the organization's ethical framework is vital. Leaders should consider how candor or opacity reflects the organization's commitment to honesty, integrity, and social responsibility.
- **Risk Assessment**: Conducting a thorough risk assessment is critical. Decision-makers should evaluate potential consequences of candor, such as reputational damage or legal implications, versus those of opacity, like stakeholder mistrust or misunderstandings.
- **Relationship Dynamics**: Consideration of existing relationships with stakeholders is essential. Long-standing partnerships or sensitive negotiations may require more diplomacy, while open communication may be suitable for well-established trust.
- **Cultural and Industry Norms**: The organizational culture and industry standards can guide the choice. In some industries, transparency is expected, while others may favor confidentiality and discretion.
- **Long-term vs. Short-term Impact**: Decision-makers should assess whether the focus is on immediate gains or long-term sustainability. Candor may lead to short-term challenges but enhance long-term trust, while opacity might yield immediate benefits but damage trust in the long run.
- **Communication Strategy Alignment**: The decision should align with the broader communication strategy. Organizations should consider how candor or opacity fits within their overall approach to communication and branding.
- **Mitigating Unintended Consequences**: Leaders must anticipate unintended consequences of their communication choices. Candor could lead to excessive scrutiny, while opacity may breed speculation. Strategies to address these consequences should be in place.
- **Transparency Plans**: Some organizations may have a structured transparency plan that outlines when, how, and to what extent candor will be practiced. Such plans can provide guidance during decision-making.

In summary, the Candor vs. Opacity dilemma is multifaceted, and the right approach depends on the specific context and the interests at stake. While candor is essential for building trust and credibility, there are situations where discretion, diplomacy, and opacity are equally important. Striking the right balance requires careful consideration of the values, interests, and ethical principles that guide an organization, as well as a keen awareness of the potential consequences of communication choices.

| 3.4 |
EXECUTION DILEMMAS

> **How will you use this chapter of the book?**
>
> If you are the founder or the CEO of a company and if you and your leadership team have a clear point of view (PoV) on the following questions and all of you are ALIGNED, then you can choose to move to the next chapter of the book. However, if you see a dissonance or have conflicting views, then we suggest digging deeper, going through this chapter and reflecting on different angles we bring in there.
>
> Here are the questions for you to discuss and ponder-
>
> - What is our organization's overall communication strategy, and how does it align with our mission, vision, and strategic goals?
> - How can we foster a culture of open, transparent, and effective communication throughout the organization?
> - What methods and channels should we use to ensure that important information reaches all levels of the organization in a timely manner?
> - How can we strike a balance between centralized control over communication for consistency and decentralized autonomy to adapt to specific needs?
> - Are we effectively using technology and tools to facilitate communication and collaboration within our organization?
> - What measures do we have in place to proactively identify and address communication challenges and opportunities?
> - How do we assess the impact and effectiveness of our communication efforts, both internally and externally?
> - What guidelines or approval processes should be in place to manage potential risks associated with communication?
> - How do we handle sensitive information and balance the need for transparency with the need for confidentiality?
>
> In times of crisis or change, how do we ensure that our communication strategy supports our ability to manage risk and maintain stakeholder trust?

Navigating the complexities of execution within an organization often presents leaders with a series of dilemmas. Balancing the need for speed with the demand for quality, deciding between quantity and quality, and choosing between consistency and adaptability are just a few of the challenges that leadership teams must confront. Furthermore, leaders must weigh the benefits of focusing on desired outcomes versus optimizing internal processes and determine the most effective approach to resource allocation. In this dynamic landscape, understanding and addressing these execution dilemmas are paramount for achieving organizational goals and ensuring long-term success.

When determining the way execution will be done in an organization, leaders need to take into account a wide range of aspects to ensure successful implementation. These aspects include:

- **Strategic Alignment**: Ensure that execution aligns with the organization's strategic goals and long-term vision. Every execution effort should contribute to the achievement of these overarching objectives.
- **Clear Objectives**: Define clear and measurable objectives for each execution effort. What are you trying to accomplish, and how will you measure success?
- **Resource Allocation**: Determine the allocation of resources, including financial, human, and technological, to support execution. Ensure that resources are available and appropriately distributed to meet the objectives.
- **Risk Assessment**: Identify potential risks and challenges that could impact execution and develop strategies for mitigating these risks.
- **Stakeholder Involvement**: Engage relevant stakeholders, both internal and external, in the planning and execution processes. Consider their input, concerns, and expectations.
- **Execution Methodology**: Choose the most suitable methodology or approach for execution, whether it's agile, waterfall, or a hybrid method. Ensure that the chosen approach aligns with the nature of the project.
- **Project Management**: Establish effective project management practices, including timelines, milestones, and key performance

indicators (KPIs) to track progress and make necessary adjustments.
- **Communication Plan**: Develop a clear and comprehensive communication plan that addresses how information will be disseminated to all stakeholders throughout the execution process.
- **Quality Assurance**: Implement quality control measures to ensure that the final outcomes meet the desired quality standards. Establish quality checkpoints and validation processes.
- **Change Management**: Consider the impact of execution on the organization's culture and its employees. Implement change management strategies to facilitate a smooth transition.
- **Monitoring and Evaluation**: Put in place mechanisms to continuously monitor and evaluate the execution progress. Regularly assess whether the project is on track and meeting its objectives.
- **Feedback Mechanisms**: Create channels for gathering feedback from team members and stakeholders. Use this feedback to make necessary adjustments and improvements during execution.
- **Adaptability**: Be prepared to adapt and pivot when necessary. Market conditions, customer preferences, and internal factors may require adjustments to the execution plan.
- **Legal and Compliance**: Ensure that execution efforts comply with all relevant laws, regulations, and industry standards. Legal issues can significantly impact execution if not addressed properly.
- **Technology and Tools**: Identify and implement the right technology and tools to support execution and enhance productivity. This may include project management software, communication platforms, and data analytics tools.
- **Training and Development**: Invest in the training and development of team members to equip them with the necessary skills and knowledge required for successful execution.
- **Sustainability**: Consider the long-term sustainability of execution efforts, including their environmental and social impact. Sustainable practices can enhance reputation and reduce long-term costs.
- **Budgeting and Cost Control**: Establish a clear budget for

execution and monitor costs throughout the process. Implement cost control measures to prevent budget overruns.
- **Ethical Considerations**: Ensure that execution efforts adhere to ethical standards and values. Ethical lapses can damage reputation and lead to legal and regulatory issues.
- **Customer-Centric Approach**: Keep the customer in mind throughout execution. Understand their needs and preferences, and ensure that the final outcomes meet or exceed their expectations.

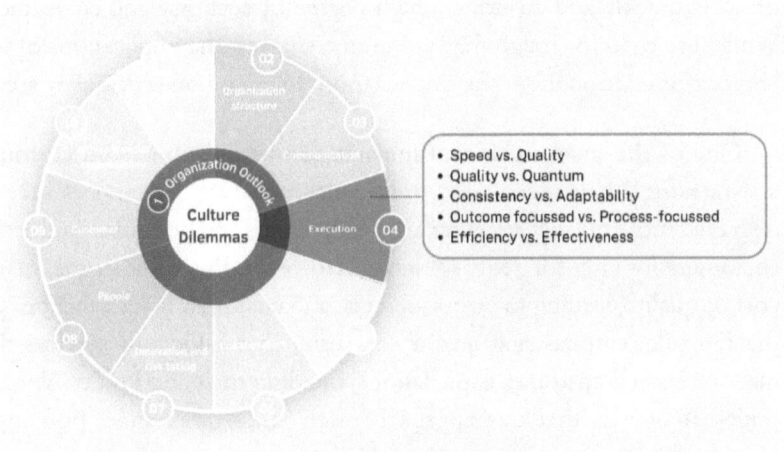

While there are countless dilemmas within the realm of execution, one must focus their attention on five pivotal ones that often take center stage:

- **Speed vs. Quality**
- **Quality vs. Quantum**
- **Consistency Vs Adaptability**
- **Outcome focused vs. Process-focussed**
- **Efficiency vs. Effectiveness**

Let's look at each of them in greater detail.

Speed vs. Quality

> **This dilemma revolves around the balance between completing tasks quickly and ensuring a high degree of accuracy and correctness**

The Speed vs. Quality dilemma lies at the heart of many organizational decisions, impacting various facets of how a company operates. At its core, this dilemma revolves around the trade-off between completing tasks or projects quickly and ensuring a high degree of accuracy and correctness. While it may seem straightforward on the surface, the implications of this choice ripple throughout the organization, touching on several key areas.

One of the most significant impacts of this dilemma is on customer satisfaction. When speed takes precedence, products or services may be delivered more quickly, meeting market demands and potentially attracting customers looking for swift solutions. However, this often comes at the cost of quality, leading to errors, defects, and customer dissatisfaction. On the flip side, emphasizing quality can result in products or services that meet or exceed customer expectations, building trust and loyalty. Yet, the trade-off here is that this approach often takes more time, potentially causing delays in meeting customer needs.

Error rates and rework are closely tied to this dilemma. Prioritizing speed may lead to increased errors and a subsequent need for rework or corrections. This not only consumes additional resources but also erodes efficiency. Conversely, a focus on quality aims to minimize errors from the outset, reducing the need for rework. However, the time spent on rigorous quality checks can slow down the execution process.

Decision-making speed is another critical aspect influenced by this dilemma. When speed is paramount, organizations tend to make decisions quickly, sometimes without exhaustive analysis. This can be advantageous in rapidly changing markets where quick adaptation is necessary. However, this approach can also lead to ill-informed decisions and unintended consequences. Conversely, a focus on quality may entail a more thorough decision-making process, which can result in better-informed choices but potentially delay responses to market shifts.

Productivity and workflow efficiency are profoundly affected by the choice between speed and quality. Prioritizing speed often pushes teams to work at a rapid pace, but this can lead to burnout and decreased efficiency over time. Conversely, an emphasis on quality may involve meticulous, time-consuming processes that can hinder workflow efficiency. Striking the right balance is crucial to maintaining a sustainable and productive work environment.

Choosing Speed Only	
Pros	**Cons**
Faster product/service delivery	Higher error rates
Quick response to market changes	Reduced customer satisfaction
Potential cost savings	Risk of damaging brand reputation
	Increased rework and correction efforts
	Potential long-term negative impacts

Choosing Quality Only	
Pros	**Cons**
High customer satisfaction and loyalty	Slower delivery times
Improved brand reputation	Higher resource and time investment
Reduced error rates	Risk of missing market opportunities
Long-term sustainability	Potentially higher costs
	May hinder rapid response to market changes

HOPE IS NOT A STRATEGY

QuickTech Solutions is a tech startup operating in the competitive tech industry, where rapid innovation and quick responses to market demands are essential. The company has firmly established itself as a speed-focused organization, valuing fast product development and delivery. This approach has yielded positive impacts: One notable advantage is *QuickTech's* market agility. The company can swiftly adapt its products and services to changing market dynamics. For instance, it can release software updates and new features faster than many competitors, which allows it to stay ahead of the curve and seize emerging opportunities. Moreover, the speed-focused approach has given *QuickTech* a competitive edge. It often outpaces larger, slower-moving competitors, gaining a foothold in the market. This strategy attracts customers looking for rapid solutions, providing a significant advantage in terms of market share and customer acquisition. However, this approach is not without its challenges. One key concern is the potential compromise on quality. Speed can sometimes lead to overlooked bugs or software glitches, which can result in customer dissatisfaction or, in severe cases, costly product recalls. Additionally, the relentless pace of innovation can lead to employee burnout, impacting morale and retention rates.

Crafted Furniture Co. stands in stark contrast to *QuickTech Solutions*. This small, artisanal furniture manufacturer places a strong emphasis on the quality of materials and craftsmanship, even if it means a longer production process. This quality-focused approach has yielded several positive impacts: First and foremost, Crafted Furniture Co. enjoys an exceptional reputation for its quality and meticulous attention to detail. Customers appreciate the craftsmanship and durability of its products, often considering them as heirloom pieces. Customer loyalty is another significant benefit of the quality-focused approach. Quality-conscious customers are willing to pay a premium for Crafted Furniture Co.'s products and often become loyal, repeat customers. This loyal customer base provides a stable source of revenue and enhances the company's long-term sustainability. However, there are challenges associated with this approach. The emphasis on quality means slower production times, limiting the volume of furniture the company can produce compared to mass manufacturers. In price-sensitive markets, Crafted Furniture Co. faces challenges competing with lower-cost alternatives, potentially limiting its market reach.

Some questions for the leaders to reflect and answer to resolve the dilemma:

- How do we decide when to prioritize getting things done quickly and when to prioritize making sure they are error-free?
- Can we identify specific tasks or projects where speed is more critical, and others where quality takes precedence?
- What impact does choosing speed over quality have on our customer relationships and satisfaction levels?
- In what situations might emphasizing quality lead to better long-term outcomes, even if it means sacrificing speed?
- How can we create a culture that encourages both speed and quality, and how do we communicate this balance to our teams?
- Are there processes or technologies that can help us achieve both speed and quality simultaneously?

There could be several factors that could influence this decision in the context of your organization like:

Customer Expectations: Aligning with what customers expect – whether they prioritize speed or quality – is a key influencer.

Complexity of the Task/Project: The nature and intricacy of the task or project determine whether speed or quality should take precedence.

Competition: The competitive landscape of the industry guides the choice, with speed often favored in competitive markets.

Resources: The availability of resources, including finances and skilled personnel, influences the capacity to balance speed and quality.

Regulatory Requirements: Compliance with industry regulations can dictate the necessity for quality over speed.

Brand Reputation: Decisions impact the company's reputation, with a focus on quality often leading to a positive brand image.

> **Market Demand/Trends**: Rapidly evolving markets may require a speed-focused approach, while stable markets may favor quality.
>
> There are other areas that get impacted because of a choice of this dilemma like:
>
> - Customer satisfaction
> - Error rates and rework
> - Decision-making speed
> - Productivity and workflow efficiency

Slack, the communication and collaboration platform, operates in a rapidly evolving tech space. To remain competitive and meet users' changing needs, they prioritize speed when it comes to product updates and feature releases. They understand that quick responses to market trends and user feedback are crucial. For example, during the COVID-19 pandemic, when remote work became prevalent, Slack swiftly introduced features to enhance virtual collaboration, such as improved video conferencing integration and enhanced notification settings. While there might be occasional minor bugs, Slack's commitment to rapid iterations allows them to address issues promptly and keep users engaged. In areas where security and user privacy are paramount, Slack places a strong emphasis on quality. They understand the significance of safeguarding user data and ensuring a secure platform for their customers, especially in industries like healthcare and finance. For instance, when launching Slack Enterprise Grid, a solution designed for large enterprises with heightened security needs, they conducted rigorous security testing and compliance assessments to meet industry standards and regulatory requirements. This quality-first approach reassures clients that their data is protected and instills trust in Slack's services. Slack also recognizes the importance of a seamless user experience. They aim to strike a balance between speed and quality when it comes to user interface and user experience (UI/UX) design. While they want to quickly roll out enhancements, they are equally focused on maintaining a high-quality, intuitive platform. For example, Slack frequently introduces UI updates and new features to enhance usability and productivity. These updates are carefully designed to maintain the quality of the user experience while also responding to user demands for innovation. By striking this balance, Slack keeps its user base engaged and satisfied. Slack's approach highlights the versatility of balancing speed and quality in different aspects of their business. They adapt their strategy to meet market dynamics, user expectations, and the specific requirements of various industries, showcasing how a real company can navigate the complexities of execution by making context-specific choices.

Let's explore some deeper and more nuanced aspects that commonly influence the decision of whether to prioritize Speed or Quality in different scenarios:

- **Product Lifecycle Stage**: The stage of a product's lifecycle can be a determining factor. During product development or market entry, speed may be crucial to gain a competitive edge. In contrast, for mature products, maintaining quality can be essential to sustain customer loyalty.
- **Customer Segmentation**: Companies may segment their customer base and tailor their approach accordingly. For some customer segments, quality may be paramount, while others may prioritize speed.
- **Risk Tolerance**: The organization's risk tolerance plays a significant role. Companies with a higher risk appetite may be more inclined to experiment with speed-focused strategies, while risk-averse companies may lean towards quality to minimize potential setbacks.
- **Innovation vs. Replication**: When introducing innovative products or services, speed can be a strategic advantage. Conversely, replicating existing products often necessitates maintaining or even improving upon existing quality standards.
- **Supply Chain Considerations**: The intricacies of the supply chain can influence the decision. For instance, a global supply chain with long lead times may encourage companies to focus on quality to avoid costly errors.
- **Market Entry Strategy**: The choice between speed and quality can be influenced by the chosen market entry strategy. For companies entering new markets, speed may be necessary to establish a presence quickly, while quality can be vital for long-term success.
- **Customer Feedback**: Ongoing analysis of customer feedback and preferences can guide the decision-making process. If customers consistently highlight the importance of one aspect over the other, it may influence the company's strategy.
- **Economic Environment**: Economic conditions, such as economic downturns or periods of rapid growth, can impact the decision. During economic downturns, cost-conscious consumers may

prioritize speed, while in prosperous times, quality may gain more attention.
- **Competitor Actions**: Observing how competitors balance speed and quality can inform a company's strategy. If competitors prioritize one aspect, it may be an opportunity to differentiate by focusing on the other.
- **Operational Capabilities**: The organizations own operational capabilities, including technology, workforce expertise, and infrastructure, influence its ability to execute speed or quality-focused strategies effectively.
- **Long-Term Vision**: The Company's long-term vision and goals can guide decisions. Companies with a vision for sustainable growth and lasting brand reputation may lean towards quality, while those aiming for rapid market expansion may prioritize speed.

These nuanced aspects, when considered in combination, help companies make informed decisions about whether to emphasize speed or quality in various scenarios. It's important to recognize that the balance between these factors may shift over time as market conditions, customer preferences, and organizational capabilities evolve.

Quality vs. Quantum

> This dilemma concerns the trade-off between producing a limited quantity of high-quality products or services versus producing a larger quantity of lower-quality items or figuring a balance between the two.

The Quality vs. Quantum dilemma presents organizations with a critical conundrum in their execution strategy. At its core, this dilemma revolves around the choice between two fundamental approaches to producing and delivering products or services. On one side of the spectrum is the pursuit of impeccable quality – producing a limited quantity of high-quality items or services. On the other side stands the quest for quantity – generating a larger volume of products or services, often at the expense of individual quality. Striking the right balance between these two approaches or choosing one over the other can have profound implications for an organization.

This dilemma is far from a simplistic choice; it delves into the very essence of an organization's identity and strategic positioning. The decision to prioritize quality or quantity influences how a company is perceived in the market, how it serves its customers, and how it manages its resources. The consequences are multifaceted, touching on various aspects of the organization's functioning.

Choosing Quality Only	
Pros	**Cons**
Enhanced brand reputation and customer loyalty.	Limited market reach due to higher prices.
Potential for premium pricing and higher profit margins.	Reduced revenue potential compared to quantity-focused competitors.
Strong differentiation in the	Greater resource and time

Choosing Quality Only	
Pros	**Cons**
Enhanced brand reputation and customer loyalty.	Limited market reach due to higher prices.
market.	investment in production.

Choosing Quantum only	
Pros	**Cons**
Broad market reach and potential for higher sales volume.	Risk of damaging brand reputation with lower-quality offerings.
Economies of scale can lead to cost savings.	Potential for higher customer churn and lower customer loyalty.
Quick response to market demand fluctuations.	Competitive challenges from other quantity-focused providers.

Bowers & Wilkins, a renowned British audio equipment manufacturer, has built its reputation around an unwavering commitment to audio quality. The company specializes in producing high-end speakers, headphones, and sound systems that are revered by audiophiles worldwide. B&W's quality-driven approach has a range of positive impacts on the company. Firstly, their emphasis on quality has resulted in a prestigious reputation for delivering exceptional audio experiences. This reputation acts as a magnet for discerning customers who are willing to pay a premium for top-tier products. B&W's dedication to quality cultivates strong customer loyalty. Those who experience B&W's products often become long-term advocates, leading to repeat business and positive word-of-mouth marketing. Moreover, B&W's quality-first strategy allows them to command premium prices for their products. This not only translates into higher profit margins but also contributes to sustained profitability. However, there are also potential downsides to this approach. B&W's high prices and exclusive focus on quality *limit their market reach. They primarily cater to a niche market of audiophiles and enthusiasts, missing out on price-sensitive consumers. Additionally, in a market saturated with audio equipment options, B&W faces intense competition, often from quantity-focused brands offering more affordable alternatives.*

On the other hand, Xiaomi, a Chinese electronics company, has gained recognition for its quantity-focused approach in the smartphone industry. They produce a wide range of smartphones with varying price points, aiming to target a broad consumer base. Xiaomi's quantity-driven strategy has had several positive impacts on the company. Foremost, Xiaomi's strategy of offering affordable smartphones in large quantities has helped it capture significant market share, particularly in emerging markets. They have become one of the top smartphone manufacturers by sales volume. By prioritizing quantity, Xiaomi provides cost-effective smartphones that appeal to budget-conscious consumers. This affordability allows them to penetrate markets with large, price-sensitive populations. Furthermore, producing in large quantities enables Xiaomi to achieve economies of scale, reducing production costs per unit and increasing profitability. However, there are also potential downsides to this approach. While Xiaomi has made strides in quality, the initial quantity-focused strategy led to perceptions of lower quality and reliability compared to premium competitors. Additionally, Xiaomi's focus on affordability often results in lower profit margins per unit compared to high-end smartphone manufacturers.

Some questions for the leaders to reflect and answer to resolve the dilemma:

- How do we determine the right mix between quality and quantity that aligns with our organization's goals and customer expectations?
- Are there specific product lines or customer segments where emphasizing quality or quantity is more strategically advantageous?
- What impact does a focus on quality have on customer loyalty, and how does this compare to the impact of providing a larger quantity of products or services?
- In what scenarios does emphasizing quantity align with our market strategy, and what risks or trade-offs should we be aware of?

- Can we adapt our approach based on changing market conditions and customer preferences, striking a dynamic balance between quality and quantity?
- How does the choice between quality and quantity influence our reputation and differentiation in the market?

There could be several factors that could influence this decision in the context of your organization like:

Market Demand: Understanding customer preferences and demand for high-quality or mass-produced items.

Competitive Landscape: Analyzing competitors' strategies and how they position themselves in the market.

Resource Availability: Assessing available resources, including production capacity, skilled labor, and capital.

Customer Segmentation: Segmenting the customer base to identify groups with varying quality and quantity preferences.

Profit Margins: Evaluating the impact on profit margins for both quality and quantity-focused approaches.

Brand Image: Considering how the chosen strategy affects the organization's brand image and reputation.

Market Trends: Monitoring industry trends and shifts in consumer preferences.

Regulatory Requirements: Ensuring compliance with industry regulations and quality standards.

There are other areas that get impacted because of a choice of this dilemma like:

- Brand reputation
- Market reach and share
- Customer loyalty

- Production costs and resource allocation

Quality and quantity can coexist within an organization through strategic portfolio management. By offering a range of products or services that cater to different customer segments, organizations can balance quality-driven and quantity-driven approaches effectively.

For instance, a furniture manufacturer may offer a high-end, handcrafted furniture line (quality) alongside a more affordable, mass-produced line (quantity). This way, the company can capture a broader market while maintaining its reputation for quality. *For example, let's take a look at "Gourmet Delights," a mid-sized food production company, and how they skillfully balance between Quality and Quantity in different scenarios - In their premium product line, Gourmet Delights specializes in creating artisanal, high-quality gourmet foods, such as handcrafted chocolates and small-batch olive oils. In this scenario, they prioritize quality over quantity. Their commitment to using the finest ingredients, traditional production methods, and rigorous quality control processes ensures that every product that bears their label represents excellence. This approach positively impacts the company in several ways. Their premium products command premium prices, leading to higher profit margins per unit. Additionally, their reputation for uncompromising quality has earned them a loyal customer base of discerning food enthusiasts who appreciate the exquisite taste and craftsmanship of their offerings. Gourmet Delights' focus on quality not only reinforces their brand image as a purveyor of premium gourmet products but also opens doors to collaborations with renowned chefs and luxury retailers. In their everyday product line, which includes staples like pasta, canned goods, and sauces, Gourmet Delights adopts a quantity-driven strategy. Here, they prioritize efficiency and affordability without compromising on safety and taste. By leveraging modern production techniques and economies of scale, they can offer these products at competitive prices, making them accessible to a wider consumer base. This quantity-focused approach enables Gourmet Delights to capture a larger market share and compete effectively with mass-market brands. It allows them to cater to price-conscious consumers looking for quality without the premium price tag. Although profit margins per unit may be lower than their premium offerings, the sheer volume of sales compensates for it. During holiday seasons and special occasions, Gourmet Delights strikes a balance between quality and quantity. They introduce limited-edition, high-quality products like gourmet gift baskets and festive treats. While these products maintain the company's reputation for quality, they are produced in larger quantities to meet seasonal demand.*

This balanced approach positively impacts the company by allowing them to capture seasonal revenue opportunities while still upholding their quality standards. Customers appreciate the combination of exceptional taste and the convenience of readily available seasonal products. In this way, Gourmet Delights showcases how a food production company can effectively navigate the Quality vs. Quantity dilemma by tailoring their approach to different product lines and consumer needs. They maintain their reputation for quality in premium offerings, expand their market reach with quantity-driven staples, and strike a balance during special occasions, ultimately ensuring sustained growth and customer satisfaction.

A more nuanced set of factors that commonly influence the decision of Quality vs. Quantum include:

- **Market Segmentation**: Companies often assess their customer base and segment it based on preferences. Understanding which segments prioritize quality and which prioritize quantity allows for tailored strategies for each.
- **Competitive Positioning**: The competitive landscape plays a crucial role. Companies analyze how competitors position themselves and whether there are opportunities to differentiate by focusing on quality, quantity, or a combination of both.
- **Market Maturity**: The stage of the market's development influences the choice. In emerging markets, quantity may be more critical to establish a presence, while in mature markets, quality often becomes a differentiating factor.
- **Customer Lifecycle**: Companies consider where their customers are in their lifecycle. Acquiring new customers might require quantity-driven strategies, while retaining long-term customers may necessitate quality-driven approaches.
- **Resource Availability**: Assessing the resources available, including production capacity, skilled labor, and capital, is essential. Quality-focused strategies often require more resources per unit, while quantity-focused ones aim for economies of scale.
- **Profit Margin Goals**: The desired profit margins impact the decision. High-quality products can often command premium prices, resulting in higher profit margins per unit. In contrast, quantity-focused strategies may aim for lower margins with higher sales volumes.

- **Product Complexity**: The complexity of the product or service affects the decision. Highly complex products may require a quality-focused approach to ensure they meet customer expectations and regulatory standards.
- **Brand Strategy**: Companies align their choice with their brand strategy. Brands known for quality will likely continue with a quality-driven approach, while those emphasizing accessibility and affordability may lean toward quantity.
- **Innovation vs. Replication**: The nature of the products or services matters. Innovations often require a quality-first approach to establish their value, while replication of existing offerings may focus on quantity to capture market share.
- **Regulatory Environment**: Compliance with industry regulations and quality standards influences the decision. Industries with strict regulations necessitate quality as a non-negotiable aspect.
- **Customer Feedback**: Companies actively gather and analyze customer feedback to understand preferences and needs. Adapting the quality-quantity balance based on this feedback is common.
- **Risk Tolerance**: The organization's risk tolerance and appetite for experimentation play a role. Companies with a higher risk tolerance may experiment with quantity-focused strategies to explore new markets or customer segments.
- **Long-Term Strategy**: The company's long-term vision and goals guide the decision. Companies aiming for sustainable growth and lasting brand reputation may lean toward quality, while those looking for rapid market expansion may prioritize quantity.
- **Operational Capabilities**: The organization's own operational capabilities, including technology, workforce expertise, and infrastructure, influence its ability to execute quality or quantity-focused strategies effectively.

In essence, the Quality vs. Quantum dilemma encapsulates the pivotal trade-off between offering fewer, high-quality products or services that cater to a specific market segment or providing a larger volume of potentially lower-quality offerings to reach a broader audience. Organizations must carefully navigate this decision, recognizing that it affects their brand, customer relationships, resource allocation, competitive position, and long-term prospects. Ultimately, the choice depends on the organization's strategic objectives and its understanding of customer needs and market dynamics.

Consistency vs. Adaptability

> This dilemma revolves around striking a balance between maintaining a consistent approach and adapting to changing circumstances and market dynamics.

The Consistency vs. Adaptability dilemma is a pivotal challenge in execution that shapes the very core of an organization's operational philosophy. It revolves around the perpetual struggle to strike the right balance between maintaining a consistent approach and being open to adaptation in response to changing circumstances and market dynamics. This dilemma is nothing short of critical because it goes to the heart of how organizations operate, innovate, and ultimately thrive in an ever-evolving business landscape.

On one end of the spectrum, consistency implies adherence to established processes, routines, and strategies. It signifies a commitment to reliability, predictability, and the preservation of existing structures and methodologies. Consistency brings stability, allows for the development of tried-and-true methods, and can reinforce a sense of order within the organization. It fosters a dependable environment where employees know what to expect and can execute tasks efficiently.

On the other end lies adaptability, which denotes a readiness to embrace change, innovation, and flexibility. It signifies the ability to pivot, adjust, and evolve in response to new challenges, market shifts, and emerging opportunities. Adaptability is the engine of innovation, enabling organizations to stay relevant, meet evolving customer needs, and respond effectively to external disruptions. It encourages a dynamic work culture where creative solutions are valued, and employees are empowered to experiment and learn.

This dilemma impacts several areas of business:

- The choice between consistency and adaptability has a profound impact on how efficiently an organization operates. Consistency streamlines processes and routines, minimizing deviations and errors. In contrast, adaptability may introduce experimentation

and variation, which can lead to agility but may also entail inefficiencies during transition periods.
- The approach an organization adopts affects the morale and engagement of its workforce. Consistency can provide a sense of stability and security, but if taken to extremes, it may stifle employee creativity and enthusiasm. Adaptability, when managed well, can invigorate employees, but excessive change without clear direction can create uncertainty and disengagement.
- Innovation is often closely tied to adaptability. Organizations that prioritize adaptability are more likely to foster a culture of innovation and creativity. However, those overly focused on consistency may miss out on opportunities for breakthrough ideas and novel approaches.
- The choice impacts an organization's risk profile. A consistent approach may provide a sense of control and risk mitigation, but it can also make the organization vulnerable to disruptions if market conditions change rapidly. Adaptability can help navigate uncertain environments but may introduce risk through experimentation and change.
- Customer preferences play a significant role in the decision. Consistency may lead to dependable, standardized products and services that meet known customer expectations. Adaptability can allow the organization to respond quickly to evolving customer needs but carries the risk of inconsistent offerings.
- The competitive landscape is influenced by this choice. Consistency can help establish a clear brand identity and a reputation for reliability. Adaptability can provide a competitive edge by responding swiftly to emerging trends or seizing new opportunities.
- Resource allocation decisions, including financial investments and talent allocation, depend on the chosen approach. Consistency may lead to resource allocation based on established processes, while adaptability requires flexibility in resource allocation to support change and innovation.

Choosing Consistency Only	
Pros	**Cons**
Establishes a sense of stability and predictability.	Risks becoming stagnant or resistant to change.
Enhances efficiency through established processes.	Could lead to missed opportunities for innovation.
May cultivate a strong organizational culture.	May not effectively respond to rapidly changing markets.

Choosing Adaptability Only	
Pros	**Cons**
Allows for swift responses to market changes.	Can create instability and inconsistency.
Encourages innovation and creativity.	May lead to resource fragmentation and inefficiencies.
Enhances the organization's agility and competitive advantage.	Employee morale and engagement may suffer due to constant change.

McDonald's, the global fast-food giant, is renowned for its unwavering commitment to consistency. This consistency-first approach permeates every aspect of the company's operations, from its menu to its processes and customer experience. McDonald's consistency-first strategy has several positive impacts on the company. When customers visit a McDonald's restaurant, they have a clear expectation of what they will receive. Whether you're in Tokyo or New York, a Big Mac tastes the same, which creates a sense of comfort and reliability for customers. The standardized menu and processes also contribute to operational efficiency. Employees can quickly and consistently prepare orders, leading to faster service and minimized errors. McDonald's consistency has resulted in a globally recognized brand identity. The company is synonymous with fast food, and its iconic Golden Arches are easily identifiable worldwide. However, there are also some negative impacts associated with McDonald's consistency-focused approach. McDonald's menu is known for its stability, with core items remaining largely unchanged for years. While this consistency is appreciated by loyal customers, it can limit the company's ability to introduce innovative menu items to cater to evolving tastes and dietary trends. When entering new markets or regions with diverse culinary preferences, McDonald's may face challenges in adapting its offerings while maintaining consistency. Striking the right balance can be complex.

Contrast that with Chipotle Mexican Grill, a popular fast-casual restaurant chain, is recognized for its adaptability in the food industry. The company has a strong commitment to sourcing fresh, sustainable ingredients and offering customizable menu options. This adaptability-first approach has positively impacted the company's growth and customer loyalty. Chipotle's adaptability-first strategy allows customers to customize their meals, choosing from a variety of fresh ingredients and proteins. This adaptability caters to diverse dietary preferences, including vegetarian, vegan, and gluten-free options, enhancing the customer experience. Chipotle also places a strong emphasis on sourcing high-quality, sustainable ingredients. They adapt their ingredient sources based on changing supplier practices and customer demands for ethical and eco-friendly sourcing. However, there are also some negative impacts associated with Chipotle's adaptability-focused approach. Ensuring a consistent supply of fresh ingredients while adhering to sustainability standards can introduce supply chain complexities and challenges in sourcing. As customers have a high degree of customization, maintaining operational consistency and speed during peak hours can be a challenge, and quality may vary between locations.

Some questions for the leaders to reflect and answer to resolve the dilemma:

- How do we determine when consistency is essential, and when adaptability is required in our organization's operations and decision-making?
- Are there specific areas within our organization where maintaining a consistent approach is more critical, while in others, adaptability is a strategic advantage?
- What impact does a consistent approach have on employee

morale and creativity compared to an adaptable approach?
- Can we cultivate a culture of adaptability without sacrificing the valuable aspects of consistency in our organization?
- How does our approach to consistency or adaptability influence our ability to manage risk and uncertainty effectively?
- What strategies can we employ to transition between consistency and adaptability when the situation demands it?

There could be several factors that could influence this decision in the context of your organization like:

Market Dynamics: Understanding how quickly market conditions change and whether agility or stability is more advantageous.

Competitive Landscape: Analyzing competitors' ability to adapt and whether differentiation through consistency or adaptability is more favorable.

Customer Expectations: Recognizing how customer preferences evolve and whether consistent offerings or adaptive customization is preferred.

Industry Regulation: Considering the level of regulatory stability and whether industry changes necessitate adaptability or adherence to established standards.

Resource Availability: Evaluating the organization's capacity for change, including technology, workforce capabilities, and financial resources.

Risk Tolerance: Assessing the organization's appetite for risk and how consistency or adaptability affects risk management strategies.

There are other areas that get impacted because of a choice of this dilemma like:

- Way of working in the organization
- Innovation and creativity

- Risk management
- Competitive advantage

Consistency and adaptability can coexist within an organization through strategic planning and clear communication. By establishing when and where each is most relevant, leaders can ensure that processes and routines remain consistent in areas where stability is vital, while remaining open to adaptation in response to dynamic circumstances. *Starbucks is a classic example of a company that balances consistency and adaptability to gain competitive advantage. While the company maintains core menu items like its iconic brewed coffee and popular espresso-based beverages consistently across locations, it also embraces adaptability by regularly introducing new seasonal or region-specific items. For instance, during the holiday season, Starbucks introduces seasonal drinks and food items like the Pumpkin Spice Latte. This adaptability allows Starbucks to cater to changing customer preferences and regional tastes while ensuring a consistent Starbucks experience worldwide. In terms of store design, Starbucks maintains a degree of consistency through its globally recognizable ambiance, featuring comfortable seating, earth-toned decor, and the familiar aroma of coffee. However, they also exhibit adaptability by tailoring store layouts to suit different locations and customer preferences. In some urban locations, you may find smaller, more streamlined stores, while in suburban or tourist-heavy areas, Starbucks stores often have more spacious seating areas and unique design elements.*

Factors that commonly influence the decision of Consistency vs. Adaptability, taking into account different scenarios and organizational contexts include

- **Nature of Industry**: The industry in which the organization operates plays a significant role. Highly regulated industries like finance and healthcare may require a greater degree of consistency to ensure compliance with stringent standards. In contrast, industries characterized by rapid technological advancements, such as tech startups, may prioritize adaptability to stay competitive.
- **Customer Segmentation**: Understanding the diversity of customer segments is crucial. Consistency may be preferred for serving long-term, loyal customers who seek reliability, while adaptability may be essential when catering to diverse customer

needs and preferences.
- **Competitive Landscape**: The intensity of competition and the pace of change in the competitive landscape are key factors. In highly competitive markets, adaptability can be a strategic advantage, while in more stable environments, consistency may help maintain market share.
- **Organizational Culture**: The existing culture within the organization can impact the decision. A culture that values tradition and established processes may lean toward consistency, whereas a culture that fosters innovation and experimentation may favor adaptability.
- **Leadership Style**: The leadership style of top executives influences the choice. Leaders who are risk-averse or have a preference for stability may opt for consistency, while visionary leaders may champion adaptability to drive innovation.
- **Resource Constraints**: Resource availability, including financial, human, and technological resources, can determine the extent to which an organization can afford to be adaptable. Limited resources may necessitate a more conservative approach.
- **Market Position**: The organization's current market position is critical. Established market leaders may focus on consistency to preserve their dominant position, while newcomers may prioritize adaptability to disrupt the status quo.
- **Regulatory Environment**: The level of regulation within the industry and region is a significant factor. Strict regulatory environments may demand consistency to ensure compliance, while less regulated sectors may have more flexibility.
- **Technology Adoption**: The organization's readiness and ability to adopt new technologies can influence the decision. A tech-savvy organization may find it easier to adapt and leverage emerging technologies.
- **Customer Feedback**: Actively gathering and analyzing customer feedback can provide insights into whether customers are seeking consistency or adaptability in products and services. Customer preferences should guide the decision.
- **Risk Appetite**: The organization's appetite for risk plays a central role. Risk-averse organizations may gravitate toward consistency as a means of risk mitigation, whereas risk-tolerant ones may

embrace adaptability as a means of seizing opportunities.
- **Strategic Goals**: The organization's long-term strategic goals and objectives guide the choice. Organizations aiming for steady growth and market stability may opt for consistency, while those pursuing rapid expansion or transformation may prioritize adaptability.
- **Economic Conditions**: Economic conditions, including economic stability or volatility, can impact the decision. In uncertain economic times, organizations may lean toward consistency to weather financial challenges.

In essence, the Consistency vs. Adaptability dilemma has far-reaching implications that extend across the organization, shaping its culture, operations, employee experiences, and its ability to navigate the complexities of an ever-changing business environment. Organizations must carefully assess their strategic goals, market conditions, and internal capabilities to make informed decisions about the degree of consistency and adaptability that best suits their context.

Outcome Focused vs. Process Focused

> This dilemma is all about prioritizing either achieving desired outcomes or refining and optimizing internal processes or striking a balance between the two.

The Outcome focused vs. Process focused dilemma is a pivotal challenge in the realm of execution within organizations. At its core, it involves deciding whether to prioritize achieving specific outcomes or concentrating on refining and optimizing internal processes. This decision carries profound implications for the organization's overall success, shaping its culture, operations, and long-term effectiveness. This dilemma is critical because it guides an organization's approach to achieving its goals.

The nuances of this choice impact various aspects of the organization:

- **Goal Clarity**: Leaders must ask themselves whether their primary focus should be on defining clear, measurable outcomes or on perfecting the methods and procedures used to reach those outcomes.
- **Resource Allocation**: The decision influences how resources, including budget and personnel, are distributed. Organizations must determine whether they allocate resources to projects and initiatives with distinct, measurable goals (outcome-focused) or invest in enhancing internal workflows and infrastructure (process-focused).
- **Risk Management**: It dictates how an organization deals with risk. An outcome-focused approach may encourage calculated risks to achieve ambitious goals, while a process-focused one may prioritize risk mitigation to ensure the reliability of internal operations.
- **Innovation and Creativity**: The balance between outcome and process orientation shapes innovation efforts. An outcome-focused organization may seek innovations that directly contribute to better results, while a process-focused organization may emphasize continuous improvement in internal procedures,

indirectly supporting innovation.
- **Employee Engagement**: The choice influences employee motivation and engagement. An outcome-focused approach provides employees with a clear sense of purpose tied to achieving results, while a process-focused approach may focus on improving day-to-day tasks, which can also be fulfilling but may feel less directly tied to broader goals.
- **Adaptability:** Organizations must consider their willingness to adapt to changing circumstances. An outcome-focused organization may be more flexible if adaptation aligns with achieving its goals, while a process-focused organization may resist changes that disrupt established procedures.

Choosing To Be Outcome Focused Only	
Pros	**Cons**
Clarity of purpose and goals.	Risk of overlooking internal efficiency.
Motivates employees with a clear sense of achievement.	Potential neglect of long-term process improvements.
Drives innovation focused on achieving results.	Pressure to meet short-term goals at the expense of long-term sustainability.

Choosing To Be Process Focused Only	
Pros	**Cons**
Emphasizes operational efficiency and reliability.	May lead to a lack of goal clarity.
Encourages continuous improvement.	Employee motivation may suffer without clear outcome-related objectives.

| Reduces the likelihood of errors and inefficiencies. | Potential resistance to change and innovation. |

Consider two vehicle manufacturers. Tesla, the electric vehicle (EV) manufacturer led by Elon Musk, is an example of an outcome-focused company. Tesla's primary objective is to revolutionize the automotive industry by producing high-quality electric vehicles and advancing clean energy solutions. Tesla's relentless focus on outcomes drives continuous innovation in EV technology and sustainable energy solutions. They have rapidly introduced groundbreaking products like the Model S and Model 3, changing the perception of EVs. Tesla's commitment to delivering high-performance electric cars aligns with customer expectations. Their vehicles have garnered a loyal fan base and received accolades for their quality and performance. Tesla's ability to bring new EV models to market quickly has given them a competitive edge. They set the standard for EV range, technology, and autonomous driving capabilities. There are also drawbacks of being exclusively outcome focused. Tesla's emphasis on outcomes sometimes leads to operational challenges, including production bottlenecks and quality control issues. Rapid expansion and ambitious goals can strain resources. Balancing innovation projects, such as battery technology and self-driving features, with essential process improvements, like manufacturing efficiency, can be a complex task.

On the other hand, Toyota, one of the world's largest automakers, is often cited as an example of a process-focused company. They are known for their commitment to the Toyota Production System (TPS) and a strong focus on operational excellence. Toyota's process-focused approach ensures that they consistently produce high-quality vehicles with minimal defects. The Toyota brand is synonymous with reliability and longevity. Toyota's dedication to process optimization has led to efficient manufacturing processes and cost control. Their lean production methods minimize waste and enhance profitability. Toyota's commitment to processes aligns with the strict regulatory standards of the automotive industry, ensuring compliance and safety. However, Toyota's strong focus on process optimization can sometimes hinder rapid innovation. They may be cautious about adopting new technologies, potentially missing opportunities in emerging markets like electric vehicles. In rapidly evolving industries, such as EVs, Toyota's meticulous processes may lead to slower product development and time-to-market, making it challenging to compete with more agile companies.

Some questions for the leaders to reflect and answer to resolve the dilemma:

- What defines success for our organization: achieving specific outcomes or perfecting internal processes?
- Are our goals clear, measurable, and directly tied to desired outcomes, or do we need to refine our processes before setting ambitious goals?
- How do we allocate resources: to projects with clear, measurable outcomes or to enhancing internal processes and infrastructure?
- How do we approach risk: are we willing to take calculated risks to achieve ambitious goals, or do we prioritize risk mitigation to ensure process reliability?
- What is our stance on innovation and creativity: do we seek innovations that directly contribute to better results, or do we prioritize continuous improvement in internal procedures?
- How do we keep our employees engaged and motivated: by providing a clear sense of purpose tied to outcomes or by focusing on improving daily tasks and processes?

There could be several factors that could influence this decision in the context of your organization like:

Industry Dynamics: The nature of the industry and its pace of change

Competitive Landscape: The level of competition in the market.

Customer Expectations: What customers value and demand.

Regulatory Requirements: Compliance and industry regulations.

Market Maturity: The stage of the market's development.

Financial Considerations: Resource availability and financial health of the organization.

> **There are other areas that get impacted because of a choice of this dilemma like:**
>
> - Goal achievement
> - Employee satisfaction and engagement
> - Resource allocation
> - Strategic alignment

Outcome-focused and process-focused approaches can coexist in an organization to varying degrees. Finding the right balance is essential, as both have their pros and cons. *For example, Mazda adopts a mix of outcome-focused and process-focused approach. They adopt an Outcome-focused approach when designing and innovating vehicles. They prioritize creating unique and appealing cars that resonate with customers by using "KODO" design philosophy, which emphasizes the beauty of movement and aesthetics and by investing in innovative engineering solutions, such as their SKYACTIV technology, to improve vehicle performance, fuel efficiency, and safety. Mazda closely studies customer preferences and market trends to deliver vehicles that align with customer expectations. On the other hand, when it comes to manufacturing and quality control, Mazda takes a Process-focused approach to ensure consistent quality and efficiency in their production lines by using lean production, quality assurance to minimize defects and ensure reliability. It standardizes production procedures to maintain consistent quality across their vehicle lineup. This process-driven approach helps them meet industry standards and regulatory requirements.*

Factors that commonly influence the decision between an Outcome-focused and a Process-focused approach:

- **Market Volatility**: The level of market volatility and uncertainty can impact the choice. In turbulent markets, an Outcome-focused approach may be favored to quickly adapt to changing conditions, while in stable markets, Process-focused approaches may provide stability.
- **Product Lifecycle**: Where a product or service is in its lifecycle matters. In the early stages, Outcome focus can drive innovation, while Process focus may be crucial in mature stages for efficiency and cost control.
- **Customer Segmentation**: Different customer segments may have

varying expectations. Organizations often balance Outcome and Process approaches to meet the unique needs of diverse customer groups.

- **Technology Infrastructure**: The state of an organization's technology infrastructure plays a role. Robust technology may enable an Outcome focus, while outdated systems may necessitate Process focus for optimization.
- **Talent and Skills**: The availability of skilled talent influences the decision. Organizations with highly skilled teams may lean towards Outcome focus, while those needing skill development may prioritize Process improvements.
- **Strategic Goals**: The organization's strategic goals and long-term vision guide the choice. Goals for growth and differentiation align with Outcome focus, while goals for stability and reliability align with Process focus.
- **Resource Constraints**: Resource availability, including budget and personnel, is a critical factor. Limited resources may necessitate a more balanced or prioritized approach.
- **Customer Feedback**: Listening to customer feedback can be a compass. Feedback on product quality may drive Process improvements, while feedback on innovation may steer towards Outcome focus.
- **Risk Tolerance:** An organization's willingness to take risks influences the choice. High-risk tolerance encourages Outcome focus, while low-risk tolerance may promote Process focus.
- **Crisis Situations**: In crisis scenarios, organizations may temporarily shift towards an Outcome focus to address urgent challenges, then return to Process focus for stability.
- **Global Market Dynamics**: International operations introduce complexities. Organizations may adopt different approaches based on regional market dynamics.
- **Change Management Capacity**: The organization's capability to manage change plays a role. Strong change management supports transitions between Outcome and Process focuses.
- **Ecosystem Partnerships**: Collaborations with partners, suppliers, and stakeholders impact the choice. Alignment with ecosystem expectations can influence the approach.
- **Innovation Strategy**: Organizations with a deliberate innovation

strategy may lean towards Outcome focus to drive breakthroughs.
- **Customer Loyalty**: High customer loyalty may allow more flexibility in balancing Outcome and Process approaches, as loyal customers often tolerate minor inefficiencies.

In essence, the Outcome focused vs. Process focused dilemma is not just a theoretical choice; it is a fundamental decision that permeates an organization's culture, operations, and success. It touches upon goal clarity, resource allocation, risk appetite, innovation, employee motivation, and adaptability, all of which are pivotal elements in determining an organization's overall effectiveness and competitiveness.

Efficiency vs. Effectiveness

> The choice between doing things efficiently (minimizing resource use) and doing things effectively (achieving desired results) or striking a balance between the two.

The Efficiency vs. Effectiveness dilemma is a pivotal challenge organizations face in their pursuit of success and sustainability. This dilemma revolves around the fundamental choice of how an organization allocates its resources, be it time, money, labor, or other assets. It's a choice that can significantly impact various aspects of an organization's functioning.

Efficiency, as one side of this dilemma, is the relentless pursuit of resource optimization. It's about doing things in the most economical way, minimizing waste, and maximizing productivity. When organizations prioritize efficiency, they streamline processes, automate tasks, and seek to reduce unnecessary costs. It often leads to a well-oiled machine, where every action is geared towards minimizing resource consumption. The result can be a lean operation, capable of delivering products or services with fewer resources. However, there's a flip side to efficiency. In the pursuit of resource optimization, organizations can sometimes lose sight of the bigger picture. The focus on trimming expenses may lead to a myopic view that prioritizes short-term gains over long-term goals. Efficiency-driven decisions can also stifle innovation and creativity, as these often require a willingness to invest resources in unproven ideas or processes.

Effectiveness, on the other hand, is all about achieving desired results and meeting objectives. Organizations that prioritize effectiveness are outcome-driven. They emphasize the importance of delivering on promises, meeting customer expectations, and fulfilling strategic goals. Effectiveness often requires a more flexible approach, where resource allocation is based on what it takes to get the job done successfully. Yet, effectiveness can come at a cost. Achieving desired results sometimes necessitates a willingness to allocate more resources than initially anticipated. This approach may be perceived as resource-intensive and could lead to inefficiencies if not managed properly. The pursuit of effectiveness may also make an organization less adaptable to changing circumstances, as it can be resistant to altering established processes or strategies.

Choosing Efficiency Only	
Pros	**Cons**
Cost savings.	Potential sacrifice of innovation.
Streamlined processes.	Reduced adaptability to changing market conditions.
Improved resource allocation.	Lower employee engagement.

Choosing Effectiveness Only	
Pros	**Cons**
Achievement of desired outcomes.	Resource-intensive.
Enhanced customer satisfaction.	May lead to inefficiencies.
Innovation and adaptability.	Potential financial strain.

Let's take the example of two fictitious companies. XYZ Electronics is a mid-sized consumer electronics manufacturer that prioritizes efficiency in its operations. The company aims to produce electronic devices at the lowest possible cost to maximize profitability. By focusing on efficiency, XYZ Electronics can offer competitive prices for its products. This cost leadership strategy attracts budget-conscious consumers, increasing market share and revenue. Also, the company's emphasis on process optimization leads to streamlined operations, reducing waste and resource consumption. This efficiency allows for higher production volumes and profitability. Moreover, XYZ Electronics invests in quality control processes to ensure product consistency while maintaining efficiency. This approach builds a reputation for reliable, affordable electronics.

HOPE IS NOT A STRATEGY

However, the strong emphasis on efficiency sometimes hampers XYZ Electronics' ability to innovate and develop cutting-edge products. They may lag behind competitors in terms of technological advancements. The company's focus on cost control might make it less agile in responding to changing consumer preferences or market trends, potentially missing opportunities for growth. An overemphasis on efficiency can lead to repetitive, monotonous tasks for employees, potentially affecting job satisfaction and creativity.

Company 2 - TechSolutions Innovations is a technology startup that emphasizes effectiveness in its approach. The company's primary goal is to develop innovative solutions to address specific customer pain points. TechSolutions Innovations' focus on effectiveness drives continuous innovation. They are often the first to introduce novel solutions, differentiating them in the market and attracting early adopters. So, they achieve high customer satisfaction by delivering tailored solutions that effectively solve customer problems. The organization's agility allows it to swiftly adapt to market changes and emerging trends. This responsiveness positions them as industry leaders in adapting to shifting consumer needs.

However, pursuing effectiveness often requires significant resource investments in research, development, and customization. This can strain the company's finances and slow down scalability. Innovations may not always yield the expected results, leading to potential financial setbacks and uncertain outcomes. A focus on effectiveness may lead to complex operations and project management, which could introduce inefficiencies in the organization.

Some questions for the leaders to reflect and answer to resolve the dilemma:

- Are we prioritizing resource optimization or achieving specific outcomes in our current initiatives?
- Do we have a clear understanding of our resource constraints and their impact on our ability to achieve desired results?
- How can we balance the need for efficiency with the imperative of achieving meaningful outcomes?
- Are there areas within the organization where efficiency should take precedence, and others where effectiveness is more critical?
- What metrics are we using to measure efficiency and

> effectiveness, and are they aligned with our strategic objectives?
> - How can we foster a culture that encourages both efficiency-driven process improvements and effectiveness-driven innovation?
>
> **There could be several factors that could influence this decision in the context of your organization like:**
>
> **Resource Availability**: The availability of financial, human, and time resources.
>
> **Market Dynamics**: Competitive pressures and market conditions.
>
> **Organizational Culture**: The prevailing culture regarding efficiency and innovation.
>
> **Regulatory Requirements**: Compliance obligations that impact resource allocation.
>
> **Customer Expectations**: The demands and preferences of customers.
>
> **Industry Standards**: Benchmarks and industry best practices.
>
> **There are other areas that get impacted because of a choice of this dilemma like:**
>
> - Cost management
> - Resource allocation and optimization
> - Strategic planning
> - Long-term sustainability and competitiveness

Efficiency and effectiveness can coexist in the organization when leaders make informed decisions about where to allocate resources efficiently and where to prioritize effectiveness. A strategic approach involves a dynamic balance that adapts to specific goals and circumstances. *For example, consider the case of InnovaTech Solutions. It recognizes the importance of innovation in the highly competitive tech industry. When developing new products, the company emphasizes effectiveness - so they invest in dedicated innovation labs, place a strong emphasis on understanding customer pain points, gather extensive feedback and data to tailor products that effectively address customer needs, ensuring high user satisfaction. They are also quick to adopt emerging technologies and trends. By staying ahead of the curve, they can deliver novel solutions that set them apart from competitors.*

To maintain profitability and operational excellence, they also take an efficiency-focused approach- they implement lean manufacturing principles to optimize production processes. They optimize its supply chain for efficiency, ensuring timely delivery of components while minimizing inventory costs and fostering a culture of continuous improvement, where employees are encouraged to identify and eliminate inefficiencies in their workflows. This results in streamlined operations and cost savings.

Factors that influence the decision between Efficiency vs. Effectiveness, include:

- **Resource Availability and Constraints**: The availability and limitations of resources, including financial, human, and time resources, play a fundamental role in the decision. Organizations with abundant resources may have more flexibility to prioritize effectiveness, while those with limited resources often lean towards efficiency.
- **Strategic Goals and Priorities**: The organization's strategic goals and immediate priorities significantly influence the choice. If the primary goal is rapid growth or market expansion, effectiveness may take precedence. Conversely, if cost reduction or operational streamlining is paramount, efficiency becomes the focal point.
- **Market and Competitive Landscape**: The organization's position within its market and the competitive landscape can drive the decision. In highly competitive markets, effectiveness may be necessary to differentiate from competitors, while mature markets may require a stronger focus on efficiency to maintain profitability.
- **Regulatory and Compliance Requirements**: Industries subject to strict regulatory standards may need to allocate resources for compliance, affecting the balance between efficiency and effectiveness. Compliance often demands specific processes, potentially limiting resource optimization.

- **Customer Expectations and Demands**: Customer expectations play a pivotal role. Organizations striving for high customer satisfaction and loyalty may prioritize effectiveness to meet or exceed customer demands. In contrast, cost-conscious customers may favor efficiency-driven offerings.
- **Risk Tolerance**: An organization's risk tolerance influences the decision-making process. Risk-averse organizations may lean towards efficiency to reduce uncertainties, while those more comfortable with risk may prioritize effectiveness to pursue innovative strategies.
- **Industry Life Cycle**: The stage of the industry life cycle matters. In emerging industries, effectiveness is often critical for market entry and establishing a presence. In mature industries, efficiency becomes vital for maintaining profitability.
- **Organizational Culture**: The prevailing culture within the organization can steer the decision. A culture that values creativity and innovation may favor effectiveness, while a culture centered on process optimization may lean towards efficiency.
- **Technology and Tools**: The availability of advanced technology and tools can impact the decision. Technology can enhance efficiency through automation and streamlined processes, but it can also enable effectiveness by facilitating data-driven decision-making.
- **Leadership and Management** Style: Leadership's approach to decision-making is crucial. Leadership that values data-driven decision-making may lean towards effectiveness, while leaders who prioritize cost control may emphasize efficiency.
- **Customer Segmentation**: Organizations may segment their customer base, tailoring their approach based on customer preferences. High-value customers may receive more personalized, effective solutions, while cost-sensitive segments may receive more efficient, standardized offerings.
- **Environmental and Social Responsibility**: Growing concerns about environmental and social responsibility may influence the decision. Organizations committed to sustainability may allocate resources for environmentally friendly practices, impacting efficiency goals.

Therefore, this dilemma is at the heart of organizational decision-making, influencing how resources are allocated and how goals are achieved. Effectiveness prioritizes achieving desired outcomes and meeting customer demands, fostering innovation and market responsiveness. However, it may require significant resource investments and entail risks. Efficiency, on the other hand, focuses on resource optimization, reducing waste, and streamlining processes to maximize profitability. Yet, it can sometimes hinder innovation and market adaptability. Companies must navigate this dilemma judiciously, considering their unique circumstances and objectives, to achieve long-term success and resilience in a dynamic business landscape.

| 3.5 |
DECISION-MAKING DILEMMAS

How will you use this chapter of the book

If you are the founder or the CEO of a company and if you and your leadership team have a clear point of view (PoV) on the following questions and all of you are ALIGNED, then you can choose to move to the next chapter of the book. However, if you see a dissonance or have conflicting views, then we suggest digging deeper, going through this chapter and reflecting on different angles we bring in there.

Here are the questions for you to discuss and ponder-

- How do we balance between centralized and decentralized decision-making to ensure both efficiency and agility?
- How can we involve a wide range of stakeholders in our decision-making processes while still making timely and effective decisions?
- What is our strategy for integrating data-driven insights into our decision-making process, while also valuing intuitive judgment and experience?
- How can we align our decision-making with both our internal strengths and external market dynamics to maximize our competitiveness?
- How do we allocate resources to optimize existing operations while also investing in new opportunities to foster growth and innovation?
- What mechanisms should we put in place to ensure clear accountability and responsibility for decision outcomes across the organization?
- How can we foster a culture of effective communication and collaboration, regardless of our decision-making approach?
- How do we ensure that our decision-making processes encourage innovation and the inclusion of diverse

> perspectives?
> - Are our decision-making approaches consistent with our organization's core values and long-term vision?
> - How will we continuously monitor the impact of our decision-making approaches and adjust them to meet evolving business needs and market conditions?

In the realm of organizational leadership, decision-making holds a pivotal role, yet it often presents leaders with intricate challenges to address. These challenges encapsulate critical choices that can significantly impact a company's trajectory. Leaders must grapple with questions related to centralized versus decentralized decision-making, striking a balance between inclusivity and efficiency, the role of data-driven versus intuitive decision-making, the emphasis on internal priorities versus external market dynamics, and the allocation of resources between optimizing existing operations and pursuing new opportunities. In this dynamic landscape, the decisions leaders make reverberate across the organizational structure, affecting accountability, innovation, stakeholder engagement, and more. To effectively navigate these dilemmas, CEOs and leadership teams must engage in thoughtful reflection, constructive dialogue, and mutual agreement on the principles and approaches that will guide their organization's decision-making processes.

Leaders should consider a wide range of aspects when determining how decision-making will be done in their organization like

- **Organizational Goals and Strategy**: Ensure that decision-making aligns with the organization's overarching goals and long-term strategy.
- **Company Culture**: Consider how the decision-making approach aligns with the existing culture and whether it promotes values and behaviors that are desired.
- **Size and Structure**: Assess the organization's size and structure to determine the most appropriate level of centralization or decentralization.
- **Industry and Market Dynamics**: Understand the specific industry and market conditions, as well as competitive forces, to adapt decision-making accordingly.

- **Stakeholder Expectations**: Take into account the expectations and needs of various stakeholders, including employees, customers, investors, and regulatory bodies.
- **Resource Availability**: Evaluate the availability of resources, including financial, human, and technological, to support different decision-making processes.
- **Risk Tolerance**: Determine the organization's risk tolerance and how it relates to decision-making, particularly in terms of pursuing new opportunities.
- **Information and Data Infrastructure**: Consider the organization's data capabilities and infrastructure to support data-driven decision-making if applicable.
- **Leadership Style**: Assess the leadership style and preferences of key leaders and how they impact decision-making approaches.
- **Historical Performance**: Review past decision-making approaches and their outcomes to inform future choices.
- **Regulatory and Compliance Requirements**: Ensure that decision-making processes comply with legal and regulatory requirements in the relevant industry.
- **Competitive Positioning**: Analyze how decision-making affects the organization's competitive positioning and ability to adapt to market changes.
- **Employee Engagement**: Consider how decision-making approaches impact employee engagement, satisfaction, and morale.
- **Innovation and Creativity**: Evaluate how different decision-making methods influence innovation, creativity, and the ability to adapt to emerging trends.
- **Communication and Transparency**: Determine how decision-making processes impact communication and transparency within the organization.
- **Customer-Centricity**: Assess whether decision-making aligns with a customer-centric approach and enhances customer satisfaction and loyalty.
- **Long-Term Sustainability**: Consider the sustainability of decision-making methods over the long term and their impact on the organization's stability and growth.
- **Adaptability and Agility**: Evaluate the organization's ability to

adapt to changing circumstances and whether decision-making methods facilitate agility.
- **Ethical and Social Responsibility**: Ensure that decision-making processes uphold ethical standards and social responsibility commitments.
- **Feedback Loops**: Establish mechanisms for collecting feedback from employees and stakeholders to continuously improve decision-making.

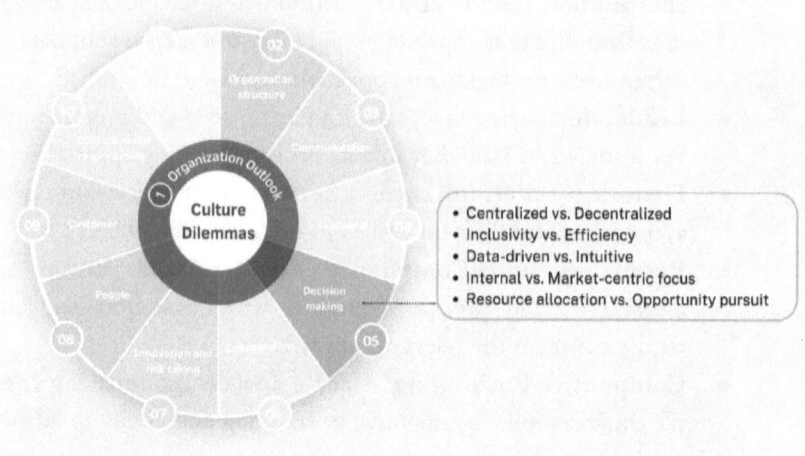

While there are many dilemmas when we think of decision-making, we will focus on five pivotal ones that often take center stage:

- **Centralized vs Decentralized**
- **Inclusivity vs Efficiency**
- **Data Driven vs. Intuitive**
- **Internal Focus vs. Market-Centric**
- **Optimization vs. Pursuit of New Opportunities**

Let's look at each of them in greater detail.

Centralized vs Decentralized Decision-Making

> The dilemma involves deciding whether decision-making authority should be concentrated at the top of the organizational hierarchy (centralized) or distributed across different teams or levels (decentralized) or there could be a balance between the two.

Centralized decision-making involves a hierarchical structure in which a select group of top-level executives or leaders retains the authority to make key decisions for the entire organization. This approach offers a clear and structured chain of command, where decisions are efficiently communicated from the top down. Centralized decision-making can provide consistency and uniformity in the execution of strategic initiatives and policies. This can be particularly beneficial in industries where regulatory compliance and adherence to standardized procedures are critical.

However, centralization comes with its own set of challenges. Decision-making is often concentrated in the hands of a few, which can lead to a bottleneck in the process. As decisions cascade down the hierarchy, they may lose sight of the nuanced details of local or departmental needs, potentially resulting in decisions that are less responsive to rapidly changing market conditions or customer requirements. Moreover, over-centralization can limit innovation and employee engagement, as those further from the top may feel disempowered and excluded from the decision-making process.

In contrast, Decentralized decision-making empowers individuals and teams at various levels of the organization to make decisions that are more closely aligned with their specific roles and responsibilities. It fosters a culture of trust, autonomy, and innovation, as employees feel a sense of ownership over their decisions and actions. Decentralization encourages frontline employees, who often have the most direct contact with customers and operations, to contribute valuable insights and adapt quickly to evolving circumstances.

Nonetheless, decentralization is not without its challenges. In a highly decentralized environment, the risk of inconsistent decision execution arises, as different teams or departments may make choices that diverge from the overarching organizational strategy. Coordinating disparate decisions can become challenging, potentially leading to confusion and inefficiency. Ensuring accountability can also be more complex, as decision-makers across the organization must be held responsible for their actions.

The impact of this decision-making dilemma extends across multiple dimensions of organizational functioning. It influences not only the speed and effectiveness of decision-making but also the organization's culture, employee engagement, and alignment with its strategic goals. The choice between centralized and decentralized decision-making should be made with careful consideration of the organization's size, industry, culture, and objectives. It's important to note that some organizations find that a hybrid model, balancing centralized and decentralized decision-making for different types of decisions, offers the benefits of both approaches. Ultimately, the decision-making approach chosen can significantly shape the organization's identity and its ability to thrive in a dynamic business environment.

Choosing Centralized Decision-Making Only	
Pros	**Cons**
Clear direction and consistency	Slower response to market changes
Efficient resource allocation	Reduced employee autonomy and motivation
Stronger control over operations	Potential bottleneck at the top

Choosing Decentralized Decision-Making Only	
Pros	**Cons**
Quick response to local needs	Potential lack of coordination
Empowered and motivated employees	Risk of inconsistent decisions
Enhanced innovation and creativity	Challenges in maintaining alignment

Grubhub, an online food delivery and ordering platform, operates with a relatively centralized decision-making approach. Key decisions, including pricing strategies, partnerships, and marketing campaigns, are often made by the corporate leadership at the top level of the organization. Centralization in decision-making allows Grubhub to maintain a consistent brand image and pricing structure across its markets. This consistency can contribute to better brand recognition and customer loyalty. Moreover, centralized decision-making can lead to more efficient resource allocation and a clear corporate direction, facilitating the execution of strategic initiatives. However, this centralized approach can also have drawbacks. Grubhub operates in a highly competitive industry where local preferences and market dynamics vary significantly. Centralized decisions may not always be responsive to local customer demands or competitor actions, potentially leading to missed opportunities or slower responses to market changes.

On the other hand, Lush Cosmetics, a global cosmetics retailer, is known for its decentralized decision-making approach. The company empowers its store managers and employees to make decisions related to store layout, product selection, and customer engagement. Decentralization aligns with Lush's commitment to individual store customization and a strong emphasis on customer experience. This approach fosters innovation at the local level, as store managers can tailor their offerings to suit the preferences of their specific customer base. It also enhances employee engagement and motivation, as staff members have a say in how their stores operate. However, decentralization can present challenges in maintaining consistency and brand standards across all Lush stores. It may lead to variations in customer experience and product availability. Furthermore, decentralized decision-making requires robust communication and support systems to ensure alignment with the company's broader goals and values.

> **Some questions for the leaders to reflect and answer to resolve the dilemma:**
>
> - Should decisions be made by those closest to daily operations or higher up in the company?
> - Is it more critical to make decisions quickly, or can we afford to take our time?
> - Do we trust our teams to make the right decisions, or do we prefer more control from the top?
> - How do decisions impact alignment within the organization? Which approach maintains better alignment?
> - Do employees thrive when they have more decision-making power, or do they prefer clear directions from above?
> - Can we find a balance between centralized and decentralized decision-making as circumstances change over time?
>
> **There could be several factors that could influence this decision in the context of your organization like:**
>
> **Size of the Organization**: Larger organizations may benefit from some level of centralization to maintain control, while smaller ones might be more flexible with decentralization.
>
> **Industry and Market Dynamics**: Industries with rapid changes may lean towards decentralization for quicker responses, while stable industries may favor centralization.
>
> **Organizational Structure and Culture**: A culture of trust and empowerment may support decentralization, while a more hierarchical culture may lean towards centralization.
>
> **Complexity of Decisions**: Highly complex decisions may require expertise from different levels, encouraging a balance.
>
> **Resource Availability**: The availability of resources, including time

and talent, can influence the choice.

Competitive Landscape: A competitive environment may necessitate quicker decisions, favoring decentralization.

There are other areas that get impacted because of a choice of this dilemma like:

- Organizational hierarchy and structure
- Decision speed and agility
- Accountability and responsibility
- Communication and collaboration dynamics

Centralization and decentralization in decision-making can coexist in an organization through a hybrid model. Certain decisions may be centralized for consistency and alignment, while others can be decentralized to empower teams and encourage innovation. *Let's consider the example of "The Honest Company," a consumer goods company founded by actress Jessica Alba. The Honest Company manufactures and sells a variety of household and personal care products, emphasizing transparency and using eco-friendly ingredients. They maintain a centralized approach to product development and quality control. Key decisions regarding product formulation, quality standards, and ingredient sourcing are typically made at the corporate level to ensure consistency, safety, and adherence to the company's mission of providing non-toxic and environmentally friendly products. This centralized approach aligns with the company's commitment to delivering trustworthy products to customers. When it comes to market expansion and retail partnerships, The Honest Company strikes a balance between centralization and decentralization. Corporate leadership often makes high-level decisions regarding the company's overall growth strategy and major retail partnerships. However, local market teams are empowered to make decisions related to market-specific strategies, promotions, and collaborations with local retailers. This balanced approach allows them to adapt to local market conditions and preferences while maintaining a cohesive national and global strategy. It fosters agility and responsiveness at the local level while preserving alignment with the company's overarching goals. They consciously promote a decentralized decision-making approach when it comes to employee empowerment and workplace practices. Employees are encouraged to share their ideas, feedback, and suggestions for improving workplace culture and practices. This approach aligns with the company's commitment to creating a positive and inclusive work environment. This helps foster a sense of ownership, and promotes a more inclusive and collaborative work culture. It allows for continuous improvement based on insights from those closest to day-to-day operations.*

The decision of whether to adopt a centralized or decentralized decision-making approach in running a business is influenced by a wide range of factors:

- **Organizational Size**: Larger organizations may require more centralized decision-making to maintain control, while smaller ones may benefit from decentralization to encourage agility and innovation.
- **Complexity of Operations**: The complexity of a company's operations can dictate the level of centralization needed. Highly complex operations may require more centralized decision-making for coordination.
- **Industry and Market Dynamics**: Industries with rapid changes or high competition may lean towards decentralization for quicker responses, while stable industries may favor centralization for consistency.
- **Corporate Culture**: The prevailing organizational culture can strongly influence the choice. Companies valuing autonomy and employee empowerment may opt for decentralization, while those valuing hierarchy may prefer centralization.
- **Decision Urgency**: The speed at which decisions need to be made plays a role. Time-sensitive decisions often benefit from decentralization, while less urgent ones may be centrally managed.
- **Resource Allocation**: The allocation of resources, including financial and human resources, can impact the decision. Centralization may optimize resource allocation, while decentralization may require additional resources for coordination.
- **Risk Tolerance**: The organization's risk tolerance is a significant factor. Risk-averse companies may prefer centralization for tighter control, while risk-tolerant organizations may embrace decentralization for agility.
- **Regulatory Environment**: Compliance with regulations can influence the decision. Heavily regulated industries may lean towards centralization to ensure adherence to legal standards.

- **Geographical Spread**: Businesses operating in multiple regions may opt for decentralization to account for local variations and needs.
- **Historical Precedent**: Past experiences with decision-making models can sway the choice. Previous successes or failures may influence the preference for one approach over the other.
- **Employee Engagement**: The level of employee engagement and satisfaction is crucial. Decentralization often empowers employees, leading to higher job satisfaction, while centralization may be preferred for consistency.
- **Innovation Focus**: Companies emphasizing innovation may prefer decentralization to foster creative thinking, whereas centralization may prioritize efficiency over innovation.
- **Alignment with Strategy**: The decision-making approach should align with the organization's strategic goals and objectives to ensure consistent progress towards long-term targets.
- **Customer-Centricity**: Companies striving for a customer-centric approach may opt for decentralization to be more responsive to customer feedback and changing needs.
- **Long-Term Sustainability**: Sustainability and adaptability are essential. The chosen approach should be sustainable over the long term and adaptable to changing circumstances
- **Adaptability and Agility**: Rapidly changing markets may necessitate decentralization to respond effectively to emerging trends, while stable markets may favor centralization.
- **Ethical Considerations**: Ethical practices and social responsibility commitments may influence the choice. Companies valuing ethical conduct may prefer centralization to ensure compliance.
- **Feedback Mechanisms**: Establishing feedback mechanisms from employees and stakeholders can aid in decision-making. Regular feedback can help adjust the chosen approach to evolving needs.
- **Resource Availability**: Resource constraints may impact the decision. Organizations with limited resources may opt for centralization to optimize resource allocation.
- **Technology Infrastructure**: The availability and capabilities of technology infrastructure can influence decision-making,

particularly for data-driven processes.

Therefore, striking the right balance between centralized and decentralized decision-making is key, as both approaches offer distinct advantages and drawbacks. Centralization can provide consistency and control, while decentralization empowers innovation and agility. Companies that excel in decision-making recognize the need for flexibility, often adopting a hybrid model that aligns with their unique context and values. Ultimately, the path chosen shapes an organization's identity, impact, and its ability to navigate the complexities of today's business landscape.

Inclusivity vs. Efficiency

> This dilemma revolves around the balance between involving multiple stakeholders and perspectives in the decision-making process (inclusivity) and making decisions quickly and efficiently (efficiency).

Inclusivity in decision-making places a premium on involving diverse voices, both internal and external, in the decision-making process. This approach recognizes that multiple perspectives can lead to more comprehensive problem-solving and better decision outcomes. Inclusive decision-making fosters a sense of ownership and engagement among stakeholders, as they feel valued and heard. Moreover, it often leads to a stronger sense of trust and alignment within the organization and with external partners, as decisions are made collectively.

However, the pursuit of inclusivity can also present challenges. It often involves a more time-consuming decision-making process, as the need for consensus or input from various stakeholders can slow down progress. Moreover, too much inclusivity can lead to decision fatigue, making it challenging to reach a conclusion. Additionally, it may not always be feasible or necessary to involve every stakeholder, particularly in urgent or routine decisions.

On the other hand, Efficiency in decision-making emphasizes quick and streamlined processes. This approach is often necessary when decisions must be made rapidly, such as in response to emergencies or fast-changing market conditions. Efficiency can lead to swift execution, allowing organizations to capitalize on opportunities and respond to challenges promptly. It is particularly valuable in scenarios where time-sensitive decisions are critical.

However, an exclusive focus on efficiency can also have drawbacks. Decisions made in haste may overlook important perspectives, leading to suboptimal outcomes or resistance from stakeholders who feel excluded. Over time, this can erode trust and engagement within the organization, impacting employee morale and teamwork. Moreover, an efficiency-centric approach may hinder innovation and limit the organization's ability to adapt to evolving circumstances.

The impact of this decision-making dilemma extends beyond the speed of decision-making. It touches upon organizational culture, stakeholder engagement, and alignment with strategic objectives. The choice between inclusivity and efficiency should be context-specific, considering factors such as the nature of the decision, its urgency, the organizational culture, and the stakeholders involved. Organizations that excel in decision-making often adopt a flexible approach, striking a balance tailored to the unique needs of each situation. Achieving this equilibrium enables organizations to harness the advantages of inclusivity while maintaining efficiency, ultimately contributing to their resilience and adaptability in today's dynamic business landscape.

Choosing Inclusivity in Decision-Making Only	
Pros	Cons
Diverse perspectives lead to well-rounded decisions.	Slower decision-making process.
Enhanced employee morale and engagement.	Potential for conflicts and disagreements.
Mitigation of risks associated with exclusion.	Resource-intensive, especially for large groups.

Choosing Efficiency in Decision-Making Only	
Pros	Cons
Quick response to urgent situations.	Risk of overlooking critical perspectives.
Streamlined decision-making process.	Potential for alienating stakeholders.

Resource-efficient, saving time and effort.	Reduced buy-in and employee engagement.

Buffer is a social media management platform known for its commitment to transparency and inclusivity in decision-making. The company takes an open and collaborative approach, involving its employees and even customers in various aspects of decision-making. Buffer's emphasis on inclusivity has yielded several positive outcomes. By involving employees in decisions, the company has cultivated a strong sense of ownership and engagement among its workforce. This approach has led to innovations in product development and improved customer service, as employees directly contribute to shaping the company's direction. Furthermore, Buffer's transparency has built trust and loyalty among customers, who appreciate the company's openness regarding pricing and strategy. However, this inclusive approach could also be time-consuming. Decision-making may take longer due to the need to gather input from various stakeholders. Additionally, achieving consensus can be challenging, leading to delays in execution. Moreover, not all decisions require extensive inclusivity, so finding the right balance is crucial to avoid decision fatigue.

On the other hand, Domino's Pizza, a global fast-food chain, is known for its efficiency-driven decision-making. The company has a streamlined approach to menu changes, marketing campaigns, and operations, allowing it to respond swiftly to market demands. Domino's focus on efficiency has enabled rapid responses to changing customer preferences and market dynamics. The company's ability to make quick decisions regarding menu offerings and delivery services has kept it competitive in the fast-food industry. This efficiency has also contributed to cost control, allowing Domino's to offer competitive prices to customers while maintaining profitability. While the efficiency-driven decision-making allows Domino's to move quickly, it may result in missed opportunities for innovation or the potential for overlooking critical customer feedback. Additionally, an overemphasis on efficiency can strain employee morale and creativity, as employees may feel excluded from the decision-making process.

Some questions for the leaders to reflect and answer to resolve the dilemma:

- Whose perspectives are crucial in making decisions? Should it be a select few or a broader range of stakeholders, and why?

- How urgent are the decisions we make? Are there situations where speedy decisions are essential, and are there others were taking more time is acceptable?
- What are the potential consequences of excluding certain voices or perspectives from the decision-making process? What risks does this pose to the organization?
- How do we balance efficiency and inclusivity?
- Do we value collaboration and diverse input, or do we prioritize efficiency and quick action?
- Are there decisions where inclusivity is paramount and others where efficiency takes precedence? Can we adapt to different situations?

There could be several factors that could influence this decision in the context of your organization like:

Decision Complexity: The complexity of the decision can influence the choice. Highly complex decisions may require diverse input for better outcomes.

Time Sensitivity: The urgency of the decision can dictate whether inclusivity or efficiency takes precedence.

Organizational Working Style: The organization's culture, whether it promotes collaboration or efficiency, plays a significant role.

Stakeholder Impact: The potential impact on various stakeholders, including employees, customers, and partners, can shape the decision.

Resource Availability: The availability of resources, including time and manpower, can impact the level of inclusivity in the decision-making process.

Industry Norms: Industry standards and practices can influence the choice, as some sectors prioritize inclusivity more than others..

There are other areas that get impacted because of a choice of this dilemma like-

- Stakeholder engagement and satisfaction
- Decision speed and adaptability
- Organizational culture and collaboration
- Innovation and diversity of thought

Etsy is an organization that skillfully strikes a balance between inclusivity and efficiency in different decision-making scenarios. When it comes to managing the vast number of product listings on its platform, Etsy employs efficiency-driven decision-making. The company uses algorithms and automated processes to ensure product listings meet certain quality standards, such as image quality and accurate descriptions. This approach allows Etsy to efficiently maintain the quality of its marketplace and swiftly address issues. It also allows the company to scale its platform effectively, accommodating a wide range of sellers and products. On the other hand, Etsy places a strong emphasis on inclusivity when engaging with its seller community. The company regularly seeks input from sellers through surveys, forums, and direct communication. This fosters a sense of ownership and partnership. It empowers sellers and provides Etsy with valuable insights into their needs and challenges, which can lead to platform enhancements and improved seller satisfaction. Etsy strikes a balance between inclusivity and efficiency in its sustainability initiatives. While the company sets sustainability goals and strategies at the corporate level, it actively involves employees in implementing eco-friendly practices in their daily work. Etsy also encourages sellers to adopt sustainable packaging practices.

Factors that commonly influence the decision of whether to prioritize Inclusivity or Efficiency in decision-making within the context of running a business include:

- **Decision Complexity**: The complexity of the decision often dictates the level of inclusivity required. Highly intricate decisions may necessitate involving a diverse group of experts and stakeholders to ensure a comprehensive understanding of all facets.
- **Time Sensitivity**: The urgency of the decision plays a pivotal role. Time-sensitive decisions may lean towards efficiency, while those with longer timeframes can afford a more inclusive approach.

- **Organizational Culture**: The prevailing organizational culture significantly influences the choice. Companies that value collaboration, diverse input, and democratic decision-making are more inclined toward inclusivity, while those with a culture emphasizing speed and agility may prioritize efficiency.
- **Stakeholder Impact**: The potential impact of the decision on various stakeholders, including employees, customers, partners, and investors, shapes the approach. Decisions with broad stakeholder implications often require inclusivity to gain consensus and ensure alignment.
- **Resource Availability**: The availability of resources, including time, manpower, and technology, impacts the decision-making process. A resource-constrained environment may push organizations toward more efficient decision-making.
- **Industry Norms**: Industry-specific standards and practices can sway the choice. Some industries, like healthcare or environmental sustainability, may inherently prioritize inclusivity due to the multifaceted nature of their decisions.
- **Regulatory Requirements**: Compliance with regulations can significantly influence the decision-making approach. Highly regulated industries may have mandated inclusivity in decision-making to ensure adherence to legal standards.
- **Risk Tolerance**: The organization's risk tolerance plays a vital role. Risk-averse organizations may favor efficiency to maintain control, while risk-tolerant ones may opt for inclusivity to mitigate risks through comprehensive analysis.
- **Innovation Emphasis**: Companies that prioritize innovation may lean towards inclusivity as it often leads to more creative problem-solving and breakthrough ideas. In contrast, organizations focused on optimization may prioritize efficiency.
- **Organizational Size**: The size of the organization can impact the decision. Larger organizations may find inclusivity more challenging to manage efficiently, while smaller ones may have a more collaborative culture.
- **Leadership Style**: The leadership style within the organization is critical. Leaders who value transparency and participation are more likely to embrace inclusivity, while autocratic leaders may lean towards efficiency.

- **Customer-Centricity**: Organizations committed to a customer-centric approach often value inclusivity to capture diverse customer insights. However, they may prioritize efficiency in certain operational decisions.
- **Nature of the Decision**: The specific nature of the decision, whether strategic, operational, financial, or cultural, can guide the choice. Some decisions may naturally require more inclusivity, while others can benefit from efficiency.
- **Long-Term Impact**: Considering the long-term implications of the decision is crucial. Decisions with enduring consequences may require a more inclusive approach to minimize unforeseen risks.
- **Decision History**: Past experiences with decision-making models can influence the choice. Organizations that have had success with inclusivity or efficiency may lean towards their preferred approach.
- **Geographical Spread**: The geographical dispersion of an organization's operations can influence the approach. Multinational companies may need to adapt their decision-making approach to account for regional variations and needs.
- **Ethical Considerations**: Ethical practices and social responsibility commitments may guide the choice. Organizations emphasizing ethical conduct may prefer inclusivity to ensure fairness and transparency.
- **Feedback Mechanisms**: The presence of robust feedback mechanisms for employees and stakeholders can guide the decision. Regular feedback can help adjust the approach to meet evolving needs and preferences.

Balancing inclusivity and efficiency is a nuanced challenge, and organizations often find that a flexible approach, tailored to the specific context of each decision, yields the best results. Understanding these factors and their interplay is essential for making informed decisions that align with the organization's values, objectives, and the nature of the situation at hand.

Data-Driven vs. Intuitive Decision-making

> This dilemma involves the choice between relying on data, analytics, and quantitative information to make decisions (data-driven) versus trusting instinct, experience, and qualitative judgment (intuitive) or striking a middle ground

Data-driven decision-making is a methodical, analytical approach that relies on empirical evidence, metrics, and quantitative information to guide choices. It's the realm of spreadsheets, algorithms, and predictive models. Organizations embracing this approach invest heavily in data collection, analytics, and technology to ensure that decisions are grounded in factual, measurable insights.

When organizations prioritize data-driven decision-making, several advantages emerge. Decision precision and accuracy tend to improve significantly, as choices are driven by tangible, evidence-based information. Accountability is also enhanced, as decisions can be traced back to specific data sources and analytical processes. Furthermore, efficiency gains are often realized, as data can illuminate inefficiencies and drive optimization efforts.

However, data-driven decision-making is not without its challenges. The sheer volume of data available in today's digital landscape can lead to information overload, making it challenging to discern meaningful insights from the noise. Moreover, this approach may inadvertently stifle creativity and innovation, as it tends to favor solutions rooted in historical data, potentially missing out on novel or unconventional approaches. Finally, data-driven decisions may overlook the intangible aspects of human experience, emotions, and social dynamics, which can be pivotal in certain contexts.

Intuitive decision-making, in contrast, is characterized by the reliance on personal judgment, experience, and instinct. It often entails making choices swiftly, drawing from a reservoir of tacit knowledge and relying on the wisdom of experience rather than quantifiable data.

One of the primary advantages of intuitive decision-making is agility.

Decisions are made quickly, which can be invaluable in rapidly changing environments. This approach can also foster creative problem-solving, encouraging individuals to think outside the box and explore innovative solutions. Furthermore, intuitive decisions often have a human touch, considering emotions and empathy in choices, which can be particularly meaningful in people-centric fields.

However, intuitive decisions come with their own set of challenges. They can be highly subjective and prone to bias, potentially leading to inconsistency or favoritism in decision outcomes. Justifying or explaining these choices can also be challenging, as they often lack a clear data-driven rationale. Moreover, there is a higher risk of error or misjudgment, especially in complex or data-rich contexts.

Choosing Data-Driven Decision-Making Only	
Pros	**Cons**
Objective and fact-based decisions.	Potential for data overload.
Better accountability and traceability.	May miss unconventional or creative solutions.
Enhanced analytical capabilities and insights.	May not account for intangible factors.

Choosing Intuitive Decision-Making Only	
Pros	**Cons**
Speed and agility in decision-making.	Subjective and potentially biased decisions.
Adaptability to unique or novel situations.	Difficulty in justifying or explaining choices.

| Acknowledgment of human experience and expertise. | Higher risk of overlooking data-backed insights. |

Netflix, the global streaming giant, relies heavily on a data-driven approach to shape its content strategy and user experience. By meticulously collecting and analyzing viewer data, the company offers highly personalized content recommendations, enhancing user engagement and satisfaction. This data-driven content strategy has also contributed to Netflix's success in creating original series and films that resonate with audiences. Additionally, data analysis enables Netflix to allocate resources efficiently, investing in content that aligns with viewer preferences. However, the data-driven approach has its downsides, such as content overload, where the sheer volume of options can overwhelm viewers, and a potential risk of content homogeneity, where creativity may take a backseat to data-driven formulas.

On the other hand, SpaceX, the pioneering aerospace manufacturer and space exploration company led by Elon Musk, is characterized by its visionary and intuitive decision-making approach. Musk's instincts and willingness to take calculated risks have resulted in remarkable achievements. His intuitive leadership has driven rapid innovation, exemplified by the successful landing and reuse of rocket boosters, a groundbreaking development in space travel cost-efficiency. Moreover, Musk's intuition has inspired audacious projects like the Starship spacecraft, poised to revolutionize interplanetary travel. SpaceX's intuitive decision-making gives it a competitive edge, securing crucial contracts and partnerships in the aerospace industry. However, this approach comes with higher risks, as evidenced by occasional setbacks and rocket launch failures, and demands substantial resources, potentially straining the company's finances and resources.

Some questions for the leaders to reflect and answer to resolve the dilemma:

- To what extent do we trust our instincts and intuition when making decisions? Are there situations where our gut feeling has proven valuable?
- Can we objectively measure the outcomes of the decisions we make? Are there metrics or data points that we capture from the same?

- How have previous experiences shaped our approach to similar decisions?
- Do we need to strike a balance between data-driven and intuitive decision-making? Are there scenarios where a combination of both approaches might yield better results?
- How are the technology and tools that we are adopting influencing our choices?
- Is our approach to decision-making consistent or do we tend to rely on data in some cases and intuition in others?

There could be several factors that could influence this decision in the context of your organization like:

Data Availability: The presence or absence of relevant data and information significantly influences the decision. Data-driven decisions require access to accurate and timely data.

Decision Complexity: The complexity of the decision often determines whether data-driven or intuitive approaches are more suitable. Highly complex decisions may benefit from data-driven analysis.

Time Constraints: The amount of time available for making the decision plays a crucial role. Data-driven analysis can be time-consuming, while intuitive decisions may be quicker.

Organizational Culture: The prevailing culture within the organization shapes the decision-making approach. Data-driven cultures prioritize evidence-based decisions, while intuitive cultures may value experience and intuition.

Industry Standards: Industry norms and regulations can dictate the level of data-driven decision-making required. Highly regulated industries often lean towards data-driven approaches.

Risk Tolerance: The organization's risk tolerance affects the choice. Risk-averse organizations may prefer data-driven decisions to mitigate uncertainty.

> There are other areas that get impacted because of a choice of this dilemma like:
>
> - Decision accuracy and precision
> - Data infrastructure and analysis capabilities
> - Innovation and adaptability
> - Organizational culture and leadership style

Data-driven and intuitive decision-making can coexist in an organization. This can be achieved by recognizing that each approach has its strengths and weaknesses and applying them appropriately. Data can inform decisions, while intuition can guide strategy and innovation. *For example, Warby Parker, the eyewear innovator, masterfully harmonizes Data-driven and Intuitive decision-making across its diverse business functions. While they trust their instincts for product design, crafting stylish and affordable eyewear through an intuitive lens, their inventory management and digital marketing strategies are firmly grounded in data analytics. By leveraging sales data, customer preferences, and market trends, they ensure efficient inventory management and optimize digital marketing campaigns, enhancing their online presence.*

Warby Parker's balanced approach extends to their pricing strategy, where they integrate data on production costs with their mission of affordability. Moreover, they create an exceptional customer experience in their physical stores, using intuition to design layouts and interactive features that prioritize customer comfort and satisfaction. This equilibrium between data-backed precision and intuition-driven innovation has propelled Warby Parker's success, reinforcing their position as a disruptive force in the eyewear industry.

The factors that commonly influence the decision of whether to adopt a Data-driven or Intuitive decision-making approach in a business context include-

- **Nature of the Decision**: The complexity and nature of the decision often dictate the approach. Decisions involving highly structured data, such as financial forecasting, may lean toward data-driven methods. In contrast, strategic decisions with

uncertain variables may require intuitive judgment.
- **Data Availability and Quality**: The availability and quality of data play a critical role. If reliable data is scarce or unreliable, intuitive decision-making may be the only viable option. Conversely, when robust data sources are accessible, data-driven approaches become more feasible.
- **Time Constraints**: The urgency of the decision influences the choice. In time-sensitive situations, intuitive decisions may be more practical, while data-driven analysis may take too long to yield insights.
- **Risk Tolerance**: Organizations with a higher risk tolerance may be more inclined to embrace intuitive decision-making, as it often involves calculated risks. Data-driven decisions may be preferred in risk-averse environments for their potential to mitigate uncertainty.
- **Decision-Maker Expertise**: The expertise and experience of the decision-maker are crucial. Seasoned leaders may rely on intuition in familiar contexts, while data-driven analysis may empower less experienced decision-makers.
- **Resource Availability**: The availability of resources, including technology and data analytics tools, can influence the choice. Organizations with robust data infrastructure may naturally lean toward data-driven methods.
- **Organizational Culture**: The prevailing culture within an organization can shape the decision-making approach. Data-driven cultures prioritize evidence-based decisions, while intuitive cultures may value experience and instinct.
- **Industry Norms and Regulations**: Industry-specific norms and regulatory requirements may dictate the level of data-driven decision-making required. Highly regulated industries, such as healthcare and finance, often lean toward data-driven approaches for compliance.
- **Stakeholder Expectations**: Stakeholder expectations, including those of customers, investors, and employees, can influence the choice. Some stakeholders may demand data-driven transparency, while others may appreciate intuitive leadership.
- **Past Successes and Failures**: An organization's history of decision-making successes and failures can shape its approach.

Past triumphs with data-driven strategies may reinforce their use, while intuition may be favored when past data-driven decisions have faltered.

- **Balance between Short-Term and Long-Term Goals**: The balance between short-term and long-term objectives is critical. Data-driven approaches may excel in achieving short-term targets, while intuitive strategies may be better suited for long-term vision and innovation.
- **Customer-Centric Focus**: Organizations that prioritize a customer-centric approach may use data-driven insights to understand and meet customer needs. However, they may also employ intuition to anticipate evolving customer preferences and desires.
- **Adaptability and Agility**: The organization's ability to adapt to change and its agility in responding to dynamic environments can influence the choice. Data-driven methods may be slower to adapt, while intuition may foster quicker responses.

The choice between data-driven and intuitive decision-making is not a binary one; it's a spectrum, and organizations often find themselves navigating this spectrum based on the context and nature of the decision at hand. Striking the right balance is the key, leveraging data-driven insights where data is abundant and reliable, while relying on intuition when speed and adaptability are paramount. This nuanced approach allows organizations to harness the advantages of both methods while mitigating their respective drawbacks, ultimately contributing to their resilience and effectiveness in a complex and dynamic business landscape.

Internal Focus
vs
Market-Centric Decision-Making

> This dilemma concerns whether decision-making should prioritize internal organizational strengths, capabilities, and priorities (internal focus) or external market dynamics, customer needs, and competitive forces (market-centric focus) or strike a balance between the two.

When an organization leans toward an internal focus in decision-making, it places a strong emphasis on leveraging its existing strengths and capabilities. This approach can lead to a sense of stability and consistency within the organization. Decisions often align with the organization's established competencies, which can result in streamlined operations and efficient resource allocation. Additionally, internal focus may reinforce a sense of organizational identity and culture, as decisions are rooted in the organization's core strengths.

However, choosing internal focus can also have its downsides. An organization that becomes too internally focused may risk becoming rigid and resistant to change. This rigidity can hinder the organization's ability to adapt to evolving market conditions, customer preferences, and competitive landscapes. Over time, this approach may lead to a disconnect between the organization and its market, potentially resulting in a loss of market relevance and missed growth opportunities.

On the other hand, organizations that prioritize a market-centric decision-making approach direct their focus outward to the dynamic forces of the market. This involves staying attuned to customer needs, market trends, and competitive forces. Market-centric decisions are often driven by the desire to gain a competitive edge, respond rapidly to changing customer preferences, and capitalize on growth opportunities.

A market-centric approach can be highly adaptive and responsive to market dynamics, fostering innovation and the ability to meet evolving customer demands effectively. It can enable organizations to identify and seize market opportunities, potentially leading to a stronger market position and greater profitability. However, it also carries its own set of challenges. Overemphasizing market-centric decision-making can expose the organization to higher levels of risk, as market conditions can be volatile and unpredictable.

Resource allocation can become less efficient if market-centric strategies are not carefully managed. The focus on meeting immediate market demands can sometimes result in inconsistent product or service quality. Balancing short-term market responsiveness with long-term sustainability and maintaining alignment with the organization's core strengths can be a delicate and challenging task.

Choosing Internal Focus Decision-Making Only	
Pros	**Cons**
Internal focus provides stability by relying on existing strengths and capabilities.	Overemphasis on internal focus may lead to rigidity, making it challenging to adapt to market shifts.
It can lead to consistent product or service quality.	The organization may lose touch with evolving customer needs.
Resources are often allocated efficiently, minimizing waste.	It can result in missed growth opportunities or competitive advantages.

Choosing Market-Centric Decision-Making Only	
Pros	**Cons**
Market-centric decisions facilitate quick responses to changing customer preferences.	Over-reliance on market-centric approaches can expose the organization to higher risks and market volatility.

Staying attuned to market dynamics can lead to a competitive advantage.	It may lead to resource inefficiencies if not carefully managed.
It encourages innovation to meet evolving customer demands.	Rapid changes to meet market demands can sometimes result in inconsistent quality.

Imagine a medium-sized factory called Company A that builds machines for other factories. Company A likes to do things the way they always have. This means they focus on what they're good at and don't change much. On the plus side, their machines work well, and customers trust them for making good-quality machines. They also save money by not trying new things and keep making their machines even better. However, the downside is that they don't respond quickly when customers want something new. They might miss opportunities to grow or make more money. They're also a bit scared to take risks, which can hold them back from exploring new markets or ideas. Over time, they might not understand what customers want anymore, which can lead to fewer sales and less growth.

Now, let's talk about a small tech startup called Company B that makes phone apps. Company B is always looking for the next big thing. They move fast and try to keep up with what people want. On the good side, they're quick to change and adapt. They keep making new apps for different needs, which helps them grow and find more customers. They also do better than their competitors because they move fast and stay on top. However, there are some downsides too. To keep up with what people want, they spend a lot of money and time, which can make it harder to make a profit. Their apps might not always work perfectly because they move so quickly, which can make some customers unhappy. Plus, trying to keep up all the time can make employees tired and leave the company.

Some questions for the leaders to reflect and answer to resolve the dilemma:

- Should the organization prioritize internal needs or external market demands when making critical decisions?
- Are we agile and adaptable enough to respond effectively to

shifting market dynamics while leveraging internal strengths?
- Do we truly understand the needs and preferences of our target audience, and are we using this understanding in our decisions?
- Are our decisions effectively harnessing the organization's internal strengths and unique capabilities?
- Should we focus on outperforming competitors or building from internal resources in our decision-making strategy?
- Is it possible to strike a balance between internal and market-centric decision-making, capitalizing on strengths while adapting to market conditions?

There could be several factors that could influence this decision in the context of your organization like:

Market Volatility: The degree of market volatility and unpredictability can push leaders to prioritize a market-centric approach for agility or internal focus for stability.

Customer Insights: Access to comprehensive customer insights and feedback can steer decisions toward a market-centric perspective.

Organizational Culture: The prevailing culture within the organization can influence the decision-making approach, with some cultures favoring internal strengths while others prioritize customer-centricity.

Resource Availability: The availability of resources, including talent and capital, can impact the organization's capacity for market-centric initiatives or internal development.

Competitive Landscape: The intensity of competition and the organization's competitive positioning may dictate whether it should adopt a more market-centric strategy or strengthen internal capabilities.

Long-Term vs. Short-Term Goals: The organization's balance between short-term profitability and long-term sustainability can guide the choice between internal focus and market-centric strategies.

> There are other areas that get impacted because of a choice of this dilemma like:
>
> - Strategic planning and execution
> - Product/service innovation and market positioning
> - Customer satisfaction and loyalty
> - Competitive advantage and adaptability to market changes

Internal focus and market-centric decision-making can coexist through strategic alignment. Organizations can leverage their core competencies while remaining responsive to market changes. This balance involves integrating customer feedback and market insights into internal processes without losing sight of the organization's strengths. *Think of a local bakery in your town as an example. This bakery strikes a balance between focusing on its internal strengths and staying in tune with market demands. They excel at their signature pastries and bread, ensuring customers can always rely on these consistent crowd-pleasers. However, to cater to market trends and seasonal demands, they introduce new pastries and themed treats. They actively engage with the local community through social media and customer feedback, listening to what their customers want and adapting their offerings accordingly. This approach has led to customer loyalty as their quality core products keep regulars coming back, ensuring a steady stream of business. At the same time, by introducing new, market-driven products, they attract new customers and remain relevant even as tastes change. This balance allows them to maintain profitability by minimizing waste and optimizing their core products' production while still exploring new opportunities.*

Factors that commonly influence the decision of whether to adopt an internal focus or market-centric decision-making approach in a business context:

- **Market Volatility**: The degree of market volatility plays a significant role in this decision. In a highly volatile market, a market-centric approach may be favored for its agility in responding to rapid changes. Conversely, in a stable market, an internal focus may suffice to maintain consistency and efficiency.
- **Customer Insights**: Access to comprehensive customer insights

and feedback can steer decisions toward a market-centric perspective. Understanding customer behaviors and preferences is crucial in aligning products and services with market needs.

- **Organizational Culture**: The prevailing culture within the organization can significantly influence the decision-making approach. Organizations with a deeply ingrained internal focus may resist shifting towards a market-centric approach and vice versa.
- **Resource Availability**: The availability of resources, including talent and capital, can significantly impact the organization's capacity for market-centric initiatives or internal development. Limited resources may lead to a more cautious internal focus.
- **Competitive Landscape**: The intensity of competition and the organization's competitive positioning are vital factors. In a highly competitive market, a market-centric strategy may be necessary to stay ahead, whereas in a less competitive sector, internal strengths might suffice.
- **Long-Term vs. Short-Term Goals**: The balance between short-term profitability and long-term sustainability can guide the choice between internal focus and market-centric strategies. Organizations looking for quick returns may prioritize market-centric approaches, while those with a long-term vision may focus internally.
- **Leadership Philosophy**: The leadership's philosophy and decision-makers' inclinations are instrumental. Visionary leaders may lean towards market-centric strategies to pursue innovation and expansion, while more conservative leaders may favor internal stability and efficiency.
- **Market Maturity**: The stage of market maturity also plays a role. In emerging markets, organizations may adopt a market-centric approach to seize growth opportunities, while in mature markets, they may shift towards internal optimization.
- **Regulatory Environment**: Industry-specific regulations and compliance requirements may dictate the degree of market-centricity needed. Highly regulated industries often require careful alignment with market regulations.
- **Customer-Centric Focus**: Organizations that prioritize a customer-centric approach may use data-driven insights to

understand and meet customer needs. However, they may also employ intuition to anticipate evolving customer preferences and desires.

- **Adaptability and Agility**: The organization's ability to adapt to change and its agility in responding to dynamic environments can influence the choice. Data-driven methods may be slower to adapt, while intuition may foster quicker responses.
- **Stakeholder Expectations**: Stakeholder expectations, including those of customers, investors, and employees, can influence the choice. Some stakeholders may demand data-driven transparency, while others may appreciate intuitive leadership.

The choice between internal focus and market-centric decision-making often shapes an organization's strategic direction, impacting its competitive position and ability to adapt to changing market conditions. Leaders must weigh these factors and consider striking a balance that aligns with their organization's goals and capabilities.

Optimization vs. Pursuit of New Opportunities

> It revolves around the balance between allocating resources to optimize existing operations and maintain stability (resource allocation) versus investing in new opportunities with higher growth potential (opportunity pursuit).

Optimization primarily revolves around the allocation of resources, efforts, and focus on improving and refining existing operations. Organizations choosing this path prioritize stability, efficiency, and consolidation. They seek to enhance productivity, reduce costs, and fine-tune their core competencies. This approach can lead to a steady and reliable performance, ensuring that customers receive consistent products or services. However, it may also result in a limited scope for growth and innovation.

Conversely, the Pursuit of new opportunities entails diverting resources and attention towards exploring uncharted territories, innovating, and seizing fresh growth avenues. Organizations following this route often embrace calculated risks, venturing into new markets, introducing novel products or services, or adopting innovative business models. While this approach can lead to exciting prospects for expansion and diversification, it also carries a higher level of uncertainty and resource intensity.

The impact of this dilemma is widespread. In terms of financial stability, organizations leaning towards optimization may experience stable financial performance, lower resource expenditure, and better risk management. Conversely, those embracing new opportunities may face higher financial volatility, substantial resource allocation, and increased risk exposure.

Customer satisfaction is another area affected. Optimization can enhance existing customer relationships by ensuring consistent quality and reliability, fostering loyalty. Pursuing new opportunities, on the other hand, may attract new customers but can sometimes result in lower customer satisfaction due to the experimental nature of new ventures.

Employee morale and innovation are also influenced. Pursuing new opportunities often energizes employees by fostering a culture of innovation and creativity. However, it can also lead to burnout and stress from the demand for rapid adaptation. Optimization, meanwhile, may offer stability but can potentially stifle innovation and discourage talent retention.

Choosing Optimization Only	
Pros	**Cons**
Stability and predictability.	Limited growth potential.
Efficient resource use.	Reduced adaptability to market changes.
Strong focus on core competencies.	Potential stagnation and decreased competitiveness.

Choosing Pursuit Of New Opportunities Only	
Pros	**Cons**
High growth potential.	Higher risk.
Innovation and market expansion.	Resource-intensive.
Attracting new customers and markets.	May divert attention from core operations.

One company that strongly advocates optimization is Ecolab Inc. Ecolab is a global leader in water, hygiene, and energy technologies and services. They focus on optimizing their solutions to help customers reduce water and energy consumption, improve food safety, and minimize environmental impact. This approach has positively impacted the company by not only reducing costs for their clients but also aligning with sustainability goals. Ecolab's optimization efforts have not only made them more efficient but also positioned them as a responsible corporate citizen, attracting environmentally-conscious customers.

On the other hand, a company known for its pursuit of new opportunities is Zoom Video Communications. Zoom became a household name during the COVID-19 pandemic by offering a video conferencing platform that was easy to use and adaptable to various situations. Their pursuit of new opportunities in the form of virtual meetings, webinars, and virtual events skyrocketed their growth. This approach has had a highly positive impact on the company, as it allowed them to capture a massive market share and generate significant revenue. However, it also brought challenges related to security and privacy, which they had to address swiftly to maintain trust among users. Nevertheless, Zoom's agility in pursuing new opportunities allowed them to thrive in a rapidly changing environment.

Some questions for the leaders to reflect and answer to resolve the dilemma:

- Are we more inclined to prioritize stability and optimization or to seek new growth opportunities?
- Do we primarily invest in improving current operations, or are we more open to investing in new ventures?
- Can our organization effectively respond to both optimization and new opportunities without becoming overwhelmed or losing focus?
- Are we comfortable with the potential risks associated with pursuing new opportunities, or do we prefer the security of optimization?
- Are we striking a balance between maintaining short-term stability and pursuing long-term growth, or are we leaning more towards one over the other?
- Is our definition of success primarily based on incremental improvements and stability, or is it tied to growth and innovation?

There could be several factors that could influence this decision in the context of your organization like

Market Conditions: The decision depends on whether the market is stable (favoring optimization) or changing rapidly (favoring new opportunities).

Competitive Landscape: If competitors are innovating, organizations may lean towards new opportunities; if competitors focus on stability, optimization becomes attractive.

Customer Demands: The decision aligns with what customers want, whether it's incremental improvements (optimization) or new solutions (new opportunities).

Financial Health: Organizations with strong finances may explore new opportunities, while those with limited resources often prioritize stability.

Market Research and Data: Access to data guides the decision by revealing market trends and customer behaviors.

Regulatory Environment: Regulations can either support or hinder pursuing new opportunities, depending on the industry's level of regulation

There are other areas that get impacted because of a choice of this dilemma like:

- Financial stability and profitability
- Growth strategy and market expansion
- Risk management and resource efficiency
- Competitive positioning and diversification

Optimization and Pursuit of New Opportunities can coexist within an organization. This requires effective resource allocation and clear prioritization based on the organization's strategic goals and capacity for managing both simultaneously. *One notable example of a company that strikes a balance between optimization and the pursuit of new opportunities is Owlet Baby Care. Owlet is a tech company that specializes in baby monitoring products, particularly the*

Owlet Smart Sock, which tracks a baby's heart rate and oxygen levels. In terms of optimization, Owlet places a strong emphasis on product quality and customer satisfaction. They continually refine their existing products, focusing on making them more accurate, user-friendly, and reliable. This optimization approach has helped them establish a loyal customer base and maintain a strong reputation for safety and reliability in the baby monitoring industry. Simultaneously, Owlet has demonstrated a willingness to pursue new opportunities. For instance, they expanded their product line to include the Owlet Cam, a baby video monitor, and introduced a subscription service that provides parents with additional insights and features. These new opportunities have allowed Owlet to diversify their revenue streams and cater to a broader range of customer needs.

The factors that commonly influence the decision between Optimization and Pursuit of new opportunities in different business scenarios include:

- **Market Maturity and Growth Potential**: The stage of the market can be a deciding factor. In mature markets with limited growth opportunities, organizations often lean towards Optimization to maintain their market share. In contrast, emerging or dynamic markets may encourage Pursuit of New Opportunities to capitalize on growth potential.
- **Competitive Intensity**: The level of competition in the industry plays a pivotal role. In highly competitive markets, organizations may opt for Pursuit of New Opportunities to differentiate themselves and gain a competitive edge. In less competitive environments, Optimization may suffice to maintain a strong position.
- **Customer Expectations**: Understanding and responding to customer demands is crucial. If customers seek innovation and new features, pursuing new opportunities aligns with their expectations. Alternatively, when customers prioritize reliability and consistency, Optimization becomes more relevant.
- **Resource Availability**: The availability of financial, human, and technological resources can influence the decision. Organizations with abundant resources may be more inclined to explore new opportunities, while those with limited resources may opt for Optimization to maximize efficiency.
- **Risk Tolerance**: The organization's risk appetite is a significant

determinant. Organizations comfortable with higher risk may lean towards Pursuit of New Opportunities, while risk-averse organizations may prioritize Optimization to minimize uncertainties.

- **Regulatory Environment**: Industry regulations can impact the decision. Heavily regulated sectors may face barriers to pursuing new opportunities, whereas less regulated industries may find it easier to innovate and expand.
- **Organizational Culture**: The prevailing culture within the organization matters. Organizations fostering a culture of innovation and agility are more likely to embrace Pursuit of New Opportunities, while those with a conservative culture may gravitate towards Optimization.
- **Long-term Strategy**: The organization's long-term strategic goals and vision play a critical role. The decision aligns with whether the organization aims for steady growth and stability (Optimization) or desires to be at the forefront of industry transformation and disruption (Pursuit of New Opportunities).
- **Leadership Vision and Commitment**: The leadership's vision and commitment to innovation versus stability significantly impact the decision. Leaders who champion innovation may drive the organization towards Pursuit of New Opportunities, while conservative leaders may prefer Optimization.
- **Customer Feedback and Market Insights**: Regular feedback from customers and market insights can guide the decision. Customer feedback highlighting changing preferences or unmet needs may signal the need for pursuing new opportunities.
- **Technological Advancements**: Advances in technology can open up new possibilities for innovation. Organizations at the forefront of technology may be more inclined to explore new opportunities enabled by these advancements.
- **Economic Conditions**: Economic factors, such as economic growth, inflation, and interest rates, can influence the decision. In robust economic conditions, organizations may be more confident in pursuing new opportunities, while economic uncertainties may lead to a preference for Optimization.

Ultimately, the choice between Optimization and Pursuit of New Opportunities hinges on the organization's goals, risk appetite, and its

HOPE IS NOT A STRATEGY

capacity to manage both paths simultaneously. Striking a balance between stability and innovation is a perpetual challenge, and the right equilibrium varies from one organization to another and may shift over time. In this complex decision, organizations must carefully assess their circumstances, industry dynamics, and long-term objectives to ensure sustained growth and success.

| 3.6 |

COLLABORATION DILEMMAS

How will you use this chapter of the book?

If you are the founder or the CEO of a company and if you and your leadership team have a clear point of view (PoV) on the following questions and all of you are ALIGNED, then you can choose to move to the next chapter of the book. However, if you see a dissonance or have conflicting views, then we suggest digging deeper, going through this chapter and reflecting on different angles we bring in there.

Here are the questions for you to discuss and ponder-

- How do we balance top-down efficiency with empowering employees through collaborative decision-making and fostering innovation?
- Should we prioritize task completion or team relationship-building in our collaboration efforts, and how can we achieve both?
- What level of formalization is needed for efficient collaboration, and where can we incorporate informality to enhance creativity?
- How can we encourage cross-functional collaboration without introducing bureaucracy and inefficiency?
- How should we balance proactive issue anticipation and reactive problem-solving in collaboration for effective risk management and resource allocation?
- What strategies promote ownership and accountability among all employees in collaborative efforts, regardless of decision-making structure?
- How can we ensure inclusive decision-making, especially in top-down structures, to value diverse perspectives?
- What mechanisms foster bottom-up innovation while aligning innovative ideas with organizational goals?

> - How do we balance structured and informal communication channels to facilitate open dialogue and idea sharing among team members?
> - How can we ensure all collaboration efforts align with our strategic objectives for long-term organizational success?

In the realm of business, collaboration is the cornerstone of innovation and progress. Yet, the road to effective collaboration is often marked by a series of dilemmas that leaders must navigate. These dilemmas, ranging from top-down vs. bottom-up approaches to structured vs. informal processes, significantly influence how organizations work together. In this chapter, we delve into these collaboration dilemmas, exploring the essential aspects leaders need to consider when defining how collaboration takes shape within their organizations. By addressing these dilemmas thoughtfully, leaders can cultivate a collaborative environment that fosters creativity, efficiency, and sustainable growth for their businesses.

When leaders are determining the way collaboration will be done in their organization, they should consider a wide range of aspects to ensure that the chosen approach aligns with the company's goals, values, and culture. Here are key aspects to take into account:

- **Organizational Goals and Strategy**: Ensure that collaboration aligns with the overall strategic objectives of the organization and contributes to achieving long-term goals.
- **Company Culture**: Consider how the chosen collaboration approach fits with the existing culture and values of the organization. Will it reinforce or require cultural changes?
- **Leadership Style**: Reflect on the leadership style within the organization and how it influences decision-making and collaboration. Leaders should set an example for the desired collaboration style.
- **Clear Objectives**: Define clear and specific objectives for collaboration efforts, ensuring that all stakeholders understand what is expected and why it matters.
- **Decision-Making Structure**: Determine whether a top-down, bottom-up, or hybrid approach to decision-making is most appropriate for various situations and initiatives.

- **Communication Channels**: Identify the most effective communication channels for collaboration, including both formal and informal methods, and ensure they are accessible to all team members.
- **Team Composition**: Consider how teams are structured and composed. Cross-functional teams can enhance collaboration by bringing diverse perspectives.
- : Evaluate the technology and tools available for collaboration **Technology and Tools**, ensuring they support efficient communication, information sharing, and project management.
- **Inclusivity and Diversity**: Promote inclusivity and diversity in collaborative efforts to harness a wide range of perspectives and experiences.
- **Ownership and Accountability**: Clearly define roles and responsibilities to establish ownership and accountability for collaborative initiatives.
- **Feedback Mechanisms**: Establish feedback loops that encourage continuous improvement and allow employees to voice their opinions and concerns.
- **Resource Allocation**: Allocate resources, including time, budget, and personnel, to support collaborative projects effectively.
- **Training and Development**: Provide training and development opportunities to enhance employees' collaboration skills and ensure they are aligned with the chosen approach.
- **Risk Management**: Consider the potential risks and challenges associated with collaboration efforts and develop strategies to mitigate them.
- **Measuring Success**: Define key performance indicators (KPIs) and metrics to measure the success and impact of collaboration efforts.
- **Adaptability**: Recognize that the chosen collaboration approach may need to evolve over time to adapt to changing business environments and needs.
- **Customer and Stakeholder Expectations**: Take into account the expectations of customers, clients, partners, and other stakeholders who may be affected by collaboration efforts.
- Legal and Compliance **Considerations**: Ensure that collaboration efforts comply with relevant laws, regulations, and

industry standards.
- **Budget and Resources**: Assess the financial implications of collaboration initiatives and allocate a budget accordingly.
- **Competitive Landscape**: Consider how collaboration can provide a competitive advantage and differentiate the organization in the market.

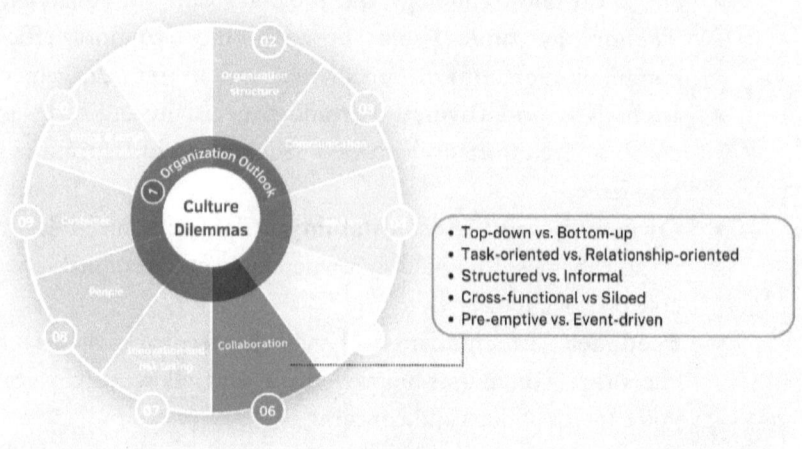

While there are many dilemmas when we think of collaboration, we will focus on five pivotal ones that often take center stage:

- **Top-down vs. Bottom-up**
- **Task-oriented vs. Relationship oriented**
- **Structured vs. Informal**
- **Cross-functional vs. Siloed**
- **Pre-emptive vs. Event-driven**

Let's look at each of them in greater detail.

Top-Down vs. Bottom-Up Collaboration

> This dilemma is all about balancing the decision-making structure within collaboration efforts, choosing between a traditional hierarchical approach with clear authority levels (top-down) or a flatter structure with more shared decision-making and input from employees at all levels (bottom-up).

Opting for a top-down collaboration approach typically means that decisions are made by a select group of individuals or a single authority figure within the organization. This model is often associated with efficiency and streamlined processes. With clear lines of authority, it can lead to quicker decision-making and the ability to maintain consistency in operations. However, this efficiency can come at a cost. In a top-down structure, there is often limited room for employee input, and innovation may be stifled as decisions tend to follow established patterns. Over time, this can lead to employee disengagement, as they may feel detached from the decision-making process and undervalued in their roles.

On the flip side, adopting a bottom-up collaboration approach encourages input and decision-making from employees at various levels within the organization. This approach taps into the diverse perspectives, experiences, and ideas that employees bring to the table. It fosters a sense of empowerment and ownership among employees, which can result in higher engagement and a stronger commitment to the organization's goals. Additionally, it often leads to greater innovation as creative ideas and solutions emerge from different corners of the organization. However, this approach can also have drawbacks. Decision-making processes may become slower and more complex, as consensus-building and coordination take time. There is a risk of misalignment with the organization's strategic objectives, as decisions may be made with a narrower focus on individual or departmental priorities.

Choosing Top-Down Collaboration Only	
Pros	**Cons**
Clear Decision Authority	Limited Innovation
Streamlined Processes	Employee Disengagement
Consistency	Potential Resistance
Efficient Execution	Lack of Diverse Input

Choosing Bottom-Up Collaboration Only	
Pros	**Cons**
Diverse Perspectives	Slower Decision-Making
Employee Empowerment	Potential Lack of Alignment
Innovation	Complexity in Coordination
Higher Engagement	Inefficiency in Certain Processes

One example of a company that advocates top-down collaboration is SpaceX, the aerospace manufacturer and space transportation company founded by Elon Musk. SpaceX operates in a highly regulated and technically complex industry where precise coordination and adherence to safety standards are paramount. The top-down collaboration approach, with Elon Musk at the helm providing strategic direction and making key decisions, has enabled SpaceX to maintain a remarkable record of success in launching rockets and achieving ambitious goals in space exploration. However, this top-down approach also means that employees may have limited involvement in high-level strategic decisions, which can potentially stifle innovation or creativity at the lower levels of the organization.

Conversely, Semco Partners, a Brazilian conglomerate, is an example of a company that embraces bottom-up collaboration. Under the leadership of Ricardo Semler, Semco has decentralized decision-making and empowered employees to have a say in company matters. This approach has led to greater employee engagement, job satisfaction, and a culture of trust. Employees at Semco have the freedom to set their own work hours, choose their salaries, and even participate in the hiring process. This bottom-up approach has positively impacted the company by fostering a culture of innovation and adaptability. However, it also presents challenges in terms of maintaining clear strategic alignment and ensuring consistent decision-making across diverse business units. Nevertheless, Semco's bottom-up collaboration model has been celebrated for its success in creating a more democratic and innovative workplace.

Some questions for the leaders to reflect and answer to resolve the dilemma:

- How comfortable are we with employees at various levels having a say in decisions that directly impact their work, and how much influence should they have?
- Are we prioritizing efficiency and consistency in our processes, or are we open to embracing innovation that might come from diverse perspectives in a more bottom-up approach?
- What message does our decision-making structure send to employees about their role and value in the organization, and how does this align with our culture and values?
- How do we ensure accountability for decisions made in both top-down and bottom-up collaboration, and how can we balance this effectively?
- Are we prepared to manage potential resistance to change if we shift towards a more bottom-up approach, and how can we address it constructively?
- How do we maintain alignment with our strategic goals and objectives in a bottom-up collaboration model while still encouraging employee input?

There could be several factors that could influence this decision in the context of your organization like:

Industry and Market Dynamics: The competitive landscape and market volatility may affect the need for agility and innovation, influencing the collaboration approach.

Employee Skillsets: The skills and competencies of employees can determine their readiness for decision-making involvement.

Decision Complexity: Complex decisions may require more centralized control, while simpler ones could benefit from a bottom-up approach.

Innovation Goals: The organization's emphasis on innovation can push it toward a more bottom-up approach to tap into creative ideas.

Change Management Capabilities: Strong change management abilities can help address resistance when shifting to a more collaborative model.

Risk Tolerance: Tolerance for risk can influence the degree of empowerment given to employees in decision-making.

There are other areas that get impacted because of a choice of this dilemma like-

- Empowerment in decision-making and ownership
- Innovation
- Decision Speed
- Inclusivity
- Alignment

The choice between top-down and bottom-up collaboration isn't necessarily an all-or-nothing decision. Many organizations find value in striking a balance, adopting a hybrid approach. In this model, some decisions are made top-down for the sake of efficiency and strategic alignment, while others involve input from employees to encourage innovation and engagement. *One organization that effectively strikes a balance between top-down and bottom-up collaboration in various scenarios is W.L. Gore & Associates, a multinational manufacturing company known for its innovative products, including Gore-Tex fabric. In the context of innovation, Gore encourages bottom-up collaboration through a unique approach to idea generation and project development.*

Employees have the freedom to work on projects of their choice, and innovative ideas can come from any level within the company. This bottom-up approach has been instrumental in driving product development and fostering a culture of creativity and ownership. On the other hand, in matters related to organizational strategy and long-term vision, W.L. Gore & Associates employs a top-down collaboration approach. Senior leaders provide clear direction and make strategic decisions to ensure alignment with the company's overall goals and objectives. This top-down guidance helps maintain a cohesive organizational structure and ensures that individual efforts contribute to the company's strategic priorities.

The decision of whether to adopt a top-down or bottom-up collaboration approach in running a business is multifaceted and influenced by a range of factors. While each organization's circumstances may vary, there are common factors that often play a pivotal role in shaping this decision:

- **Organizational Culture**: The existing culture within the organization is a crucial factor. If the culture is traditionally hierarchical and values top-down decision-making, it may require significant cultural shifts to embrace bottom-up collaboration, and vice versa.
- **Leadership Style**: The leadership style of top executives and senior managers is a key determinant. Leaders who are open to employee involvement and empowerment are more likely to favor a bottom-up approach, while those who prefer control may opt for a top-down model.
- **Industry and Market Dynamics**: The competitive landscape and market conditions in the industry can influence the choice. Fast-changing industries with a need for rapid innovation may lean towards bottom-up collaboration, while more stable industries may favor top-down structures for efficiency.
- **Decision Complexity**: The complexity of decisions is a critical consideration. Complex, high-stakes decisions may require centralized control for consistency and alignment with the organization's strategy, whereas simpler decisions can benefit from employee input.
- **Employee Skillsets**: The skills and competencies of the workforce play a role. Organizations with highly skilled and

knowledgeable employees may be more inclined to seek their input, especially in areas where employees possess expertise.

- **Employee Engagement**: The level of employee engagement within the organization is a significant factor. Engaged employees are more likely to contribute meaningfully to collaborative efforts, making bottom-up collaboration more feasible.
- **Innovation Goals**: If the organization prioritizes innovation, it may opt for a bottom-up approach to tap into diverse ideas and creative solutions that emerge from all levels of the workforce.
- **Change Management Capabilities**: The organization's ability to manage change effectively is essential. Shifting from a top-down to a bottom-up model, or vice versa, often requires change management efforts to address potential resistance and ensure a smooth transition.
- **Organizational Structure**: The existing organizational structure can either enable or hinder the implementation of certain collaboration models. Flat, decentralized structures may naturally align with bottom-up collaboration, while highly hierarchical structures may favor a top-down approach.
- **Risk Tolerance**: The organization's tolerance for risk and its willingness to experiment can influence the decision. Bottom-up collaboration may involve more experimentation and risk-taking, while top-down approaches may focus on risk mitigation.
- **Resource Availability**: The availability of resources, including time and budget, can affect the decision. Bottom-up collaboration may require additional resources for communication, training, and coordination.
- **Regulatory and Compliance Requirements**: In heavily regulated industries, compliance with external regulations may necessitate a top-down approach to ensure consistency and adherence to legal requirements.
- **Strategic Goals**: The organization's strategic goals and long-term vision can guide the choice of collaboration approach. The selected approach should align with these overarching objectives.

Ultimately, the decision between top-down and bottom-up collaboration profoundly influences an organization's culture, its ability to innovate, the speed of decision-making, and the level of employee engagement. Leaders must carefully weigh these factors and consider the unique needs and goals of their organization when choosing the collaboration approach that best aligns with their vision for success.

Task-Oriented vs. Relationship-Oriented Collaboration

> Deciding whether collaboration should primarily focus on completing tasks efficiently (task-oriented) or on building strong relationships, trust, and consensus among team members (relationship-oriented) or striking a balance between the two.

When organizations emphasize task-oriented collaboration, their primary focus is on efficiently completing tasks, projects, and objectives. This approach is characterized by clear goals, timelines, and a structured workflow that seeks to maximize productivity and meet targets. Task-oriented collaboration can be particularly effective in industries with tight deadlines and where precision and efficiency are paramount, such as manufacturing or project management. However, this approach can have its drawbacks. A singular focus on tasks may lead to strained relationships among team members, reduced employee morale, and hindered innovation. Over time, it can create a workplace culture that prioritizes task completion over the well-being of the individuals performing those tasks, potentially impacting retention and overall job satisfaction.

Conversely, relationship-oriented collaboration prioritizes building strong bonds among team members, fostering trust, and consensus-building. In this approach, teams invest time and effort in developing personal relationships, valuing open communication, and encouraging collaboration through consensus and shared decision-making. Relationship-oriented collaboration can lead to enhanced team cohesion, a supportive work environment, and improved conflict resolution capabilities. It can be especially beneficial in creative industries, where innovation and the exchange of ideas are critical. However, this approach may also have its challenges. The emphasis on relationships and consensus-building can sometimes slow down task completion and decision-making, making it less suitable for industries where agility and rapid execution are vital.

Choosing Task-Oriented Collaboration Only	
Pros	**Cons**
Efficient Task Completion	Limited Relationship Building
Clear Focus on Goals	Potential for Low Morale
Streamlined Processes	Challenges in Conflict Resolution
Accountability	May Negatively Affect Employee Satisfaction

Choosing Relationship-Oriented Collaboration Only	
Pros	**Cons**
Strong Trust and Team Cohesion	May slow down Task Completion
Enhanced Innovation	Resource-Intensive
Positive Workplace Culture	Potential for Task Neglect
Effective Conflict Resolution	Difficulties in Measuring Impact on Outcomes

One notable example of a company that advocates task-oriented collaboration is FedEx, a global courier delivery services company. FedEx operates in a highly competitive and time-sensitive industry where efficiency and precision are paramount. The company's success is built on a task-oriented approach that emphasizes streamlined processes, on-time deliveries, and a rigorous focus on meeting customer demands. This approach has allowed FedEx to consistently deliver packages with speed and reliability. However, it can also have its challenges, such as high-pressure work environments and potential employee burnout due to the relentless emphasis on task completion, which may affect employee satisfaction and retention.

HOPE IS NOT A STRATEGY

Conversely, Zappos, an online shoe and clothing retailer, is an example of a company that prioritizes relationship-oriented collaboration. Zappos places a strong emphasis on creating a positive and inclusive workplace culture, fostering trust and camaraderie among employees. The company's core values prioritize employee happiness and engagement, which extends to how it interacts with customers. Zappos is known for its exceptional customer service, which is built on strong employee-customer relationships. While this approach positively impacts employee satisfaction, customer loyalty, and innovation, it may require more resources and time investment in building and maintaining relationships, potentially affecting operational efficiency compared to task-oriented models.

Some questions for the leaders to reflect and answer to resolve the dilemma:

- How do we balance the need to efficiently complete tasks with the importance of building strong relationships among team members?
- What role do relationships and trust play in achieving our long-term organizational goals, and how can task efficiency complement this?
- How do team dynamics change when we emphasize task completion over relationship-building, and what impact does this have on collaboration?
- How does our chosen collaboration focus affect employee satisfaction, and how does satisfaction influence productivity and innovation?
- How do task-oriented and relationship-oriented approaches impact our ability to resolve conflicts within teams, and how does this affect team morale?
- What role do strong internal relationships play in building and maintaining positive customer relationships, and how does this influence business success?

There could be several factors that could influence this decision in the context of your organization like:

Leadership Style: The leadership style of top executives and managers often sets the tone for collaboration priorities.

Industry and Market Dynamics: Industry norms and market conditions may require a focus on task efficiency or relationship-building.

Project Complexity: The complexity of projects and tasks can determine whether a task-oriented or relationship-oriented approach is more appropriate.

Employee Skill sets: The skills and interpersonal abilities of employees may favor one approach over the other.

Customer Expectations: Customer expectations and demands can also influence the collaboration approach, as strong relationships may be critical for customer retention.

There are other areas that get impacted because of a choice of this dilemma like:

- Project Delivery
- Team Cohesion
- Employee Satisfaction
- Customer Relationships
- Innovation

Task-oriented and relationship-oriented collaboration can coexist by finding a balance where each approach complements the other. For instance, task-oriented collaboration can drive efficiency in routine tasks, while relationship-oriented collaboration can be prioritized in team-building, innovation, and conflict resolution efforts. *An organization that effectively strikes a balance between task-oriented and relationship-oriented collaboration in various scenarios is REI (Recreational Equipment, Inc.), an American retail and outdoor recreation services corporation. REI operates in the retail industry while maintaining a strong commitment to environmental stewardship and promoting outdoor activities. In their retail operations, they often emphasize task-oriented collaboration, ensuring efficient inventory management, supply chain logistics, and customer service to meet customer demands effectively. However, where REI truly shines in striking a balance is through its commitment to building relationships with both employees and customers. They foster a positive workplace culture that encourages employees to share their passion for outdoor activities, creating strong relationships within the company. Additionally, REI maintains close relationships with customers through its outdoor programs, events, and initiatives that promote outdoor exploration, reflecting a relationship-oriented approach. By blending task-oriented efficiency with relationship-oriented community building, REI has successfully cultivated brand loyalty, employee engagement, and a thriving outdoor enthusiast community.*

The decision between task-oriented and relationship-oriented collaboration is multifaceted and influenced by several common factors that cut across various scenarios within an organization-

- **Organizational Culture**: The prevailing culture within the organization plays a pivotal role. Companies with a strong culture of collaboration and interpersonal relationships may naturally lean toward relationship-oriented collaboration, while those with a results-driven or performance-oriented culture may emphasize task-oriented collaboration
- **Leadership Style**: The leadership style of senior executives and managers significantly influences the collaboration approach. Leaders who prioritize relationships and consensus-building tend to foster relationship-oriented collaboration, while those who focus on efficiency and productivity may favor a task-oriented approach.
- **Industry and Market Dynamics**: The nature of the industry and market conditions can dictate the collaboration approach. In highly competitive and fast-paced industries, task-oriented collaboration may be essential to meet tight deadlines and maintain a competitive edge. Conversely, industries where innovation and creativity are paramount may lean more towards relationship-oriented collaboration.
- **Project Complexity**: The complexity of projects and tasks plays a crucial role in determining the collaboration approach. Complex, multifaceted projects often require a balance between task-oriented and relationship-oriented collaboration to ensure both efficiency and effective coordination among team members.
- **Employee Skillsets**: The skills and competencies of the

workforce also influence the choice. Highly skilled and motivated employees may be more inclined to engage in relationship-oriented collaboration, as they can handle the intricacies of task completion while building strong interpersonal connections.

- **Customer Expectations**: Customer expectations and demands can sway the collaboration approach. In industries where strong customer relationships are essential, relationship-oriented collaboration may take precedence to enhance customer satisfaction and loyalty.
- **Resource Constraints**: Resource availability, including time, budget, and personnel, can impact the decision. Limited resources may lead organizations to prioritize task-oriented collaboration to maximize efficiency, while ample resources may allow for a more balanced approach
- **Risk Tolerance**: An organization's tolerance for risk also plays a role. Task-oriented collaboration may be favored in risk-averse environments, where precision and predictability are essential. In contrast, organizations with a higher risk tolerance may be more open to relationship-oriented collaboration, which can involve more experimentation and adaptability.
- **Project Urgency**: The urgency of projects and tasks can dictate the collaboration approach. Time-sensitive projects may necessitate a task-oriented focus to meet deadlines, while long-term initiatives may allow for a more relationship-oriented approach.
- **Organizational Values**: The values and principles upheld by the organization influence the collaboration approach. Organizations that prioritize employee well-being, trust, and inclusivity may gravitate towards relationship-oriented collaboration to align with their core values.
- **Team Dynamics**: The dynamics within teams and departments can impact the choice. High-performing teams may be more inclined to adopt a task-oriented approach, while teams that require cohesion and improved collaboration may benefit from a relationship-oriented strategy.

The key to navigating the task-oriented versus relationship-oriented collaboration dilemma lies in achieving a balance that aligns with the organization's goals and industry demands. Striking this equilibrium allows organizations to harness the benefits of both approaches. For instance, task-oriented collaboration can ensure that projects are completed efficiently, while relationship-oriented collaboration can create a positive workplace culture that fosters innovation, engagement, and employee satisfaction. The ideal mix varies depending on the nature of the work, industry requirements, and the organization's values. Therefore, leaders must carefully assess their organization's unique needs and objectives to determine the most appropriate blend of task-oriented and relationship-oriented collaboration, recognizing that a one-size-fits-all approach may not be suitable for every scenario.

Structured vs. Informal Collaboration

> Deciding whether collaboration processes should follow formalized, structured processes or allow for more spontaneous and informal interactions or figure a balance between the two.

Structured collaboration relies on well-defined processes, clear guidelines, and established workflows. It offers a systematic approach that enhances predictability and accountability. Organizations that prioritize structured collaboration benefit from efficient execution of routine tasks, consistent quality standards, and a clear audit trail for decision-making. Structured processes are often essential in industries with strict regulatory requirements, such as finance or healthcare, where compliance and risk mitigation are paramount. However, this approach can have downsides. Excessive structure may lead to bureaucracy, slowing decision-making, stifling innovation, and limiting employee autonomy. It can create a rigid environment that discourages creative thinking and adaptability.

In contrast, informal collaboration fosters spontaneity, encourages creativity, and places a premium on building strong relationships among team members. It values open communication, flexibility, and the free exchange of ideas. Organizations that emphasize informal collaboration often see benefits such as enhanced innovation, improved team morale, and rapid adaptation to change. This approach can be particularly effective in creative industries, research and development, or startups, where ideation and experimentation are central. However, informal collaboration also presents challenges. Without structure, there may be a lack of clear accountability, leading to potential inefficiencies and miscommunication. Decision-making can become less transparent, and there may be difficulties in measuring the impact of efforts.

Choosing Structured Collaboration Only	
Pros	**Cons**
Clear Processes	Potential for Bureaucracy
Accountability	Inhibits Spontaneity
Compliance	Innovation May Suffer
Efficiency in Repetitive Tasks	Reduced Autonomy

Choosing Informal Collaboration Only	
Pros	**Cons**
Encourages Creativity	Lack of Accountability
Promotes Innovation	Potential for Disorganization
Builds Strong Relationships	Inefficiency in Complex Tasks
Fosters Employee Autonomy	May Lead to Information Gaps

Siemens Healthineers, a global leader in medical technology, is an example of a company that places a strong emphasis on structured collaboration. Given its involvement in the healthcare industry, Siemens Healthineers operates within a highly regulated and quality-focused environment. Their commitment to structured collaboration is evident in the precision and compliance with which they design, manufacture, and deliver medical devices and solutions. This approach positively impacts the company by ensuring the safety and reliability of their products, adhering to strict regulatory standards, and maintaining a strong reputation for quality and consistency. However, the downside can be a potential slowdown in decision-making processes and a need for extensive documentation, which may hinder agility and innovation in rapidly evolving healthcare markets.

Etsy, an e-commerce platform focused on handmade and vintage goods, exemplifies a company that leans toward informal collaboration. Etsy's success is closely tied to its creative and diverse community of sellers and buyers. The company values open communication, creativity, and innovation, fostering an environment where employees are encouraged to think outside the box. This informal collaboration approach positively impacts Etsy by driving continuous innovation, supporting a thriving creative marketplace, and maintaining a strong sense of community among its users. However, it may pose challenges in terms of scalability, consistent quality control, and potential risks associated with informal processes, such as disputes among sellers or intellectual property concerns. Nonetheless, Etsy's informal collaboration model has contributed significantly to its unique brand identity and competitive advantage in the e-commerce industry.

Some questions for the leaders to reflect and answer to resolve the dilemma:

- How do structured collaboration processes impact our efficiency, and does this efficiency come at the cost of spontaneity and creativity?
- Can formalized processes stifle innovation, and how can we ensure that innovation thrives even within structured collaboration?
- How does our choice between structured and informal collaboration affect employee autonomy and decision-making freedom?
- Do structured processes hinder open communication, and how can we ensure that important information flows seamlessly in an informal setting?
- How does each collaboration style adapt to changes in the business environment, and how can we remain agile while being structured or informal?
- How does the chosen approach impact employee engagement and satisfaction, and how does this influence overall productivity?

There could be several factors that could influence this decision in the context of your organization like:

> **Nature of Projects**: The nature of the projects or tasks being undertaken may require a particular collaboration style. Complex, high-stakes projects may lean towards structured processes, while creative endeavors may prefer informality.
>
> **Industry Regulations**: In regulated industries, adherence to formal processes may be necessary to ensure compliance.
>
> **Resource Availability**: Resource constraints, including time and budget, can impact the decision. Structured processes may require more resource allocation.
>
> **Leadership Style**: The leadership style and preferences of top executives often play a role in the chosen collaboration approach.
>
> **Employee Skillsets**: The skills and abilities of employees may favor one approach over the other, depending on the need for structure or creative freedom.
>
> **There are other areas that get impacted because of a choice of this dilemma like:**
>
> - Workflow Efficiency
> - Creativity & innovation
> - Adaptability, agility
> - Employee Engagement
> - Communication

Structured and informal collaboration can coexist through a hybrid approach. Structured processes can be used for routine tasks and projects requiring precision, while informal interactions can be encouraged for brainstorming, idea generation, and team building. *Buffer is known for its innovative social media management tools and its commitment to creating a positive workplace culture. In this organization, a dynamic approach to collaboration is vital. When it comes to product development and customer support, Buffer implements structured collaboration. They have well-defined processes for product feature planning, development sprints, and customer support ticket management. This structure ensures that their tools are reliable, customer queries are addressed promptly, and the quality of their product remains consistent.* However, *Buffer also places a strong emphasis on informal collaboration, particularly in the areas of team communication, feedback, and ideation. They foster open and transparent communication channels among team members and encourage employees to share ideas freely. The company's commitment to asynchronous communication allows employees to work at their own pace while maintaining effective collaboration. This informal approach positively impacts Buffer by promoting innovation, building strong relationships within remote teams, and creating a work environment where employees feel valued and empowered.*

When deciding between structured and informal collaboration, organizations consider a range of factors that influence their choice. These common factors cut across various scenarios and play a crucial role in determining the appropriate approach:

- **Organizational Culture**: The existing culture within the organization is a primary factor. Companies with a culture that values formal processes and procedures are more likely to lean towards structured collaboration, while those with a culture that encourages creativity, autonomy, and open communication may favor informality.
- **Nature of Projects**: The type of projects or tasks being undertaken significantly impacts the collaboration approach. Complex, high-stakes projects that require precision and adherence to regulations may necessitate structured collaboration. Conversely, creative endeavors, brainstorming, and innovation-focused projects may thrive in an informal environment.
- **Industry Regulations**: In regulated industries like finance, healthcare, or pharmaceuticals, adherence to formalized processes is often a legal requirement to ensure compliance and minimize risk. This can heavily influence the choice of structured collaboration.
- **Resource Availability**: The availability of resources, including time and budget, can be a determining factor. Structured processes may require more resource allocation in terms of planning, documentation, and training.
- **Leadership Style**: The leadership style of top executives and managers plays a significant role. Leaders who prioritize structure,

control, and adherence to guidelines are more inclined towards structured collaboration, while those who value empowerment, innovation, and employee autonomy may favor informality.

- **Employee Skillsets**: The skills, competencies, and preferences of the workforce influence the collaboration approach. Highly skilled and self-motivated employees may thrive in an informal environment, while those who require clear guidance may perform better in structured processes.
- **Customer Expectations**: Customer expectations and demands can sway the collaboration approach. Some customers may require a structured approach to ensure consistency and reliability, while others may appreciate a more informal, flexible, and personalized experience.
- **Project Urgency**: The urgency of projects and tasks can dictate the collaboration approach. Time-sensitive projects may necessitate structured processes to meet tight deadlines, while long-term initiatives may allow for a more informal and exploratory approach.
- **Organizational Values**: The values and principles upheld by the organization influence the collaboration approach. Organizations that prioritize transparency, trust, and open communication may lean towards informality, while those that emphasize stability and predictability may prefer structure.
- **Team Dynamics**: The dynamics within teams and departments can impact the choice. High-performing teams may be more inclined to adopt a structured approach, while teams that require cohesion, creativity, and relationship-building may benefit from informality.

The key to navigating the structured versus informal collaboration dilemma lies in finding a balance that aligns with an organization's goals, industry requirements, and cultural values. Many successful organizations recognize the value of both approaches. They use structured collaboration for tasks that require precision, compliance, and efficiency, while reserving informal collaboration for creative brainstorming, innovation, and relationship-building. This hybrid model ensures that organizations can benefit from the best of both worlds, maintaining efficiency and structure where necessary while fostering an environment that encourages creativity, adaptability, and strong relationships. Leaders must carefully assess their organization's unique needs and objectives to strike this balance, recognizing that it may vary depending on the nature of tasks and projects undertaken within the organization.

Cross-Functional vs. Siloed Collaboration

> Deciding whether collaboration efforts should encourage cooperation and communication among different departments and teams (cross-functional) or allow teams to work independently within their own silos (siloed) or strike a balance between the two.

Cross-Functional Collaboration involves breaking down departmental barriers and forming teams that include members from different functional areas. This approach aims to leverage diverse expertise and perspectives to address complex challenges and foster innovation. In such teams, individuals bring their unique skills to the table, leading to comprehensive problem-solving. For instance, in a cross-functional team for product development, engineers, marketers, and designers collaborate to ensure a product not only meets technical specifications but also aligns with customer needs and market trends. While cross-functional collaboration can be highly effective in promoting innovation and holistic problem-solving, it comes with its own set of challenges. Decision-making can become more complex, as multiple perspectives must be considered, potentially slowing down the process. Additionally, establishing effective communication channels and overcoming departmental silos can be challenging.

Siloed Collaboration, on the other hand, involves organizing teams and departments based on functional specialization. Each department operates independently, focusing on its specific tasks and objectives. This approach can lead to streamlined processes and clear lines of accountability. For example, in a manufacturing company, siloed departments for production, quality control, and logistics may operate with well-defined roles and responsibilities, ensuring efficiency in their respective areas. However, siloed collaboration can also have drawbacks. It may hinder innovation and holistic problem-solving, as teams may lack exposure to different perspectives. Communication barriers can emerge between departments, leading to information silos and delayed decision-making. Moreover, employees may become narrowly focused on their department's goals, potentially overlooking opportunities for improvement or collaboration.

Choosing Cross-Functional Collaboration Only	
Pros	**Cons**
Diverse Perspectives	Complex Decision-Making
Enhanced Innovation	Potential for Bureaucracy
Efficient Resource Utilization	Resistance to Change
Improved Communication	Resource Allocation Challenges

Choosing Siloed Collaboration Only	
Pros	**Cons**
Specialization	Limited Cross-Functional Learning
Clear Accountability	Reduced Innovation
Streamlined Decision-Making	Communication Barriers
Autonomy	Duplication of Effort

Zalando SE, a leading European e-commerce fashion platform, strongly advocates cross-functional collaboration. In the fast-paced fashion industry, Zalando brings together diverse teams spanning technology, logistics, marketing, and fashion expertise to create a seamless online shopping experience. This approach positively impacts the company by enabling rapid adaptation to evolving fashion trends, efficient supply chain management, and personalized customer experiences. Cross-functional collaboration allows Zalando to innovate swiftly and respond to market demands, ultimately enhancing customer satisfaction. However, it also poses challenges related to complex decision-making processes, requiring effective communication and alignment among diverse teams.

Michelin, a global tire manufacturer, often adheres to a more siloed collaboration model within its manufacturing and research divisions. Michelin's specialization in tire production requires meticulous quality control and a focus on engineering excellence. The siloed approach positively impacts the company by ensuring rigorous quality standards and production efficiency in a highly specialized industry. However, it can also lead to challenges in terms of innovation, as siloed teams may have limited exposure to diverse perspectives and market trends. To address this, Michelin balances siloed manufacturing with cross-functional innovation teams to maintain a competitive edge in tire technology.

Some questions for the leaders to reflect and answer to resolve the dilemma:

- How does our choice between cross-functional and siloed collaboration impact the efficient use of resources, and can we ensure that valuable expertise is leveraged effectively?
- Does a cross-functional approach foster innovation by bringing together diverse perspectives, and how do we maintain innovation within siloed teams?
- How does siloed collaboration affect information flow and communication bottlenecks, and how can cross-functional teams ensure open and efficient dialogue?
- Does cross-functional collaboration enhance decision-making by incorporating input from multiple departments, and how can we balance this with the autonomy of siloed teams?
- How does each approach impact employee morale and job satisfaction, and how does this relate to overall productivity?
- How does our collaboration style influence the customer experience, and can we provide seamless service through cross-functional teams or specialized service through siloed teams?

There could be several factors that could influence this decision in the context of your organization like:

Organizational Culture: Companies with a culture of cooperation and open communication are more inclined towards cross-functional collaboration, while those with a culture of autonomy and specialization may lean towards siloed collaboration.

> **Nature of Industry**: Some industries, like healthcare, require cross-functional collaboration to ensure comprehensive patient care, while others, like manufacturing, may prioritize specialization for efficiency.
>
> **Complexity of Projects**: Complex, multifaceted projects may require cross-functional teams to ensure all aspects are adequately addressed, while simpler tasks may be managed more effectively within siloed teams.
>
> **Leadership Style**: Leaders who value collaboration and synergy may promote cross-functional teams, while those who prioritize individual departmental achievements may favor siloed teams.
>
> **Resource Availability**: Cross-functional collaboration may require more resource allocation for coordination, while siloed teams can operate with fewer interdepartmental dependencies.
>
> **There are other areas that get impacted because of a choice of this dilemma like:**
>
> - Efficiency of processes
> - Innovation and creativity
> - Communication, information flow and knowledge sharing.
> - Alignment and teamwork
> - Decision-Making

The choice between cross-functional and siloed collaboration is not binary; many organizations find success in adopting a hybrid approach. They create cross-functional teams for projects that require diverse expertise and innovation while maintaining siloed departments for tasks that demand specialization and efficiency. This hybrid model aims to strike a balance between leveraging diverse perspectives and maintaining streamlined operations. *Let's consider Epic Games, the video game and software developer known for its popular game engine Unreal Engine and the immensely popular game Fortnite. Epic Games exemplifies an organization that successfully strikes a balance between cross-functional and siloed collaboration in different scenarios. Within the realm of video game development, Epic Games adopts cross-functional collaboration when creating and innovating its game engines and game design. Cross-functional teams consisting of engineers, designers, artists, and marketing specialists collaborate closely to ensure the creation of groundbreaking gaming experiences. This approach allows Epic Games to leverage diverse expertise to deliver innovative and visually stunning games and game development tools.*

However, Epic Games also employs siloed collaboration within its various departments responsible for different aspects of its business, such as Unreal Engine development and Fortnite operations. These departments often operate with specialized teams focused on specific tasks, which ensures efficiency and expertise within those areas. For instance, the technical team working on the Unreal Engine may function independently to maintain the high quality and performance expected by developers worldwide. This balanced approach allows Epic Games to harness the creative and innovative potential of cross-functional teams when developing cutting-edge technologies and games, while also maintaining streamlined and specialized operations in different facets of their business.

Let's delve deeper into the factors influencing the decision between cross-functional and siloed collaboration. These factors play a pivotal role in determining the most suitable approach for an organization:

- **Organizational Culture**: The prevailing culture within the organization is a foundational factor. A culture that values openness, cooperation, and innovation is more inclined toward cross-functional collaboration, while a culture emphasizing autonomy and specialization may favor siloed collaboration.
- **Nature of Industry**: The industry in which the organization operates plays a significant role. In highly regulated industries such as healthcare or finance, where compliance and comprehensive solutions are paramount, cross-functional collaboration may be favored. In contrast, industries that require rapid innovation and specialization, such as technology startups, may lean toward siloed collaboration.
- **Complexity of Projects**: The complexity of projects or tasks can dictate the collaboration approach. Complex, multifaceted projects that demand expertise from various disciplines often benefit from cross-functional teams. Simpler, repetitive tasks may be handled more efficiently within siloed teams.
- **Leadership Style**: Leadership preferences and styles of top

executives influence the choice. Leaders who prioritize collaboration, synergy, and innovation are more likely to promote cross-functional teams. Those who emphasize individual departmental achievements may favor siloed teams

- **Resource Availability**: Resource constraints, including budget and personnel, can impact the decision. Cross-functional collaboration may require more resource allocation for coordination and training, whereas siloed teams may operate with fewer interdepartmental dependencies.
- **Customer Demands**: The demands and expectations of customers or clients can sway the collaboration approach. Customers seeking integrated solutions or comprehensive services may be better served by cross-functional teams, while those valuing specialized expertise may prefer siloed teams.
- **Project Urgency**: The urgency of projects and tasks can dictate the collaboration approach. Time-sensitive projects may necessitate cross-functional teams to ensure rapid decision-making and problem-solving, while long-term initiatives may allow for a more structured, siloed approach.
- **Historical Practices**: Established practices within the organization, including historical departmental structures and communication norms, can influence the choice. Long-standing siloed structures may require a deliberate effort to transition toward cross-functional collaboration.
- **Change Management Capacity**: An organization's readiness and capacity for change are vital. Implementing cross-functional collaboration may require change management efforts to address resistance and ensure a smooth transition.
- **Performance Metrics**: The key performance indicators (KPIs) used to measure success can impact the collaboration approach. Organizations emphasizing holistic outcomes and customer satisfaction may lean toward cross-functional collaboration, while those focusing on department-specific metrics may prefer siloed teams.

In summary, the choice between cross-functional and siloed collaboration significantly impacts how an organization functions. It affects decision-making processes, innovation, communication, employee engagement, and the overall ability to adapt to complex challenges. Organizations must carefully consider their goals, industry, and culture when determining which approach best suits their unique needs.

Pre-Emptive vs. Event-Driven Collaboration

> Balancing the choice between initiating collaboration proactively to anticipate and prevent issues (pre-emptive) or responding to situations reactively as they arise (event-driven).

Pre-emptive Collaboration, often associated with proactive planning and risk mitigation, involves identifying potential issues before they materialize and taking measures to prevent or mitigate their impact. Organizations that adopt this approach prioritize thorough planning, data analysis, and predictive strategies. For instance, in the context of project management, pre-emptive collaboration would involve meticulous project planning, risk assessments, and resource allocation to minimize potential disruptions. This approach offers the advantage of enhanced predictability, reduced risks, and improved preparedness. It can lead to cost savings by avoiding costly crises. However, it can also be resource-intensive and potentially constrain innovation if it overly prioritizes risk aversion.

Conversely, Event-driven Collaboration emphasizes reacting to situations as they arise, often in response to unforeseen challenges or opportunities. This approach is characterized by agility and adaptability, with organizations relying on their ability to mobilize quickly in response to changing circumstances. For instance, in the context of crisis management, event-driven collaboration entails assembling cross-functional teams to address emerging issues promptly. This approach offers the benefit of agility in crisis situations, resource efficiency as resources are allocated based on immediate needs, and the potential for innovative problem-solving. However, it can be reactive in nature, introducing uncertainty and potential escalations. It may also impact customer experience if organizations are perceived as unprepared for challenges.

Choosing Pre-Emptive Collaboration Only	
Pros	**Cons**
Risk Mitigation	Resource Intensive
Enhanced Predictability	Potential for Over-caution
Improved Preparedness	Reduced Adaptability
Potential Cost Savings	Innovation Constraint

Choosing Event-Driven Collaboration Only	
Pros	**Cons**
Agility in Crisis	Reactive Nature
Resource Efficiency	Uncertainty
Innovation Potential	Potential for Escalation
Adaptive Problem-Solving	Customer Impact

Take any of India's large IT services companies, they strongly advocate pre-emptive collaboration. They operate in a highly competitive and rapidly evolving industry. Their pre-emptive approach involves collaborating closely with clients, industry experts, and technology partners to anticipate market trends and emerging technologies. By proactively identifying clients' evolving needs and potential challenges, they can develop customized solutions and service offerings ahead of competitors. This pre-emptive approach positively impacts their market leadership, customer satisfaction, and ability to stay at the forefront of technology trends. However, it also demands continuous investment in research and development and a keen focus on talent development to maintain their competitive edge.

Zomato, a prominent Indian food delivery and restaurant discovery platform, often relies on event-driven collaboration. Operating in the dynamic and competitive food *delivery industry, Zomato faces a range of unforeseen challenges such as fluctuating demand, logistical issues, and market disruptions. Their event-driven approach allows them to quickly adapt to these challenges by mobilizing delivery personnel, adjusting operational strategies, and responding to customer feedback. This event-driven collaboration positively impacts their ability to provide efficient food delivery services and maintain customer satisfaction during unforeseen events. However, it also introduces challenges related to operational scalability, resource allocation, and maintaining quality standards during peak demand periods. Zomato's event-driven collaboration is essential for navigating the unpredictable nature of the food delivery business.*

Some questions for the leaders to reflect and answer to resolve the dilemma:

- How do we balance preemptive measures to mitigate risks with event-driven responses when unforeseen challenges arise?
- What level of resources should be allocated to proactive planning versus reactive crisis management, and how does this impact our overall efficiency?
- Does pre-emptive collaboration stifle innovation by overemphasizing risk aversion, and how can we inject creativity into event-driven solutions?
- How does each approach influence our ability to deliver a consistent and exceptional customer experience, and how can we ensure alignment?
- How do our collaboration choices affect employee engagement and job satisfaction, and what role do they play in attracting and retaining talent?
- Are we agile enough to pivot from pre-emptive strategies to event-driven responses when necessary, and vice versa, while maintaining strategic focus?

There could be several factors that could influence this decision in the context of your organization like:

Industry Dynamics: Industries with rapidly changing landscapes, such as technology, may lean toward event-driven collaboration, while highly regulated industries like finance may prioritize pre-emptive measures.

Historical Data: The availability and reliability of historical data can influence the choice. Organizations with extensive data may lean toward predictive analytics (pre-emptive), while those with limited data may rely on event-driven responses.

Resource Availability: The availability of resources, including financial and human capital, can impact the decision. Organizations with ample resources may invest more in pre-emptive collaboration, while resource-constrained entities may rely on event-driven approaches.

Regulatory Environment: Regulatory requirements can play a significant role. Industries with strict compliance standards may emphasize pre-emptive measures to avoid legal issues, while less regulated sectors may adopt a more event-driven approach.

There are other areas that get impacted because of a choice of this dilemma like:

- Crisis Management
- Resource Allocation
- Communication
- Decision-Making Speed
- Risk Management

Pre-emptive and event-driven collaboration can coexist by establishing a well-defined framework. Organizations can proactively plan for known risks and challenges (pre-emptive) while maintaining the flexibility to adapt swiftly to unexpected situations (event-driven). Effective communication and clear protocols enable a seamless transition between the two approaches. *Consider Apollo Hospitals, a leading healthcare organization in India, as an example of an organization that strikes a balance between pre-emptive and event-driven collaboration in different scenarios. In the context of pre-emptive collaboration, Apollo Hospitals places a strong emphasis on proactive healthcare planning and preventive measures. They collaborate with medical researchers, public health experts, and government agencies to anticipate healthcare trends and potential health crises. For example, they actively participate in vaccination campaigns to prevent the outbreak of infectious diseases like seasonal flu or pandemics. This pre-emptive collaboration positively impacts public health by reducing the incidence of preventable illnesses and minimizing the strain on healthcare resources.*

Simultaneously, Apollo Hospitals also excels in event-driven collaboration. In the healthcare industry, unexpected medical emergencies and crises are a common occurrence. Apollo's event-driven approach involves swift coordination among healthcare professionals, disaster management teams, and government authorities to respond to natural disasters, accidents, and disease outbreaks. Their expertise in event-driven collaboration enables them to provide critical medical care during emergencies, such as setting up makeshift hospitals during disasters or deploying medical teams to disease hotspots. This balanced approach allows Apollo Hospitals to effectively manage both routine healthcare needs and respond to unforeseen healthcare challenges. By combining pre-emptive measures for long-term health planning with event-driven responses for crisis situations, Apollo Hospitals ensures comprehensive and adaptable healthcare services for the community.

Let's delve deeper into the factors influencing the decision between pre-emptive and event-driven collaboration. These factors provide valuable insights into why organizations may lean toward one approach over the other:

- **Nature of Industry**: The type of industry in which an organization operates plays a significant role. Industries with fast-changing landscapes, such as technology and fashion, often favor event-driven collaboration to adapt swiftly to market shifts. In contrast, highly regulated sectors like healthcare may prioritize pre-emptive measures to comply with stringent regulations and manage risks proactively.
- **Organizational Culture**: The prevailing culture within the organization influences the choice. Organizations with a risk-averse culture that values thorough planning and compliance may lean toward pre-emptive collaboration. Those with a culture that encourages innovation, agility, and adaptability may favor event-driven approaches.
- **Resource Availability**: Resource constraints, including budget and personnel, impact the decision. Organizations with ample

resources may invest more in pre-emptive collaboration, as they have the capacity for data analysis, risk assessments, and preventive measures. Resource-constrained organizations may opt for event-driven strategies due to cost considerations.
- **Regulatory Environment**: Regulatory requirements and compliance obligations can strongly influence the choice. Industries subject to strict regulations often prioritize pre-emptive measures to avoid legal issues and penalties. Event-driven collaboration may be seen as reactive and risky in such contexts.
- **Historical Data**: The availability and reliability of historical data are crucial. Organizations with access to comprehensive and accurate data may lean toward pre-emptive collaboration, leveraging data analysis for predictive strategies. In contrast, those with limited historical data may rely more on event-driven approaches based on real-time information.
- **Leadership Style**: The leadership style and preferences of top executives can shape the decision. Leaders who value planning, risk management, and compliance are more likely to promote pre-emptive collaboration. Leaders emphasizing adaptability, innovation, and quick decision-making may favor event-driven strategies.
- **Competitive Landscape**: The competitive landscape also matters. Organizations operating in highly competitive markets may prioritize event-driven collaboration to seize emerging opportunities and respond to competitive threats rapidly. Less competitive industries may focus on pre-emptive measures to maintain stability.
- **Customer Expectations**: Customer expectations and preferences can influence the decision. Customers seeking reliable, well-planned services may prefer organizations that prioritize pre-emptive collaboration. Others seeking flexibility, innovation, and responsiveness may favor event-driven approaches.
- **Global Factors**: Global events, such as economic recessions, natural disasters, or public health crises, can impact the choice. These events may necessitate event-driven collaboration to address immediate challenges, even for organizations that

typically prioritize pre-emptive measures.
- **Adaptability**: The organization's capacity for adaptability and change management plays a role. An organization with a strong change-ready culture can more easily transition between preemptive and event-driven approaches as circumstances evolve.

The impact of this choice is far-reaching. It influences risk management, resource allocation, innovation, customer experience, employee engagement, and adaptability. Organizations must carefully evaluate their unique needs, goals, and industry dynamics to strike the right balance between pre-emptive and event-driven collaboration. A well-thought-out framework that combines proactive planning with adaptive responsiveness can provide the flexibility needed to navigate the complex and dynamic business landscape effectively.

| 3.7 |

INNOVATION AND RISK-TAKING DILEMMAS

> **How will you use this chapter of the book?**
>
> If you are the founder or the CEO of a company and if you and your leadership team have a clear point of view (PoV) on the following questions and all of you are ALIGNED, then you can choose to move to the next chapter of the book. However, if you see a dissonance or have conflicting views, then we suggest digging deeper, going through this chapter and reflecting on different angles we bring in there.
>
> Here are the questions for you to discuss and ponder-
>
> - Are we balancing small, gradual improvements with big, game-changing innovations to stay competitive?
> - How are we dividing resources between improving existing products and pursuing new, groundbreaking ideas?
> - Are we investing in employee skills and training to ensure we stay relevant in our market?
> - Do we encourage employees to take calculated risks, or do we prioritize caution?
> - Are we exploring new opportunities and technologies, or are we focusing more on what we already have?
> - How does our innovation strategy support our long-term growth and sustainability?
> - Do we actively seek partnerships for innovation, or do we rely mainly on our internal capabilities?
> - Are we more focused on preventing risks or on recovering from them when they occur?
> - What kind of culture are we nurturing – one that encourages innovation or one that minimizes risk?
> - How does our approach to innovation and risk-taking contribute to our competitive positioning?

In the dynamic landscape of today's business world, leaders face critical decisions when it comes to innovation and risk-taking. These decisions can shape the future of their organizations. Should they make gradual improvements to existing products or take bold leaps into uncharted territories? Should they explore new opportunities or stick with what's familiar? Should they collaborate with external partners or rely solely on their internal expertise? These dilemmas, rooted in the fundamental aspects of business strategy, require careful consideration and thoughtful planning. In this chapter, we will explore these essential choices that leaders must make to navigate the complex terrain of innovation and risk-taking in their organizations.

Leaders need to consider various aspects when determining the way innovation and risk-taking will be approached in the organization. Here's a comprehensive list of these aspects:

- **Strategic Alignment**: Ensure that innovation efforts align with the organization's overall strategic goals and mission.
- **Market Dynamics**: Analyze the competitive landscape, market trends, and customer demands to identify opportunities for innovation.
- **Resource Allocation**: Allocate financial, human, and technological resources to support innovation initiatives effectively.
- **Risk Assessment**: Evaluate the potential risks associated with innovation projects and develop risk mitigation strategies.
- **Innovation Culture**: Foster a culture that encourages creativity, experimentation, and learning from failures.
- **Leadership Commitment**: Demonstrate leadership commitment to innovation by setting an example and providing support.
- **Talent Management**: Recruit, retain, and develop talent with the necessary skills and mindset for innovation.
- **Collaboration and Partnerships**: Determine the level of collaboration with external partners, such as customers, suppliers, or startups, to enhance innovation.
- **Intellectual Property**: Establish clear policies and practices for managing intellectual property rights related to innovations.

- **Metrics and KPIs**: Define key performance indicators (KPIs) and metrics to measure the success of innovation efforts.
- **Innovation Process**: Develop a structured innovation process that outlines how ideas are generated, evaluated, and implemented.
- **Communication and Transparency**: Communicate the innovation strategy and progress transparently throughout the organization.
- **Risk Tolerance**: Define the organization's risk tolerance and communicate it to employees to guide their decision-making.
- **Change Management**: Implement effective change management practices to ensure a smooth transition to an innovation-focused culture.
- **Feedback Loops**: Establish feedback mechanisms to gather input from employees, customers, and stakeholders to improve innovation efforts.
- **Regulatory Compliance**: Ensure that innovation projects comply with relevant regulations and standards.
- **Market Testing**: Conduct market testing and validation of new innovations before full-scale implementation.
- **Sustainability**: Consider the environmental and social impact of innovations and prioritize sustainability where applicable.
- **Learning from Failure**: Encourage a mindset that views failure as a learning opportunity and not a deterrent to innovation.
- **Long-term vs. Short-term**: Balance short-term gains with long-term sustainability when making innovation and risk-taking decisions.
- **Budgeting**: Allocate budgets for both incremental and radical innovation, and adjust as needed based on project priorities.
- **Competitive Analysis**: Continuously monitor competitors' innovation efforts and adjust strategies accordingly.
- **Customer-Centricity**: Keep the customer's needs and preferences at the center of innovation efforts.
- **Scalability**: Consider the scalability of innovation initiatives to accommodate future growth.
- **Ethical Considerations**: Address ethical implications and potential ethical dilemmas associated with innovations.

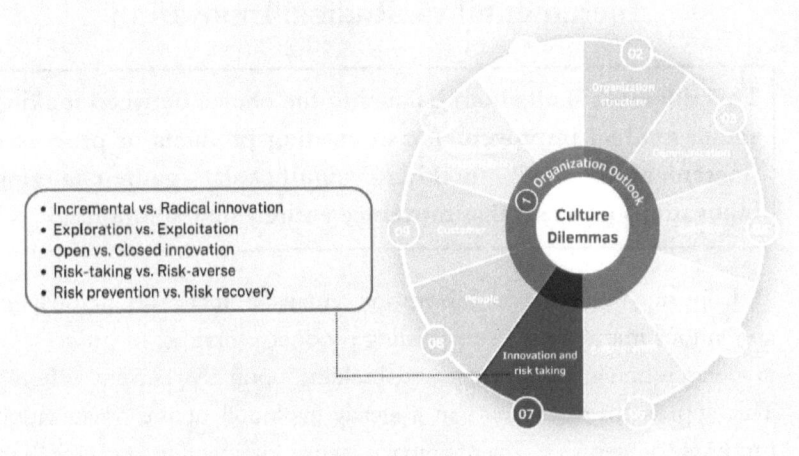

While there are many dilemmas when we think of innovation, we will focus on five pivotal ones that often take center stage:

- **Incremental vs. Radical innovation**
- **Exploration vs. Exploitation**
- **Open innovation vs. Closed innovation**
- **Risk-taking vs. Risk-averse**
- **Risk prevention vs. Risk recovery**

Let's look at each of them in greater detail.

Incremental vs. Radical Innovation

> This dilemma is all about balancing the choice between making small, gradual improvements to existing products or processes (incremental) and making significant, game-changing innovations (radical) that introduce entirely new solutions.

Choosing incremental innovation entails a focus on gradual and continuous improvements to existing products, services, or processes. It involves refining, optimizing, and building upon the current offerings. This approach often results in a steady evolution of the organization's products or services, maintaining a sense of stability and reliability. Companies that opt for incremental innovation prioritize short-term gains and are typically risk-averse in their approach. They tend to be more resource-efficient as they build upon existing knowledge and infrastructure. However, the downside is that this strategy may lead to a lack of competitive differentiation and innovation fatigue over time.

On the other hand, radical innovation involves the pursuit of groundbreaking, disruptive changes. It is characterized by the development of entirely new solutions or the introduction of products or services that challenge established norms. Organizations that embrace radical innovation are willing to take significant risks and allocate substantial resources to explore uncharted territories. This approach can lead to revolutionary breakthroughs that transform industries and capture significant market share. However, it also comes with higher uncertainty, resource demands, and the potential for failure.

Choosing Incremental Innovation Only	
Pros	**Cons**
Stable and predictable progress	Limited long-term competitiveness
Lower short-term risks	Potential stagnation and loss of market share
Efficient resource utilization	Reduced innovation excitement among employees

Choosing Radical Innovation Only	
Pros	**Cons**
Potential for disruptive breakthroughs	High short-term risks and uncertainty
Competitive differentiation	Resource-intensive and costly
Attracting top talent and investors	Potential internal resistance and cultural challenges

Take the example of Zoom. Zoom continuously improves its video conferencing platform by adding small, user-friendly features and enhancing performance. This approach has paid off significantly during the pandemic when remote work and virtual meetings surged in demand. Zoom's regular updates and user-friendly interface have positively impacted its market position and revenue. However, this incremental approach also made it vulnerable to privacy and security concerns that emerged as it gained more users, leading to scrutiny and the need for quick remedial actions. Nevertheless, by staying focused on small, user-centric improvements, Zoom has maintained its relevance and continues to be a preferred choice for virtual meetings.

On the other hand, Tesla's approach is rooted in radical innovation, aiming to revolutionize the automotive industry. Tesla introduced electric cars with longer ranges and cutting-edge technology, challenging the status quo. This radical approach has propelled Tesla to a leadership position in the EV market, attracting a devoted following and driving the industry toward sustainability. However, the rapid pace of innovation and expansion has also posed challenges. Tesla faces production bottlenecks and quality issues that have garnered attention. Despite these challenges, Tesla's commitment to radical innovation has not only reshaped the automotive industry but also influenced the way people perceive and adopt electric vehicles, positively impacting its market share and brand perception.

Some questions for the leaders to reflect and answer to resolve the dilemma:

- Are our customers looking for small, gradual improvements in our products, or do they need entirely new and groundbreaking solutions?
- What is our competition doing? Are they making small improvements or coming up with radically new ideas?
- Do we have the resources, both in terms of money and talent, to support radical innovation, or should we focus on incremental changes within our means?
- How comfortable are we with taking risks? Are we prepared for the uncertainties that come with radical innovation?
- What are our long-term goals? Does our innovation choice align with where we want to be in the future?
- Is this the right time for a radical change, or should we wait until the market is more receptive to it?

There could be several factors that could influence this decision in the context of your organization like:

Market Demand and Trends: Understanding what customers want and the current market trends guides the choice.

Available Resources and Budget: The resources at hand, including financial and human capital, play a significant role.

> **Competitive Landscape and Industry Disruption**: Assessing the competitive environment and potential industry disruptions is crucial.
>
> **Organizational Culture and Risk Tolerance**: The organization's culture and its willingness to embrace risk affect the decision.
>
> **Long-Term Strategic Goals**: Alignment with long-term strategic objectives shapes the innovation choice.
>
> **Customer Feedback and Preferences**: Listening to customer feedback and preferences informs the decision-making process.
>
> **There are other areas that get impacted because of a choice of this dilemma like:**
>
> - Product development and differentiation
> - Competitive advantage and market relevance
> - Resource allocation and budgeting
> - Employee skill sets and training
> - Risk assessment and management strategy

Incremental and radical innovation can coexist in the organization. Companies can allocate resources and teams specifically for incremental improvements while also having separate teams or initiatives dedicated to radical innovation. This allows for a balanced approach to meet different market needs. *Slack continuously refines and enhances its team collaboration software with small, user-focused improvements. They regularly release updates that address user feedback, streamline workflows, and provide incremental features that enhance the user experience. These incremental innovations contribute to user satisfaction and help Slack maintain its position as a leading communication and collaboration platform.*

On the other hand, Slack also embraces radical innovation by exploring new avenues to expand its platform. For example, they have ventured into the development of a new category called the "Slack Platform," which offers developers a canvas to build customized apps and integrations within Slack. This radical approach opens up a world of possibilities for businesses to create unique, tailored solutions that go beyond traditional team communication. Slack's willingness to embrace both incremental and radical innovation has allowed it to cater to a wide range of customer needs and stay competitive in a rapidly evolving tech landscape.

The decision of whether to pursue incremental or radical innovation is influenced by a complex interplay of factors within the organization and the broader business environment. While the specific circumstances can vary, here's a common set of factors that commonly influence this decision:

- **Market Stability and Maturity**: In stable and mature markets, incremental innovation may be more suitable as it allows organizations to maintain their market position and cater to existing customer needs. In contrast, industries characterized by rapid change and disruption may necessitate radical innovation to stay relevant.
- **Customer Expectations**: Understanding customer expectations and preferences is crucial. If customers are content with gradual improvements, incremental innovation may suffice. However, if there is a growing demand for groundbreaking solutions, radical innovation becomes imperative.
- **Competitive Landscape**: The competitive environment plays a significant role. If competitors are primarily engaged in incremental innovation, radical innovation can provide a unique selling proposition. Conversely, in highly dynamic industries, staying ahead may require radical innovation efforts.
- **Resource Availability**: The availability of financial resources, skilled talent, and technological infrastructure can dictate the feasibility of radical innovation. Organizations with ample resources may be more inclined to take risks in pursuit of radical innovations.
- **Risk Tolerance**: An organization's risk appetite is a critical factor. Those with a low tolerance for risk may opt for incremental innovation to minimize uncertainties, while risk-tolerant organizations may embrace radical innovation despite the higher inherent risks.
- **Organizational Culture**: Organizational culture profoundly influences innovation choices. Companies with a culture that encourages experimentation, risk-taking, and adaptability are

more likely to embrace radical innovation.
- **Industry Regulations**: Regulatory constraints can impact the feasibility of radical innovation. Highly regulated industries may find it more challenging to introduce radical changes due to compliance requirements.
- **Technological Readiness**: The organization's technological capabilities and readiness to adopt cutting-edge technologies can influence the choice. Radical innovation often relies on advanced technology, and a lack of technological readiness can hinder its implementation.
- **Long-term Vision**: The organization's long-term strategic vision and goals are paramount. Decisions should align with where the company envisions itself in the future. Radical innovation may be a means to achieve transformative long-term objectives.
- **Customer Segmentation**: Understanding different customer segments is essential. Companies may choose to pursue both incremental and radical innovation simultaneously to cater to diverse customer needs.
- **Market Timing**: The timing of market entry or product launch can impact the success of an innovation. Deciding when to introduce incremental improvements or radical innovations can be strategic.
- **Resource Allocation Strategy**: The organization's overall resource allocation strategy, including budget allocation for research and development, can guide the innovation approach.
- **Customer Feedback and Market Research**: Ongoing customer feedback and thorough market research can provide valuable insights into whether incremental enhancements or radical innovations are more likely to resonate with the target audience.
- **Partnerships and Collaborations**: Collaborative partnerships with external entities, such as startups or research institutions, can influence the choice by providing access to cutting-edge ideas and technologies.
- **Historical Performance**: Past innovation successes and failures can shape the organization's willingness to pursue incremental or radical paths based on their historical track record.
- **Ecosystem Dynamics**: Consideration of the broader business

ecosystem, including suppliers, distributors, and partners, can impact the feasibility and acceptance of radical innovations.

In essence, the choice between incremental and radical innovation is a strategic decision that ripples through the organization, influencing product development, competitive positioning, resource allocation, employee skills, and risk management. It is a decision that requires careful consideration and alignment with the organization's long-term vision and goals.

Exploration vs. Exploitation

> Deciding whether to explore new opportunities, technologies, and markets (exploration) or exploit existing resources, products, and capabilities (exploitation) to maximize short-term gains or strike a balance between the two.

Choosing exploration entails a proactive pursuit of innovation and new frontiers. Organizations embracing exploration actively seek out uncharted territories, experiment with novel technologies, and enter unfamiliar markets. This approach is characterized by a willingness to take risks, a tolerance for uncertainty, and an eagerness to push boundaries. Exploration can lead to the discovery of new revenue streams, expansion into untapped markets, and the development of cutting-edge products or services. It fosters creativity and adaptability within the organization and can position it for long-term growth and sustainability. However, exploration can be resource-intensive, with uncertain returns in the short term, potentially leading to financial challenges and market instability.

On the other hand, exploitation focuses on maximizing the value of existing resources, products, and capabilities. Organizations following an exploitation strategy concentrate their efforts on refining and optimizing what they already have. They seek to extract maximum efficiency and profitability from their current operations and offerings. Exploitation often leads to short-term gains, steady revenue streams, and improved operational efficiency. It can be a prudent approach in stable markets where incremental improvements and cost control are paramount. However, over-reliance on exploitation may lead to complacency and missed opportunities for innovation. It can hinder an organization's adaptability in the face of changing market dynamics and technological disruptions.

Choosing Exploration Only	
Pros	**Cons**
Potential for discovering new markets and revenue streams	Higher risk of failure and resource allocation challenges
Keeps the organization adaptable and forward-thinking	May lead to short-term financial instability
Encourages creativity and innovation	Can create uncertainty among employees

Choosing Exploitation Only	
Pros	**Cons**
Stability and predictability in the short term	Vulnerable to market changes and competition
Efficient resource utilization and cost control	May lead to stagnation and missed opportunities for growth
Builds on existing strengths and expertise	Can hinder long-term competitiveness

A company that advocates exploration is Biocon Limited. Biocon is a leading biopharmaceutical company that has consistently pursued exploration within the pharmaceutical and biotechnology sectors. Their approach involves a strong commitment to research and development, including the development of biosimilars and innovative biopharmaceutical products. This exploration-driven strategy has positively impacted Biocon's market position by enabling the creation of a diverse portfolio of drugs and therapies. It has allowed the company to expand its presence in global markets and establish itself as a leader in the biopharmaceutical industry. However, this exploration-focused approach also comes with challenges, such as the need for substantial investments in research, regulatory hurdles, and the inherent risks associated with drug development.

Nevertheless, Biocon's commitment to exploration has been instrumental in its growth and success.

An Indian company that predominantly follows an exploitation strategy is HDFC Bank. HDFC Bank, one of India's leading private sector banks, emphasizes the efficient use of its existing resources and capabilities in the banking and financial services sector. The bank's approach centers on providing a wide range of financial products and services while optimizing operational efficiency and customer service within its established business model. This exploitation-focused strategy has positively impacted HDFC Bank's profitability and customer satisfaction. The bank's reputation for reliability and customer-centric banking practices has led to a loyal customer base and consistent growth in its market share. However, it can be challenging for HDFC Bank to explore radically new business models or technologies beyond its core banking operations, potentially limiting its ability to adapt to evolving fintech innovations or changing customer preferences in the long term.

Some questions for the leaders to reflect and answer to resolve the dilemma:

- How should we allocate our resources - on exploring new ideas or exploiting existing ones?
- Are we more focused on immediate gains, or are we considering long-term sustainability?
- How comfortable are we with the uncertainty and risks that come with exploration?
- Do changing market trends require us to explore new opportunities, or can we continue to profit from existing ones?
- Are we exploiting our current strengths to the fullest, or should we explore new avenues to gain a competitive edge?
- Does our organizational culture lean towards exploring new possibilities or optimizing existing processes?

There could be several factors that could influence this decision in the context of your organization like:

Market Conditions: Market stability and competitive activity drive the decision.

> **Resource Availability**: The availability of money, talent, and technology is crucial.
>
> **Organizational Culture**: The company's risk-taking culture shapes the choice.
>
> **Long-Term Goals**: Strategic objectives guide the decision.
>
> **Customer Needs**: Customer preferences and trends play a key role.
>
> **There are other areas that get impacted because of a choice of this dilemma like:**
>
> - Long-term growth and sustainability
> - Operational stability and efficiency
> - Resource allocation and investment focus
> - Organizational culture and adaptability
> - Competitive positioning and market share

Exploration and exploitation can coexist in the organization by carefully balancing resources and creating separate teams or initiatives focused on each. This allows the organization to maximize both short-term gains and long-term innovation. *An example of an organization that strikes a balance between exploration and exploitation in different scenarios is Muthoot Finance Ltd. Muthoot Finance is an Indian financial services company that primarily operates in the gold loan segment. In terms of exploitation, Muthoot Finance efficiently leverages its existing resources and expertise to maximize short-term gains. The company's core business model revolves around providing gold loans, and it has honed this operation to achieve operational efficiency and profitability. This exploitation-driven strategy has allowed Muthoot Finance to establish a strong presence in the gold loan market and generate consistent revenue. On the exploration side, Muthoot Finance has also ventured into new opportunities within the broader financial services sector. They have explored areas such as microfinance, housing finance, and insurance, diversifying their portfolio and expanding their reach. This exploration-driven strategy has positively impacted the company by opening up new revenue streams and reducing its dependence on a single line of business. Muthoot Finance's ability to strike a balance between the exploration of new financial services and the exploitation of its core gold loan business has allowed it to remain competitive, adapt to changing market dynamics, and continue its growth trajectory in the financial services industry.*

Here's a common set of factors that influence the decision of whether to pursue exploration or exploitation in the running of a business:

- **Market Dynamics**: The state of the market, including its growth rate, competitive intensity, and customer demands, plays a fundamental role in the decision. Rapidly changing markets may necessitate exploration, while mature and stable markets may favor exploitation.
- **Resource Availability**: The organization's access to financial resources, skilled talent, and technological infrastructure significantly impacts the choice. Abundant resources may enable exploration, while resource constraints may encourage exploitation.
- **Risk Tolerance**: The organization's appetite for risk and its willingness to embrace uncertainty are critical. Risk-tolerant organizations may be more inclined towards exploration, while risk-averse ones may favor exploitation.
- **Organizational Culture**: The prevailing culture within the organization, including its attitude toward innovation, risk-taking, and adaptability, profoundly influences the choice. Cultures that encourage experimentation tend to favor exploration, while those emphasizing efficiency may lean toward exploitation.
- **Long-Term Strategic Goals**: Alignment with the organization's long-term strategic objectives is essential. Companies emphasizing sustainable growth and market disruption often prioritize exploration, whereas those focused on short-term profitability may favor exploitation.
- **Customer Needs and Trends**: Keeping a pulse on customer preferences, market trends, and evolving demands is crucial. Organizations that prioritize customer-centricity and responsiveness may opt for exploration, while those aiming to meet current demands may prioritize exploitation.
- **Technological Advancements**: The pace of technological advancement in the industry can influence the decision. Industries

undergoing rapid technological change may require exploration to stay competitive, while stable industries may rely on exploitation to maximize existing technologies.

- **Regulatory Environment**: Compliance with industry-specific regulations and legal constraints can be a determining factor. Strict regulatory environments may limit the scope for exploration, while more permissive regulations may encourage it.
- **Talent and Skill Sets**: The organization's internal talent pool and the availability of specific skills within the workforce can impact the choice. A highly skilled and adaptable workforce may favor exploration, while a specialized workforce may be more aligned with exploitation.
- **Cost of Innovation**: The expenses associated with exploring new opportunities and technologies versus optimizing existing ones can influence the decision. Organizations with cost-effective innovation capabilities may be more inclined towards exploration.
- **Time-to-Market**: The speed required to introduce innovations into the market is a critical consideration. Industries with rapidly changing consumer preferences may require swift exploration, while industries with longer product lifecycles may emphasize exploitation.
- **Historical Performance**: An organization's past experiences with exploration and exploitation can shape its approach. Successful explorations may encourage further exploration, while past exploitation successes may reinforce that strategy.
- **Competitive Landscape**: Assessing the competitive environment and the strategies of key competitors can provide insights. Organizations seeking to outmaneuver competitors may opt for exploration, while those consolidating market share may favor exploitation.
- **Ecosystem Dynamics**: Consideration of the broader business ecosystem, including supplier relationships, distribution channels, and partner collaborations, can influence the feasibility and acceptance of exploration or exploitation.

In summary, the exploration vs. exploitation dilemma underscores the need for organizations to carefully assess their market context, available resources, risk tolerance, and strategic objectives. Striking the right balance between the two strategies is essential for long-term success, as it determines the organization's adaptability, competitiveness, and capacity for sustainable growth in an ever-changing business landscape.

Open Innovation vs. Closed Innovation

> Choosing between collaborating with external partners, such as customers, suppliers, or startups (open innovation), or keeping innovation efforts within the organization's boundaries and relying on internal expertise (closed innovation) or striking a balance for optimizing output.

Choosing open innovation means actively seeking external input and partnerships to drive innovation. Organizations following this approach recognize that valuable ideas and expertise exist beyond their own boundaries. They engage in collaborations, open innovation contests, or partnerships with startups to tap into fresh perspectives and complementary skills. This open innovation strategy can lead to a wider range of ideas, accelerated innovation, and a deeper understanding of customer needs. However, it also comes with challenges, including the need to manage external relationships, safeguard intellectual property, and align external partners with the organization's goals.

In contrast, closed innovation relies primarily on the internal capabilities and expertise of the organization. Companies following this path often have a strong belief in their in-house talent and resources. They prioritize internal R&D, product development, and innovation processes. Closed innovation can be characterized by a focus on protecting intellectual property and maintaining tight control over the innovation process. This approach can result in proprietary innovations, a high level of control, and reduced risk of intellectual property leakage. However, it can also lead to a lack of exposure to diverse perspectives, potentially slower innovation cycles, and a risk of insularity.

Choosing Open Innovation Only	
Pros	**Cons**
Access to diverse external expertise and ideas.	Risk of intellectual property leaks or disputes.
Faster innovation and adaptability to market changes.	Challenges in aligning external partners with internal goals.
Potential cost savings through external partnerships.	Resource allocation complexities and management.

Choosing Closed innovation only	
Pros	**Cons**
Greater control over the innovation process.	Limited exposure to external perspectives and ideas.
Enhanced protection of proprietary knowledge.	Slower innovation and response to market shifts.
Easier alignment with organizational objectives.	Potential for innovation stagnation or insularity.

An excellent example of a company that strongly advocates open innovation is "LEGO Group." LEGO has embraced a culture of collaboration with external partners, including its enthusiastic user community. Through initiatives like LEGO Ideas, the company invites customers and fans to propose and vote on new product ideas. This open innovation approach has had a profoundly positive impact on LEGO's business. It has not only led to the creation of innovative product lines but has also strengthened customer engagement and loyalty. However, it also comes with challenges, such as managing the volume of ideas, ensuring alignment with the brand, and addressing intellectual property concerns. Overall, LEGO's open innovation strategy has fostered a dynamic relationship with its user community and sustained its position as a market leader in the toy industry.

A company that predominantly follows a closed innovation strategy is "ZARA," a leading fashion retailer. ZARA keeps its product development, design, and manufacturing processes tightly integrated within the organization. This closed innovation approach allows the company to maintain strict control over every aspect of its supply chain and product offerings. The positive impact of this strategy is notable in ZARA's ability to quickly respond to fashion trends, reduce lead times, and deliver fresh collections to stores at an astonishing pace. However, the closed innovation strategy may also limit the diversity of design ideas and potentially overlook external market insights. Nonetheless, ZARA's tightly controlled approach has enabled it to become a fast-fashion giant known for its efficiency and adaptability within the fashion industry.

Some questions for the leaders to reflect and answer to resolve the dilemma:

- Are we ready to collaborate with external partners, or do we prefer to rely on internal capabilities?
- How comfortable are we with sharing our innovation journey with external entities?
- Should we allocate resources for internal R&D or invest in external partnerships?
- Is our priority to innovate quickly, and if so, can external collaboration expedite this?
- Does our organizational culture favor internal expertise, or are we open to diverse external perspectives?
- Are external partners aligned with our long-term innovation goals?

There could be several factors that could influence this decision in the context of your organization like:

Industry Dynamics: Highly competitive industries may favor open innovation for rapid adaptation (e.g., tech sector).

Resource Availability: Organizations with limited resources (financial, skilled talent, infrastructure) may turn to open innovation to access external expertise.

Intellectual Property Concerns: Industries with valuable proprietary information may lean toward closed innovation (e.g., pharmaceuticals).

Speed-to-Market Goals: Companies with rapid innovation goals may opt for open innovation to access external solutions quickly (e.g., startups).

Market Feedback and Trends: Industries reliant on consumer preferences may embrace open innovation to stay responsive (e.g., consumer electronics).

There are other areas that get impacted because of a choice of this dilemma like:

- Idea generation and diversity of perspectives
- Speed of innovation and time-to-market
- Intellectual property management and ownership
- Resource allocation and partnership strategy
- Market positioning and competitive advantage

Open and closed innovation can coexist in an organization by creating distinct innovation pathways. Closed innovation can focus on core capabilities, while open innovation can explore external collaborations to supplement or diversify the innovation portfolio. *An example of an organization that strikes a balance between open innovation and closed innovation in different scenarios is "Hindustan Zinc Limited" (HZL). HZL is a mining and metals company based in India, and it operates in a highly regulated and technology-intensive industry. In the context of closed innovation, HZL places a strong emphasis on internal expertise and research when it comes to safety and core mining processes. The company invests in closed innovation to continuously improve the safety of its mining operations, with a focus on reducing accidents and enhancing environmental sustainability. By relying on its internal expertise and experience, HZL has been able to maintain high safety standards and compliance with industry regulations.*

On the other hand, HZL also embraces open innovation in certain areas, particularly in technology and environmental sustainability. The company collaborates with external partners and research institutions to explore innovative technologies for waste management, resource conservation, and energy efficiency. By engaging in open innovation partnerships, HZL gains access to external expertise and ideas that help it reduce its environmental footprint and improve resource utilization.

A common set of factors that influence the decision of whether to adopt open innovation or closed innovation in the running of a business include:

- **Industry Ecosystem**: The nature of the industry plays a crucial role. Industries characterized by rapid technological advancements and dynamic ecosystems may favor open innovation to tap into external expertise.
- **Resource Availability**: The availability of financial resources, skilled talent, and infrastructure can impact the choice. Organizations with abundant resources may have the capacity to explore open innovation options.
- **Risk Tolerance**: The organization's appetite for risk and willingness to collaborate externally affect the decision. Risk-tolerant companies may be more inclined toward open innovation, while risk-averse ones may prefer closed innovation.
- **Intellectual Property (IP) Considerations**: The importance of protecting intellectual property can be a determining factor. Industries with valuable IP may lean toward closed innovation to safeguard proprietary knowledge.
- **Speed-to-Market Objectives**: The urgency to bring innovations to market can guide the decision. Companies aiming for rapid innovation may opt for open innovation to access external solutions quickly.
- **Market Feedback and Trends**: The relevance of customer feedback and emerging market trends can drive the choice. Industries reliant on consumer preferences may embrace open innovation to stay responsive to changing market dynamics.
- **Competitive Landscape**: An assessment of the competitive environment and the strategies of key competitors can provide insights. Organizations seeking a competitive edge may opt for

open innovation to outmaneuver rivals.
- **Technology Readiness**: The maturity of technologies in the industry can influence the decision. Mature industries may lean toward closed innovation, while emerging fields may benefit from open innovation to access cutting-edge technologies.
- **Cost Efficiency**: The cost-effectiveness of internal R&D versus external collaborations can play a role. Companies looking to optimize costs may explore open innovation for cost-effective solutions.
- **Market Entry or Expansion Goals**: Organizations with plans to enter new markets or expand their product/service offerings may consider open innovation to access external market knowledge and insights.
- **Customer-Centric Approach**: The extent to which an organization values customer input and co-creation can affect the choice. Customer-centric companies may prioritize open innovation to incorporate customer feedback.
- **Regulatory Environment**: Compliance with industry-specific regulations and legal constraints can be a determining factor. Strict regulations may limit the scope for open innovation.

The open innovation vs. closed innovation dilemma underscores the need for organizations to carefully assess their industry context, available resources, risk tolerance, and strategic objectives. Striking the right balance between the two strategies is essential for long-term success, as it shapes the organization's adaptability, competitiveness, and capacity for sustainable innovation in an ever-evolving business landscape.

Risk-Taking vs. Risk-Averse

> This dilemma involves balancing a culture that encourages calculated risk-taking, experimentation, and innovation (risk-taking) with a culture that prioritizes caution, risk avoidance, and minimizing potential risks (risk-averse).

Opting for a risk-taking culture is akin to fostering an environment where employees are encouraged to think creatively, challenge the status quo, and explore uncharted territories. It encourages calculated risk-taking, where decisions are made with the acknowledgment that not all ventures will succeed. This approach often leads to innovative breakthroughs, agility in adapting to market changes, and the attraction of creative talents seeking opportunities for expression and growth. However, a risk-taking culture is not without its challenges. It can introduce uncertainty and potential financial losses, as not every innovative venture will yield the desired results. It also demands a high tolerance for failure and a willingness to pivot quickly in response to setbacks. Managing and mitigating risks while pursuing innovation becomes a delicate balancing act.

Conversely, a risk-averse culture prioritizes the minimization of potential risks and the protection of existing assets. This approach can be especially beneficial in industries with strict regulations, where the consequences of failure are high, or when maintaining a stable and predictable operation is paramount. Risk-averse organizations may excel at maintaining their current market positions and safeguarding their financial stability. However, a risk-averse culture may also inhibit creativity and slow the pace of innovation. It can lead to missed opportunities for growth, market leadership, and the attraction of innovative talent. Furthermore, an excessive focus on risk avoidance can sometimes result in a resistance to change, stagnation, and a failure to adapt to evolving market dynamics.

Choosing Risk-Taking Approach Only	
Pros	**Cons**
Faster innovation and adaptability to market changes.	Higher potential for financial losses.
Potential for breakthrough innovations and market leadership.	Greater tolerance for failure may lead to inefficient resource allocation.
Attraction of creative talent.	Risk of alienating risk-averse stakeholders.

Choosing Risk-Averse Approach Only	
Pros	**Cons**
Greater stability and predictability.	Slower innovation cycles and potential stagnation.
Enhanced protection against financial losses.	Missed opportunities for growth and market leadership.
Reduced exposure to reputational risks.	Challenges in attracting and retaining innovative talent.

An example of a company that advocates a risk-taking approach is SpaceX, known for its audacious goals in the aerospace industry, including the development of reusable rockets and plans for interplanetary travel. SpaceX's willingness to take significant risks has propelled it to the forefront of the space exploration sector. By innovating rapidly and pushing boundaries, the company has achieved remarkable successes, such as landing and reusing rockets, drastically reducing launch costs, and securing contracts with NASA. However, this risk-taking approach has also led to high-profile failures, such as rocket explosions. Nonetheless, SpaceX's daring and innovative culture has enabled it to disrupt the space industry, win numerous contracts, and set ambitious goals for the future, illustrating the power of calculated risk-taking in achieving groundbreaking innovation.

A company exemplifying a risk-averse approach is "Hindustan Unilever Limited" (HUL), a subsidiary of Unilever. HUL operates in the fast-moving consumer goods (FMCG) sector and maintains a strong focus on market stability and brand protection. The company's risk-averse stance is evident in its cautious product launches, where extensive market research and testing precede any new product introduction. This approach has helped HUL maintain its market leadership in various consumer product categories in India. While HUL may not be known for groundbreaking innovations, its risk-averse strategy ensures that its core brands remain reliable and consistent, catering to the preferences of a risk-averse consumer base. This approach has proven successful in the FMCG sector by offering stability and maintaining consumer trust, even though it may miss out on some opportunities for disruptive innovation.

Some questions for the leaders to reflect and answer to resolve the dilemma:

- Are our innovation and risk-taking efforts aligned with our organization's overall risk appetite and strategic objectives?
- How comfortable are we with accepting and learning from failures as a part of the innovation process?
- Does our organizational culture actively promote experimentation and reward calculated risk-taking?
- Are we willing to allocate resources and budgets for innovative projects, even if they carry inherent risks?
- To what extent do we prioritize understanding customer needs and preferences when considering innovation risks?
- Are we focused on short-term gains or do we consider the long-term benefits of innovation and calculated risk-taking?

There could be several factors that could influence this decision in the context of your organization like:

Market Dynamics: The competitive nature of the industry and market volatility can influence the decision. Highly competitive markets may favor risk-taking for differentiation.

Financial Health: The organization's financial stability and capacity to absorb potential losses impact the risk-taking approach.

Customer Expectations: The level of innovation expected by customers and the industry can shape the decision. Customer-driven industries may lean toward risk-taking.

Regulatory Environment: Strict regulations or compliance requirements may necessitate a risk-averse approach to ensure legal and ethical adherence.

Resource Availability: The availability of resources, including talent, technology, and capital, can determine the extent to which risks can be managed effectively.

There are other areas that get impacted because of a choice of this dilemma like:

- Employee behavior and decision-making
- Creativity, idea generation, and innovation speed
- Project success rates and failure tolerance
- Organizational adaptability and change readiness
- Corporate governance and risk management strategy

Risk-taking and risk-averse approaches can coexist within an organization by creating distinct innovation pathways. Different divisions or teams may adopt varying risk profiles depending on their objectives. *Let's take the example of Mahindra & Mahindra," an Indian multinational automobile manufacturing corporation. In the context of risk-taking, Mahindra & Mahindra has demonstrated a willingness to innovate and venture into new markets and segments. For instance, the company's foray into electric vehicles with the Mahindra e2o was a bold move in response to changing consumer preferences and environmental concerns. This risk-taking approach allowed Mahindra & Mahindra to position itself as a leader in the Indian electric vehicle market. Conversely, the company also exhibits a risk-averse approach when it comes to its core business of manufacturing utility vehicles and tractors. Mahindra & Mahindra has a long-standing reputation for producing reliable and rugged vehicles, and it maintains a cautious and quality-centric approach to ensure that its core products meet customer expectations and regulatory requirements. By combining these two approaches, Mahindra & Mahindra manages to balance innovation and stability effectively. The company leverages its risk-taking spirit to explore emerging opportunities while maintaining a risk-averse stance to protect its core businesses.*

Here's a deeper exploration of factors that commonly influence the decision of whether to adopt a risk-taking or risk-averse approach within a business:

- **Industry and Market Dynamics**: The nature of the industry and the level of competition play a significant role. Highly competitive and rapidly evolving industries often favor a risk-taking approach, while stable, regulated sectors may lean toward risk aversion.
- **Financial Stability**: The financial health of the organization determines its capacity to absorb potential losses. Companies with strong financial reserves may be more inclined to take calculated risks.
- **Regulatory Environment**: Stringent regulatory requirements can influence the approach. Industries with strict compliance standards may prioritize risk aversion to avoid legal and reputational risks.
- **Customer Expectations**: The expectations of customers regarding innovation and risk-taking are crucial. Customer-centric businesses may embrace risk-taking to meet evolving demands.
- **Innovation Goals**: The organization's innovation goals and strategies are central. Companies aiming for disruptive innovation and market leadership may opt for risk-taking, while those focused on incremental improvements may prefer risk aversion.
- **Resource Allocation**: The allocation of resources, including budget and talent, affects the approach. Companies willing to invest in innovation and allocate resources for experimentation are more likely to be risk-takers.
- **Risk Management Capabilities**: The organization's ability to effectively manage and mitigate risks influences the decision. Strong risk management capabilities can mitigate potential downsides of risk-taking.
- **Organizational Culture**: The existing culture within the

organization plays a vital role. Cultures that encourage creativity, experimentation, and learning from failure are conducive to risk-taking.

- **Market Position**: The current market position and competitive standing of the organization impact the approach. Market leaders may have the freedom to take calculated risks, while newcomers may prioritize risk aversion for stability.
- **Leadership Philosophy**: The leadership's risk appetite and philosophy shape the organization's culture and approach to risk. Visionary leaders may promote risk-taking, while cautious leaders may favor risk aversion.
- **Technological Landscape**: The maturity of technology in the industry influences the approach. Emerging technologies may prompt risk-taking to harness new opportunities, while mature industries may focus on risk aversion to protect existing assets.
- **Global Economic Conditions**: Broader economic factors, such as economic downturns or growth cycles, can impact the decision. Economic uncertainties may lead to a more risk-averse approach.

In conclusion, the risk-taking vs. risk-averse dilemma encapsulates a critical choice that organizations must make in shaping their culture and approach to innovation. Striking the right balance is key, as both approaches have their merits and challenges. Ultimately, the chosen path deeply impacts the organization's adaptability, competitive standing, and capacity for sustainable innovation in an ever-evolving business landscape.

Risk Prevention vs. Risk Recovery

> Deciding whether to invest resources and efforts in preventing risks through proactive measures and safeguards (risk prevention) or focusing on responding to and mitigating risks after they have occurred (risk recovery) or choosing between the two in different situations.

A proactive risk prevention approach involves identifying potential risks and implementing safeguards, processes, and controls to mitigate or eliminate them. This approach is akin to building a sturdy fence to prevent intruders from entering a property. Organizations that prioritize risk prevention tend to emphasize foresight, planning, and adherence to rigorous standards. They aim to reduce the likelihood of adverse events and their potential impact. For example, in the context of cyber security, a company may invest in robust firewalls, encryption, and employee training to prevent data breaches.

Conversely, a risk recovery approach focuses on responding to and mitigating risks after they have manifested. This strategy entails having contingency plans, crisis management teams, and resources in place to address unexpected events effectively. It is akin to having firefighters ready to respond to a fire outbreak. Organizations favoring risk recovery often prioritize flexibility, adaptability, and the ability to bounce back from adverse situations. In the context of supply chain management, a company may rely on a diverse supplier network and disaster recovery plans to recover quickly from disruptions like natural disasters.

Choosing Risk Prevention Only	
Pros	**Cons**
Reduced likelihood of major disruptions and incidents.	Upfront resource allocation may divert funds from immediate needs.
Potential cost savings in the long term.	Complexity and costs associated with prevention measures.
Enhanced reputation and stakeholder trust.	Risk of overinvesting in prevention, potentially neglecting other important areas.

Choosing Risk Recovery Only	
Pros	**Cons**
Lower immediate resource allocation requirements.	Potential for higher overall costs in the long term due to reactive responses.
Greater flexibility to adapt to unexpected risks.	Higher likelihood of reputation damage and stakeholder trust erosion.
Focus on addressing risks as they arise, potentially with simpler solutions.	Limited ability to prevent recurring issues or learn from past incidents.

Ford Motor Company, a prominent player in the automotive industry, places a strong emphasis on risk prevention. Given the sector's high safety standards and regulatory requirements, Ford invests extensively in research, development, and quality control. They have implemented robust manufacturing processes and stringent safety protocols to prevent defects and ensure vehicle safety. While this proactive approach demands significant upfront investments, it has allowed Ford to maintain a reputation for producing reliable and safe vehicles. They have a lower recall rate compared to some competitors, contributing to long-term customer trust. However, this strategy can also result in a slower pace of innovation compared to companies that take more risks in product development.

On the contrary, Airbnb, a leading player in the sharing economy and vacation rental industry, leans towards a risk recovery strategy. In an industry marked by rapid expansion and evolving regulations, Airbnb prioritizes adaptability over extensive risk prevention measures. They have faced various regulatory and legal challenges in different markets, leading to temporary suspensions and legal battles. However, Airbnb's flexibility and ability to pivot quickly have allowed them to recover and continue expanding into new regions. Their risk recovery approach enables them to address emerging issues reactively, which is essential in a dynamic and highly competitive industry. However, it can also lead to occasional disruptions for hosts and guests due to legal constraints.

Some questions for the leaders to reflect and answer to resolve the dilemma:

- How does our organization perceive and assess risks – as potential threats to prevent or as inevitable challenges to recover from?
- Are we willing to allocate resources upfront for risk prevention, even if it diverts resources from other immediate needs?
- To what extent do we learn from past incidents and incorporate those lessons into our risk prevention and recovery strategies?
- Are we more focused on short-term goals, which may favor risk recovery, or do we prioritize long-term sustainability, encouraging risk prevention?
- How do the expectations of our stakeholders, such as customers, investors, and regulators, influence our approach to risk management?
- Are we willing to embrace complex and costly risk prevention measures, or do we prefer simpler, reactive risk recovery solutions?

There could be several factors that could influence this decision in the context of your organization like:

Industry Dynamics: The nature of the industry and its susceptibility to various risks significantly influence the approach. Highly regulated industries may lean towards risk prevention.

Financial Resources: The organization's financial strength and available resources play a crucial role. Well-financed organizations may have the capacity for proactive risk prevention.

Regulatory Environment: Stringent regulatory requirements can necessitate a focus on risk prevention to ensure compliance and avoid penalties.

Market Competition: The competitive landscape and the need to differentiate in the market can impact the decision. In competitive markets, risk prevention can be a source of competitive advantage.

Past Incidents: The organization's history of risk incidents and their consequences may shape its approach. Repeated incidents may drive a shift towards prevention.

There are other areas that get impacted because of a choice of this dilemma like:

- Crisis management and response effectiveness
- Resource allocation for risk mitigation
- Decision-making speed and adaptability during crises
- Organizational culture and emphasis on preparedness
- Reputation management and stakeholder trust

Risk prevention and risk recovery can coexist within an organization. Different departments or teams may adopt varying risk management strategies depending on their specific functions and objectives. For instance, finance teams may focus on risk prevention to safeguard financial assets, while crisis management teams may specialize in risk recovery. *The Clorox Company, known for its household cleaning and consumer products, is an excellent example of an organization that effectively balances risk prevention and risk recovery strategies. Clorox places a strong emphasis on risk prevention, particularly in the context of product safety and quality. They invest heavily in research and development, adhering to strict quality control measures and regulatory compliance to prevent product defects and ensure consumer safety. This proactive approach is essential in the consumer goods industry, where product recalls can damage a company's reputation and result in substantial financial losses. Clorox's commitment to risk prevention has helped them maintain a strong reputation for producing reliable and safe products. Despite their focus on prevention, Clorox also recognizes the need for effective risk recovery strategies, especially in responding to unforeseen events such as supply chain disruptions or market fluctuations. They maintain contingency plans and crisis management teams to swiftly address unexpected challenges. For instance, during the COVID-19 pandemic, Clorox ramped up production of disinfectants to meet heightened demand. Their ability to adapt and recover from disruptions demonstrates their agility and preparedness. Clorox's balanced approach to risk management enables them to maintain product quality and safety while also being agile in responding to changing market conditions. This approach has contributed to their long-term success in the consumer goods industry.*

Let's explore the factors that commonly influence the decision of whether to follow risk prevention or risk recovery in a business:

- **Supply Chain Complexity**: The complexity of a company's supply chain can impact the decision. Businesses with intricate supply chains may be more inclined toward risk prevention to ensure continuity.
- **Strategic Importance**: The strategic importance of a particular operation or process can influence the approach. Critical operations may require a stronger focus on risk prevention to avoid disruptions.
- **Market Volatility**: In volatile markets, organizations may prioritize risk prevention to mitigate market-related risks, while in stable markets, they may emphasize risk recovery.
- **Customer Expectations**: Customer demands and expectations can guide the approach. Businesses catering to customers who value reliability and consistency may lean toward risk prevention.
- **Nature of Risks**: The specific types of risks an organization faces

matter. Some risks, such as cyber security threats, may demand robust prevention measures, while others, like natural disasters, necessitate effective recovery plans.

- **Insurance Coverage**: The extent of insurance coverage for different risks can influence the approach. Organizations with comprehensive coverage may rely more on risk recovery.
- **Legal Liability**: The potential legal liability associated with certain risks can be a determining factor. Businesses exposed to high legal risks may prioritize prevention to avoid litigation.
- **Corporate Culture**: The organization's culture and values play a crucial role. A culture that values safety and preparedness may favor risk prevention, while a more agile culture may emphasize recovery.
- **Leadership Experience**: The experience and risk management philosophy of top leadership can shape the approach. Leaders with a background in risk prevention may advocate for this approach.
- **Competitive Advantage**: Some organizations view risk prevention as a source of competitive advantage. By minimizing disruptions, they can gain a reputation for reliability in the market.
- **Global Operations**: Companies with global operations face diverse risks across different regions. Their approach may vary based on the geographic context.
- **Scalability**: Scalability requirements can influence the decision. Businesses with growth ambitions may invest in scalable prevention measures, while smaller companies may opt for recovery.
- **Environmental Sustainability**: Environmental concerns and sustainability goals may influence the approach. Companies committed to sustainability may prioritize risk prevention to minimize environmental impacts.
- **Human Resources**: The availability of skilled personnel for risk management can be a factor. Organizations with a capable risk management team may lean toward prevention.
- **Customer Base**: The diversity of the customer base can be a consideration. Companies with a broad customer base may have more flexibility to recover from isolated incidents.
- **Economic Conditions**: Economic factors, such as economic

downturns or periods of growth, can impact the approach. Economic uncertainties may lead to a more risk-averse stance.

The decision to prioritize one approach over the other is influenced by various factors, including the organization's industry, financial resources, regulatory environment, past incidents, and the risk tolerance of its leadership. Moreover, some organizations adopt a hybrid strategy, selectively applying risk prevention and risk recovery principles depending on the nature of the risk and its potential impact. In summary, the risk prevention vs. risk recovery dilemma is a multifaceted challenge that requires organizations to carefully consider the implications of their chosen approach. Striking the right balance is crucial, as it directly affects an organization's resilience, reputation, financial stability, and overall ability to navigate a complex and unpredictable business landscape.

| 3.8 |
PEOPLE DILEMMAS

How will you use this chapter of the book?

If you are the founder or the CEO of a company and if you and your leadership team have a clear point of view (PoV) on the following questions and all of you are ALIGNED, then you can choose to move to the next chapter of the book. However, if you see a dissonance or have conflicting views, then we suggest digging deeper, going through this chapter and reflecting on different angles we bring in there.

Here are the questions for you to discuss and ponder-

- How do we balance developing our current employees' skills with hiring from outside?
- Are we promoting from within and building a talent pipeline effectively?
- Do we prioritize experience or potential when hiring and promoting?
- Are we open to hiring for potential to bring in fresh perspectives and diverse skills?
- Do we rely solely on metrics or consider intangible qualities in evaluations?
- How do our evaluation methods align with our culture and values?
- How do we manage costs and quality by balancing in-house talent and outsourcing?
- What measures are in place to protect intellectual property when outsourcing?
- Are we hiring for specific expertise or prioritizing adaptability?
- Does our talent strategy prepare us for industry changes and challenges?

In the ever-evolving landscape of business, leaders are confronted with critical decisions in the realm of people management. These choices, ranging from talent development and recruitment to performance evaluation and diversity promotion, are pivotal in shaping an organization's success. Striking the right balance between these people-related dilemmas can determine the vitality and longevity of a company. In this chapter, we delve into these fundamental considerations, exploring the facets that leaders must navigate to make sound and strategic decisions in managing their most valuable asset—their people.

Leaders need to consider various aspects when determining how people-related decisions will be made in the organization. Here's a comprehensive list of these aspects:

- **Strategic Alignment**: Ensure that people-related decisions align with the organization's overall strategic goals and mission.
- **Talent Development**: Invest in employee training and development to build a skilled and adaptable workforce.
- **Succession Planning**: Develop a robust succession plan to identify and nurture future leaders from within the organization.
- **Recruitment Strategy**: Define a clear recruitment strategy that balances internal promotions with external hires.
- **Diversity and Inclusion**: Promote diversity and inclusion in hiring and promotion practices to foster innovation and equality.
- **Performance Evaluation**: Establish fair and transparent performance evaluation processes that consider both quantitative metrics and qualitative factors.
- **Cultural Fit**: Assess how candidates or employees align with the organizational culture and values.
- **Training and Onboarding**: Develop effective training and onboarding programs to integrate new hires seamlessly into the organization.
- **Cost Management**: Manage labor costs effectively by considering the balance between in-house talent and outsourcing.
- **Knowledge Retention**: Implement knowledge management strategies to retain critical institutional knowledge.
- **Leadership Development**: Invest in leadership development programs to cultivate future leaders from within the organization.
- **Adaptability**: Ensure that the workforce has the flexibility and adaptability needed to respond to changing industry demands.

- **Employee Engagement**: Foster a culture of employee engagement to boost morale and productivity.
- **Ethical Considerations**: Address ethical concerns related to hiring, promotion, and talent management.
- **Legal Compliance**: Ensure all people-related decisions comply with labor laws and regulations.
- **Communication**: Communicate people-related decisions transparently to build trust and maintain employee morale.
- **Workforce Planning**: Continuously assess the workforce's skills and capabilities to meet current and future needs.
- **Retention Strategies**: Develop strategies to retain top talent and reduce turnover.
- **Performance Improvement**: Implement performance improvement plans for underperforming employees.
- **Employee Well-being**: Prioritize employee well-being, including physical and mental health.
- **Feedback Mechanisms**: Establish feedback mechanisms for employees to voice their concerns and suggestions.
- **Change Management**: Implement effective change management strategies when introducing new people-related policies or practices.
- **Labor Market Trends**: Stay informed about labor market trends to adapt hiring and talent management strategies accordingly.
- **Data Analytics**: Use data analytics to make informed decisions regarding talent acquisition, development, and retention.
- **Alignment with Organizational Values**: Ensure that all people-related decisions align with the organization's core values and long-term vision.

HOPE IS NOT A STRATEGY

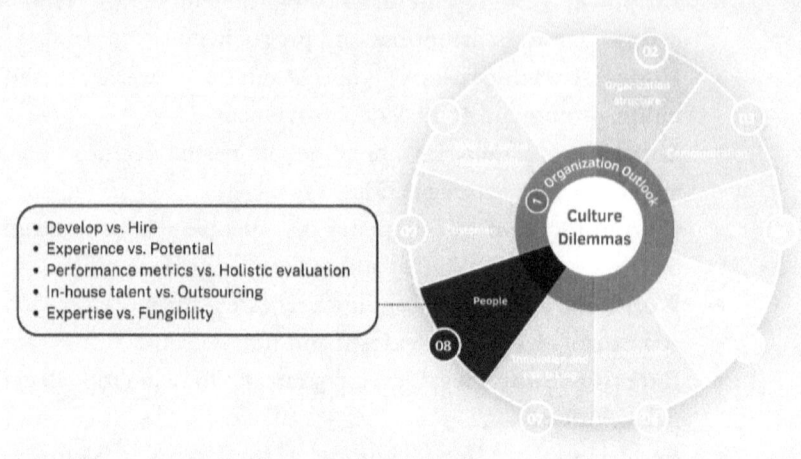

While there are many dilemmas when we think of people related aspects, we will focus on five pivotal ones that often take center stage:

- **Develop vs. Hire**
- **Experience vs. Potential**
- **Performance Metrics vs. Holistic Evaluation**
- **In-House Talent vs. Outsourcing**
- **Expertise vs Fungibility**

Let's look at each of them in greater detail.

Develop vs. Hire

> This dilemma is all about balancing the investment in developing existing employees' skills and promoting from within versus hiring external candidates to meet specific skill or role requirements.

When an organization leans toward the Develop side of this spectrum, it often places a strong emphasis on its current workforce. In such cases, the organization commits resources, time, and effort to training, up skilling, and mentoring its employees. The goal is to foster a culture of continuous learning, where employees are empowered to grow, adapt, and evolve within the organization. This approach can lead to higher employee morale and job satisfaction, as it demonstrates a genuine investment in the professional development of staff. Additionally, it can promote loyalty and a sense of belonging among employees, contributing to long-term retention. However, the Develop approach may not be suitable for all scenarios. Organizations may find that it takes time to build the necessary skills internally, potentially delaying the fulfillment of immediate skill gaps. Moreover, certain roles may demand highly specialized skills or expertise that cannot be developed in-house within a reasonable timeframe. Over reliance on internal development may also require continuous investment in training and development programs, which can strain the organization's budget and resources.

On the other side of the spectrum lies the Hire approach. In this scenario, organizations prioritize external recruitment to swiftly address specific skill shortages or meet immediate role requirements. External hires can bring fresh perspectives, diverse experiences, and external expertise, injecting new life and ideas into the organization. They can fill gaps quickly and efficiently, enabling the company to respond to evolving market demands and competitive pressures. However, the Hire approach is not without its drawbacks. It may lead to lower employee morale if internal talent feels overlooked or undervalued. There can be a sense of missed opportunities for career growth among existing employees, potentially resulting in attrition. Moreover, the costs associated with recruitment, onboarding, and integration of external hires can be substantial, impacting the organization's financial bottom line.

Choosing Develop Only	
Pros	**Cons**
Fosters employee loyalty and retention.	May take longer to fill immediate skill gaps.
Builds a skilled and knowledgeable workforce from within.	Not suitable for roles requiring highly specialized skills.
Supports a culture of continuous learning.	Requires ongoing investment in training and development programs.

Choosing Hire Only	
Pros	**Cons**
Quickly addresses immediate skill shortages.	Can lead to decreased employee morale if internal talent is overlooked.
Brings in fresh perspectives and external expertise.	May result in higher recruitment and onboarding costs.
May help in diversifying the workforce.	Could disrupt team dynamics and company culture if not integrated effectively.

Take the example of Joe's Bakery, a small, family-owned bakery that has been a neighborhood favorite for decades. Instead of frequently hiring experienced bakers from outside, Joe's Bakery takes a "Develop" approach by investing in training and nurturing local talent. They hire individuals with a passion for baking, even if they have limited experience, and then provide extensive on-the-job training and mentorship. This *strategy has created a dedicated team of bakers who are deeply connected to the bakery's traditions and values. The positive impact is evident in the consistent quality of their products and the strong sense of community that surrounds Joe's Bakery. However, it may take longer to develop expertise in specialized techniques, and they may occasionally face challenges in keeping up with high demand during peak seasons.*

On the other hand, Zappos leans towards a Hire strategy, especially for specialized roles and leadership positions. Zappos values the infusion of fresh perspectives and external expertise to drive innovation and customer-centricity. While they maintain a unique and dynamic company culture, Zappos acknowledges that external hires can bring new ideas and energy to the organization. This approach positively impacts the company by quickly filling roles with individuals possessing specific skill sets or industry experience. However, it can also pose challenges in terms of integrating new hires into the company culture and may lead to occasional disruptions in team dynamics.

Some questions for the leaders to reflect and answer to resolve the dilemma:

- Have we assessed the existing skill sets within our organization, and do we see potential talent that can be developed to meet future needs?
- Have we identified specific skills or roles that require immediate attention, and have we determined whether these can be fulfilled through internal development or external hiring?
- Does our company's culture encourage learning and growth from within, or does it place a high value on external expertise?
- Have we conducted a detailed analysis of the costs associated with training and development versus the expenses related to recruitment and onboarding for external hires?
- How does our organization's talent strategy align with our long-term goals, and what measures are in place to ensure this alignment?
- Have we considered how our decision may affect employee morale and engagement, given that both internal development and external hiring can have implications for team dynamics?

> **There could be several factors that could influence this decision in the context of your organization like:**
>
> **Market Availability**: The availability of external talent with the required skills in the job market.
>
> **Time Sensitivity**: Urgency in filling a role may influence whether you choose to develop or hire.
>
> **Training Infrastructure**: The existing capacity and resources for employee development within the organization.
>
> **Employee Engagement**: The willingness of employees to learn and grow within the company culture.
>
> **Succession Planning**: Whether there is a clear succession plan in place for key roles and positions within the organization.
>
> **There are other areas that get impacted because of a choice of this dilemma like:**
>
> - Employee morale and engagement
> - Talent pipeline and succession planning
> - Onboarding and training costs
> - Organizational culture and loyalty

Develop and hire can coexist effectively. Companies often blend these approaches by investing in employee development while strategically hiring for roles that demand specialized skills or experience. *In-N-Out Burger, a popular fast-food chain based in the United States, has earned a reputation for its commitment to employee development while strategically hiring external talent when needed. The company takes a "Develop" approach when it comes to its front-line employees. In-N-Out invests heavily in training and developing its associates, emphasizing the importance of providing excellent customer service and maintaining the brand's high standards. However, when it comes to higher-level positions and specialized roles, In-N-Out is open to external hiring. For example, they may hire experienced managers or professionals in areas like supply chain management or information technology to meet specific needs. This balanced approach allows In-N-Out to maintain its strong internal culture and commitment to employee development while ensuring that it has the expertise required to support its growth and operations. This approach positively impacts the company by fostering a sense of pride and loyalty among its employees, many of whom have long tenures with the company. Simultaneously, it allows In-N-Out to access external expertise to meet evolving business demands, maintaining a competitive edge in the highly competitive fast-food industry.*

When organizations face the decision of whether to Develop or Hire, several factors come into play, influencing their choice. Here are common factors that influence this decision:

- **Skill Gap Analysis**: Organizations assess their current workforce's skills and capabilities against the skills required for various roles. A significant skill gap may lean them towards hiring externally to fill immediate needs.
- **Business Strategy**: The organization's strategic goals and growth plans play a vital role. If rapid expansion is a priority, hiring externally may be necessary to scale quickly.
- **Time Sensitivity**: Urgency is a significant factor. If there's a time-sensitive project or a need to respond swiftly to market changes, hiring externally can be a quicker solution.
- **Cost-Benefit Analysis**: A comprehensive analysis of costs associated with internal development (e.g., training, mentorship) versus external hiring (e.g., recruitment, onboarding) is essential. This analysis helps determine the cost-effectiveness of each approach.
- **Leadership Development**: Organizations with strong leadership development programs may prefer internal development to groom future leaders from within their ranks.
- **Organizational Culture**: The culture and values of the organization play a critical role. Companies with a culture of promoting from within may prioritize internal development.
- **Employee Morale**: The morale and engagement of existing employees should not be underestimated. A focus on internal development can boost morale and job satisfaction.
- **Market Availability**: External hiring depends on the availability

of suitable candidates in the job market. In competitive industries, it may be challenging to find qualified external candidates.

- **Succession Planning**: Organizations with a well-defined succession plan may choose to develop employees to ensure a pipeline of future leaders.
- **Employee Loyalty**: Internal development can foster loyalty and a sense of belonging among employees, reducing turnover.
- **Diversity and Inclusion**: Companies may choose to hire externally to bring in diverse perspectives and experiences, enhancing their workforce's diversity.
- **Innovation Needs**: For roles requiring innovative thinking or fresh perspectives, external hires may be preferred.
- **Industry Dynamics**: The specific demands and dynamics of the industry can influence the choice. Some industries may require constant external hiring due to high turnover or specialized skills.
- **Resource Constraints**: Organizations with limited resources for training and development may rely more on external hiring to meet skill requirements.
- **Flexibility and Adaptability**: The organization's ability to adapt to changing circumstances and market conditions can influence the choice between developing or hiring talent.

In essence, the Develop vs. Hire dilemma is about striking the right balance. Successful organizations often find ways to blend these approaches, recognizing the value of nurturing their internal talent while also strategically hiring external candidates when necessary. The choice should align with the organization's specific needs, long-term objectives, and industry dynamics. It is not a one-size-fits-all decision but rather a dynamic process that requires thoughtful consideration of the organization's unique circumstances and goals.

Experience vs. Potential

> **This dilemma is all about choosing between hiring or promoting individuals with proven experience in a role versus individuals with potential but less experience or striking a strategic balance between the two.**

Choosing to prioritize experience often means opting for candidates who have a track record of successfully handling similar roles or responsibilities. These individuals come with a known set of skills and a demonstrated ability to perform in their respective fields. Consequently, organizations that lean towards experience might expect a more immediate impact from their hires, as these individuals are presumed to require less training and can potentially deliver results from day one. In established industries or roles where predictability and stability are paramount, the preference for experience is understandable.

On the other hand, opting for potential implies a willingness to invest in candidates who may not have a lengthy history of experience but exhibit qualities that suggest they can grow into the role. This approach values attributes such as adaptability, a willingness to learn, creativity, and the ability to bring fresh perspectives to the organization. Organizations that prioritize potential believe in nurturing talent from within and are often more open to giving opportunities to less experienced candidates, facilitating their development and growth over time.

The impact of this decision is multifaceted. Prioritizing experience can provide immediate benefits in terms of performance but may lead to stagnation in terms of innovation and fresh thinking. Over-reliance on experienced individuals may also perpetuate a lack of diversity within the organization, both in terms of demographics and thought. Conversely, a strong focus on potential can bring in fresh perspectives, foster innovation, and create a more diverse workforce. However, it may require significant investments in training and mentorship to bridge the gap between potential and performance.

Choosing Experience Only	
Pros	**Cons**
Immediate impact	Limited innovation
Reduced training needs	Potential for stagnation
Stability	Lack of fresh perspectives.

Choosing Potential Only	
Pros	**Cons**
Fresh perspectives	Longer learning curve
Adaptability	Higher training investments
Potential for long-term growth.	Potential for initial performance gaps.

Tata Motors, one of India's largest automotive manufacturers, has traditionally leaned towards hiring experienced professionals in key roles within its manufacturing and engineering divisions. The company's emphasis on experience has contributed to its reputation for producing reliable and well-engineered vehicles. Seasoned engineers and production managers have played a crucial role in maintaining quality and efficiency. However, this approach has at times resulted in slower adaptation to rapidly changing consumer preferences and emerging technologies in the automotive industry. Tata Motors faced challenges in keeping up with the demand for electric vehicles and connected technologies due to the entrenched culture of experience. While stability and quality remained strengths, the company recognized the need to balance this with an infusion of fresh talent and potential to drive innovation.

Flipkart, India's leading e-commerce platform, has been known for its focus on potential over experience, particularly in its technology and data science teams. The company actively recruits young talent from top universities and startups, valuing innovative thinking and adaptability. This approach has allowed Flipkart to stay at the forefront of e-commerce technology, pioneering solutions like AI-driven recommendations and supply chain optimization. However, it also requires significant investments in training and development to bridge the experience gap. Flipkart's strategy has created a dynamic and forward-thinking culture but sometimes results in initial learning curves for new hires. Nonetheless, the company's ability to continually evolve its platform and services showcases the positive impact of prioritizing potential in a fast-paced industry.

Some questions for the leaders to reflect and answer to resolve the dilemma:

- Do we prioritize the experience of candidates, or do we believe in nurturing potential even if it means less experience on paper?
- Considering that fresh perspectives often come from those with potential, how does our hiring strategy impact innovation within the organization?
- How does our choice between experience and potential align with the long-term vision and growth plans of the organization?
- Does our approach promote diversity and inclusion by considering individuals with potential who may bring unique perspectives?
- Does our organization have a culture that encourages continuous learning and skill development, which can complement potential?
- How does our choice affect leadership diversity, considering that potential hires may bring fresh voices to leadership positions?

There could be several factors that could influence this decision in the context of your organization like:

Role Complexity: More complex roles may require experienced candidates.

Industry Dynamics: Fast-changing industries may favor potential to adapt to new challenges.

Market Competition: In highly competitive markets, the need for experienced candidates to hit the ground running may be more pronounced.

Resource Availability: The availability of resources for training and mentorship can influence the choice, especially in smaller organizations.

Organizational Maturity: The maturity of your organization and its existing talent pool can shape the decision, as established organizations may lean more toward experience.

There are other areas that get impacted because of a choice of this dilemma like:

- Short-term versus long-term performance
- Innovation and fresh perspectives
- Succession planning and leadership development
- Skill diversity within the workforce

Striking a strategic balance between experience and potential is another approach that many organizations adopt. This approach acknowledges that certain roles may benefit from the stability and expertise that experienced candidates bring, while others may require the dynamism and innovative thinking that potential candidates offer. Balancing these two facets of talent can be challenging but allows organizations to harness the best of both worlds, driving performance while fostering growth and innovation. *Dabur India Ltd., a leading Indian consumer goods company known for its health and wellness products, effectively balances between experience and potential in its talent strategy. In its core manufacturing and quality control functions, Dabur often prioritizes experience, especially when it comes to ensuring the consistency and safety of its products. Experienced professionals in these areas play a crucial role in upholding the company's reputation for quality. However, in its marketing and product development teams, Dabur actively seeks fresh talent and individuals with potential.*

HOPE IS NOT A STRATEGY

This approach helps the company stay innovative and responsive to changing consumer preferences and market trends, particularly in the wellness and Ayurvedic products sector. By strategically blending the expertise of experienced professionals with the fresh perspectives of potential talent, Dabur can maintain its legacy of quality while continually introducing new and innovative products to meet evolving consumer demands.

Here are some additional factors that influence the decision of choosing between Experience and Potential:

- **Nature of the Role**: The specific requirements of the role in question play a significant role in the decision-making process. Roles that demand specific technical expertise or extensive industry knowledge may lean more toward experienced candidates, while roles that require creativity and adaptability might favor potential.
- **Industry Dynamics**: The dynamics of the industry in which the organization operates can be a critical factor. Industries characterized by rapid change and innovation, such as technology or startups, may prioritize potential to stay agile and responsive. In contrast, highly regulated or traditional industries might prioritize experience for compliance and stability.
- **Company Culture**: The prevailing culture within the organization can strongly influence the decision. Companies with a strong commitment to mentorship and internal growth are more likely to favor potential, while those with a culture of stability and risk aversion may prioritize experience.
- **Resource Availability**: The availability of resources for training and development can impact the decision. Organizations with robust training programs and mentorship opportunities may be more inclined to hire for potential, as they have the means to bridge skill gaps.
- **Talent Pipeline**: Consideration of the existing talent pipeline within the organization is crucial. If there are promising internal candidates who exhibit potential, organizations may choose to develop these individuals to fulfill key roles.
- **Market Competition**: The competitive landscape within the industry can influence the decision. In a highly competitive job

market where experienced candidates are in high demand, it may be more challenging to attract top talent with potential.

- **Long-Term Strategy**: The organization's long-term strategic goals and vision play a significant role. If the strategy includes rapid growth and expansion into new markets or industries, potential may be favored to adapt to changing circumstances.
- **Team Dynamics**: The dynamics of existing teams can also be a factor. Hiring for potential can bring fresh perspectives but may disrupt existing team dynamics. Conversely, hiring experienced candidates may ensure stability but can lead to a lack of diversity in thought.
- **Succession Planning**: Consideration of succession planning is essential. Organizations that focus on grooming future leaders from within may prioritize potential to identify and nurture emerging talent.
- **Risk Tolerance**: The organization's appetite for risk is a critical factor. Hiring individuals with potential carries some level of uncertainty and risk, whereas experienced candidates offer a more predictable performance.

In essence, the decision between experience and potential is a pivotal one for organizations, shaping not only the composition of their workforce but also their capacity for growth, adaptability, and long-term success. It's a decision that requires careful consideration of the specific needs, culture, and goals of the organization in question.

Performance Metrics vs. Holistic Evaluation

> Deciding whether to primarily rely on quantitative performance metrics, be meritocratic or adopting a more holistic evaluation approach that considers loyalty, cultural fit, and intangible qualities or strike a balance somewhere in between.

Emphasizing performance metrics means relying heavily on quantitative data and objective measures to evaluate employees. This approach often involves setting clear and measurable goals, using Key Performance Indicators (KPIs), and assessing employees based on their ability to meet these predefined targets. Choosing this path can have several implications for the organization. On one hand, it offers a structured and objective way of evaluating employees' performance. It provides a clear understanding of who meets the set standards and who falls short, enabling precise differentiation. Additionally, it can foster a meritocratic culture, where rewards and promotions are directly linked to performance outcomes. However, the exclusive use of performance metrics has its downsides. It can sometimes lead to tunnel vision, where employees focus solely on meeting quantitative targets, potentially neglecting other crucial aspects of their roles. This approach may discourage risk-taking and experimentation, as individuals might be hesitant to deviate from established metrics.

On the other hand, adopting a holistic evaluation approach considers a broader spectrum of factors beyond just performance metrics. It takes into account intangible qualities such as cultural fit, adaptability, leadership potential, and loyalty to the organization. This approach aims to create a more comprehensive and nuanced understanding of an employee's contributions. Opting for holistic evaluation can have several advantages. It recognizes that not all valuable contributions can be quantified, and it values qualities that are critical for long-term organizational success. It can foster a more inclusive and engaged workforce, as employees feel that their unique skills and attributes are acknowledged. Additionally, it encourages innovation and adaptability, as these intangible qualities are essential in a rapidly changing business landscape. However, the holistic evaluation approach can also introduce subjectivity and bias into the assessment process. It may be challenging to establish clear benchmarks for qualities like cultural fit or adaptability, making evaluations less precise. Moreover, it requires effective communication and documentation to ensure that employees understand the criteria and the reasons behind their evaluations.

Choosing Performance Metrics-Based Evaluation Only	
Pros	Cons
Provides clear, objective benchmarks.	May lead to a narrow focus on quantitative targets.
Encourages goal-oriented performance.	Can neglect intangible qualities.
Easily measurable and comparable.	May discourage risk-taking and innovation.

Choosing Holistic Evaluation Only	
Pros	Cons
Considers employee contributions beyond numbers.	Can be subjective and prone to bias.
Encourages a more inclusive and engaged workforce.	May lack clear benchmarks for performance.
Fosters innovation and adaptability.	Requires effective communication and documentation.

Company A, a mid-sized manufacturing firm, heavily relies on performance metrics-based evaluation. They have implemented key performance indicators (KPIs) for various roles, tracking factors like production output, efficiency, and quality control. This approach has led to improved operational efficiency and increased profitability. Employees are incentivized to meet and exceed their KPIs, resulting in a highly competitive work environment. However, it has also created a culture where employees are solely focused on meeting individual targets, potentially stifling collaboration and innovation. Moreover, there have been concerns about employee burnout due to the constant pressure to achieve quantifiable results.

Company B, a boutique design agency, prioritizes a holistic evaluation approach. They value qualities like creativity, collaboration, and cultural fit as much as quantifiable performance metrics. This approach has fostered a highly creative and innovative work environment where employees feel valued for their unique contributions. Teamwork is encouraged, leading to the development of groundbreaking design projects. However, it can be challenging to quantify the impact of individual contributions, making it harder to reward high-performing employees or identify areas for improvement. Additionally, some employees may feel that their efforts are not adequately recognized if they don't align with specific metrics.

Some questions for the leaders to reflect and answer to resolve the dilemma:

- How do we strike a balance between quantitative performance metrics and a more holistic evaluation approach to ensure a fair assessment of our employees?
- Are our current evaluation methods aligned with our organizational values and long-term goals?
- How can we effectively measure intangible qualities like cultural fit and innovation in our workforce?
- What role does employee feedback and self-assessment play in our evaluation process, and how can we make it more meaningful?
- Can we identify areas where performance metrics are crucial and others where holistic evaluation adds significant value?
- How do we communicate the shift towards a more holistic approach to our employees and ensure their buy-in?

There could be several factors that could influence this decision in the context of your organization like:

Nature of the Industry: The level of competition and industry

> dynamics can determine the need for performance metrics or a more holistic approach.
>
> **Employee Skill Sets**: The type of skills and roles within the organization may require different evaluation methods.
>
> **Employee Engagement**: High levels of employee engagement may favor a more holistic approach.
>
> **Market Position**: The company's market position and competitive strategy may influence the need for innovation and intangible qualities in evaluation.
>
> **There are other areas that get impacted because of a choice of this dilemma like:**
>
> - Employee motivation and fairness perception
> - Retention and loyalty
> - Diversity and inclusion efforts
> - Alignment with organizational values and culture

In practice, many organizations find that a balance between performance metrics and holistic evaluation is the most effective approach. By combining quantitative measures with qualitative assessments, organizations can reap the benefits of both methods. This balance allows for the recognition of outstanding achievements while also considering the intangible qualities that contribute to a vibrant and successful workplace culture. Ultimately, the choice between performance metrics and holistic evaluation should align with the organization's values, goals, and the nature of its workforce. *Take the example of ABC Consultants. ABC Consultants specializes in providing management and strategy consulting services to various industries. The company recognizes the importance of both quantitative performance metrics and holistic evaluation in their operations. For client projects, ABC Consultants employs performance metrics such as project completion timelines, client satisfaction ratings, and revenue generated from each project. These metrics help in assessing the efficiency and profitability of their consulting services. It allows the firm to identify areas for improvement and reward high-performing project teams. When it comes* to employee development and promotions, ABC Consultants values holistic evaluation. They consider not only project performance but also employees' teamwork, leadership potential, creativity, and adaptability. This approach helps identify future leaders within the organization and ensures a diverse skill set among their consultants.

To encourage innovation and idea generation, ABC Consultants holds brainstorming sessions and innovation challenges where employees are evaluated based on the novelty and feasibility of their ideas. This holistic approach fosters a culture of innovation and continuous improvement. Recognizing the importance of employee well-being, ABC Consultants also assesses work-life balance through holistic evaluation. They encourage employees to maintain a healthy work-life balance and consider this factor when evaluating job satisfaction and performance.

The decision of whether to choose Performance Metrics or Holistic Evaluation is influenced by various factors that revolve around the organization's culture, industry, and goals. Here is a common set of factors that can influence this decision:

- **Nature of the Industry**: The industry in which the organization operates can impact the choice. For instance, highly regulated industries like finance and healthcare may rely more on performance metrics to ensure compliance, while creative industries may value holistic evaluation for fostering innovation.
- **Company Size**: The size of the organization can influence the decision. Smaller companies may have more flexibility to implement holistic evaluations, as they can maintain a closer connection with employees. Larger corporations may rely on performance metrics for consistency and scalability.
- **Employee Roles**: The nature of employees' roles within the organization can also be a determining factor. Sales teams, for example, often have quantifiable targets, making performance metrics essential. Meanwhile, roles that require creativity or teamwork may benefit more from holistic evaluation.
- **Long-Term vs. Short-Term Goals**: The organization's goals, especially its long-term vision, can impact the choice. If long-term success and adaptability are crucial, holistic evaluation may be favored to identify employees with leadership potential and adaptability.

- **Market Competitiveness**: The competitiveness of the market can drive the need for specific skills and quick results. In highly competitive markets, organizations may prioritize performance metrics to ensure they are on par with or ahead of competitors.
- **Employee Feedback and Engagement**: Listening to employee feedback and assessing engagement levels can guide the decision. If employees express dissatisfaction with rigid performance metrics or suggest a more inclusive approach, it might be time to consider holistic evaluation.
- **Innovation Requirements**: Organizations that heavily rely on innovation may opt for holistic evaluation to identify and nurture employees who contribute creatively and think outside the box.
- **Regulatory Compliance**: In industries with strict regulatory requirements, compliance can heavily influence the choice. Performance metrics may be necessary to ensure adherence to regulations.
- **Employee Development**: Consider whether the organization places a strong emphasis on employee development. If so, holistic evaluation may be used to identify individuals with high potential for growth and leadership roles.
- **Historical Practices**: The organization's historical practices and traditions in performance assessment can be a strong influence. Companies that have traditionally used one method may be hesitant to switch to another.
- **Resource Availability**: The availability of resources, including time, technology, and expertise, can impact the choice. Holistic evaluation may require more resources in terms of training and data collection.

In practice, organizations often find that a balanced approach, where they use performance metrics for certain roles and incorporate holistic evaluation for others, can provide a comprehensive view of employee performance and potential. This approach allows organizations to adapt to changing needs and goals while acknowledging the complexity of human contributions in the workplace.

In-House Talent vs. Outsourcing

> This dilemma revolves around balancing the use of in-house employees for core functions versus outsourcing to contract or gig workers for specialized or temporary needs.

At its core, this dilemma involves striking a balance between relying on in-house employees to perform essential functions and opting to delegate specific tasks or roles to external contractors, gig workers, or third-party service providers. One of the fundamental aspects of this decision revolves around cost. Maintaining in-house talent typically entails fixed costs such as salaries, benefits, office space, and equipment. In contrast, outsourcing offers a more variable cost structure, allowing organizations to pay for services as needed. While outsourcing can lead to cost savings, it may also mean less control over the quality and reliability of the work performed.

In-house talent provides organizations with a higher degree of control over their workforce. This control extends to the hiring process, training, and the ability to align employees with the company's values and culture. However, it may limit flexibility, making it challenging to quickly scale up or down in response to changing market demands. Outsourcing, on the other hand, offers greater flexibility in adapting to short-term needs but may come at the expense of direct control. Security and risk management are paramount concerns for organizations. In-house teams generally offer better control over data security and confidentiality, which is crucial in industries where privacy and regulatory compliance are top priorities. Outsourcing, while often cost-effective, can introduce risks related to data security, quality control, and compliance. Organizations must carefully assess these risks and implement measures to mitigate them.

Choosing To Have In-House Talent Only	
Pros	**Cons**
Better control and alignment with organizational culture.	Higher fixed costs, including salaries and benefits.
Immediate response to changes and challenges.	Limited scalability and flexibility.
Enhanced data security and confidentiality.	Skill gaps may require additional training.

Choosing Outsourcing Only	
Pros	**Cons**
Cost-effective for non-core tasks.	Reduced control and communication challenges.
Access to specialized skills and expertise.	Risk of quality control and data security issues.
Scalability and flexibility to meet changing demands.	May not align with organizational culture and values.

Symphony Limited, a well-known manufacturer of air coolers, places a strong emphasis on in-house talent for its product design and manufacturing processes. By investing in nurturing its in-house engineering and R&D teams, Symphony maintains strict quality control over its products. This approach allows them to innovate and adapt their products to changing consumer preferences swiftly. Symphony's engineers deeply understand the company's product lines and customer expectations, fostering a culture of innovation and product excellence. However, this strategy incurs higher fixed costs, including salaries and manufacturing facilities expenses, which can impact short-term profitability. Additionally, it requires continuous talent development efforts and may limit the company's flexibility in adjusting production capacity to market fluctuations.

HOPE IS NOT A STRATEGY

UrbanCompany, a rapidly growing online marketplace for local services, heavily relies on outsourcing for specific functions like customer support and digital marketing. By outsourcing these non-core functions to specialized service providers, UrbanCompany achieves cost efficiency and scalability. They can quickly adapt their workforce based on demand and seasonal fluctuations. This outsourcing strategy allows them to concentrate their in-house teams on core technology development and business expansion tasks, increasing their agility and responsiveness to customer needs. However, it introduces challenges related to maintaining consistent service levels and brand representation, as they depend on external partners. Moreover, the outsourced teams may not fully understand UrbanCompany's brand culture, potentially affecting customer interactions and service quality.

Some questions for the leaders to reflect and answer to resolve the dilemma:

- Does outsourcing align with our strategic goals, or does in-house talent better support our long-term objectives?
- Are we willing to invest more in in-house talent for higher quality, or is cost-efficiency more critical, even if it means outsourcing?
- What functions or tasks are core to our business, and should these be handled in-house, while outsourcing non-core activities?
- How do we mitigate risks associated with outsourcing, such as data security and quality control?
- Does outsourcing align with our organizational culture and values, or does it create a disconnect among employees?
- Can our in-house team adapt to fluctuations in demand, or is outsourcing more flexible for scaling up or down as needed?

There could be several factors that could influence this decision in the context of your organization like:

Nature of Work: The complexity and criticality of tasks influence the decision. Core functions may be kept in-house for better control, while non-core tasks can be outsourced.

> **Cost Analysis:** The financial impact, including salary expenses, training costs, and outsourcing fees, plays a significant role in the decision-making process.
>
> **Industry Regulations:** Compliance requirements may necessitate in-house talent for specific functions, especially in regulated industries.
>
> **Availability of Skills:** The availability of specific skills in the job market may affect whether it's feasible to hire in-house or outsource.
>
> **Technological Requirements:** For tasks requiring specialized technology or tools, outsourcing might be more practical than investing in in-house infrastructure.
>
> **There are other areas that get impacted because of a choice of this dilemma like:**
>
> - Cost management and flexibility
> - Control over quality and processes
> - Knowledge retention and intellectual property
> - Employee stability and job security

The decision between in-house talent and outsourcing should be made strategically, considering the nature of the work, cost implications, regulatory requirements, and long-term business goals. It's often a mix of both that offers the best balance of control, cost-effectiveness, and flexibility. *Quess Corp Limited, a leading Indian business services provider, exemplifies a balanced approach between in-house talent and outsourcing. Quess offers a wide range of services, including staffing, facilities management, and technology solutions, to various industries. Quess recognizes the importance of maintaining in-house expertise for its core services. It invests significantly in building and nurturing its internal teams, especially in areas like technology, innovation, and domain-specific knowledge. For instance, the company has its own technology development division that focuses on creating digital solutions and software products.*

While Quess excels in core services, it also leverages outsourcing for complementary functions. For instance, it may outsource certain back-office processes, customer support, or non-core IT operations to specialized service providers. This allows the organization to manage costs efficiently and maintain flexibility. Quess has strategically acquired other companies to expand its service offerings. These acquisitions often involve bringing specialized skills and services in-house while respecting the unique strengths of the acquired entities. This approach enhances Quess's capabilities without entirely outsourcing critical functions. Quess's flexibility in balancing in-house talent and outsourcing is largely driven by its client-centric approach. The company tailors its solutions to meet each client's specific needs, allowing for a customized mix of in-house and outsourced services.

The decision between in-house talent and outsourcing is influenced by a range of factors that can be categorized into different dimensions. Here's a common set of factors that can influence this decision:

- **Nature of the Task or Service**: The type of task or service required plays a significant role. Complex and core functions are often kept in-house, as they require a deep understanding of the company's operations and culture. In contrast, non-core or specialized tasks are more likely to be outsourced.
- **Cost Considerations**: Cost-effectiveness is a primary driver. Organizations assess the financial impact of hiring in-house employees, including salaries, benefits, training, and infrastructure costs, compared to the expenses associated with outsourcing.
- **Expertise and Skills**: Availability and accessibility of specific skills and expertise can influence the decision. If specialized skills are scarce in the job market or required only periodically, outsourcing becomes an attractive option.
- **Scalability and Flexibility**: Consideration of scalability is crucial. Outsourcing offers flexibility in quickly scaling up or down to meet changing demands, while in-house teams may face limitations in adapting to fluctuating workloads.
- **Quality Control**: The organization's ability to maintain quality standards is vital. In-house teams often provide better control over the quality of work and adherence to company standards, whereas outsourcing may introduce concerns about consistency.
- **Strategic Alignment**: The alignment of the task or service with the organization's strategic goals and core competencies is a key factor.

Tasks closely aligned with the organization's mission and strategy are more likely to be kept in-house.
- **Risk Management**: Risk considerations, including data security, intellectual property protection, and regulatory compliance, heavily influence the decision. Organizations may opt for in-house talent when stringent risk management is required.
- **Cultural Fit**: The extent to which the task or service requires alignment with the company's culture and values can be a determining factor. Core functions that contribute to the organizational culture may be handled in-house.
- **Regulatory Environment**: Industry-specific regulations and legal requirements can dictate whether certain tasks must be handled in-house. Organizations need to comply with regulations governing outsourcing if applicable.
- **Cost of Transition**: Transitioning from in-house to outsourcing or vice versa can have associated costs. Organizations must factor in these transition costs when making the decision.
- **Communication and Collaboration**: Considerations about communication and collaboration within teams and with external partners play a role. In-house teams can foster stronger collaboration, while outsourcing may require effective communication mechanisms.
- **Long-Term vs. Short-Term Needs**: The organization's outlook, whether focused on long-term stability or short-term efficiency, can influence the decision. Long-term strategic needs may favor in-house talent development.
- **Available Technology**: The availability of technology and tools necessary for the task or service can impact the decision. Outsourcing may require investments in technology integration.
- **Geographical Considerations**: Geographic location can be a factor. Certain tasks or services may be more cost-effective when outsourced to regions with lower labor costs.
- **Market Dynamics**: Market conditions, including competition and customer expectations, can influence the decision. Rapid market changes may favor outsourcing for flexibility.
- **Employee Morale**: The morale and job satisfaction of existing employees should be considered. Outsourcing decisions can affect the motivation and engagement of in-house teams.
- **Track Record of Providers**: Evaluating the reputation and track

record of potential outsourcing partners is essential. It helps ensure reliability and quality.

- **Sustainability and Social Responsibility**: Organizations focused on sustainability and social responsibility may factor in considerations related to outsourcing, such as ethical labor practices.

In conclusion, the decision to utilize in-house talent or outsourcing should be made strategically, taking into account the nature of the work, cost implications, regulatory requirements, and long-term business objectives. Many organizations find that a balanced approach, where core functions are kept in-house, and non-core or specialized tasks are outsourced, offers the best compromise between control, cost-effectiveness, and flexibility. Ultimately, the choice must align with the organization's unique circumstances and goals.

Expertise vs. Fungibility

> This dilemma is all about choosing between hiring individuals with deep expertise in a specific field versus those with a broader skill set and adaptability or selectively striking a balance between the two.

Hiring individuals with deep expertise in a specific field provides immediate benefits in terms of subject matter proficiency. These experts excel at tackling complex problems, driving innovation within their specialized domains, and establishing the organization's credibility in niche areas. They are often seen as the go-to resources for intricate challenges, which can elevate the company's reputation and build client trust. Moreover, their specialized knowledge can lead to industry recognition and thought leadership, further solidifying the organization's position. However, there are downsides to leaning exclusively towards expertise. Relying heavily on specialists can result in rigidity within the workforce. This rigidity may limit the organization's adaptability to market shifts or evolving customer needs. Over time, it may also create silos within the company, making collaboration across departments challenging. Additionally, the risk of succession vulnerabilities arises when there's an overdependence on experts, as it can be challenging to find replacements with comparable knowledge.

Opting for individuals with broader skill sets and adaptability, or fungibility, emphasizes versatility within the workforce. These professionals can quickly pivot between roles and responsibilities, responding adeptly to changing business demands. Fungible employees bring agility to the organization, allowing it to optimize resources efficiently. They can cover various functions, reducing the need for specialized hires in every domain. This versatility may also lead to innovative problem-solving, as employees draw from a diverse skill pool. Yet, choosing fungibility over expertise can introduce its own set of challenges. Versatility often implies a shallower level of expertise. While these employees can handle a range of tasks, they may lack the depth of knowledge required for complex, specialized tasks. Competency gaps may emerge in critical areas, potentially affecting the quality of work and overall efficiency. Overloading versatile employees with diverse responsibilities can lead to burnout and reduced productivity, which may negatively impact team morale and the organization's performance.

Choosing Expertise Only	
Pros	**Cons**
Specialized experts can tackle complex issues with precision.	Overemphasizing expertise can hinder adaptability to market shifts.
High expertise can lead to breakthroughs in specialized domains.	Lack of fungibility may result in siloed departments.
Attracting top experts can enhance industry credibility.	Heavy reliance on experts can create succession vulnerabilities.

Choosing Fungibility Only	
Pros	**Cons**
Fungible talent can swiftly adapt to changing roles and responsibilities.	Lack of specialization may lead to suboptimal solutions in complex scenarios.
Multi-skilled employees can cover various functions, optimizing resources.	Focusing solely on fungibility can result in skills gaps in critical areas.
Versatile professionals may offer creative solutions by drawing from diverse skills.	Overloading versatile employees can lead to burnout and reduced productivity.

An architectural firm known as "DesignMasters" places a strong emphasis on expertise. They hire renowned architects and designers with decades of specialized experience in designing iconic skyscrapers. While this strategy has allowed them to create some of the world's most stunning and innovative buildings, it also comes with challenges. They face higher labor costs due to the premium paid to top experts, and project timelines can be longer as they wait for the right specialist. However, their reputation for architectural excellence has attracted high-profile clients seeking bespoke designs. In this case, their commitment to expertise positively impacts their brand and quality but may limit scalability and speed of project completion.

"TechFlex Solutions" is a software development startup that leans towards fungibility. They hire developers with versatile skill sets who can work on a variety of programming languages and technologies. This approach allows them to quickly adapt to changing client needs and take on diverse projects. While it promotes flexibility, it may sometimes result in shallower expertise in certain areas. However, their ability to handle a wide range of projects has led to rapid growth and client retention. The downside is that they may not excel in highly specialized projects, but their agility and ability to diversify into new tech areas have been their strengths.

Some questions for the leaders to reflect and answer to resolve the dilemma:

- What is the primary driver for our talent acquisition strategy – specialized expertise or adaptability and versatility?
- How does our current talent mix align with our organizational goals and evolving market dynamics?
- Are we optimizing our human resources to adapt to changing business needs and industry disruptions?
- In which areas do we require deep subject matter experts, and where can we benefit from more flexible, multi-skilled professionals?
- How do our talent decisions impact our innovation and problem-solving capabilities?
- Are we fostering a culture that encourages continuous learning and development, regardless of whether employees lean more towards expertise or fungibility?

There could be several factors that could influence this decision in the context of your organization like:

Nature of Industry: Industries with rapidly changing landscapes may favor fungibility to adapt quickly, while highly regulated sectors often require deep expertise.

Organizational Strategy: Alignment with the company's strategic goals will dictate whether expertise or fungibility takes precedence.

Market Demand: Understanding customer demands and market trends guides the talent mix.

Technology Landscape: Tech-driven industries may prioritize adaptable, tech-savvy professionals.

Employee Development: A focus on fostering adaptability and learning can bridge the gap between expertise and fungibility.

There are other areas that get impacted because of a choice of this dilemma like:

- Project and task allocation
- Problem-solving and innovation
- Team dynamics and collaboration
- Success in rapidly changing industries

The most effective approach often lies in striking a strategic balance between expertise and fungibility. This balance allows organizations to leverage the strengths of both. Specialized experts can handle intricate tasks, while versatile employees adapt to dynamic challenges. Cross-functional training and fostering a culture of continuous learning can bridge the gap between these two ends of the spectrum. This balance optimizes the organization's ability to tackle complex problems, adapt to market shifts, and maintain a versatile, innovative workforce while minimizing the risks associated with extreme choices in either direction.

Let's consider a mid-sized consulting firm called "StrategyLink". This consulting firm specializes in providing strategic advice to businesses across various industries. They've found success by carefully balancing expertise and fungibility in their workforce. For complex industries like healthcare and finance, StrategyLink assigns projects to highly specialized teams comprising experts with deep industry knowledge. This approach ensures that they provide precise, industry-specific solutions that meet stringent regulatory requirements. In industries like retail and technology, where needs can change rapidly, StrategyLink maintains a pool of versatile consultants with broad skill sets.

These consultants can quickly adapt to new challenges and offer cross-industry insights that help clients stay agile. By maintaining a roster of specialized experts while also having adaptable consultants, StrategyLink can offer tailored solutions for their clients in various sectors. This balanced approach allows them to address a wide range of client needs effectively, contributing to their reputation and client satisfaction.

Several factors come into play when deciding whether to prioritize expertise or fungibility within an organization. Here's a common set of factors that influence this decision:

- **Nature of Industry and Market Dynamics**: In industries with complex, highly specialized requirements (e.g., healthcare, aerospace), deep expertise is often essential for compliance and quality. In rapidly evolving markets where adaptability is key (e.g., technology, startups), a more fungible workforce may be advantageous.
- **Organizational Goals and Strategy**: If the organization aims to be a market leader in a specific niche, expertise is crucial to establish dominance and build reputation whereas when the strategic focus is on agility and diversification, fungible talent can help seize opportunities in various domains.
- **Resource Constraints**: Organizations with substantial resources may afford specialized experts for in-depth tasks. Smaller organizations or those with budget constraints may rely on versatile talent to handle multiple roles.
- **Risk Tolerance**: Lower tolerance for errors, especially in areas like healthcare or finance, may necessitate specialized expertise. Higher risk tolerance and openness to experimentation may favor fungible talent.
- **Innovation Requirements**: For groundbreaking innovations, specialized knowledge can be a catalyst whereas fungible employees can facilitate cross-pollination of ideas, fostering innovation through diverse perspectives.
- **Long-Term vs. Short-Term Goals**: Long-term objectives may require deep domain knowledge, while short-term goals may lean towards flexibility. Short-term projects or quick market entry may benefit from fungible resources.

- **Client or Customer Expectations**: Client expectations for specialized knowledge may drive the need for expertise. When clients seek versatility or customized solutions, fungible teams may be more suitable.
- **Technology and Automation**: Increasing automation may reduce the need for expertise in certain repetitive tasks while fungible employees may be better suited to managing and adapting to automated processes.
- **Competition and Talent Availability**: In highly competitive fields, attracting top specialists may be challenging whereas a larger pool of versatile talent may be readily available.
- **Regulatory and Compliance Requirements**: Industries with strict regulations (e.g., pharmaceuticals) may require deep expertise to ensure compliance. Less-regulated industries may have more room for fungible talent.

In conclusion, the Expertise vs. Fungibility dilemma has profound implications for an organization's adaptability, problem-solving capabilities, and workforce dynamics. The decision should align with the organization's strategic goals and its ability to navigate the ever-evolving business landscape effectively.

| 3.9 |
CUSTOMER DILEMMAS

How will you use this chapter of the book?

If you are the founder or the CEO of a company and if you and your leadership team have a clear point of view (PoV) on the following questions and all of you are ALIGNED, then you can choose to move to the next chapter of the book. However, if you see a dissonance or have conflicting views, then we suggest digging deeper, going through this chapter and reflecting on different angles we bring in there.

Here are the questions for you to discuss and ponder-

- Are our decisions in sync with our strategic goals and values for both customers and employees?
- How can we allocate resources wisely to address these dilemmas without neglecting anyone?
- Are we regularly evaluating the effects of our decisions on customer loyalty, employee morale, and our brand's image?
- Do our choices prioritize long-term relationships over short-term gains?
- Is our culture fostering innovation and adaptability to address these dilemmas?
- Is our organizational culture supportive of finding the right balance between customer and employee priorities?
- How do our choices affect our competitive position, considering both customer retention and acquisition?
- How do we define and measure success in these areas, and how can we improve continually?
- Are we considering ethics when making choices that affect customers and employees?

Are our leadership actions consistent with our decisions regarding these dilemmas, setting the right tone for the organization?

In business, decisions concerning customers are at the heart of success. These customer-related dilemmas require careful consideration and strategic thinking. In this section, we delve into the essential dilemmas that business leaders encounter when crafting customer-centric strategies. By exploring these dilemmas, leaders can better understand the intricacies of meeting customer expectations, fostering loyalty, and achieving sustainable growth in today's competitive marketplace.

When determining the way customer-related decisions will be taken in an organization, leaders need to take into account a wide range of aspects to ensure that these decisions align with the organization's goals, values, and customer-centric strategies. Here are several key aspects to consider:

- **Organizational Strategy and Goals**: Ensure that customer-related decisions align with the overall strategic objectives and long-term goals of the organization.
- **Customer Expectations**: Understand the specific needs, expectations, and preferences of your target customer segments.
- **Market Research**: Conduct thorough market research to gain insights into market trends, customer behavior, and competitors.
- **Data and Analytics**: Utilize data-driven insights to inform decision-making, including customer feedback, sales data, and customer journey analytics.
- **Customer Segmentation**: Segment your customer base to tailor decisions and strategies to different customer groups effectively.
- **Customer Lifetime Value (CLV)**: Consider the CLV of customers to assess their long-term value to the organization.
- **Customer Feedback**: Collect and analyze direct feedback from customers through surveys, reviews, and other feedback mechanisms.
- **Employee Engagement**: Ensure that employees are engaged and empowered to deliver exceptional customer experiences.
- **Resource Allocation**: Allocate resources, including budget, personnel, and technology, to support customer-centric initiatives.
- **Technology and Tools**: Invest in the right technology and tools to enhance customer interactions and streamline processes.

- **Customer Journey Mapping**: Map out the customer journey to identify pain points and opportunities for improvement.
- **Customer Service and Support**: Develop and maintain efficient customer service and support systems.
- **Marketing and Communication**: Create effective marketing strategies and messaging that resonate with your target audience.
- **Customer Retention**: Implement customer retention strategies such as loyalty programs and relationship-building initiatives.
- **Pricing Strategy**: Determine pricing strategies that balance profitability with customer affordability and value perception.
- **Brand Reputation**: Protect and enhance the brand's reputation by delivering consistent quality and value.
- **Ethical Considerations**: Ensure that customer-related decisions adhere to ethical standards and are aligned with corporate social responsibility (CSR) values.
- **Compliance and Regulations**: Stay informed about relevant industry regulations and compliance requirements related to customer data and interactions.
- **Innovation**: Encourage innovation to meet evolving customer needs and stay ahead of competitors.
- **Competitor Analysis**: Continuously monitor and analyze competitors to identify opportunities and threats in the market.
- **Training and Development**: Invest in employee training and development to equip them with the skills needed for exceptional customer interactions.
- **Risk Management**: Assess and mitigate potential risks associated with customer-related decisions.
- **Crisis Management**: Develop strategies and plans for handling customer-related crises or issues effectively.
- **Customer-Centric Culture**: Cultivate a customer-centric organizational culture that emphasizes the importance of customer satisfaction and loyalty.

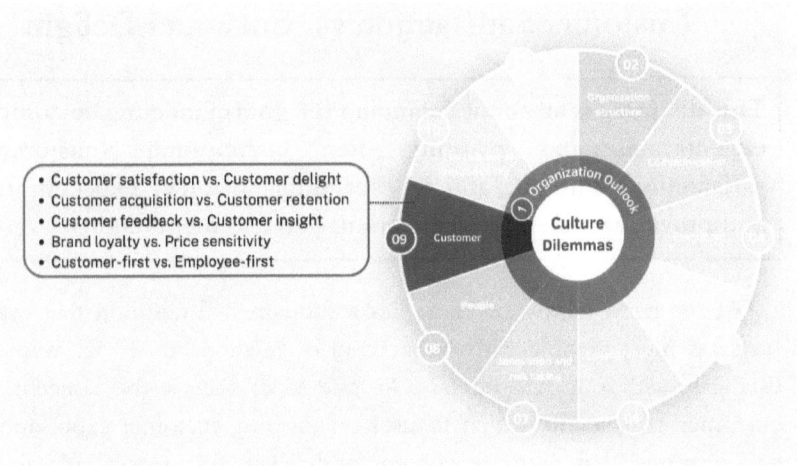

While there are many dilemmas when we think of customer, we will focus on five pivotal ones that often take center stage:

- **Customer satisfaction vs. Customer delight**
- **Customer acquisition vs. customer retention**
- **Customer feedback vs. Market research**
- **Brand loyalty vs. Price sensitivity**
- **Customer first vs. Employee first**

Let's look at each of them in greater detail.

Customer Satisfaction vs. Customer Delight

> **This dilemma is all about balancing the goal of meeting customer expectations and ensuring their contentment (customer satisfaction) with the aim of exceeding customer expectations and providing exceptional experiences (customer delight).**

At the heart of this dilemma lies a fundamental question that every business must grapple with: What kind of relationship do we want to establish with our customers? On one side, there's the concept of customer satisfaction, which focuses on meeting customer expectations and ensuring that they are content with their experiences. It's about delivering on promises, being consistent, and providing a baseline level of quality and service.

On the other side of the spectrum, we have customer delight. This approach is more ambitious, aiming not just to meet but to exceed customer expectations. It's about going above and beyond, creating memorable and exceptional experiences that leave customers pleasantly surprised. Delightful experiences are the kind that customers share with friends and family, fostering loyalty and advocacy.

The choice between satisfaction and delight is far from trivial, as it can significantly impact various facets of the organization. When a business opts for customer satisfaction, it often follows a more conservative and risk-averse approach. The focus is on operational efficiency, consistency, and minimizing the chance of negative experiences. While this can lead to stability and reduced costs, it may limit the organization's ability to stand out in a competitive market. Conversely, businesses that prioritize customer delight understand that remarkable experiences often require more investment, both in terms of resources and creativity. This approach can foster strong customer loyalty and positive word-of-mouth marketing. However, it can also be resource-intensive and potentially unsustainable in the long run if not managed carefully.

Moreover, the decision to aim for customer satisfaction or delight ripples through various aspects of the organization, influencing marketing strategies, product or service design, employee training, and even the company's overall culture. It can impact hiring practices, employee empowerment, and the emphasis placed on customer feedback and innovation.

Choosing Customer Satisfaction Only	
Pros	**Cons**
Higher customer retention	Limited customer loyalty
Reduced churn	Missed opportunities for growth
Cost-effective	Vulnerability to competitive disruption

Choosing Customer Delight Only	
Pros	**Cons**
Strong customer loyalty	Resource-intensive
Positive word-of-mouth	Potential inconsistency in exceeding expectations
Competitive advantage	Not always feasible in all situations

McDonald's, a global fast-food chain, places a strong emphasis on customer satisfaction. They have streamlined their menu to provide consistent and familiar options at affordable prices. Customers can expect the same taste and quality at any McDonald's location worldwide. The focus on satisfaction ensures that customers receive what they expect, leading to a sense of reliability and comfort when choosing McDonald's. However, this approach may not provide the same level of excitement and delight as other dining experiences.

The Walt Disney Company, known for its theme parks and entertainment offerings, prioritizes customer delight as a core strategy. Disney goes above and beyond to create magical and immersive experiences for its visitors. They constantly innovate by introducing new attractions, shows, and experiences that exceed visitor expectations. The emphasis on delight ensures that visitors leave with unforgettable memories and a strong desire to return. However, achieving this level of delight often involves substantial investments in creativity and innovation.

Some questions for the leaders to reflect and answer to resolve the dilemma:

- How important is it for us to not only meet customer expectations but to exceed them?
- Do we understand the difference between customer satisfaction and customer delight and how it applies to our business?
- What kind of customer relationships do we aim to build - those based on contentment or those that create loyal advocates?
- Are we willing to invest in resources and efforts to consistently provide exceptional experiences for our customers?
- How do we measure and track customer satisfaction and delight, and how does this information guide our decisions?
- Do we have a strategy in place to handle situations where exceeding customer expectations may not be feasible or sustainable?

There could be several factors that could influence this decision in the context of your organization like:

Industry Competition: The level of competition in your industry can drive the need for delight over satisfaction or vice versa.

Target Market: Understanding your customer's preferences and expectations is crucial in making this decision.

Product or Service Type: The nature of your offerings can influence whether you aim for satisfaction or delight.

> **Brand Positioning**: Your brand's identity and positioning in the market play a significant role.
>
> **Resource Availability**: The resources you can allocate to customer experience efforts affect your choice.
>
> There are other areas that get impacted because of a choice of this dilemma like:
>
> - Customer loyalty and advocacy
> - Resource allocation for customer service
> - Brand image and reputation
> - Employee engagement and motivation
> - Customer retention and repeat business

Customer satisfaction and customer delight can coexist in the organization. Many companies aim for a baseline of satisfaction while striving to exceed expectations for certain customer segments or on specific occasions.

For example, "The Rustic Kitchen" is a regional restaurant chain with a focus on providing a pleasant dining experience for its customers. Here's how they balance customer satisfaction and customer delight:

- *The Rustic Kitchen ensures that every visit offers customers consistent quality in terms of food taste, portion size, and service. They maintain a standardized menu and well-trained staff to meet customer expectations for reliability and satisfaction.*
- *While the restaurant maintains a core menu for consistency, they periodically introduce seasonal or special dishes that surprise and delight customers. These innovative offerings provide an element of excitement for returning customers and create buzz among new visitors.*
- *The Rustic Kitchen uses customer data and feedback to personalize the dining experience. They might offer personalized recommendations based on past orders or celebrate birthdays with a complimentary dessert. This personal touch contributes to both satisfaction and delight.*

- *The restaurant actively seeks feedback from customers and listens to their suggestions and concerns. This feedback loop helps them identify areas where they can enhance satisfaction by addressing common issues while also finding opportunities to introduce delightful changes based on customer preferences.*
- *The Rustic Kitchen pays attention to creating an engaging ambiance with occasional live music, themed décor, or seasonal decorations. These elements go beyond the meal itself to create memorable dining experiences.*
- *Employees are trained not only to provide efficient service but also to recognize opportunities for delight. They have the flexibility to make small, unexpected gestures like offering a complimentary appetizer or engaging in friendly conversation, enhancing both satisfaction and delight.*

Here's a deeper exploration of the factors influencing the decision between customer satisfaction and customer delight:

- **Industry and Competitive Landscape**: The nature of your industry plays a vital role. In highly competitive markets, businesses often lean towards customer delight as a means to differentiate themselves. In contrast, in mature industries, the focus might be more on maintaining customer satisfaction as it can be challenging to introduce truly unique offerings.
- **Customer Segmentation**: Understanding your customer segments is crucial. Some customer segments may value consistency and reliability (satisfaction), while others may be more receptive to unique, delightful experiences. Segmenting your audience helps tailor your approach.
- **Resources and Budget**: The allocation of resources, especially budget, is a significant factor. Delivering delightful experiences often requires more investment in training, technology, and creative initiatives. Smaller businesses might find it more challenging to sustain a delight-focused strategy.
- **Organizational Culture**: Your Company's culture and values can influence the direction you choose. A culture that encourages innovation, empowerment, and a customer-centric mindset is more likely to pursue customer delight.
- **Technological Capabilities**: Advancements in technology can enable more personalized and delightful experiences. Assessing

your technological capabilities and readiness can help determine your path.

- **Customer Feedback:** Analyzing customer feedback and preferences is essential. If your customers consistently express a desire for innovative, delightful experiences, it's a signal to move in that direction.
- **Employee Training and Engagement:** Employees are key in delivering exceptional experiences. The level of training, empowerment, and engagement your employees receive can determine your ability to provide delight.
- **Long-Term vs. Short-Term Goals:** Consider your organization's long-term vision. While delight can foster customer loyalty, it may take time to yield results. Satisfaction, on the other hand, might yield quicker gains.
- **Risk Tolerance:** Assess your organization's risk tolerance. Pursuing delight often involves experimentation, which can lead to occasional failures. Determine how comfortable your organization is with such risks.
- **Customer Lifetime Value:** Evaluate the lifetime value of your customers. In industries where customers make repeat purchases over time, the value of delighting and retaining customers can be significant.
- **Regulatory Environment:** Some industries, such as finance or healthcare, have stringent regulations that might limit the extent to which you can pursue customer delight. Compliance requirements should factor into your decision.
- **Market Trends:** Monitor market trends and shifts in consumer behavior. A trend towards heightened customer expectations for exceptional experiences may push you towards delight.
- **Competency and Expertise:** Assess your organization's competency in delivering delightful experiences. Do you have the expertise and creative talent to consistently create remarkable moments?
- **Brand Positioning:** Consider your brand's current positioning and whether it aligns better with satisfaction or delight. Changing your positioning can be challenging and may require significant rebranding efforts.

HOPE IS NOT A STRATEGY

In the end, this dilemma underscores the importance of aligning the customer experience strategy with the organization's broader goals and capabilities. Striking the right balance between satisfaction and delight is not a one-size-fits-all proposition. It requires a nuanced understanding of your industry, target audience, and competitive landscape, as well as a commitment to continuous improvement in delivering exceptional value to customers. Ultimately, it's about choosing a path that aligns with your organization's identity and long-term vision in an ever-evolving marketplace.

Customer Acquisition vs. Customer Retention

> This dilemma is all about deciding whether to focus efforts and resources on attracting new customers (customer acquisition) or on retaining existing customers through loyalty programs and relationship-building (customer retention) or striking a balance between the two.

The dilemma of customer acquisition versus customer retention is a pivotal one for businesses across various industries. It essentially involves making a strategic choice between two fundamental approaches to managing a customer base: whether to channel efforts and resources towards acquiring new customers or to prioritize retaining existing ones. The decision, while seemingly straightforward, has far-reaching consequences that can significantly impact different aspects of an organization.

At the heart of this dilemma is the allocation of resources. Opting for customer acquisition often means investing in marketing campaigns, sales efforts, and lead generation to bring in fresh clientele. Conversely, choosing customer retention directs resources towards loyalty programs, customer support, and relationship-building activities aimed at nurturing and satisfying the existing customer base. The allocation of budget, personnel, and time must be carefully considered, as it can influence the overall financial health and efficiency of the organization. The choice between acquisition and retention can have a direct impact on a company's revenue stream. Acquiring new customers can provide an immediate revenue boost, especially in industries with substantial market potential. However, the initial acquisition cost can be high, and it may take time to recoup the investment. On the other hand, retention strategies are focused on maximizing the lifetime value of existing customers, which often results in a stable and predictable revenue stream.

The choice between acquisition and retention can influence how a company is perceived in the market. Aggressive acquisition strategies may position a company as growth-oriented and innovative, attracting investors and partners. Conversely, a strong emphasis on customer retention can signal stability and customer-centricity, which can build trust and brand reputation. Another key consideration is the overall customer experience. Retention strategies typically prioritize delivering exceptional experiences to existing customers. In contrast, acquisition strategies may focus on attracting a larger volume of customers without necessarily delivering personalized experiences. The choice made can influence customer satisfaction and word-of-mouth recommendations.

Choosing Customer acquisition only	
Pros	**Cons**
Potential for rapid growth.	High initial costs.
Opportunity to tap into new markets.	Uncertainty regarding customer loyalty.
Fresh perspectives and insights from new customers.	Market saturation may lead to fierce competition.

Choosing Customer retention only	
Pros	**Cons**
Stable revenue from loyal customers.	May limit immediate growth.
Lower acquisition costs.	Requires continuous investment in relationship-building.
Opportunity to cross-sell or upsell to existing customers.	Vulnerable to customer churn in a changing market.

Uber is a prime example of a company that has traditionally focused on customer acquisition. Uber aggressively expanded into new markets, offering attractive promotions and discounts to attract riders and drivers. Their goal was to quickly gain a large user base and dominate the ride-sharing industry. While this strategy led to rapid growth and market dominance, it also resulted in significant losses due to high customer acquisition costs and driver incentives. Uber's emphasis on customer acquisition has sometimes overshadowed concerns about customer retention, leading to occasional issues with customer loyalty and trust.

HOPE IS NOT A STRATEGY

Amazon Prime is a notable example of a company that prioritizes customer retention. Amazon invested in creating a loyalty program that offers a wide range of benefits, including free shipping, streaming services, and exclusive deals. They aim to keep customers engaged and loyal to the Amazon ecosystem, encouraging frequent purchases and long-term memberships. While Amazon also invests in customer acquisition through advertising and marketing, their primary focus is on retaining existing Prime members. This strategy has contributed to Amazon's long-term success, as Prime members tend to spend more and shop more frequently on the platform.

Some questions for the leaders to reflect and answer to resolve the dilemma:

- What is our long-term vision for the company, and how does it align with customer acquisition and retention strategies? Are we looking for rapid growth or long-lasting relationships?
- How are we allocating our resources, both in terms of budget and manpower, between customer acquisition and customer retention efforts?
- Do we understand the lifetime value of our customers? How does this information impact our strategy? Are we willing to invest in retaining high-value customers even if it means reducing acquisition efforts?
- What are our competitors doing? Are they primarily focused on acquisition, retention, or a balance of both? How should our strategy align with or differentiate from theirs?
- What is the state of our industry or market? Is it growing, saturated, or evolving rapidly? How should this influence our customer strategy?
- Are we actively seeking and listening to customer feedback? How can customer input guide our decision between acquisition and retention strategies?

There could be several factors that could influence this decision in the context of your organization like:

Industry Type: In some industries with high competition and frequent market entrants, acquisition may be a priority. In others, like subscription-based services, retention is critical for profitability.

Customer Acquisition Costs: The cost of acquiring a new customer can be significant. This cost needs to be balanced against the potential revenue generated from that customer over time.

Customer Churn Rate: Understanding how quickly customers leave (churn) can impact the decision. High churn rates may necessitate a stronger focus on retention efforts.

Product or Service Maturity: For new products or services, acquisition might be crucial for initial growth. Mature products may require stronger retention efforts.

Market Share: In a crowded market, acquisition may be necessary to gain a foothold, while in a niche market, retention can be more critical.

There are other areas that get impacted because of a choice of this dilemma like:

- Sales and revenue growth
- Marketing strategy and budget allocation
- Customer lifetime value
- Organizational culture and customer-centricity
- Competitor analysis and market share

Customer acquisition and customer retention can coexist. In fact, they often should. Companies can balance these strategies by investing in acquisition to fuel growth while also nurturing and retaining valuable existing customers. *Buffer is a social media management company that offers tools to schedule, publish, and analyze content across various social media platforms. They have successfully struck a balance between customer acquisition and customer retention. Buffer actively invests in content marketing and social media advertising to attract new users to their platform. They create valuable blog posts, webinars, and guides on social media best practices to draw in potential customers. By targeting relevant keywords and providing helpful content, they acquire new users interested in social media management. On the other hand, Buffer places a strong emphasis on retaining existing customers.*

They offer excellent customer support, including a responsive help center and personalized email support. Buffer also provides a user-friendly platform with features that cater to the needs of their current customers. They keep users engaged through regular updates and improvements to their tool, ensuring that customers continue to find value in their service.

Several common factors influence the decision of choosing between customer acquisition and customer retention:

- **Market Maturity**: In a mature market where most potential customers are already using a product or service, the emphasis might shift toward customer retention. Conversely, in emerging markets, acquiring new customers may be a higher priority.
- **Competitive Landscape**: The level of competition in the industry plays a significant role. In highly competitive markets, acquiring new customers might require more aggressive strategies, while in less competitive markets, retaining existing customers could be easier and more cost-effective.
- **Customer Lifetime Value (CLV)**: Understanding the long-term value of a customer is crucial. If the CLV is high, businesses may be more inclined to invest in customer retention efforts. If it's relatively low, they might prioritize acquisition to grow the customer base.
- **Resource Availability**: The availability of resources, both in terms of budget and personnel, can impact the decision. Smaller companies with limited resources may opt for retention strategies that are less costly.
- **Product or Service Nature**: Some products or services are more suited to frequent purchases or subscriptions, making customer retention essential. Others, like one-time purchases or specialized products, may require continuous customer acquisition efforts.
- **Customer Behavior**: Analyzing customer behavior is critical. If customers frequently switch brands or products, businesses may need to focus more on retention. However, if customers tend to stay loyal to a brand, acquisition strategies could be prioritized.
- **Customer Feedback**: Customer feedback can provide insights into whether there are issues with the product, service, or

customer experience that need to be addressed for better retention. Listening to customers can guide the decision-making process.

- **Profit Margins**: Understanding the profit margins associated with acquisition and retention strategies is vital. Sometimes, acquiring a new customer can be costly upfront but profitable in the long run, while retaining existing customers may yield immediate returns.
- **Industry Regulations**: Some industries have regulations that affect customer acquisition and retention strategies. For instance, data privacy laws can impact how customer data is used for acquisition and retention efforts.
- **Customer Segment Differences**: Diverse customer segments may require tailored approaches. High-value customers might warrant special retention efforts, while acquisition strategies might target a broader audience.
- **Technology and Tools**: The availability of technology and tools for customer acquisition and retention can influence the choice. Advanced analytics and customer relationship management (CRM) systems can enhance both approaches.
- **Economic Conditions**: Economic factors, such as inflation or economic downturns, can influence customer behavior and purchasing decisions, impacting the effectiveness of acquisition or retention strategies.
- **Brand Reputation**: A strong brand reputation can facilitate both acquisition and retention. Customers are more likely to stay with a reputable brand, while a positive brand image can attract new customers.

In reality, most organizations strike a balance between customer acquisition and retention. This balance depends on factors like industry, growth stage, available resources, and market conditions. Successful companies often recognize that both strategies are interconnected and can feed into each other. Acquiring new customers is essential for growth, while retaining existing customers can provide a stable foundation for long-term success. The challenge lies in finding the right equilibrium that suits the specific goals and circumstances of the organization.

Customer Feedback vs. Market Research

> This dilemma is all about balancing the reliance on direct customer feedback, surveys, and data (customer feedback) with comprehensive market research, industry analysis, and data-driven insights (market research) for decision-making.

Customer feedback involves listening to the voices of your existing customers. It's about collecting direct insights, opinions, and experiences from those who have interacted with your products or services. This can take the form of surveys, reviews, social media comments, or direct communication with customers. The advantage of customer feedback is its immediacy. It provides a real-time pulse on customer sentiment and preferences. On the other hand, market research is a systematic approach to understanding the broader market landscape. It involves analyzing industry trends, studying competitors, and gathering data from various sources to make informed decisions. Market research provides a more comprehensive view of market dynamics, helping organizations identify emerging opportunities and potential threats.

There could be several impacts of choosing one over the other like:

- **Decision Timeliness**: Relying primarily on customer feedback can lead to faster decision-making, allowing organizations to respond quickly to customer needs. However, it might miss longer-term market trends that require in-depth research.
- **Resource Allocation**: Focusing extensively on market research can be resource-intensive in terms of time and budget. This may divert resources from addressing immediate customer concerns.
- **Risk Management**: Depending on customer feedback alone might expose organizations to risks associated with not understanding broader market shifts. Relying on market research alone may lead to missing out on specific customer pain points.
- **Competitive Edge**: Customer feedback can help in retaining and nurturing existing customers, ensuring their satisfaction. Market research can provide insights into how to gain an edge over competitors in the wider market.

- **Product Development**: Customer feedback is invaluable for improving existing products and services. Market research is crucial when considering new product launches, expansions, or diversifications.
- **Innovation**: Market research can uncover new market niches and unmet needs. Customer feedback guides incremental improvements based on current offerings.

Choosing Customer Feedback Only	
Pros	Cons
Immediate insights	Limited scope
Cost-effective	Potential bias
Strengthens customer relationships.	Lack of broader market context.

Choosing Market Research Only	
Pros	Cons
Comprehensive data	Time-consuming
Industry insights	Expensive
Reduced bias	May not capture real-time trends

Apple is well-known for its emphasis on customer feedback in product development. The company actively seeks input from its user base through surveys, feedback forms, and online forums. This approach has allowed Apple to refine its products based on real user experiences, leading to highly user-centric designs and innovations such as the iPhone and iPad. By prioritizing customer feedback, Apple has built a loyal customer base and achieved remarkable success in the consumer electronics industry.

Conversely, Microsoft, a leading technology company, places a strong emphasis on market research to drive its product development and business strategies. Microsoft conducts comprehensive market analysis to understand customer needs, competitive landscapes, and industry trends. This research informs decisions regarding product launches, feature updates, and market positioning. Microsoft's commitment to market research has played a crucial role in the success of products like Windows, Office, and Azure, allowing the company to adapt to changing customer demands and maintain a significant presence in the tech industry.

Some questions for the leaders to reflect and answer to resolve the dilemma:

- Do we prioritize insights from existing customers or rely on broader market data when making strategic decisions?
- Are we inclined to act on real-time feedback from customers, or do we prefer comprehensive, data-driven market research that takes longer to gather?
- How do we allocate our resources between gathering customer feedback and conducting market research? What's our budget and time allocation for each?
- What level of risk are we comfortable with? Customer feedback can be immediate but might lack broader market insights, while market research offers more comprehensive data but carries the risk of delayed decision-making.
- Is our industry fast-paced and competitive, where quick adjustments are crucial (customer feedback), or do we operate in a stable environment that values extensive research (market research)?
- How do we strike a balance between the qualitative insights obtained from customer feedback and the quantitative data derived from market research?

There could be several factors that could influence this decision in the context of your organization like:

Decision Timeliness: If the organization needs to make swift decisions, customer feedback can provide real-time insights. Market research may take longer to yield results.

Budget Constraints: The availability of funds may dictate the extent of market research or customer feedback activities the organization can undertake.

Industry Dynamics: Some industries require rapid adaptation to changing customer preferences, making customer feedback critical, while others necessitate in-depth market analysis.

Product Lifecycle: The stage of a product or service in its lifecycle can influence the need for continuous customer feedback or periodic market research.

Data Availability: The amount and quality of available data sources can affect the feasibility and accuracy of both approaches.

There are other areas that get impacted because of a choice of this dilemma like:

- Product development and enhancement
- Marketing strategy and messaging
- Customer satisfaction and loyalty
- Innovation and product roadmap
- Competitive intelligence and market positioning

Balancing these approaches is key. Many successful organizations use a combination of both customer feedback and market research. They recognize that customer feedback offers immediate insights for fine-tuning existing operations, while market research is essential for long-term strategic planning and innovation. The optimal balance depends on the industry, organizational goals, and the competitive landscape, but understanding the value of both is crucial for informed decision-making. *The NorthWest Boutique, a regional retail chain specializing in outdoor apparel and equipment, excels in striking a balance between customer feedback and market research. On one hand, the company actively seeks customer feedback through surveys, online reviews, and in-store interactions. They use this direct input to improve existing product lines, enhance customer service, and refine in-store experiences. For example, after receiving feedback about the need for more sustainable product options, they introduced eco-friendly clothing lines, which received positive customer responses. On the other hand, The NorthWest Boutique also conducts market research to stay competitive in the rapidly evolving outdoor retail sector. They analyze market trends, competitor strategies, and emerging consumer preferences to make informed decisions about expanding product categories and entering new markets. For instance, their market research led to the successful introduction of a line of outdoor adventure gear, aligning with a growing interest in outdoor activities. By combining customer feedback and market research, The NorthWest Boutique maintains a loyal customer base while remaining agile and responsive to broader industry changes. This balance enables them to provide tailored products and experiences while staying competitive in a dynamic market.*

The factors that influence the decision of whether to choose customer feedback or market research:

- **Objectives and Scope**: Consider the specific objectives of the research. If the aim is to understand customer satisfaction with current products or services, customer feedback might suffice. If the goal is to identify new market opportunities or assess industry trends, market research is more appropriate.
- **Resource Constraints**: Evaluate the available resources in terms of time, budget, and expertise. Customer feedback can often be collected quickly and at a lower cost, while market research might require more extensive resources.
- **Industry Dynamics**: Different industries have varying levels of complexity and volatility. In rapidly changing industries like technology, market research may be more critical, whereas stable industries might rely more on customer feedback.
- **Competitive Landscape**: Analyze the level of competition within your industry. If competition is fierce, market research can uncover unique market gaps and positioning opportunities. In less competitive markets, customer feedback may be sufficient for maintaining customer loyalty.
- **Customer Base**: Consider the size and diversity of your customer base. If your customer base is large and diverse, market research can provide insights into different customer segments. For smaller, niche businesses, customer feedback may be more relevant.

- **Product Lifecycle**: The stage of your product or service lifecycle matters. In the introduction phase, market research helps identify market fit, while in the maturity phase, customer feedback aids in continuous improvement.
- **Regulatory Environment**: Some industries have strict regulations regarding customer data and market research practices. Ensure compliance with these regulations when choosing your research approach.
- **Geographical Expansion**: If you plan to expand into new markets, market research is vital to understanding local preferences and market conditions. Customer feedback may provide insights at a micro-level but might not cover macro-market dynamics.
- **Risk Tolerance**: Assess your organization's appetite for risk. Relying heavily on customer feedback may lead to a lower risk of product/service failure, but it might also miss out on broader market trends and opportunities.
- **Strategic Goals**: Align your research approach with your organization's strategic goals. If the goal is short-term profitability and retention, customer feedback is crucial. If long-term growth and innovation are the focus, market research plays a pivotal role.
- **Customer Engagement**: Evaluate how engaged your customers are. Highly engaged customers may provide valuable feedback, while less engaged customers might not provide representative insights.
- **Data Accessibility**: Consider the availability of historical data. If you have a rich history of customer feedback, it can complement market research efforts and provide valuable context.

Ultimately, organizations should strike a balance that aligns with their specific goals, resources, and competitive landscape, recognizing that both customer feedback and market research have their unique strengths and limitations.

Brand Loyalty vs. Price Sensitivity

> This dilemma is all about choosing between building strong brand loyalty through consistent quality and experiences (brand loyalty) and addressing price-sensitive customer demands by offering competitive pricing (price sensitivity) or choosing a middle ground.

The Brand Loyalty vs. Price Sensitivity dilemma presents a critical decision for businesses in how they position themselves in the market and cater to customer expectations. On one hand, emphasizing brand loyalty entails consistently delivering top-quality products or services and ensuring exceptional customer experiences. This approach aims to cultivate a loyal customer base that values the brand's reliability, trustworthiness, and overall value proposition. These loyal customers are often willing to pay premium prices and tend to stick with the brand over the long term. Conversely, addressing price sensitivity involves offering competitive pricing, discounts, and deals to attract and retain customers who prioritize affordability. This strategy aims to capture a broader market share by appealing to cost-conscious consumers who may be less concerned with brand loyalty and more focused on securing the best deal. Price-sensitive customers are more likely to shop around and switch brands if they find better prices elsewhere.

The impact of this dilemma extends across various facets of the organization. When leaning heavily toward brand loyalty, a business invests in maintaining high product or service standards, customer service excellence, and consistent branding. This can enhance reputation, customer satisfaction, and long-term profitability. However, it may limit the brand's reach to a specific segment of the market, potentially missing out on price-sensitive customers. A price-sensitive approach can help a business attract a larger customer base, but it may require cost-cutting measures that impact product quality or customer service. While this can lead to short-term gains, it may risk eroding brand reputation and customer loyalty over time.

Choosing Brand Loyalty Only	
Pros	**Cons**
Higher profit margins	Potentially limited market reach
Customer advocacy	Higher production costs
Long-term customer relationships	Vulnerability to economic downturns

Choosing Price Sensitivity Only	
Pros	**Cons**
Attraction of budget-conscious customers	Slim profit margins
Wider market reach	Lower customer retention
Agility in pricing	Potential brand dilution

Yeti Cycles, a manufacturer of high-end mountain bikes, places a strong emphasis on brand loyalty. Their products are known for exceptional quality, innovation, and durability. Yeti has built a loyal customer base through consistent delivery of top-tier mountain bikes and a commitment to the mountain biking community. While their bikes are premium-priced, the brand loyalty they've cultivated allows them to maintain strong sales even in a competitive market. This approach has positively impacted Yeti Cycles by fostering a dedicated customer community that supports the brand, offers word-of-mouth referrals, and provides valuable feedback for product improvement. However, the potential downside is limited market reach due to the premium pricing, which may exclude budget-conscious customers.

Xiaomi, a Chinese electronics company, places a strong emphasis on price sensitivity. They offer a wide range of consumer electronics, including smartphones, at competitive prices. Xiaomi's strategy focuses on providing affordable yet feature-rich products to a mass market. This approach has positively impacted Xiaomi by rapidly expanding its market share, especially in emerging economies, and gaining a large customer base.

However, it also comes with challenges, such as thin profit margins and the need for high sales volumes. Additionally, the focus on price sensitivity may lead to questions about product durability and after-sales service quality, which can impact customer loyalty.

Some questions for the leaders to reflect and answer to resolve the dilemma:

- Are we aware of where our target audience stands in terms of their loyalty to our brand and price sensitivity?
- Have we thoroughly assessed what our competition is doing regarding brand loyalty and price sensitivity strategies?
- Can we identify ways to differentiate ourselves in the market based on quality and brand loyalty, and how will this impact our pricing?
- Do we have flexible pricing models that can address the needs of price-sensitive customers without compromising brand loyalty?
- Have we clearly defined our long-term goals and considered how brand loyalty and price sensitivity fit into our strategic vision?
- Are there specific market segments where we can successfully serve both brand-loyal and price-sensitive customers?

There could be several factors that could influence this decision in the context of your organization like:

Market Competition: The level of competition in your industry can heavily influence your choice.

Product Differentiation: If your products or services have unique features, brand loyalty might be more attainable.

Customer Demographics: Understanding your customers' income levels, values, and preferences is vital.

Industry Trends: Stay informed about market trends, as they may favor one approach over the other.

> **Economic Conditions**: Economic stability or downturns can impact customer spending behavior.
>
> **There are other areas that get impacted because of a choice of this dilemma like:**
>
> - Customer retention and repeat business
> - Pricing strategy and revenue margins
> - Brand equity and recognition
> - Sales and market share
> - Customer perception and loyalty programs

Striking a balance between brand loyalty and price sensitivity is possible in some scenarios, where businesses can segment their offerings to cater to both types of customers. Yet, this balance can be challenging to achieve without diluting the brand's identity or complicating pricing structures. *Amul is a well-known Indian dairy cooperative that has effectively balanced Brand Loyalty and Price Sensitivity in the dairy and dairy product market. Here's how they achieve this balance:*

- **Quality and Brand Loyalty:** *Amul has built a strong brand reputation for providing high-quality dairy products. They are known for their consistency in delivering fresh and pure dairy items. Over the years, Amul has gained the trust of consumers, fostering brand loyalty among those who seek quality dairy products.*

- **Price Sensitivity:** *While maintaining quality, Amul is also conscious of price sensitivity among Indian consumers. They offer a wide range of dairy products at competitive and affordable prices, making them accessible to a broad demographic of consumers, including those with budget constraints.*

- **Product Variety:** *Amul's extensive product portfolio includes a variety of dairy items, from milk and butter to cheese and ice cream. This diversity allows them to cater to consumers with different preferences and budgets. They offer both premium and value-based products, striking a balance between quality and affordability.*

- **Advertising and Brand Promotion:** *Amul is well-known for its creative and engaging advertisements, often featuring the famous "Amul girl."*

These advertisements not only promote the brand but also create a sense of nostalgia and emotional attachment among consumers, enhancing brand loyalty.

- ***Local Sourcing and Cooperative Model**: Amul's cooperative model involves local farmers, which not only supports rural livelihoods but also contributes to the affordability of their products. This resonates with consumers who appreciate the brand's commitment to local communities.*

Several factors influence the decision of whether to prioritize Brand loyalty or Price sensitivity in a business. Here's a common set of factors that play a role in this decision:

- **Target Market and Segmentation**: Understanding the demographics, psychographics, and behavior of your target audience is crucial. If your primary market segment values quality, exclusivity, and brand trust, brand loyalty may be the priority. On the other hand, if your target market is more price-sensitive and seeks value for money, price sensitivity becomes vital.
- **Competitive Landscape**: Analyzing your competitors and their strategies is essential. If your competitors are mainly focused on price wars, you might choose to differentiate through brand loyalty. Conversely, if competitors are emphasizing premium pricing and customer experience, you might need to match or adapt to their approach.
- **Product or Service Differentiation**: The nature of your product or service matters. Some products inherently lend themselves to branding and loyalty due to unique features or benefits. Others may be commoditized, making price sensitivity a more viable strategy.
- **Cost Structure**: Evaluating your cost structure is vital. If your operational costs allow for competitive pricing without compromising quality, price sensitivity can be a strong option. If maintaining high standards significantly impacts your costs, brand loyalty may be more sustainable.
- **Brand Strength**: Assessing the strength of your brand and its existing loyalty base is critical. An established brand with a loyal customer following may be in a better position to focus on brand

loyalty. A newer or lesser-known brand may need to employ price sensitivity to attract customers initially.

- **Market Trends and Consumer Behavior**: Monitoring market trends and shifts in consumer behavior is essential. For instance, if there's a growing trend of consumers valuing sustainable and ethical practices, brand loyalty through responsible business practices may be the way forward.
- **Economic Conditions**: Economic conditions, such as recessions or economic booms, can impact consumer behavior. During economic downturns, price sensitivity often becomes more pronounced as consumers seek cost savings.
- **Long-Term vs. Short-Term Goals**: Consider your organization's long-term objectives. Building strong brand loyalty might lead to sustainable growth over time, while price sensitivity could result in short-term revenue boosts.
- **Marketing and Promotion Strategy**: Your marketing and promotion strategies should align with your chosen approach. Building brand loyalty often involves storytelling, content marketing, and relationship-building efforts. Price sensitivity may require more aggressive pricing strategies and promotions.
- **Customer Acquisition vs. Retention**: Determine whether your focus is on acquiring new customers or retaining existing ones. Brand loyalty typically aligns with customer retention, while price sensitivity can attract new customers.
- **Flexibility and Adaptability**: The ability to adapt to changing market conditions is vital. Businesses may need to switch between strategies depending on market dynamics or employ a hybrid approach.
- **Customer Feedback and Insights**: Regularly collecting and analyzing customer feedback and insights can provide valuable guidance on which strategy resonates more with your audience.

The choice between brand loyalty and price sensitivity must align with the organization's long-term goals, competitive landscape, and target market. It's a decision that impacts product development, marketing strategies, customer relationships, and overall competitiveness in the market, making it a pivotal factor in a company's success or failure.

Customer First vs. Employee First

> This dilemma is all about Deciding whether to prioritize customer needs, satisfaction, and experiences (customer first) or to focus on employee well-being, engagement, and development with the belief that satisfied employees lead to satisfied customers (employee first) or striking a balance between the two.

Prioritizing the customer experience above all else is a strategy embraced by many businesses. Here, the central belief is that happy customers are the lifeblood of any organization. This approach emphasizes delivering exceptional service, meeting customer expectations, and constantly striving to exceed them. The immediate benefits are evident: increased customer loyalty, positive word-of-mouth, and potentially higher revenue. However, the exclusive focus on customer satisfaction can have profound consequences for the organization. It often leads to relentless demands on employees to cater to every customer whim, which can result in burnout, high turnover, and decreased employee morale. Employees may feel undervalued, leading to disengagement and, ironically, lower service quality. Furthermore, this strategy can sometimes prioritize short-term gains over long-term employee development, potentially harming the company's ability to innovate and grow.

On the flip side, the "Employee first" approach asserts that a company's most valuable asset is its workforce. It posits that satisfied, motivated, and engaged employees are better positioned to deliver excellent service and create satisfied customers. This approach focuses on creating a positive workplace culture, investing in employee training and development, and ensuring a healthy work-life balance. Choosing "Employee first" can result in a loyal and dedicated workforce. Satisfied employees are more likely to stay with the company, provide superior customer service, and actively contribute to the organization's success. However, the downside is that an exclusive emphasis on employee well-being may lead to neglecting customer needs and expectations, potentially harming customer satisfaction and the bottom line.

Choosing Customer First Only	
Pros	**Cons**
High customer satisfaction	Employee burnout, turnover, decreased morale
Potential for increased revenue	Potential decline in product/service quality
Competitive advantage in service industries	Difficulty attracting top talent

Choosing Employee First Only	
Pros	**Cons**
High employee morale and loyalty	Possible neglect of immediate customer needs
Improved job performance	Potential dip in short-term profits
Positive workplace culture, better customer service due to engaged employees.	Competition challenges in customer-centric markets.

Zappos, an online shoe and clothing retailer, is known for its unwavering commitment to customer satisfaction. Their "Deliver WOW Through Service" approach places customers at the forefront of everything they do. Zappos offers free shipping both ways, a generous return policy, and 24/7 customer support. While this customer-first strategy has helped them build a loyal customer base and achieve significant success, it has also resulted in a highly competitive and often demanding work environment for employees. Customer service representatives often go to great lengths to meet customer expectations, which can be stressful. However, Zappos believes that happy employees lead to happy customers, and they offer extensive employee benefits, aiming to strike a balance between customer and employee satisfaction.

HOPE IS NOT A STRATEGY

The Motley Fool, a financial services and investment advice company, places a strong emphasis on its employees. They believe that satisfied and engaged employees are more likely to provide exceptional customer service. The Motley Fool offers a relaxed work environment, flexible schedules, and a commitment to professional development. While this employee-first approach fosters a positive and productive work culture, it may potentially have a downside when it comes to competing with customer-first companies in the financial advisory industry. The intense focus on employee well-being and development may require higher employee-related costs. However, The Motley Fool believes that their happy employees translate into long-term customer relationships and trust.

Some questions for the leaders to reflect and answer to resolve the dilemma:

- Do we believe that prioritizing customer satisfaction at all costs is the best approach, or do we think that investing in employee well-being and engagement will naturally lead to happier customers?
- How do we balance immediate customer needs and long-term employee development goals?
- Are we considering the impact on employee morale and turnover when we make customer-centric decisions, and vice versa?
- How do we navigate situations where customer demands may conflict with the well-being of our employees?
- Do we view customer and employee satisfaction as mutually exclusive, or can they complement each other in our organization?
- Are there situations where it makes sense to prioritize one group over the other, and if so, what are those scenarios?

There could be several factors that could influence this decision in the context of your organization like:

Business Model: The nature of your business, whether it's service-oriented or product-based, can significantly influence the choice.

Service-based businesses may lean more toward "customer first," while product-focused companies might emphasize "employee first."

Industry Competition: Competitive industries may prioritize customer satisfaction as a way to differentiate themselves, while less competitive sectors may focus on employee well-being to attract and retain talent.

Employee Skills: If your employees possess unique skills or expertise that contribute to your company's success, you may prioritize their well-being more to retain and develop this talent.

Company Size: Larger organizations may have more resources to simultaneously invest in both customer and employee satisfaction, while smaller businesses may need to make more targeted choices.

Leadership Philosophy: The personal beliefs and values of your leadership team can strongly influence this decision, as it often aligns with their vision for the company.

There are other areas that get impacted because of a choice of this dilemma like-

- Customer satisfaction and loyalty
- Employee motivation and retention
- Organizational culture and values
- Resource allocation for customer service and employee programs
- Employee engagement and customer-centricity

Customer first and Employee first can coexist. In fact, they often complement each other. Satisfied employees are more likely to provide better customer service, which, in turn, can lead to satisfied customers. Striking a balance ensures that the needs and expectations of both groups are met without compromising one for the other. *Tavant Technologies, an IT services and solutions company based in India, effectively balances the "Customer first" and "Employee first" approaches. They prioritize employee well-being with benefits such* as health and wellness programs and continuous learning opportunities, fostering a motivated and skilled workforce. Simultaneously, Tavant provides innovative solutions and exceptional customer service to their clients, enhancing customer satisfaction and building trust. By investing in employee growth and happiness, Tavant believes they can deliver better results for their customers, as engaged employees are more likely to meet customer expectations. This holistic approach has led to growth, customer loyalty, and employee satisfaction, exemplifying a successful blend of customer and employee focus within the organization.

Let's explore some factors that influence the decision of choosing "Customer first" versus "Employee first" in more detail:

- **Industry and Competition**: The nature of the industry plays a significant role. In industries with intense competition and commoditized products or services, customer loyalty may be hard to come by. Here, companies often prioritize customer-first approaches to stand out and retain a customer base. Conversely, industries with specialized knowledge or where employees play a crucial role (like consulting or professional services) tend to lean more towards employee-first strategies.
- **Customer Base**: Understanding the customer base is crucial. If your customers are primarily one-time buyers, you may be tempted to focus more on satisfying their immediate needs. However, if your business relies on repeat customers or subscription models, employee satisfaction becomes vital because they are the ones who maintain those relationships.
- **Leadership Philosophy**: The leadership's personal beliefs and priorities also play a role. A CEO who strongly values customer satisfaction may drive the company in that direction, while a leader who prioritizes employee development and engagement will influence the organization differently.
- **Business Lifecycle**: The stage of the business lifecycle matters. Startups may initially prioritize customer acquisition and satisfaction to gain traction, while more established companies may shift towards employee-first approaches to maintain growth and longevity.
- **Financial Resources**: The financial health of the organization is essential. Companies with limited resources may struggle to invest

heavily in both customer and employee satisfaction simultaneously. Therefore, they may need to prioritize one over the other based on their financial capabilities.

- **Employee Turnover**: High employee turnover can be a red flag. If the company faces challenges retaining employees, it may need to adopt an employee-first approach to reduce turnover and associated costs.
- **Customer Feedback**: Consistent customer feedback can provide insights. If customers consistently express dissatisfaction with employee behavior or service quality, this may signal a need to shift towards customer-first strategies.
- **Market Trends**: Monitoring industry trends and best practices can inform the decision. If industry benchmarks suggest that employee-first approaches lead to better long-term results, the company may choose to follow suit.
- **Legal and Regulatory Environment**: In some industries, regulatory requirements may mandate specific employee practices or customer service standards, influencing the decision.

The choice between "Customer first" and "Employee first" should align with a company's values, industry, and unique circumstances. What's clear is that neglecting one in favor of the other can have far-reaching consequences on the organization's overall health and success.

| 3.10 |
ETHICS AND SOCIAL RESPONSIBILITY DILEMMAS

> **How will you use this chapter of the book?**
>
> If you are the founder or the CEO of a company and if you and your leadership team have a clear point of view (PoV) on the following questions and all of you are ALIGNED, then you can choose to move to the next chapter of the book. However, if you see a dissonance or have conflicting views, then we suggest digging deeper, going through this chapter and reflecting on different angles we bring in there.
>
> Here are the questions for you to discuss and ponder-
>
> - How does our core value align with sustainability and growth goals?
> - Are we willing to make short-term sacrifices for long-term sustainability?
> - How can we balance cost savings with ethical sourcing practices?
> - What's the role of community engagement in our vision, and how does it impact profitability?
> - How do we prioritize product safety without compromising market competitiveness?
> - How can we leverage customer data while protecting privacy and complying with regulations?
> - Are we willing to invest in sustainability even if it affects short-term profits?
> - How do we balance philanthropy with financial objectives?
> - How can we build strong supplier relationships without compromising on ethics?
> - How do our ethical commitments affect our corporate culture and employee engagement?

In today's complex business landscape, leaders often grapple with critical decisions that transcend profit margins and market share. Ethical and social responsibility dilemmas lie at the heart of these choices, presenting leaders with a fundamental question: How should organizations balance their pursuit of financial success with a commitment to ethical conduct and social impact? This book delves into the core dilemmas faced by leaders, providing insights and guidance on navigating the intricate web of corporate ethics and social responsibility. Through real-world examples and practical advice, we explore the delicate equilibrium between profit and principles, shedding light on the challenges and opportunities that lie ahead.

Leaders should consider a wide range of aspects when determining how ethical and social responsibility-related decisions will be made in the organization. These aspects include:

- **Stakeholder Expectations**: Understand the expectations and concerns of various stakeholders, including customers, employees, shareholders, and the community.
- **Legal and Regulatory Compliance**: Ensure compliance with local, national, and international laws and regulations related to ethics and social responsibility.
- **Ethical Framework**: Develop a clear ethical framework or code of conduct that guides decision-making at all levels of the organization.
- **Transparency and Accountability**: Promote transparency in decision-making processes and establish accountability mechanisms for ethical lapses.
- **Risk Management**: Identify and mitigate risks associated with ethical and social responsibility decisions, including reputational, legal, and operational risks.
- **Resource Allocation**: Allocate resources, such as budget and manpower, to support ethical and responsible initiatives.
- **Long-Term Sustainability**: Consider the long-term sustainability of the organization and balance short-term gains with long-term impact.
- **Community Engagement**: Evaluate the organization's role in

the community and how it can contribute positively through philanthropy and social impact projects.
- **Supply Chain Ethics**: Assess supply chain practices, ensuring ethical sourcing, fair labor practices, and sustainable procurement.
- **Employee Welfare**: Prioritize employee well-being, engagement, and development, recognizing that satisfied employees often lead to satisfied customers.
- **Customer Data and Privacy**: Balance the use of customer data for insights with the responsibility to protect customer privacy and data security.
- **Environmental Impact**: Address the environmental impact of business operations, promoting sustainability and responsible resource management.
- **Product Safety and Quality**: Ensure the safety and quality of products and services, meeting customer expectations and regulatory requirements.
- **Philanthropy and Social Impact**: Determine the organization's philanthropic activities and social impact projects that align with its values and goals.
- **Financial Performance**: Assess how ethical and social responsibility decisions impact financial performance, considering both short-term and long-term effects.
- **Communication and Reporting**: Develop clear communication strategies for sharing ethical and responsible initiatives with stakeholders and reporting progress.
- **Continuous Improvement**: Establish mechanisms for ongoing evaluation and improvement of ethical and social responsibility practices.

HOPE IS NOT A STRATEGY

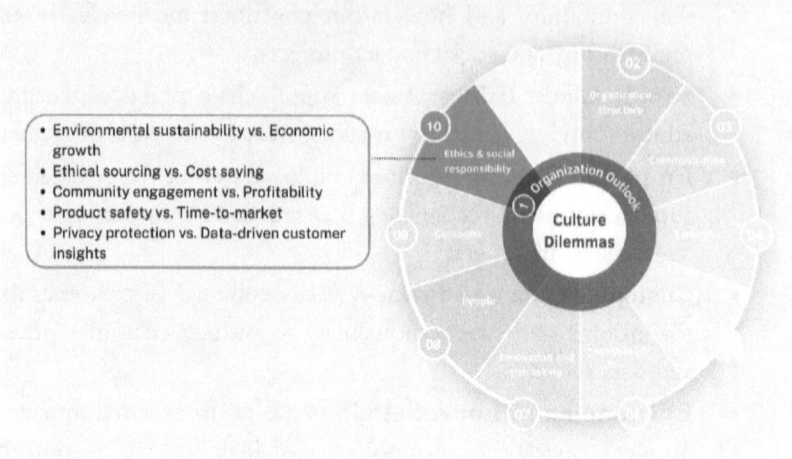

While there are many dilemmas when we think of Ethics and social responsibility, we will focus on five pivotal ones that often take center stage:

- **Environmental sustainability vs. Economic growth**
- **Ethical sourcing vs. Cost saving**
- **Community engagement vs. Profitability**
- **Product safety vs. Time-to-market**
- **Privacy protection vs. Data-driven customer insights**

Let's look at each of them in greater detail.

Environmental Sustainability vs. Economic Growth

> This dilemma is all about balancing efforts to minimize the negative environmental impact of business operations and promote sustainability (environmental sustainability) with the pursuit of economic growth and competitiveness (economic growth).

The dilemma of environmental sustainability versus economic growth revolves around a fundamental question that organizations face today: How can they harmonize their economic pursuits with their responsibility toward the environment? On one hand, there's the pressing need to reduce environmental harm, conserve resources, and transition to sustainable practices. On the other, there's the relentless drive for economic growth, competitiveness, and financial prosperity.

Choosing environmental sustainability entails a commitment to minimizing the negative ecological consequences of business activities. It involves investing in renewable energy, reducing waste, adopting eco-friendly processes, and embracing responsible sourcing and production methods. Organizations pursuing this path recognize that environmental degradation can lead to long-term economic challenges, including resource scarcity, regulatory penalties, and reputational damage. Moreover, with increasing consumer awareness and demand for sustainable products and services, environmental sustainability can also offer a competitive advantage in the market.

However, the journey towards environmental sustainability often comes with immediate financial costs. Investments in green technologies, energy-efficient infrastructure, and sustainable supply chains can strain budgets in the short term. Additionally, there's the challenge of adapting business models to meet stricter environmental regulations, which can further impact profitability. The benefits of these investments, such as reduced energy expenses and a positive brand image, may take time to materialize.

On the flip side, economic growth, driven by profit maximization and expansion, can sometimes disregard environmental concerns. Companies focusing solely on growth might prioritize cost-cutting measures that lead to resource depletion, pollution, and habitat destruction. The pursuit of economic gains can inadvertently harm ecosystems, contribute to climate change, and result in a range of social and ethical issues.

The impact of this dilemma extends beyond the balance sheet. It affects corporate reputation, stakeholder relations, and even employee morale. Organizations that prioritize environmental sustainability often find favor with eco-conscious consumers, attracting a loyal customer base and enhancing brand loyalty. They also tend to be more appealing to socially responsible investors. Conversely, those fixated solely on economic growth may face reputational damage, especially in an era where environmental issues are at the forefront of public consciousness.

Choosing Environmental Sustainability Only	
Pros	**Cons**
Enhanced brand reputation and customer loyalty.	Initial investment costs for sustainable infrastructure.
Attraction of socially responsible investors.	Potential short-term impact on profit margins.
Potential long-term cost savings through resource efficiency.	Market competition from less sustainable alternatives.

Choosing Economic Growth Only	
Pros	**Cons**
Increased revenue and market share.	Environmental degradation and resource depletion.
Job creation and economic development.	Risk of regulatory fines and legal issues.
Attraction of investors seeking high returns.	Potential reputational damage from sustainability neglect.

Let's take two examples - Company A, a mid-sized food production company, has made a deliberate choice to prioritize environmental sustainability. They've implemented eco-friendly packaging, reduced water and energy consumption, and sourced ingredients locally to reduce their carbon footprint. While these efforts initially incurred higher production costs, they have reaped significant benefits. Customers appreciate the company's commitment to sustainability, leading to increased brand loyalty and market share. Moreover, by optimizing their resource usage, Company A has achieved long-term cost savings. Their sustainability efforts have not only enhanced their reputation but also attracted investors looking for socially responsible businesses.

Company B, a regional construction firm, has chosen to prioritize economic growth over environmental sustainability. Their primary focus is on expansion and maximizing profits, often opting for cost-effective construction materials and methods, regardless of their environmental impact. This approach has allowed them to secure numerous contracts and experience rapid financial growth. However, it has also attracted criticism from environmental advocacy groups and led to several legal disputes related to environmental violations. While Company B has achieved impressive economic growth in the short term, their long-term prospects might be affected by potential regulatory penalties and damage to their reputation, which could impact their ability to secure future projects.

These examples illustrate the different paths companies can take regarding environmental sustainability and economic growth. Company A's commitment to sustainability has led to enhanced brand loyalty and cost savings, while Company B's focus on economic growth has delivered immediate financial success but carries long-term risks related to environmental concerns and reputation. The choice between the two approaches ultimately depends on a company's values, goals, and the specific industry in which it operates.

Some questions for the leaders to reflect and answer to resolve the dilemma:

- How can we strike a balance between environmental sustainability and economic growth within our organization?
- Are we willing to invest in environmentally sustainable practices, even if they may initially impact our economic growth?
- How can we communicate the importance of environmental sustainability to our stakeholders, including employees and shareholders?
- What measures can we take to ensure that our economic growth doesn't come at the expense of the environment?
- Are there opportunities for innovation that allow us to achieve both environmental sustainability and economic growth simultaneously?
- How do our competitors approach this dilemma, and what can we learn from their experiences?

There could be several factors that could influence this decision in the context of your organization like:

Regulatory Environment: The stringency of environmental regulations can significantly influence the decision, as non-compliance may result in fines and reputational damage.

Market Demand: Consumer preferences for eco-friendly products and services can drive sustainability efforts, impacting economic growth.

> **Technological Advancements**: Innovations in sustainable technologies can make eco-friendly practices more economically viable.
>
> **Stakeholder Pressure**: Pressure from investors, customers, and advocacy groups can sway decisions toward sustainability.
>
> **Long-Term Perspective**: Leaders with a long-term view may prioritize sustainability for its future economic benefits.
>
> **There are other areas that get impacted because of a choice of this dilemma like:**
>
> - Sustainability initiatives
> - Resource allocation
> - Regulatory compliance
> - Brand image
> - Market positioning

Environmental sustainability and economic growth can coexist when organizations adopt sustainable practices that drive innovation, reduce costs, and attract environmentally conscious consumers. *Let's consider the example of "The Body Shop," a well-known cosmetics and skincare company that has managed to strike a balance between environmental sustainability and economic growth. The Body Shop has consistently demonstrated its commitment to environmental sustainability while also achieving economic growth. They have made efforts to minimize their environmental impact through initiatives such as promoting the use of sustainable and ethically sourced ingredients, reducing plastic packaging, and emphasizing the importance of fair trade. These efforts align with their core values and have attracted a customer base that values ethical and sustainable products. At the same time, The Body Shop has managed to maintain economic growth by effectively marketing their environmentally friendly and ethical products. Their commitment to sustainability has become a unique selling point, attracting consumers who are willing to pay a premium for products that align with their values. This approach has not only increased customer loyalty but has also contributed to the company's bottom line.*

The decision of whether to prioritize environmental sustainability or economic growth involves a range of factors, each carrying significant weight. Here's a closer look at some of the key factors that influence this decision:

- **Regulatory Environment**: The prevailing environmental regulations and government policies play a crucial role. Companies often align their practices with these regulations to avoid legal issues and penalties. Stringent environmental laws may incentivize firms to prioritize sustainability.
- **Consumer Preferences**: Understanding consumer attitudes and preferences is essential. If customers are increasingly valuing eco-friendly products and sustainable practices, businesses are more likely to invest in sustainability to meet market demands and maintain competitiveness.
- **Industry Trends**: Different industries have varying levels of environmental impact and sustainability expectations. Companies within sectors with high environmental footprints, like manufacturing or energy, may face more scrutiny and pressure to adopt sustainable practices.
- **Resource Availability**: The availability and cost of key resources, including raw materials and energy, can affect sustainability decisions. If resources are scarce or expensive, businesses may look for sustainable alternatives.
- **Investor and Stakeholder Pressure**: Investors, shareholders, and other stakeholders are increasingly concerned about environmental responsibility. Companies often face pressure to disclose their sustainability efforts and achieve specific environmental goals to attract investments and maintain shareholder confidence.
- **Competitive Landscape**: Analyzing the actions of competitors is crucial. If competitors are investing heavily in sustainability, a company might feel compelled to do the same to remain competitive.
- **Technology Advancements**: Advances in green technologies can make sustainable practices more economically viable. Companies may prioritize sustainability when cost-effective technologies become available.

- **Long-Term Strategy**: Companies with a long-term vision are more likely to invest in sustainability, viewing it as a means to secure their future. Those focused solely on short-term profits might prioritize economic growth.
- **Supply Chain Considerations**: Sustainable supply chain practices can impact both economic and environmental aspects. Evaluating the environmental footprint of the supply chain can influence sustainability decisions.
- **Brand Image and Reputation**: A positive brand image associated with sustainability can enhance a company's reputation, attract customers, and drive loyalty. Conversely, a poor environmental track record can lead to reputational damage.
- **Cost-Benefit Analysis**: Conducting a thorough cost-benefit analysis is essential. Businesses must assess the short-term costs of sustainability initiatives against the potential long-term benefits, including cost savings and revenue generation.
- **Ethical Values**: Some companies have strong ethical values and are committed to making environmentally responsible choices, regardless of the immediate financial implications.
- **Global Context**: The global context matters, especially for multinational corporations. Companies operating in regions with different environmental norms and standards must navigate varying expectations.

In conclusion, the environmental sustainability vs. economic growth dilemma is not a binary choice but a complex balancing act. Striking the right equilibrium between the two is a critical challenge for modern organizations. It requires forward-thinking strategies that consider both short-term financial goals and the long-term health of the planet. In an increasingly environmentally conscious world, businesses that effectively navigate this dilemma are more likely to thrive, ensuring profitability while safeguarding the planet for future generations.

Ethical Sourcing vs. Cost Saving

> This dilemma is all about choosing between sourcing materials, customer leads, and people (employees) ethically, often at a higher cost (ethical sourcing), and seeking cost savings through less costly suppliers (cost savings) or striking a balance.

The ethical sourcing versus cost saving dilemma poses a fundamental question for organizations: should they prioritize ethical practices in sourcing materials, customer leads, and talent, even if it means incurring higher costs, or should they opt for cost-saving measures by selecting less expensive suppliers? Striking a balance between these two options is also on the table. When a company leans heavily toward ethical sourcing, it demonstrates a commitment to values such as sustainability, fair labor practices, and social responsibility. This can lead to positive impacts in terms of reputation and brand loyalty. However, it often translates into higher expenses, which can affect the bottom line. Additionally, ethical sourcing can sometimes limit the pool of suppliers, potentially impacting the variety and availability of resources.

On the other hand, focusing solely on cost savings can yield immediate financial benefits. It can reduce operational expenses and improve short-term profitability. However, it may come at the expense of ethical considerations. Cutting costs can sometimes lead to sourcing from suppliers who do not adhere to fair labor practices or sustainable production methods. This can expose the organization to reputational risks and damage its brand image.

Choosing Ethical Sourcing Only	
Pros	**Cons**
Enhanced brand reputation and customer trust.	Higher immediate costs.
Mitigation of legal and reputational risks.	Potential challenges in finding ethical suppliers.
Alignment with evolving consumer preferences.	Complex monitoring and compliance requirements.

Choosing Cost Saving Only	
Pros	**Cons**
Immediate financial benefits.	Risk of reputational damage.
Competitive pricing for products or services.	Potential legal liabilities.
Short-term profitability.	Long-term sustainability concerns.

Take the example of Company A, a medium-sized clothing retailer known for its commitment to ethical sourcing. This company carefully selects suppliers who adhere to fair labor practices, use sustainable materials, and minimize environmental impact. While their products are slightly pricier compared to competitors who prioritize cost savings, Company A has built a loyal customer base that appreciates their ethical stance. They have seen positive impacts on their brand reputation, with customers viewing them as socially responsible. Additionally, they've attracted ethically conscious investors who have supported their growth. Despite the higher initial costs, Company A's long-term commitment to ethical sourcing has bolstered its brand and sustainability.

On the other hand, Company B, an electronics manufacturer that competes in a highly price-sensitive market. This company prioritizes cost-saving measures in its supply chain, often choosing suppliers based on the lowest bid. While this approach has allowed them to offer products at competitive prices and capture a significant market share, it has also led to occasional quality issues and allegations of labor exploitation at some supplier facilities. Company B has faced occasional public relations challenges related to these issues, and although they've enjoyed short-term profitability, the long-term impact on their brand reputation and customer loyalty remains uncertain.

Some questions for the leaders to reflect and answer to resolve the dilemma:

- How do we define and communicate our ethical sourcing standards within the organization?
- What are the potential long-term consequences of not prioritizing ethical sourcing in our operations?
- Can we explore sustainable sourcing options that align with our ethical goals while also considering cost savings?
- How can we effectively convey our commitment to ethical sourcing to customers and stakeholders?
- What is the financial impact of incorporating ethical sourcing into our supply chain, both short-term and long-term?
- What mechanisms can we implement to monitor and ensure compliance with ethical sourcing practices across our supply chain?

There could be several factors that could influence this decision in the context of your organization like:

Consumer Expectations: Increasing consumer awareness and demand for ethically sourced products can influence the decision towards ethical sourcing.

Regulatory Environment: Stringent regulations and compliance requirements can push organizations towards ethical sourcing.

Brand Reputation: Maintaining a positive brand image can be a significant factor in favor of ethical sourcing.

> **Supplier Relationships**: Strong relationships with ethical suppliers can facilitate cost-effective ethical sourcing.
>
> **Market Competitiveness**: Ethical practices can enhance competitiveness in markets where consumers value sustainability and ethics.
>
> There are other areas that get impacted because of a choice of this dilemma like:
>
> - Supply chain transparency
> - Reputation
> - Product quality
> - Supplier/ partner relationships
> - Financial performance

Striking a balance between ethical sourcing and cost savings can be a complex endeavor. It requires organizations to identify areas where they can prioritize ethics without significantly compromising financial stability. Moreover, it demands transparency and communication with stakeholders to convey the commitment to ethical practices while also addressing the economic realities. *Consider a medium-sized food production company, "GreenHarvest Foods," that effectively balances ethical sourcing and cost-saving strategies in various scenarios. GreenHarvest sources its primary ingredient, organic quinoa, from a cooperative of small-scale farmers in South America. While they pay a premium for ethically sourced, organic quinoa, they've established long-term partnerships with these farmers, contributing to their economic well-being and community development. However, for packaging materials like recyclable cardboard, GreenHarvest chooses cost-saving options without compromising quality or environmental sustainability. This dual approach allows them to maintain competitive pricing for their products while adhering to their ethical sourcing commitments for primary ingredients. GreenHarvest has built a reputation for both ethical practices and cost-consciousness, attracting a diverse customer base that values both sustainability and affordability. This balance has contributed to the company's steady growth and positive brand image.*

When deciding between ethical sourcing and cost-saving measures, several factors come into play, influencing the choice an organization makes. Here's a common set of factors that affect this decision:

- **Customer Expectations**: Understanding customer preferences and demands is crucial. If customer's value ethically sourced products or services, it can incentivize a company to invest in ethical sourcing, even if it comes at a higher cost.
- **Regulatory Environment**: The regulatory landscape can have a substantial impact. Industries with stringent ethical and environmental regulations may be more inclined to prioritize ethical sourcing to avoid legal and reputational risks.
- **Supplier Relationships**: The relationships with suppliers are vital. Trustworthy and ethical suppliers can make ethical sourcing more feasible, while strained relationships or limited supplier options may push a company towards cost-saving measures.
- **Long-Term vs. Short-Term Perspective**: Companies with a long-term perspective might prioritize ethical sourcing as an investment in brand reputation and sustainability. Conversely, those focused on short-term gains might opt for cost savings.
- **Market Competition**: The level of competition in the market can be a deciding factor. In highly competitive markets, cost savings may be necessary to remain competitive, while in niche markets, ethical sourcing could be a unique selling point.
- **Investor and Stakeholder Pressure**: Pressure from investors and stakeholders, including environmental or socially responsible investment funds, can influence the decision. Companies with ethical investors may lean towards ethical sourcing.
- **Risk Tolerance**: Assessing risk tolerance is crucial. Companies with a low tolerance for reputational or legal risks are more likely to prioritize ethical sourcing, as unethical practices can lead to significant risks.
- **Cost-Benefit Analysis**: A thorough cost-benefit analysis is essential. It involves evaluating the long-term benefits of ethical sourcing, such as improved reputation and customer loyalty, against the short-term cost savings.
- **Transparency and Reporting**: Companies committed to

transparency and reporting on their ethical and sustainability efforts may choose ethical sourcing to align with their reporting commitments.

- **Product or Service Complexity**: The complexity of the product or service being sourced can also impact the decision. Highly complex products may require specialized suppliers, making cost-saving measures challenging.
- **Geographic Location**: The location of suppliers and their proximity to the organization's operations can affect costs and ethical considerations. Local sourcing may be more feasible for ethical practices.
- **Technology and Innovation**: Innovative technologies can sometimes provide cost-effective ethical sourcing solutions. Companies at the forefront of innovation may find ways to balance both.
- **Consumer Education**: The level of consumer awareness and education on ethical and sustainable practices can influence market dynamics and a company's decision.

The impact of this decision spans various areas within the organization. Ethical sourcing can influence supplier relationships, the quality of products and services, and the perception of the organization in the eyes of customers and investors. Cost-saving measures can affect the bottom line, operational efficiency, and short-term financial performance. The choice between these two approaches must consider these far-reaching consequences and weigh them against the organization's values and long-term goals.

Community Engagement vs. Profitability

> This dilemma is all about balancing investments in community engagement initiatives, philanthropy, and social impact projects (community engagement) with the need to maintain profitability and meet financial objectives (profitability).

Prioritizing community engagement involves investing in initiatives, philanthropy, and social impact projects that benefit society beyond the confines of the organization. This approach signifies a commitment to social responsibility and sustainability. It can encompass activities such as funding education programs, supporting local charities, or promoting environmental conservation. Choosing this path often yields various positive outcomes. First and foremost, it enhances the organization's reputation, painting it as a socially responsible and ethical entity. This can attract customers and investors who place a high value on such principles. Additionally, community engagement fosters trust among stakeholders, including customers, employees, regulators, and the broader public. It also has a direct impact on employee morale, as engagement in meaningful community work boosts job satisfaction and retention rates. Moreover, these initiatives can create lasting goodwill, building loyalty among customers and securing the company's long-term sustainability.

On the other hand, profitability remains the cornerstone of an organization's financial health. It involves making decisions that maximize financial gains while minimizing costs. A strong focus on profitability ensures financial stability, providing the resources needed for reinvestment, growth, and future sustainability. It also contributes to maintaining a competitive edge by allowing the company to control costs and offer competitive pricing. Moreover, profitability aligns with the interests of investors and shareholders, as it is often their primary goal, leading to increased shareholder value and attracting more investment.

Choosing Community Engagement Only	
Pros	**Cons**
Bolster the company's image, attracting socially conscious consumers and investors.	Strain financial resources, affecting short-term profitability.
Boost employee satisfaction and retention.	May make it challenging to match competitors' prices.
Build trust among stakeholders, including customers, investors, and regulators.	Can be demanding, potentially leading to disappointment if not managed effectively.
Sustainable growth by fostering goodwill and loyalty.	

Choosing Profitability Only	
Pros	**Cons**
Ensure financial stability, allowing for reinvestment and future growth.	May harm the company's reputation, particularly in an era where social responsibility is valued.
Lower costs may enable competitive pricing and market leadership.	A profit-only focus can lead to employee dissatisfaction and high turnover rates.
Maximizing profits can satisfy investors and shareholders, increasing stock value.	Companies may face stricter regulations and public backlash if they neglect social responsibility.

For example, Company A, a medium-sized regional bank, places a strong emphasis on community engagement. It actively supports local charities, sponsors educational programs, and encourages employees to volunteer in their communities. While these initiatives involve significant financial investments, they have had a positive impact on the bank's reputation. The local community views Company A as a trusted partner, leading to an increase in customer loyalty and a steady influx of deposits. Additionally, the bank benefits from lower employee turnover rates, as staff members take pride in their company's community involvement. However, the commitment to community engagement has limited short-term profitability compared to larger, profit-driven competitors.

On the other hand, Company B, a mid-sized manufacturing firm in a highly competitive global industry, prioritizes profitability over community engagement. It consistently seeks cost-saving measures by streamlining production processes and sourcing materials from the lowest-cost suppliers, even if they are overseas. While this approach has boosted short-term profitability and allowed Company B to weather economic downturns, it has led to occasional controversy regarding labor practices and environmental concerns. These controversies have affected the company's reputation, and it faces occasional backlash from activist groups and socially conscious consumers. In the short term, profitability remains a strength, but the company is mindful of the need to address sustainability and ethical sourcing concerns to ensure long-term viability.

Some questions for the leaders to reflect and answer to resolve the dilemma:

- How do our community engagement efforts align with our organization's values and long-term goals?
- What level of financial commitment are we willing to make for community initiatives, and how does it impact our profitability?
- Are there ways to integrate community engagement into our core business operations to achieve both social impact and financial sustainability?
- What metrics and key performance indicators (KPIs) can we establish to measure the success of our community engagement initiatives?
- How does the perception of our community engagement efforts affect our brand reputation and customer loyalty?
- How can we effectively communicate our commitment to

community engagement to stakeholders, including investors and customers?

There could be several factors that could influence this decision in the context of your organization like:

Industry and Competitive Landscape: In some industries, community engagement may be a standard practice, while in others, a focus on profitability might be more critical.

Market Dynamics: A market that values socially responsible businesses may require more community engagement efforts to remain competitive.

Regulatory Environment: Some regions may offer incentives or impose requirements related to community engagement or sustainability.

Stakeholder Expectations: The expectations of various stakeholders, including investors, customers, employees, and local communities, can shape our decisions. Meeting or exceeding these expectations is often essential for long-term success.

Financial Health: Profitability concerns may take precedence if the company is struggling financially, while a strong financial position can allow for more extensive community engagement efforts without sacrificing profitability.

There are other areas that get impacted because of a choice of this dilemma like:

- Corporate reputation
- Stakeholder relationships
- Employee morale
- Brand loyalty
- Financial performance

Community engagement and profitability can coexist within an organization through a balanced approach. This involves aligning community engagement initiatives with the core values and long-term goals of the business. By integrating community engagement into the business strategy, organizations can create shared value. For example, companies can develop social impact projects that not only benefit the community but also contribute to brand reputation and customer loyalty, ultimately boosting profitability. *Ben & Jerry's, the renowned ice cream manufacturer, effectively strikes a balance between community engagement and profitability. The company actively engages with local communities, supports social and environmental causes, and promotes fair trade practices while maintaining profitability through innovative product offerings and a strong brand built on values. Ben & Jerry's demonstrates that it's possible to align business goals with community engagement, even in the competitive food industry, showcasing the feasibility of this balancing act.*

Let's delve deeper into the factors that influence the decision of choosing between community engagement and profitability:

- **Industry and Market Dynamics**: Some industries, like technology or finance, may prioritize profitability due to fierce competition and rapidly changing market conditions. Conversely, industries such as healthcare or sustainable energy often emphasize community engagement as it aligns with their mission and societal expectations.
- **Stakeholder Expectations**: Understanding the expectations of various stakeholders, including customers, investors, employees, and the local community, is essential. Some stakeholders may prioritize ethical practices and community involvement, while others may focus solely on financial returns.
- **Long-term vs. Short-term Goals**: The time horizon for strategic planning plays a crucial role. Organizations with a long-term perspective may invest in community engagement as part of their sustainable growth strategy, even if it affects short-term profitability.
- **Regulatory Environment**: The regulatory landscape can heavily influence the decision. Some industries face stringent regulations that necessitate community engagement, while others may benefit from cost-saving measures that align with profitability goals.

- **Financial Health**: The current financial health of the organization is a critical factor. Companies with strong financial reserves are often more willing to invest in community engagement without compromising profitability.
- **Competitive Position**: The competitive landscape also matters. Companies with a unique value proposition may prioritize community engagement as a differentiator, while highly competitive industries may focus on profitability to gain an edge.
- **Risk Tolerance**: Assessing risk tolerance is vital. Pursuing community engagement might entail reputational risks, while a strict focus on profitability could pose financial risks.
- **Innovation and Adaptability**: The ability to innovate and adapt is crucial. Innovations in operations or product development can often reconcile community engagement with profitability.
- **Local and Global Impact**: Consider whether the organization operates primarily in local or global markets. International companies may need to adapt their strategies to meet diverse cultural expectations and regulatory requirements.
- **Resource Allocation**: Effective resource allocation is key. Balancing financial resources between community engagement and profitability initiatives requires careful planning and prioritization.
- **Measuring Impact**: Establishing clear metrics for assessing the impact of community engagement initiatives is essential. This allows organizations to gauge the effectiveness of their efforts and make data-driven decisions.

In this complex dilemma, organizations must find a delicate balance. Overemphasizing community engagement can strain financial resources, impacting short-term profitability. Conversely, prioritizing profitability alone may lead to negative public perception, regulatory challenges, and a potential loss of trust among stakeholders. Therefore, the challenge lies in integrating community engagement into the broader business strategy, creating shared value for the community and the organization. This requires careful planning and alignment with the company's values and long-term objectives, ultimately leading to sustainable success.

Product Safety vs. Time-To-Market

> This dilemma is all about deciding how much time and resources to invest in ensuring the safety and quality of products (product safety) versus accelerating product development to seize market opportunities and maintain competitiveness (time-to-market).

The product safety vs. time-to-market dilemma represents a crucial decision-making challenge for organizations. On one side, there's the imperative to ensure the safety and quality of products. This means conducting thorough testing, quality control measures, and adherence to regulations. It's a path that prioritizes long-term reliability and customer trust. On the other side, there's the pressing need to accelerate product development, pushing new offerings into the market quickly to seize opportunities and maintain competitiveness. This route emphasizes speed, agility, and capitalizing on market trends.

Choosing to prioritize product safety has several implications. Firstly, it requires significant investments in research, development, and testing phases, which can extend the time it takes to bring a product to market. This approach can enhance the organization's reputation for quality, build customer trust, and mitigate legal and financial risks associated with product defects. However, it may also lead to missed market windows, slower revenue growth, and potentially higher costs associated with rigorous safety measures.

Conversely, prioritizing time-to-market can be advantageous in rapidly changing industries where being the first to market with a new product or feature is crucial for success. It can lead to quicker revenue generation, increased market share, and a reputation for innovation. Nevertheless, it often involves trade-offs in terms of product safety and quality. Rushed development may result in defects, recalls, legal challenges, and reputational damage, all of which can have significant long-term consequences.

Choosing Product Safety Only	
Pros	**Cons**
Prioritizing safety builds trust with customers, enhancing your company's reputation.	Safety measures can slow down product development and time-to-market.
Lower chances of costly lawsuits and fines due to product safety issues.	Ensuring safety may increase expenses for testing and compliance.
Focus on safety often leads to higher product quality and fewer defects.	Overemphasis on safety can make you miss market opportunities.
Safe products can have a longer life in the market, ensuring sustainable revenue.	Excessive focus on safety can stifle innovation and risk-taking.

Choosing Time-To-Market Only	
Pros	**Cons**
Faster product launches can help you beat competitors and capture market share.	Rushed development may result in lower product quality and safety issues.
Speed prioritizes innovation, encouraging creative solutions and product development.	Product recalls and safety concerns can harm your brand's reputation.
Shorter development cycles often lead to lower operational costs.	Neglecting safety can lead to legal liabilities and financial losses.
Speedy product releases can boost revenue and market presence.	Unsatisfied customers due to subpar products may lead to declining sales.

HOPE IS NOT A STRATEGY

Look at this example - Company A operates in the aerospace industry, specializing in manufacturing critical components for commercial aircraft. They have firmly embraced the ethos of product safety. The organization meticulously follows rigorous safety protocols, conducts exhaustive testing, and invests heavily in quality assurance. While this approach has resulted in a stellar safety record and an excellent reputation for reliability, it has led to longer development cycles and higher costs. Customers in the aviation sector highly value safety, and Company A's commitment to product safety has translated into long-term contracts and strong brand loyalty. However, the trade-off is slower innovation and product development compared to competitors.

Conversely, Company B operates in the technology sector, specializing in consumer electronics. They have chosen to prioritize time-to-market. The organization thrives on releasing cutting-edge products quickly, often being the first to introduce new features to the market. This strategy has led to frequent product launches and staying ahead of competitors in terms of innovation. However, it also comes with some downsides. Due to the emphasis on speed, product testing and quality assurance processes may sometimes be expedited, resulting in occasional product defects. While Company B's products are known for their innovation and exciting features, they have faced occasional recalls and customer dissatisfaction due to these defects. Still, the strategy has allowed them to capture significant market share and maintain high profitability.

Some questions for the leaders to reflect and answer to resolve the dilemma:

- How do we prioritize between ensuring product safety and getting products to market quickly?
- What role do customer expectations play in our decision between product safety and time-to-market?
- How do regulatory requirements influence our approach to product safety and time-to-market?
- Are there specific industries or product categories where we need to lean more towards safety or speed?
- How do cost considerations impact our choice between product safety and time-to-market?
- Can we balance these priorities effectively to achieve both safety and speed in product development?

There could be several factors that could influence this decision

> **in the context of your organization like:**
>
> **Regulatory Environment:** Strict regulations may necessitate a stronger focus on product safety, while lenient regulations might allow for a more aggressive time-to-market approach.
>
> **Market Competition:** In highly competitive markets, organizations may prioritize speed to gain an edge, while in less competitive environments, safety may take precedence.
>
> **Customer Expectations:** Understanding what customers prioritize—whether it is product safety or the latest features—shapes the decision-making process.
>
> **Technology and Innovation:** Technological advancements may allow for faster product development while maintaining safety standards.
>
> **Historical Data and Experience:** Organizations may learn from previous successes and failures, guiding their decisions regarding product safety and time-to-market.
>
> **There are other areas that get impacted because of a choice of this dilemma like:**
>
> - Customer trust
> - Brand reputation
> - Legal liabilities
> - Innovation efforts
> - Market competitiveness

Balancing product safety considerations with other business imperatives like time-to-market is essential for organizations to achieve optimal outcomes. *For example, XYZ Electronics, a medium-sized consumer electronics manufacturer, adeptly navigates the product safety vs. time-to-market dilemma. They conduct rigorous risk assessments, efficient prototype testing, and stringent quality control to ensure safety without compromising development speed. Customer feedback is actively sought for rapid improvements. Regulatory compliance is non-negotiable, and market analysis informs product features. Their flexibility allows for prioritizing safety in high-end devices while expediting accessory releases. This balanced approach has bolstered their competitiveness, customer trust, and market position in the electronics industry.*

Several factors influence the decision of whether to prioritize product safety or time-to-market like:

- **Industry and Market Dynamics**: The nature of the industry plays a significant role. Industries with rapidly changing trends, such as technology or fashion, often favor time-to-market to stay competitive. In contrast, industries with stringent regulations, like pharmaceuticals or aerospace, lean toward product safety.
- **Regulatory Environment**: Compliance with regulations is a critical factor. Industries with strict safety standards necessitate a focus on product safety to avoid legal repercussions. Understanding the regulatory landscape is vital in making this decision.
- **Competitive Landscape**: The competitive environment can dictate the need for speed or thorough safety measures. If competitors are quickly introducing new products, it may drive the organization to prioritize time-to-market.
- **Customer Expectations**: Understanding customer preferences is key. In some markets, customers prioritize safety and quality over speed, while in others, they value innovation and new features.
- **Risk Tolerance**: Assessing risk tolerance is crucial. Some organizations are risk-averse and prefer to minimize risks associated with product defects, while others may be more risk-tolerant and willing to take chances on rapid innovation.
- **Resource Availability**: The availability of resources, including budget, manpower, and technology, can impact the decision. Organizations with ample resources may be better positioned to invest in both safety and speed.
- **Brand Reputation**: Existing brand reputation can also sway the choice. Organizations with a strong reputation for quality may be hesitant to compromise it for the sake of speed.
- **Product Complexity**: The complexity of the product itself

matters. More complex products often require longer development times to ensure safety and quality.

- **Market Window**: Timing can be everything. If there's a limited market window for a product or feature, organizations may prioritize time-to-market to seize the opportunity.
- **Innovation Strategy**: The organization's overall innovation strategy influences the decision. Some organizations focus on incremental innovations, while others prioritize disruptive innovations that often require more time and resources.
- **Customer Feedback**: Listening to customer feedback can provide valuable insights. If customers are demanding quicker product releases or emphasizing safety concerns, it can guide the decision-making process.
- **Long-Term Vision**: Consideration of the organization's long-term vision is critical. Balancing short-term gains with long-term sustainability is a strategic decision.
- **Supply Chain Management**: A well-optimized supply chain can enable faster product development. Effective supply chain management can influence the decision in favor of time-to-market.
- **Market Risks**: Assessing potential market risks, including the competition's movements and consumer behavior, can provide insights into whether speed or safety is more critical.
- **Customer Loyalty**: Existing customer loyalty can be a factor. Satisfied customers may tolerate longer development times for safer products, while new market entrants may prioritize speed.

This dilemma extends its influence throughout the organization. It impacts decision-making processes, resource allocation, innovation strategies, and even the company's culture. Leaders must carefully weigh the trade-offs, considering the specific industry, product, and market conditions. Striking the right balance is key, as extreme choices on either end of the spectrum can have far-reaching and sometimes irreversible implications for an organization's competitiveness and reputation.

Privacy Protection vs. Data-Driven Customer Insights

> This dilemma is all about balancing the ethical responsibility of protecting customer privacy and data (privacy protection) with the potential benefits of using customer data for personalized marketing and customer insights (data-driven customer insights).

The dilemma of privacy protection versus data-driven customer insights delves into a critical decision that organizations face today. On one hand, there's the ethical obligation to safeguard customer privacy and data, ensuring their trust and compliance with data protection regulations. This approach prioritizes privacy protection, emphasizing stringent data security measures, limited data collection, and consent-based practices. Conversely, there's the allure of data-driven customer insights, which can significantly benefit organizations. By harnessing customer data, companies can tailor their marketing efforts, improve customer experiences, and enhance overall operational efficiency. This path prioritizes leveraging data to gain a competitive edge and maximize business growth.

Choosing one path over the other has substantial implications. Opting for stringent privacy protection measures may limit the volume of data collected, potentially restricting opportunities for personalized marketing and insights. On the flip side, an exclusive focus on data-driven insights might lead to data breaches, customer mistrust, and legal repercussions, severely impacting reputation and customer relationships. The decision permeates various facets of an organization. It affects the effectiveness of marketing strategies, the depth of customer understanding, and, most importantly, the level of trust customers have in the company. Furthermore, it can influence resource allocation, technology investments, and even the talent needed to manage and analyze data responsibly.

Choosing Privacy Protection Only	
Pros	**Cons**
Enhanced customer trust	Limited data for insights
Compliance with laws	Potential competitive disadvantage
Reduced reputational risks	Constrained marketing
Ethical integrity	

Choosing Data-Driven Customer Insights Only	
Pros	**Cons**
Personalized marketing	Privacy risks
Improved customer experiences	Data breaches
Competitive advantage	Reputational damage
	Legal consequences

DuckDuckGo is a privacy-focused search engine that positions itself as an alternative to Google. They have built their entire business model around stringent privacy protection, not collecting or storing personal data from users' searches. This approach has garnered trust among users concerned about their online privacy. DuckDuckGo's commitment to privacy has enabled it to capitalize on the growing demand for private browsing and has attracted users who value data protection. While this focus on privacy has limited their ability to provide personalized search results and monetize data like Google, it has built a loyal user base concerned about privacy issues, and they continue to grow. DuckDuckGo's commitment to privacy has allowed it to carve a niche in the market as a trustworthy search engine. They have gained a loyal following of users who appreciate their stance on data protection and are willing to use their services because of it. The company may miss out on revenue opportunities tied to targeted advertising, as they don't utilize customer data for personalized marketing. Their growth potential in certain segments of the market may be limited due to this privacy-first approach.

Amazon, the e-commerce giant, is known for its data-driven approach to understanding customer behavior and preferences. They extensively collect and analyze customer data to provide personalized product recommendations, optimize supply chain management, and even create original content for their streaming service. This data-driven approach has significantly contributed to Amazon's dominance in the e-commerce industry and its ability to enter various other markets successfully, such as cloud computing and smart devices. Amazon's data-driven insights have allowed them to enhance the customer experience by tailoring recommendations and improving delivery efficiency. This approach has contributed to their impressive growth and diversified business portfolio. The company has faced scrutiny and criticism for its data practices, particularly concerning user privacy and the competitive advantage it gains from extensive customer data. They must continually address these concerns and comply with evolving data protection regulations.

Some questions for the leaders to reflect and answer to resolve the dilemma:

- How do we strike a balance between protecting customer privacy and leveraging data for insights?
- What is the ethical responsibility we owe to our customers regarding their data?
- Can we anonymize data effectively to preserve privacy while gaining insights?
- How can we ensure data security and compliance with privacy regulations?
- What risks are associated with data breaches, and how can they affect our reputation?
- How can we educate our employees and customers about data privacy and its importance?

There could be several factors that could influence this decision in the context of your organization like:

Legal and Regulatory Environment: Compliance with data protection laws is critical, as non-compliance can lead to severe legal consequences and fines.

Industry Standards: Benchmarking against ethical data practices in the sector ensures alignment with industry norms and customer expectations.

Customer Expectations: Aligning data use with customer preferences is essential to maintain trust and meet their expectations regarding privacy.

Technology Capabilities: Assessing data anonymization and encryption tools helps in determining the feasibility of protecting customer data.

Data Sensitivity: Weighing the sensitivity of the data collected is vital, as highly sensitive data may require stricter privacy protection measures.

There are other areas that get impacted because of a choice of this dilemma like:

- Customer trust
- Regulatory compliance
- Data security
- Marketing effectiveness
- Ethical standards

In reality, companies often find themselves navigating a delicate balance between these factors, making nuanced decisions based on their unique circumstances, industry dynamics, and customer profiles. Ultimately, the choice hinges on the organization's commitment to ethical data practices, its strategic objectives, and its ability to adapt to evolving customer expectations and regulatory landscapes. *A prime example of an organization striking a balance between privacy protection and data-driven customer insights is Mailchimp. Mailchimp, known for its email marketing and automation services, places a significant emphasis on user data privacy. They have stringent data protection measures, including robust opt-in and opt-out features for email subscribers, ensuring compliance with privacy regulations. However, Mailchimp also leverages customer data to provide insights and analytics to their users. By analyzing email open rates, click-through rates, and customer engagement data, they empower businesses to refine their email marketing strategies and drive better results. This balance allows Mailchimp to offer valuable data-driven tools while respecting user privacy, making it a trusted platform for businesses seeking to engage their audience effectively.*

The decision of choosing between privacy protection and data-driven customer insights is multifaceted, influenced by various factors that permeate different aspects of business operations:

- **Regulatory Environment**: The prevailing data protection laws and regulations in a region significantly impact this decision. Stringent data privacy laws, such as GDPR in Europe or CCPA in California, necessitate robust privacy protection measures.
- **Customer Expectations**: Understanding customer preferences and expectations regarding data privacy is paramount. Some customers are willing to share data for personalized experiences, while others prioritize data protection.
- **Industry Norms**: The industry in which an organization operates can dictate data practices. Highly regulated sectors like healthcare may lean more towards privacy protection, while e-commerce might emphasize data-driven insights.
- **Reputation and Trust**: The level of trust a company has with its customers is essential. A breach of privacy can erode trust quickly, impacting the brand's reputation and customer loyalty.
- **Competitive Landscape**: The extent to which competitors utilize customer data can influence the decision. If rivals heavily rely on data-driven insights, a company may feel compelled to follow suit.
- **Resource Availability**: Implementing strong privacy protection measures can be resource-intensive, requiring investments in cyber security, compliance, and employee training. The availability of these resources can affect the decision.
- **Data Quality**: The quality and accuracy of data available also play a role. Organizations might prioritize privacy if they deem data

unreliable or unnecessary.
- **Long-Term Strategy**: The organization's strategic goals are pivotal. If long-term sustainability and customer trust are primary objectives, privacy protection may be favored. Conversely, if rapid growth and competitiveness are paramount, data-driven insights could take precedence.
- **Technology Infrastructure**: The existing technology stack and infrastructure can influence the decision. A robust data protection framework may require specific technological investments.
- **Customer Segmentation**: Segmenting the customer base can help tailor the approach. For instance, offering opt-in data sharing options to customers who value personalized experiences while ensuring strict privacy protection for those who prioritize it.
- **Ethical Considerations**: Ethical principles and values of the organization's leadership can weigh heavily. Some leaders prioritize data ethics, while others may be more profit-oriented.
- **Legal Liabilities**: Anticipating potential legal liabilities related to data handling and privacy breaches is crucial. Legal risks can be substantial and impact the decision-making process.
- **Risk Tolerance**: The organization's risk appetite plays a role. Some companies are risk-averse and prefer conservative privacy measures, while others are more willing to embrace data-driven risks.
- **Employee Expertise**: The organization's talent pool and their expertise in data management and data protection influence the decision. An organization with skilled data analysts may be more inclined towards data-driven insights.

Ultimately, the challenge lies in striking a harmonious balance between privacy protection and data-driven insights, where organizations can harness the power of data ethically while respecting customer privacy and abiding by ever-evolving data protection regulations.

\#

| 3.11 |
LEADERSHIP DILEMMAS

How will you use this chapter of the book?

If you are the founder or the CEO of a company and if you and your leadership team have a clear point of view (PoV) on the following questions and all of you are ALIGNED, then you can choose to move to the next chapter of the book. However, if you see a dissonance or have conflicting views, then we suggest digging deeper, going through this chapter and reflecting on different angles we bring in there.

Here are the questions for you to discuss and ponder-

- How can we balance making leadership decisions with involving our teams in the decision-making process?
- Should we focus more on achieving short-term goals or inspiring our teams with a long-term vision?
- Are we leading by example, or should we delegate more responsibility to our employees?
- When it comes to leadership changes, should we promote from within or bring in external leaders for fresh perspectives?
- How can we encourage innovation while maintaining stability in our leadership?
- How do we empower employees while ensuring they remain accountable?
- What strategies can we use to balance short-term goals and long-term vision in leadership?
- Do we prioritize grooming internal talent or bringing in external leaders for leadership development?
- How can we ensure our leadership decisions align with our organization's values and culture?
- How should we adapt our leadership style to changing employee needs and the evolving business landscape while staying true to our core principles?

In the realm of business leadership, navigating through the complex landscape of decisions is akin to charting a course through uncharted waters. Leaders face a multitude of dilemmas, each presenting a distinct challenge and a unique set of consequences. These dilemmas are the crucibles in which leaders' mettle is tested, where their choices can shape the course of an organization's future.

One such crucible involves the decision-maker versus the facilitator: should a leader primarily dictate decisions or facilitate collaborative decision-making? This choice impacts the speed of decision-making, the empowerment of employees, the culture of innovation, and the accountability within the organization. These leadership dilemmas are the crucibles of leadership, demanding thoughtful consideration and deliberate choices that align with an organization's values, goals, and vision for the future.

When determining how leadership-related decisions will be made in an organization, leaders need to consider several crucial aspects:

- **Long-Term Strategy**: Consider whether leadership decisions should focus on short-term goals and task-oriented objectives or emphasize a long-term vision that inspires and guides teams.
- **Employee Engagement**: Assess how leadership decisions impact employee engagement. Decisions that empower and involve employees in the decision-making process can boost morale and commitment.
- **Innovation and Adaptation**: Reflect on how leadership choices influence innovation and the organization's ability to adapt to changing market trends and technologies.
- **Knowledge Transfer**: When deciding between leadership continuity and introducing fresh perspectives, think about how knowledge transfer occurs within the organization. Continuity may preserve institutional knowledge, while fresh perspectives can bring new ideas.
- **Risk Management**: Consider how leadership decisions affect risk management. Leaders must assess whether they should actively drive change, which may introduce risks, or prioritize stability to mitigate potential disruptions.

- **Market Competitiveness**: Evaluate how leadership strategies impact the organization's competitiveness in the market. Decisions should align with the organization's ability to stay relevant and competitive.
- **Employee Development**: Balance leadership decisions that promote employee development and those that delegate ownership, allowing employees to take responsibility and grow.
- **Workload Distribution**: Determine how leadership decisions affect the distribution of workloads and responsibilities among employees. This consideration can impact workload balance and employee satisfaction.
- **Leadership Trust**: Reflect on the level of trust between leaders and employees. Decide whether leadership decisions should emphasize leading by example to build trust or delegating ownership to empower employees.

While there are many dilemmas when we think of leadership, we will focus on five pivotal ones that often take center stage:

- **Decision-maker vs. Facilitator**
- **Task-oriented vs. Visionary**
- **Leading by example vs. Delegating ownership**
- **Leadership continuity vs. Fresh perspectives**
- **Change agent vs. Stability maintainer**

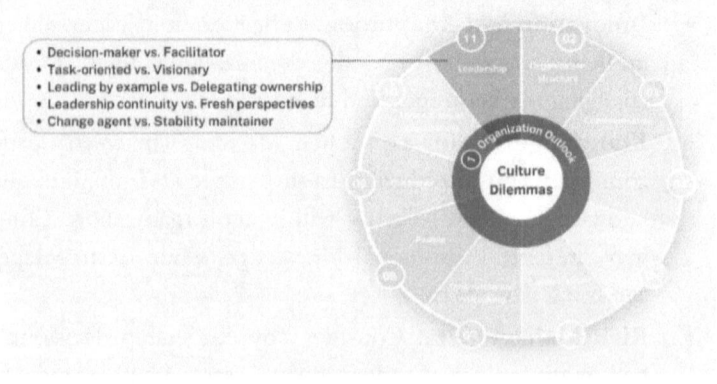

Let's look at each of them in greater detail.

Decision Maker vs. Facilitator

> This dilemma involves deciding whether a leader should primarily make decisions and provide directives (decision-maker) or act as a facilitator who enables collaborative decision-making within teams (facilitator) or strike a balance between the two styles.

The Decision Maker vs. Facilitator dilemma in leadership revolves around the fundamental question of how a leader should guide their team and make decisions within an organization. On one side of the spectrum, there's the decision-maker, a leader who takes charge, provides directives, and makes the final call in most situations. This style of leadership is often seen as efficient and effective in scenarios where quick, top-down decisions are required, especially in high-pressure or crisis situations. On the other side, there's the facilitator, a leader who promotes collaborative decision-making. In this approach, leaders encourage team members to contribute their ideas, engage in discussions, and collectively arrive at decisions. Facilitators emphasize building consensus and ensuring that everyone's voice is heard. This style is particularly valuable in fostering teamwork, creativity, and a sense of ownership among team members.

The impact of choosing one style over the other can be profound and influence various aspects of an organization. When leaders lean toward being decisive decision-makers, it can result in quicker resolutions and clearly defined accountability. However, it may also lead to reduced team engagement, stifled creativity, and a lack of diversity in perspectives. Team members might become dependent on the leader's decisions, potentially hindering their growth and problem-solving skills. Conversely, leaders who adopt a facilitative approach tend to nurture a collaborative and innovative environment. They empower team members, encourage open communication, and promote diverse viewpoints. This approach can enhance problem-solving skills, foster creativity, and lead to well-rounded decisions. However, it might slow down decision-making processes, especially in time-sensitive situations, and create ambiguity in accountability.

Choosing to be Decision maker only	
Pros	**Cons**
Faster decision-making in urgent situations.	Limited input from team members may lead to missed insights.
Clear accountability for outcomes.	Reduced engagement and ownership among team members.
Effective in highly regulated or structured environments.	Risk of decision-maker burnout.
Decisive leadership can inspire confidence in team members.	May hinder innovation and creativity in problem-solving.

Choosing to be Facilitator only	
Pros	**Cons**
Encourages collaboration and diverse perspectives.	Decision-making may be slower in urgent situations.
Fosters team cohesion and a sense of ownership.	Ambiguity in accountability.
Enhances individual and team problem-solving skills.	May not be suitable for all types of tasks.
Can lead to more creative and innovative solutions.	Requires strong facilitation and communication skills from the leader.

Pixar Animation Studios, known for producing beloved animated films like "Toy Story," "Finding Nemo," and "Inside Out," is a company that adopts a Facilitator leadership approach. Pixar encourages collaboration and creative input from all team members, regardless of their position. The company's "Braintrust" meetings exemplify this approach, where directors and creatives engage in open, candid discussions to refine their films. This approach has contributed to Pixar's consistent ability to create groundbreaking and emotionally resonant animated movies, making them a leader in the industry.

Conversely, Toyota, one of the world's largest automakers, employs a Decision Maker leadership approach, especially in its manufacturing processes. The company's well-known "Toyota Production System" emphasizes efficiency, quality, and lean manufacturing principles. Toyota's leadership values standardized processes and quick decision-making to maintain high-quality standards and meet production goals. This approach has made Toyota a leader in the automotive industry, known for its reliable vehicles and efficient manufacturing practices.

Some questions for the leaders to reflect and answer to resolve the dilemma:

- How do you perceive the role of a leader: as a decision-maker, a facilitator, or a combination of both?
- In what situations do you believe a centralized decision-making approach is most effective, and when does a collaborative approach make more sense?
- Are there specific teams or projects within the organization that might benefit more from facilitative leadership, while others require more directive leadership?
- How do you ensure that your leadership style aligns with the needs and expectations of your team members?
- Can you provide examples of successful outcomes when you adopted a decision-maker or facilitator role, and when it didn't work as expected?
- What strategies do you employ to transition between decision-maker and facilitator roles based on evolving circumstances?

There could be several factors that could influence this decision in the context of your organization like:

> **Team Dynamics**: The composition and dynamics of the team can influence whether a decision-maker or facilitative approach is more effective.
>
> **Nature of the Task**: Complex, critical tasks might necessitate a directive approach, while creative tasks often benefit from facilitation.
>
> **Organizational Culture**: The existing culture and norms in the organization can encourage one leadership style over the other.
>
> **Time Sensitivity**: Urgent situations may require quicker decision-making, favoring a directive approach.
>
> **Skill Development**: Encouraging facilitation can help team members develop decision-making and problem-solving skills.
>
> **There are other areas that get impacted because of a choice of this dilemma like:**
>
> - Decision-Making Speed
> - Employee Empowerment
> - Team Collaboration
> - Innovation Culture
> - Accountability

Finding the right balance between these two leadership styles is crucial. Leaders often need to adapt their approach based on the context, the nature of tasks, and the maturity of their team. Effective leaders can seamlessly transition between being decision-makers and facilitators, ensuring that they empower their teams while also making timely decisions when necessary. *Semco is a Brazilian conglomerate known for its unique approach to leadership and decision-making. Founded by Ricardo Semler, the company has adopted a balanced approach between the Decision maker and Facilitator leadership styles. In Semco, leaders encourage employees to participate in decision-making processes, similar to the Facilitator style. Teams are given significant autonomy, and employees have the freedom to set their work hours and salaries. This approach empowers employees, fosters creativity, and leads to a strong sense of ownership and commitment.*

However, Semco also acknowledges the need for decisive leadership, particularly in critical situations. Ricardo Semler, as the CEO, assumes the Decision maker role when it comes to strategic decisions or addressing urgent issues. This balanced approach ensures that the company benefits from both collaborative decision-making and effective leadership when necessary.

When deciding between a Decision maker and Facilitator approach in leadership, several factors come into play like:

- **Nature of the Task**: The type of work and tasks involved can dictate the leadership approach. For routine tasks with well-defined processes, a Decision Maker style might suffice. Conversely, complex, creative, or ambiguous tasks may benefit from a Facilitator approach.
- **Team Maturity**: The maturity and experience level of team members are essential. Inexperienced teams may require more guidance and decision-making from leaders, whereas experienced and self-driven teams may thrive under a Facilitator's guidance.
- **Time Sensitivity**: Time constraints can heavily influence the choice. Urgent matters may necessitate quick decisions by a Decision maker, while less time-sensitive projects may allow for collaborative discussions.
- **Risk Tolerance**: The organization's risk tolerance and the consequences of decisions are critical. Decision makers can shoulder more significant responsibility, but Facilitators may distribute decision-making to reduce risk.
- **Innovation and Creativity Needs**: Organizations that prioritize innovation and creativity may prefer a Facilitator approach, as it encourages diverse perspectives and idea generation.
- **Communication and Collaboration Tools**: The availability and effectiveness of communication and collaboration tools and technologies can influence the decision. In a digital era, facilitating remote collaboration has become more accessible, favoring a Facilitator approach.
- **Leadership Style and Skills**: The leadership style and capabilities of leaders themselves can shape the choice. Leaders comfortable with one style may naturally lean in that direction.

- **Employee Engagement**: The level of engagement and job satisfaction among employees is crucial. A Facilitator approach can often lead to higher employee engagement and retention.
- **Organizational Goals**: The organization's overarching goals and strategies should align with the chosen leadership style. For instance, a company emphasizing agility and adaptability may lean toward Facilitator to encourage innovation.
- **Regulatory and Compliance Requirements**: In industries with strict regulations, a Decision maker approach may be necessary to ensure compliance and mitigate risks.
- **Customer and Stakeholder Expectations**: Understanding the expectations and preferences of customers and stakeholders can help guide the leadership approach. Some stakeholders may appreciate transparency and collaboration, while others may prioritize results.
- **Change Management Needs**: During times of significant change, a Facilitator approach can help employees feel more involved in the transformation process, fostering acceptance and buy-in.
- **Organizational Size**: The size of the organization can impact the feasibility of a leadership style. Smaller companies may have a flatter hierarchy and more flexibility, making Facilitator leadership more accessible.
- **Cost Considerations**: The resources required for each leadership style, including training and technology, can affect the choice, especially for smaller organizations with limited budgets.

The choice between being a decision-maker or a facilitator, or finding the middle ground, should align with the organization's culture, objectives, and the specific needs of the team and tasks at hand. It's a dynamic dilemma that requires leaders to continually assess and adjust their approach to achieve the best outcomes for their organization and team members.

Task-Oriented vs. Visionary

> This dilemma centers on the balance between leaders who focus on task-oriented goals and deliverables (task-oriented) and leaders who emphasize visionary leadership by inspiring teams with a long-term vision (visionary).

The Task-oriented vs. Visionary leadership dilemma is at the heart of how leaders choose to guide their teams and organizations. Task-oriented leaders prioritize immediate goals, efficiency, and tangible results. They excel at breaking down complex projects into manageable tasks, setting clear objectives, and ensuring deadlines are met. This style of leadership can provide stability and control in the short term, ensuring that daily operations run smoothly. On the other hand, Visionary leaders are driven by a long-term perspective. They focus on inspiring and motivating their teams by painting a compelling picture of the future. They encourage creativity, innovation, and out-of-the-box thinking, which can lead to groundbreaking ideas and sustained success. Visionary leadership often attracts top talent, as employees are drawn to the exciting possibilities presented by a forward-thinking leader.

However, the choice between these leadership styles is not binary, and the decision impacts various aspects of the organization. A task-oriented approach can ensure that critical day-to-day tasks are accomplished efficiently, reducing errors and maintaining stability. Still, it may lack the capacity to foster innovation or adapt to rapid changes in the business landscape. Conversely, a visionary leadership style can set a bold direction for the company and encourage employees to strive for greatness. However, it might risk neglecting immediate challenges or failing to translate grand visions into practical execution. The impact of this dilemma extends to areas like employee morale, organizational culture, and adaptability to change. A task-oriented leader may maintain a culture of discipline and accountability but could stifle creativity. Meanwhile, a visionary leader may cultivate an innovative atmosphere but struggle with maintaining focus on short-term goals.

Choosing Task-Oriented Leadership Only	
Pros	**Cons**
Efficient task completion.	May overlook long-term opportunities.
Clear objectives and deadlines.	Can lead to burnout if not balanced.
Risk mitigation in the short term.	Limited adaptability in rapidly changing environments.

Choosing Visionary Leadership Only	
Pros	**Cons**
Inspires creativity and innovation.	May overlook immediate challenges.
Attracts and retains top talent.	Vision may not always align with practical execution.
Long-term strategic advantage.	Requires consistent communication to maintain focus.

McDonald's Corporation, a global fast-food chain, is known for its Task-oriented leadership approach. The company has a standardized operational model that focuses on efficiency, consistency, and cost control. McDonald's leaders prioritize tasks and processes to ensure that every restaurant delivers the same experience to customers worldwide. This approach has enabled McDonald's to achieve remarkable consistency and profitability. However, it has also faced criticism for being slow to adapt to changing consumer preferences and societal health concerns. Task-oriented leadership has allowed McDonald's to maintain its market position and financial stability, but it may face challenges in responding quickly to industry disruptions.

Tesla, Inc., the electric vehicle and clean energy company led by Elon Musk, exemplifies Visionary leadership. Musk is known for his visionary approach, setting audacious long-term goals for Tesla and the industry as a whole. He envisions a future where electric vehicles and sustainable energy sources play a crucial role in mitigating climate change. Tesla's leadership emphasizes innovation, rapid development, and market disruption. This approach has led to groundbreaking products like electric cars, solar energy solutions, and battery technology advancements. Tesla's visionary leadership has positioned it as a market leader in electric vehicles and renewable energy. However, this approach is not without challenges, as it requires substantial capital investment and entails significant risks associated with innovation and market volatility.

Some questions for the leaders to reflect and answer to resolve the dilemma:

- How do you balance the immediate tasks that need completion with the long-term vision of where your organization should be headed?
- What role do your leadership style and personal strengths play in determining whether you lean more towards task-oriented or visionary leadership?
- Do you believe that a focus on tasks and a visionary approach are mutually exclusive, or can they complement each other?
- How do you motivate your team to stay focused on tasks while also inspiring them with a larger vision?
- Can you identify situations in which being task-oriented is more beneficial, and others where a visionary approach is essential?
- What strategies can you implement to transition between task-oriented and visionary leadership as needed?

There could be several factors that could influence this decision in the context of your organization like:

Organizational Culture: The existing culture can influence the preference for task-oriented or visionary leadership. A culture that values innovation may lean towards visionary leadership.

Industry Dynamics: Fast-paced industries may require a more task-oriented approach, while creative sectors may benefit from visionary leadership.

Team Skills and Composition: A highly skilled and self-motivated team might thrive with a visionary leader.

Market Conditions: Market stability or volatility can determine whether a task-oriented focus on immediate challenges is necessary or if a visionary leader is needed to navigate change.

Leadership Development: Your own leadership development and experiences may shape your preferred style, as well as your ability to switch between the two.

There are other areas that get impacted because of a choice of this dilemma like:

- Goal Achievement
- Employee Morale
- Long-Term Strategy
- Creativity and Innovation
- Adaptability to Change

The optimal choice between a Task-oriented or Visionary leader may involve a hybrid approach or transitioning between styles based on changing circumstances. The key is to align leadership with the organization's goals, challenges, and culture while remaining flexible to adapt as needed. *Sweetgreen is a fast-casual restaurant chain in the United States that offers healthy salads and bowls. The company strikes a balance between Task-oriented and Visionary leadership. In the context of day-to-day operations, Sweetgreen emphasizes Task-oriented leadership. The company maintains strict quality control and operational standards across all its locations. The leaders focus on efficient food preparation, inventory management, and customer service to ensure consistency and reliability in delivering healthy meals. This Task-oriented approach enables Sweetgreen to provide a consistent customer experience and maintain operational efficiency. On the other hand, Sweetgreen's leaders also embrace Visionary leadership in their broader mission and sustainability initiatives. The company is committed to promoting healthy eating, sustainability, and environmental responsibility. They have a long-term vision of transforming the fast-food industry by providing nutritious and locally sourced food. Sweetgreen's leaders prioritize innovation in menu offerings, sustainable sourcing, and community engagement. This Visionary approach has allowed Sweetgreen to differentiate itself in the market and attract customers who value healthy and environmentally conscious dining options.*

Several factors influence the decision of whether to choose a Task-oriented or Visionary leader in an organization. Here is a common set of factors to consider:

- **Organizational Culture**: The existing culture of the organization plays a significant role. If the culture values stability, efficiency, and a focus on the present, a Task-oriented leader may be more suitable. In contrast, if the culture encourages innovation, risk-taking, and long-term thinking, a Visionary leader might be a better fit.
- **Business Life Cycle**: The stage of the organization's life cycle matters. In a startup or a high-growth phase, a Visionary leader can inspire and drive innovation. As a company matures or faces challenges, a Task-oriented leader may be needed to streamline operations and ensure financial stability.
- **Industry Dynamics**: Different industries have unique demands. For highly regulated or risk-averse industries like finance or healthcare, a Task-oriented leader can ensure compliance and safety. In contrast, dynamic industries like technology or creative fields may benefit from a Visionary leader who can drive innovation.
- **Market Conditions**: The competitiveness of the market and the pace of change are crucial. In fast-moving markets, a Visionary leader may help seize opportunities, while in stable markets, a Task-oriented leader can maintain a competitive edge through efficiency.
- **Team Composition**: The composition of the workforce matters. If the team consists of experienced professionals who require less guidance, a Visionary leader may foster creativity. Conversely, a less experienced team might benefit from a Task-oriented leader's guidance and structure.
- **Financial Health**: The financial situation of the organization is vital. When facing financial constraints or declining revenues, a Task-oriented leader may be essential for cost-cutting and

recovery efforts. In prosperous times, a Visionary leader can invest in growth and expansion.

- **Stakeholder Expectations**: Consider the expectations of various stakeholders, including investors, customers, and employees. Some stakeholders may value stability and short-term returns, while others prioritize long-term growth and innovation.
- **Risk Tolerance**: Evaluate the organization's risk tolerance. Visionary leaders often take calculated risks to drive innovation, while Task-oriented leaders may prioritize risk mitigation and stability.
- **Change Management Needs**: If significant changes are on the horizon, such as mergers, acquisitions, or restructuring, a Task-oriented leader skilled in change management may be necessary to navigate transitions smoothly.
- **Leadership Succession**: Consider the organization's future leadership needs. Developing a pipeline of leaders with complementary skills is crucial for long-term success. A balance of Task-oriented and Visionary leaders in leadership succession planning can be beneficial.
- **Customer and Market Feedback**: Actively seek feedback from customers and monitor market trends. Customer preferences and market dynamics can guide the choice of leadership style to meet evolving demands.
- **Employee Feedback**: Listen to your employees. They can provide valuable insights into the leadership style they respond to best and what drives their motivation and productivity.

Balancing these two styles, where possible, can be a powerful approach. It involves recognizing when each style is most appropriate and integrating short-term objectives into a broader, long-term vision. This hybrid approach can harness the best of both worlds, providing stability, efficiency, and innovation within an organization. Ultimately, leaders must carefully consider the unique needs and circumstances of their organization to strike the right balance between being task-oriented and visionary.

Leading By Example vs. Delegating Ownership

> This dilemma involves deciding whether leaders should lead by setting examples and actively participating in tasks (leading by example) or leaders should delegate ownership and empower employees to take responsibility (delegating ownership) or wear different hats for different scenarios.

Leading by Example is a leadership approach where leaders actively participate in tasks, showing their team members how things should be done. This style involves direct guidance, hands-on involvement, and a focus on demonstrating the desired behaviors, work ethic, and dedication to achieving goals. When leaders lead by example, they become role models, providing a clear path for their team to follow. On the other hand, Delegating Ownership is a leadership approach where leaders entrust their team members with tasks, projects, or responsibilities, giving them autonomy and accountability for successful outcomes. This approach emphasizes empowerment, where leaders encourage team members to take ownership of their work, make decisions, and drive projects forward independently.

Choosing to lead by example can have several positive impacts on the organization. It ensures clarity in expectations, as leaders set a visible benchmark for performance. Team members can benefit from hands-on guidance and may find it motivating to witness their leaders' commitment. However, it can also lead to dependency, where team members rely heavily on leaders for direction and problem-solving, potentially stifling their growth and decision-making abilities. Conversely, opting for a delegating ownership approach empowers team members to take responsibility and initiative. It encourages leadership development and independence, which can be especially beneficial when dealing with a skilled and capable team. However, it may pose challenges related to ensuring accountability, effective communication, and the potential risk of errors when team members are entrusted with significant responsibilities

Choosing Leading By Example Only	
Pros	**Cons**
Team members receive clear direction and guidance.	Team members may become overly dependent on leaders.
Leaders set an example of expected behavior.	Team development may be stunted if leaders do most tasks.
Faster resolution of issues through direct leadership.	Leading by example can be time-consuming for leaders.

Choosing Delegating Ownership Only	
Pros	**Cons**
Team members feel more empowered and responsible.	Delegating ownership may lead to mistakes if team members are not fully prepared.
Opportunity for team members to develop leadership skills.	Ensuring accountability without direct involvement can be tricky.
Leaders can focus on strategic tasks.	Effective communication is crucial when delegating tasks.

Toyota is known for its "Leading by Example" approach to leadership. The company's founder, Kiichiro Toyoda, was deeply involved in the early development of Toyota's production system, known as the Toyota Production System (TPS). This approach has trickled down through generations of leadership, with top executives actively participating in continuous improvement initiatives, also known as "Kaizen." Toyota's leaders regularly visit production lines, work with employees, and set high standards for quality and efficiency. This approach has contributed to Toyota's reputation for quality and innovation, with a strong culture of learning from the top down. However, it can also result in slower decision-making processes, as leaders are deeply involved in various aspects of the business.

HOPE IS NOT A STRATEGY

Whereas, Google, a subsidiary of Alphabet Inc., leans toward "Delegating Ownership" in its leadership style. Google's co-founders, Larry Page and Sergey Brin, have actively empowered employees to explore their ideas and initiatives through the company's famous "20% time" policy, which allows employees to work on projects of their choice. This approach has led to innovations such as Gmail and Google News. Google's leaders trust their employees to take ownership of projects and make decisions, fostering a culture of creativity and autonomy. However, it can also pose challenges in terms of alignment and coordination, as different teams may pursue diverse projects. Nevertheless, this approach has contributed to Google's status as a leader in technological innovation.

Some questions for the leaders to reflect and answer to resolve the dilemma:

- How do you view the role of a leader in your organization: as a hands-on contributor or as an enabler of your team's success?
- What is the balance between fostering a culture of self-reliance and demonstrating leadership through personal involvement?
- Are there specific situations where leading by example is more effective, and others where delegating ownership makes more sense?
- How does the level of trust you have in your team members influence your approach to leading by example or delegating ownership?
- In what ways do your team's skills, expertise, and development needs impact your decision between leading by example or delegating ownership?
- How do you strike a balance between being a role model and ensuring your team has the autonomy to excel in their roles?

There could be several factors that could influence this decision in the context of your organization like:

Team Competency: The skill set and capability of your team members play a crucial role in determining whether they need more guidance (leading by example) or can take ownership of tasks (delegating

> ownership).
>
> **Time Sensitivity**: Urgency and timelines of tasks may lead to more direct involvement (leading by example) or allow for delegation (delegating ownership).
>
> **Complexity of Tasks**: The complexity of projects or tasks may dictate whether hands-on leadership or delegation is more suitable.
>
> **Organizational Culture**: The existing culture in your organization may encourage or discourage delegation based on trust and empowerment.
>
> **Leadership Resources**: The availability of leadership resources, including time and energy, can influence your approach to leading by example or delegating ownership.
>
> **There are other areas that get impacted because of a choice of this dilemma like:**
>
> - Employee Engagement
> - Work Culture
> - Employee Development
> - Leadership Trust
> - Workload Distribution

Leading by example and delegating ownership can coexist in the organization by adapting leadership approaches to specific situations. Leaders can lead by example when team members require guidance or when setting a precedent is important. Simultaneously, they can delegate ownership to foster autonomy and responsibility in their teams when tasks align with team capabilities and strategic goals. *Imagine a medium-sized tech startup called "InnoTech Solutions." InnoTech operates in the software development industry and has found success by balancing these leadership styles effectively. InnoTech's CEO, Sarah, believes in setting the tone through "Leading by Example." She actively participates in the ideation and early development stages of key projects, working alongside the development teams. Sarah's hands-on involvement helps establish high standards of quality and demonstrates her commitment to the company's mission. This approach is particularly valuable in critical phases of product development, ensuring that innovative solutions meet the desired quality benchmarks. However, InnoTech also encourages "Delegating Ownership." In this startup, department heads and team leads are given substantial autonomy to make decisions within their domains. For instance, the head of marketing, David, has the freedom to develop marketing strategies and campaigns, aligning them with the company's overall vision. This empowers him and his team to adapt quickly to market trends and respond to changing customer needs. In scenarios where innovation and high-quality output are paramount, Sarah leads by example, actively contributing to technical discussions and problem-solving. However, when it comes to operational functions like marketing, she encourages team members like David to take ownership of their domains. This balance allows InnoTech to remain agile, competitive, and innovative while maintaining high standards of quality.*

The choice between Leading by example and Delegating ownership is influenced by several critical factors that leaders and organizations must consider:

- **Nature of Tasks and Projects**: The complexity, criticality, and type of tasks or projects at hand play a significant role. Simple, routine tasks may be better suited for delegation, while complex, high-stakes projects might require more hands-on leadership.
- **Team Experience and Competency**: The skills and experience level of team members matter. Highly skilled and experienced teams may benefit more from delegated ownership, whereas less experienced teams may require more guidance through leading by example.
- **Time Constraints**: Time-sensitive projects or tasks may necessitate quick decision-making and action, favoring the leading by example approach. Longer-term projects might allow for a more delegated ownership style.
- **Leadership Development**: Consider the long-term growth and development of team members. Delegating ownership can be a powerful tool for leadership development, as it encourages team members to take on new challenges and responsibilities.
- **Organizational Culture**: The prevailing culture within the organization can influence leadership style. A culture that values autonomy and innovation may lean towards delegating ownership, while a culture that prioritizes control and adherence to procedures may lean towards leading by example.

- **Team Size**: The size of the team can impact the feasibility of certain leadership styles. Leading by example may be more manageable in smaller teams, while larger teams may require more delegation.
- **Risk Tolerance**: Consider the organization's risk tolerance. Leading by example can mitigate risks by providing direct oversight, while delegation may introduce more risk but also more innovation opportunities.
- **Task Complexity**: The complexity of the task or project can influence the leadership style. Tasks that require precision, attention to detail, and specific methodologies may lean towards leading by example.
- **Employee Engagement**: Consider the level of employee engagement and motivation. Delegating ownership can boost motivation and job satisfaction, but only if team members are ready for the responsibility.
- **Feedback Mechanisms**: Evaluate the organization's feedback mechanisms and communication channels. Effective communication is crucial for both styles, but particularly for delegation to ensure team members are aligned with expectations.
- **Resource Availability**: The availability of resources, including time, budget, and technology, can impact the choice. Leading by example may require more immediate resource allocation, whereas delegation may spread resources over a more extended period.
- **Change Management**: During times of change or transition, leadership style can have a profound impact. Leading by example can provide stability, while delegation can foster adaptability.
- **Alignment with Organizational Goals**: Consider how each leadership style aligns with the organizations overall goals and strategies. The chosen style should support the achievement of these objectives.
- **Client or Customer Expectations**: External factors, such as client or customer expectations, can influence leadership style. Some clients may prefer a more hands-on approach, while others may appreciate a more empowered, delegated team.
- **Regulatory and Compliance Requirements**: In regulated

industries, compliance and adherence to specific standards can drive the choice of leadership style. Leading by example may be necessary to ensure strict compliance.

The choice between leading by example and delegating ownership can significantly influence the organizational culture, team dynamics, and employee development. Striking the right balance, often by wearing different hats depending on the context, enables leaders to maximize their impact on their teams and the organization as a whole. Ultimately, effective leaders are those who can adapt their leadership style to align with the evolving needs of their teams and the goals of the organization.

Leadership Continuity vs. Fresh Perspectives

> **This dilemma revolves around the decision to either maintain leadership continuity by promoting from within (leadership continuity) or bring in external leaders to inject fresh perspectives and expertise (fresh perspectives) or striking a balance between the two.**

Opting for leadership continuity, where leaders are promoted from within, carries certain advantages. It helps maintain a sense of stability and consistency, as leaders are intimately familiar with the organization's history, culture, and operations. This can lead to smoother transitions and a sense of security among employees. Moreover, internal leaders often possess a deep understanding of the company's strengths and weaknesses, enabling them to make informed decisions that align with its long-term goals. However, an overemphasis on leadership continuity can sometimes result in complacency, resistance to change, and a lack of exposure to fresh ideas.

On the other hand, embracing fresh perspectives by bringing in external leaders introduces novel approaches, industry insights, and innovative thinking into the organization. External leaders may bring a wealth of experience and a global perspective, which can be invaluable in navigating a rapidly changing business landscape. They can swiftly implement changes, challenge the status quo, and drive innovation. However, this approach may also create disruption during leadership transitions, as these leaders must adapt to the organization's culture and build trust. Additionally, there's a risk of overlooking internal talent and losing institutional knowledge when constantly opting for fresh perspectives.

Choosing Leadership Continuity Only	
Pros	**Cons**
Stability and consistency in leadership.	Potential resistance to change.
Streamlined Processes	Limited exposure to new ideas and approaches.
Smooth transitions.	Risk of complacency.

Choosing Fresh Perspectives Only	
Pros	**Cons**
Innovation and new insights.	Disruption during leadership transitions.
Broader industry expertise.	Potential cultural clashes.
Rapid adaptation to market changes.	Loss of institutional knowledge.

ABC Technologies, a mid-sized software development company, has a history of promoting leadership continuity. They believe in nurturing talent from within and have a strong leadership development program. As a result, many top-level executives have risen through the ranks. While this approach fosters a sense of loyalty and stability, it has also led to some challenges. ABC Technologies occasionally faces resistance to change and innovation, as the leadership team tends to have a deep-rooted understanding of the industry but may be less open to fresh, disruptive ideas. However, their commitment to leadership continuity has ensured a strong company culture and deep industry knowledge.

Conversely, Innovate Solutions, a dynamic startup in the renewable energy sector, has embraced a fresh perspectives approach. They actively seek leaders from diverse backgrounds and industries who can bring innovative ideas to the table. This strategy has injected new energy into the organization and enabled them to stay at the forefront of technological advancements. However, it's not without its challenges. The rapid leadership turnover can sometimes disrupt company culture and create a sense of uncertainty among employees. Moreover, aligning the diverse leadership team around a unified vision can be a complex task. Nevertheless, their choice of fresh perspectives has positioned Innovate Solutions as an industry leader in innovation and sustainability.

Some questions for the leaders to reflect and answer to resolve the dilemma:

- How do our current leaders' strengths and weaknesses align with our organization's long-term goals?
- Are there untapped talents and potential leaders within our organization who can step up into leadership roles?
- What specific expertise and fresh perspectives could external leaders bring that might benefit our organization?
- How can we strike a balance between maintaining institutional knowledge and infusing fresh ideas into our leadership?
- What are the potential challenges and opportunities in transitioning leadership from within versus bringing in external leaders?
- What leadership development and onboarding strategies can ensure a smooth transition and integration of new leaders?

There could be several factors that could influence this decision in the context of your organization like:

Organizational Strategy: The alignment of leadership decisions with the overall strategic direction of the organization.

Market Dynamics: Understanding how external market conditions and competition affect the need for fresh perspectives or continuity.

Talent Pool: Assessing the availability of internal talent with leadership potential and the external talent pool.

Leadership Succession Planning: The effectiveness of the organization's succession planning and development programs.

> **Performance Metrics**: Tracking and evaluating the impact of leadership decisions on key performance indicators.
>
> **There are other areas that get impacted because of a choice of this dilemma like:**
>
> - Knowledge Transfer
> - Innovation and Change
> - Leadership Development
> - Employee Retention

Leadership continuity and fresh perspectives can coexist through a phased approach. Organizations can groom and promote talent from within while also periodically introducing external leaders for critical roles. This dual approach balances institutional knowledge with innovative thinking. *XYZ Consulting is a mid-sized management consulting firm that has successfully struck a balance between leadership continuity and fresh perspectives. They understand the value of retaining experienced consultants who have in-depth industry knowledge and a deep understanding of client needs. At the same time, they recognize the importance of infusing new ideas and approaches into their services. To achieve this balance, XYZ Consulting employs a dual-track leadership approach. They have a core group of long-standing partners who provide stability and continuity to the organization. These partners play a crucial role in maintaining client relationships and ensuring consistent service quality. Alongside them, XYZ Consulting actively recruits and promotes younger, innovative consultants who bring fresh perspectives and the latest industry insights.*

The decision to choose between leadership continuity and fresh perspectives is influenced by a multitude of factors. These factors can vary depending on the organization's size, industry, stage of development, and specific challenges. Here's a set of factors that commonly influence this decision:

- **Succession Planning**: The availability of suitable internal candidates for leadership positions is a crucial factor. If there are well-prepared, competent leaders within the organization, leadership continuity may be a natural choice. However, a lack of internal talent may necessitate seeking fresh perspectives externally.

- **Industry Dynamics**: Industries that experience rapid technological advancements or disruptive changes often benefit from fresh perspectives. In contrast, sectors with stable market conditions may find continuity more suitable.
- **Financial Stability**: Organizations facing financial challenges or those in need of a turnaround may opt for fresh perspectives to drive change and transformation. Stable, financially sound organizations may prioritize continuity to maintain their success.
- **Competitive Landscape**: The level of competition in the industry can impact the choice. Highly competitive industries may require fresh perspectives to gain a competitive edge, while less competitive sectors might focus on stability.
- **Organizational Size**: Larger organizations often have more resources to invest in leadership development and may be more inclined to maintain leadership continuity. Smaller companies might be more flexible in bringing in fresh perspectives due to their agility.
- **Market Position**: The market position of the organization matters. Market leaders may prefer continuity to preserve their market share, while challengers may seek fresh perspectives to disrupt the status quo.
- **Strategic Goals**: The organization's strategic goals and objectives are paramount. If the strategy involves significant transformation, entering new markets, or diversification, fresh perspectives may align better. Conversely, if the strategy emphasizes consolidation and optimization, leadership continuity might be favored.
- **Risk Tolerance**: The organization's risk tolerance influences the decision. Embracing fresh perspectives carries inherent risks, such as cultural clashes and initial disruptions, which need to be weighed against potential rewards.
- **Stakeholder Expectations**: Consideration of stakeholders' preferences, including shareholders, employees, and customers, is essential. Aligning leadership choices with stakeholder expectations can enhance trust and support.

- **Regulatory Environment**: In regulated industries, adherence to compliance and industry standards can be a major factor. Leadership continuity may offer better compliance continuity, while fresh perspectives can bring innovative compliance solutions.
- **Legacy Leadership**: The reputation and legacy of previous leaders can impact the choice. If outgoing leaders have a strong legacy and positive influence, there may be a preference for continuity.
- **Time Sensitivity**: Urgency can drive the choice. Organizations facing immediate challenges may opt for fresh perspectives to address issues quickly, while those with a longer planning horizon may prioritize leadership continuity.
- **Global Considerations**: For organizations with international operations, global perspectives and understanding may influence the decision. Sometimes, a mix of leaders with regional expertise and fresh global perspectives is sought.

To strike a balance between the two approaches, organizations need to carefully evaluate their specific needs, strategic goals, and the availability of internal talent. This might involve a hybrid model, where certain leadership positions are filled from within, ensuring continuity, while others are open to external candidates to infuse fresh insights. This balance can provide the stability of experienced leaders and the dynamism of new perspectives. Ultimately, the decision hinges on the organization's vision and its capacity to adapt to change. A well-considered approach to this dilemma can shape the organization's culture, performance, and its ability to thrive in a rapidly evolving business environment.

Change Agent vs. Stability Maintainer

> This dilemma concerns whether leaders should actively drive change and innovation within the organization (change agent) or prioritize maintaining stability and continuity (stability maintainer) or striking a balance between the two.

Opting to be a Change agent involves actively driving transformation and innovation. This approach can inject fresh ideas, new processes, and innovative strategies into the organization. Leaders who embrace this role often push boundaries, challenge the status quo, and seek out new opportunities for growth and improvement. They are change catalysts who promote agility and adaptability, making the organization more responsive to market shifts and competitive challenges. However, the path of a Change Agent may be marked by short-term disruptions, resistance from employees, and the need for substantial resources and energy to implement change successfully.

On the other hand, choosing to be a Stability maintainer places a premium on preserving the organization's current state. Leaders who adopt this stance prioritize continuity, consistency, and reliability. They focus on maintaining well-established processes, ensuring that existing products or services meet quality standards, and upholding a stable working environment. Stability Maintainers can be seen as guardians of organizational traditions and values, which can be reassuring to employees and stakeholders. However, this approach might hinder adaptability and innovation, making the organization less responsive to evolving market dynamics and less attractive to top talent seeking new challenges.

Striking a balance between being a Change agent and a Stability maintainer requires finesse and a nuanced understanding of the organization's needs. Leaders who can harmonize these seemingly opposing roles can foster a culture of controlled innovation, where change is purposeful and aligned with the organization's core values and objectives. They create an environment where employees feel secure in their roles while being encouraged to explore new ideas and approaches. This approach can lead to sustainable growth, enhanced employee satisfaction, and a resilient organization capable of navigating both stability and change.

Choosing Change Agent Only	
Pros	**Cons**
Potential for rapid adaptation to market trends.	Short-term disruptions and uncertainty.
Increased innovation and competitiveness.	Resistance from employees and stakeholders accustomed to stability.
Attraction of dynamic talent seeking opportunities for growth.	Risk of strategic inconsistency.

Choosing Stability Maintainer Only	
Pros	**Cons**
Consistent operations and product/service quality.	Vulnerability to market changes and competitive pressures.
Higher employee morale and satisfaction.	Limited potential for growth and innovation.
Reduced risk of overextending resources.	Reduced appeal to forward-thinking talent.

Box Inc., a cloud content management company, is known for embracing a Change Agent approach. Under the leadership of Aaron Levie, the company has continuously evolved its services and technologies to stay ahead in the competitive cloud storage and collaboration space. Box expanded from file storage to enterprise content management, targeting enterprise clients, and diversifying its offerings. This Change Agent strategy allowed Box to adapt to shifting market dynamics and emerging technologies, positively impacting its growth and ability to attract larger enterprise customers. However, this approach also carried risks, with rapid expansion and technology shifts sometimes requiring significant resources and adaptation efforts.

Berkshire Hathaway, led by Warren Buffett, epitomizes the Stability Maintainer approach. Buffett's leadership style is characterized by a focus on long-term value investing, financial stability, and maintaining a diversified portfolio of established companies. Berkshire Hathaway typically acquires well-established businesses in traditional industries like insurance, utilities, and manufacturing. This Stability Maintainer strategy has yielded consistent, albeit not explosive, growth over the years. It offers stability and reduced exposure to market volatility, making it attractive to investors seeking a more conservative approach. However, critics argue that this approach may miss out on opportunities for disruptive growth seen in more dynamic investment portfolios.

Some questions for the leaders to reflect and answer to resolve the dilemma:

- How willing are we to embrace change and disruption in our organization's strategies and operations?
- Do we believe that stability and continuity are more critical than adaptability and innovation in our industry?
- Can we identify specific areas within our organization where change is needed, and where stability is essential?
- Are we prepared to accept short-term disruptions and uncertainties for the sake of long-term innovation and growth?
- How well do we understand the current dynamics of our industry and market, and how do they influence our decision?
- Are we open to collaborating with different leadership styles within our organization to find a balance between change and stability?

There could be several factors that could influence this decision in the context of your organization like:

Market Volatility: The level of turbulence in your industry can greatly impact the choice between change and stability.

Customer Expectations: Understanding what your customers demand—whether it's innovation or consistency—plays a vital role.

Competitive Landscape: The actions and strategies of your competitors can influence your decision to either lead change or maintain stability.

Resource Availability: The availability of resources, including time, budget, and skilled personnel, affects your ability to drive change.

Organizational Culture: The existing culture of your organization can either support or resist change initiatives.

There are other areas that get impacted because of a choice of this dilemma like:

- Organizational Resilience
- Adaptation to Market Trends
- Employee Satisfaction
- Risk Management
- Market Competitiveness

Change agents and Stability maintainers can coexist in an organization by creating a structured approach that balances innovation and continuity. This requires clear delineation of responsibilities, effective communication, and a shared vision of the organization's goals.*Etsy, an online marketplace for unique and handcrafted goods, demonstrates a remarkable balance between being a Change Agent and a Stability Maintainer. Etsy is known for its commitment to sustainability and social responsibility. It actively encourages sellers on its platform to use eco-friendly materials and practices. This change-driven approach aligns with evolving consumer preferences for sustainable products and ethical business practices. Etsy continually updates its policies to promote these values, reflecting its role as a Change agent in promoting responsible and ethical commerce. At the same time, Etsy maintains a stable and user-friendly platform that empowers small business owners and artisans. It provides a stable and reliable marketplace for sellers, ensuring they have a consistent platform to showcase their products. This approach aligns with its role as a Stability Maintainer, offering a reliable platform for sellers to grow their businesses over time. Etsy's ability to balance these roles has contributed to its sustained growth and success. By promoting change in line with societal and environmental values while providing stability for its users, Etsy has positioned itself as a platform that appeals to both socially conscious consumers and small business owners seeking reliable and consistent support. This balance allows Etsy to adapt to changing market dynamics while maintaining the trust and loyalty of its user base.*

The decision of whether to choose a Change agent or a Stability maintainer as a leader within an organization is influenced by various factors beyond just culture and leadership style. Here's a set of key factors that play a pivotal role in this decision:

- **Organizational Life Cycle**: The stage of the organization's life cycle can heavily influence the leadership approach needed. Startups and early-stage companies often require Change agents to drive growth and innovation, while more mature organizations may benefit from Stability maintainers to optimize processes and maintain consistency.
- **Market Dynamics**: The competitive landscape and market volatility are critical considerations. Fast-changing markets might require change agents to stay ahead, while stable markets might favor stability maintainers to sustain success.
- **Industry Type**: Certain industries, like technology or fashion, are inherently dynamic and favor change agents. Conversely, regulated industries, such as finance or healthcare, may lean toward stability maintainers due to compliance and risk management.
- **Financial Health**: The financial state of the organization matters. Change initiatives can be resource-intensive, so financial stability may determine whether a company can afford to be innovative.
- **Employee Skills and Attitudes**: The existing skills and attitudes of the workforce are crucial. An employee base open to change and possessing adaptable skills can align with a Change agent's approach, while a more risk-averse workforce may prefer Stability maintainers.
- **Leadership Team's Composition**: The leadership team's

makeup can influence the decision. If the executive team is already filled with Change agents, bringing in a Stability maintainer may provide balance and vice versa.

- **External Pressures**: External factors such as regulatory changes, customer demands, or disruptive technologies can force organizations to adopt a Change agent approach to remain competitive.
- **Strategic Goals**: The organization's strategic goals and objectives play a pivotal role. If the goal is rapid expansion or market disruption, a Change agent might be preferable. In contrast, if stability and efficiency are paramount, a Stability maintainer could be the choice.
- **Employee Turnover**: High turnover rates might necessitate a Change agent approach to continually attract and retain talent. In contrast, low turnover may signal a stable work environment, favoring Stability maintainers.
- **Historical Performance**: Past performance and the organization's track record can influence the decision. If previous change initiatives were successful, leaders may opt for a Change agent approach.
- **Customer Expectations**: Customer preferences and expectations can guide the leadership style. In industries where customers demand constant innovation, change agents may be necessary.
- **Risk Tolerance**: The organization's appetite for risk is a critical factor. Change initiatives inherently carry risks, and an organization with a low risk tolerance may opt for Stability maintainers.
- **Global Presence**: If the organization operates globally, it might require leaders who can adapt to diverse markets and cultures, which could favor Change agents with cross-cultural experience.
- **Resource Availability**: The availability of resources, including time, capital, and personnel, can impact the choice. Organizations with limited resources may lean toward Stability maintainers who can maximize efficiency.

In summary, the decision between being a Change Agent or a Stability

Maintainer is pivotal, as it shapes the organization's culture, strategy, and long-term success. While each approach has its merits and drawbacks, the most effective leaders often find ways to balance both roles, leveraging stability as a foundation for innovation and using change as a means of ensuring the organization's relevance and competitiveness in a rapidly evolving world.

Step 4

DISCOVER YOUR COMPANY'S CORE AND NON-NEGOTIABLE VALUES

Identify the beliefs, philosophies and principles that drive your business

Core company values shape your company culture and impact your business strategy. They help you create a purpose, improve team cohesion, and create a sense of commitment in the workplace. Non-negotiable values are those that are integral to your business and cannot be compromised for optimization or profits.

Every company has a unique way of doing things, a special character that sets it apart. This character is shaped by values. But how do we find these genuine values, especially when there's a trend to just pick popular buzzwords? Let's dive into understanding the real essence of values and why it's crucial to find ones that truly represent a company.

The Trap of Fancy Values

Many organizations, in a bid to emulate industry giants, often cherry-pick values from the playbook of successful companies. This approach is flawed. Adopting values merely because they've worked for another doesn't guarantee success. It's akin to wearing someone else's shoes; no matter how stylish they might be, if they don't fit, they'll only cause discomfort.

The Power of Authentic Values

Authentic values aren't about sounding impressive; they're about being genuine reflections of an organization's ethos. They're the principles that have naturally guided a company's decisions, especially during challenging times. The benefits of such authenticity are manifold:

- Creating a Unique Identity: Authentic values carve out a distinct identity, setting a company apart in a saturated market.
- Attracting and Retaining Talent: Employees resonate more with genuine values, leading to higher engagement and retention rates.
- Guiding Decision-making: Authentic values serve as a reliable compass during decision-making processes, ensuring consistency and alignment with the company's core beliefs.

Understanding Different Types of Values

- **Permission-to-Play Values or non-negotiable values:** Basic standards or behaviors expected within an industry or company. They don't differentiate a company but are essential for operation.
- **Core Values:** The fundamental beliefs guiding a company's

actions and decisions. They remain consistent over time and are intrinsic to the company's identity.
- **Aspirational Values:** Values that a company aspires to achieve in the future. They reflect where the company wants to be.
- **Accidental Values:** These emerge spontaneously, often reflecting the personalities of early employees or specific circumstances.

Types of Values with Examples

Type of Value	Description	Example
Core Values	Fundamental beliefs guiding behavior.	Amazon's 'Customer Obsession'.
Aspirational Values	Values a company aims to have in the future.	A small company aspiring for global reach might value 'diversity'.
Permission-to-Play Values	Basic behavioral standards.	In pharmaceuticals, 'safety' and 'integrity'.
Accidental Values	Values that arise spontaneously.	A tech startup's early employees might create a value of 'playfulness'.

Discovering Authentic Values

True values aren't about picking phrases that resonate well in boardrooms or sound impressive in annual reports. They are deeply rooted in the very fabric of an organization's decision-making process, especially during challenging times. To truly identify these genuine values, one must revisit the deliberations and thought processes that leaders underwent during Step 3, when resolving the dilemmas. It's in these moments of introspection and decision-making that the organization's authentic values shine through.

It's not about selecting values that sound trendy or appealing to the masses. It's about digging deep and recognizing what the organization genuinely identifies with. What are the principles that are non-negotiable, no matter the circumstances? What aspirations does the company hold for its future? By aligning with values that genuinely reflect the organization's beliefs and aspirations, companies not only set a clear path for their present but also lay a foundation for the future they envision. These values become the guiding principles, ensuring that every decision, big or small, is a step towards that envisioned future.

Translating Values into Behaviors

Identifying values is just the beginning. The real challenge lies in translating these abstract concepts into tangible behaviors. This involves defining what each value means in practice and, equally importantly, what it doesn't. For instance, if 'integrity' is a value, it might translate to behaviors like 'honoring commitments' and 'transparent communication.'

How to Use These Values

Values, once identified and translated into behaviors, should be embedded into the company's DNA. They should guide hiring decisions, performance reviews, and even strategic planning. They should be celebrated, reinforced, and, when necessary, defended. As you navigate the journey of defining your company's culture, remember to be genuine. Let your unique experiences and beliefs guide your values. And for those seeking further inspiration, the end of this book offers examples of common value words, their meanings, and their behaviors. Use them as a starting point, but remember, the true essence of your company lies within its unique experiences and beliefs.

You can see a few sample values translated to behaviours and actions and explained in different scenarios at https://www.alignbydesign.in/hopeisnotastrategy#

Step 5

BRING IT ALL TOGETHER

Document to get everybody in the organization on the same page

The "Culture Manifesto" serves as a guiding star for companies, offering a clear beacon of what the company believes in and stands for. On the other hand, the "Culture Handbook" functions as a detailed map, offering guidance on how things operate within the company.

The output of resolving the dilemmas will give us a clear view of who we want to be and what is acceptable and not acceptable in the company. We also get a clear view on how things work in the company - like how decisions are made, how accountability is given, how communication is done etc. These inputs go into the culture manifesto and the culture handbook.

The Culture Manifesto: Your Company's Guiding Star

Imagine you're on a big ship in the middle of the sea. The sea is like the business world - vast and sometimes unpredictable. Now, every ship needs a bright light to guide it, especially when it gets dark or stormy. That's what the Culture Manifesto is for a company. It's like a shining star that shows the way.

In simple words, the Culture Manifesto tells everyone what the company believes in and stands for. It's like a story that tells people what to expect when they join the company or work with it. It's not just about making the company look good; it's about being honest about what the company is like.

The Culture Handbook: Your Company's Map

Now, while the guiding star shows the direction, you also need a map to know the paths to take on your journey. That's where the Culture Handbook comes in. It's a detailed guide about how things work in the company.

The Culture Handbook is like a rulebook, but it's not just about rules. It tells new people how to fit in and what's expected of them. It also shares stories and traditions that make the company special. So, it's like a welcome guide for newcomers, helping them feel at home and do their best.

Using Both Tools for Success

Together, the Culture Manifesto and the Culture Handbook help everyone in the company know where they're going and how to get there. They help attract the right people to the company and make sure everyone works well together. Just like a ship needs both a guiding star and a map to reach its destination, a company needs both these tools to succeed in the business world. You can see a few sample values translated to behaviors and actions and explained in different scenarios at https://www.alignbydesign.in/hopeisnotastrategy

Step 6

BRING CULTURE TO LIFE

Defining is the first step. Getting it to life is when magic happens

To enliven the culture, providing guidance on what and how things are done, leadership behaviors aligning to the company values, emphasizing consistent demonstration and recognition of desired behaviors and adapting by acquiring new skills and communication methods, ensuring resilience and success are key.

Culture is the heartbeat of an organization. It's the way people think, act, and interact. While it's easy to write down a list of values or beliefs, the real challenge is making them come alive in the daily life of the company. This chapter will break down how to do just that, in a way that's easy to understand and implement.

Why Culture Matters

Think of culture as the personality of a company. Just like a person, if a company says one thing and does another, it can feel confusing or even dishonest. That's why it's not enough to have a list of values on a wall. Those values need to be seen in action every day. When this happens, everyone knows what to expect and how to behave, making work smoother and more enjoyable.

Four Simple Aspects of Making Culture Real

- **Processes and Playbooks**: Think of these as the rulebook or guidebook for your company. It's not just about what you do, but how you do it. This isn't about strict rules, but giving everyone a clear idea of how things work. It's like having a recipe when cooking a new dish. The recipe helps you know what ingredients to use and the steps to follow, but you can still add your own touch.#
- **Leadership Behaviors**: Leaders are like the captains of a ship. If the captain is calm and confident, the crew feels safe and works well. But if the captain is unsure or dishonest, the crew gets worried and things fall apart. So, leaders need to show the values of the company in everything they do. If they want honesty, they need to be honest. If they want hard work, they need to work hard too.#
- **Sustained Reinforcement**: Imagine trying to grow a plant. You can't just water it once and expect it to grow. You need to water it regularly. The same goes for culture. You need to keep showing and rewarding the behaviors you want to see. This could be through awards, stories, or just simple thank you. The key is to do it regularly.
- **New Knowledge and Behaviors**: As the world changes,

companies need to change too. This means everyone might need to learn new things or act differently. This could be new skills for a job or new ways to communicate. The important thing is to keep learning and growing, so the company stays strong and successful.

CREATING PROCESSES AND PLAYBOOKS

Clear Processes: The Blueprint for Daily Work

Processes are like recipes. They give step-by-step instructions on how to get things done in the organization. By having clear processes, everyone knows what to do and how to do it. This helps in making sure things run smoothly and consistently. Imagine a kitchen where everyone is trying to bake a cake. If there's no recipe, everyone might do it differently. Some cakes might turn out great, while others might not. But if there's a clear recipe to follow, every cake has a better chance of turning out delicious.

In the same way, when a company has clear processes, everyone knows the "recipe" for their work. This means fewer mistakes, less confusion, and a better outcome for everyone. But it's not enough to just have these processes in our heads. Writing them down is important. This way, everyone can refer to them, and new people can learn them easily. It's like having a cookbook for the company!

Playbooks: The Guide to Company Culture

While processes are like recipes, playbooks are like guidebooks. They don't just tell us how to do things; they tell us why we do them and what's important to the company. For new people joining the company, a playbook is like a welcome guide. It helps them understand what the company values and how they fit in. It's like joining a new sports team and getting a handbook that tells you the team's history, its star players, and its winning strategies.

For example, think of a company that believes in treating every customer like family. Their playbook might have stories of employees going above and beyond for customers. It might talk about the importance of listening and understanding. New employees can read this and quickly understand that in this company, customers are not just numbers; they're like family.

Real-Life Impact of Processes and Playbooks

Let's look at two examples to understand this well.

First, think of a tech company that started small but grew very quickly. In the beginning, everyone knew what they were doing because they were a small team. But as they grew, they wrote down their processes. This helped the new people they hired understand their work quickly. Even as they became a big company, they still felt like a close-knit team because of these processes.

Next, consider a shop that believes every customer should feel special. They created a playbook that talked about the importance of a personal touch. Every new employee read stories of how other employees made customers feel special. This inspired them to do the same. As a result, customers loved coming to this shop because they always felt valued.

In both these examples, the companies used processes and playbooks to make sure everyone was on the same page. This helped them work better and stay true to what they believed in.

In conclusion, having clear processes and playbooks is like having a map and guidebook for a journey. They help everyone know where they're going and how to get there, making the journey smoother and more enjoyable for everyone.

LEADERSHIP ACTIONS - LEADERS AS ROLE MODELS

Leaders are like the captains of a ship. They guide the direction, set the pace, and inspire the crew. Their actions and words shape the environment, or in business terms, the culture of the organization.

Why Leaders Matter in Culture Building

Leaders are the ones who set the tone. If they act with honesty, the team learns to value trust. If they encourage new ideas, the team feels free to innovate. Simply put, the way a leader behaves becomes a mirror for the team. So, if a leader wants a positive, hard-working, and innovative culture, they need to show those traits first.

Understanding and Living the Values

Before leaders can inspire others, they need to know what they stand for. This means taking time to think about the values that are important to the organization. It's not just about picking nice words but choosing values that leaders truly believe in. Once they have these values, leaders need to show them in their actions every day. This way, the team knows that these aren't just words on paper but principles to live by.

How Leaders Can Show and Share the Culture

- **Clear Communication:** Leaders should talk about the values often. They can share stories that show these values in action or explain why certain values are important. This helps the team see the bigger picture.#
- **Celebrate Good Work:** When someone does something great, leaders should celebrate it. This shows the team what behaviors are appreciated and encourages more of the same.#
- **Create a Safe Space:** Teams should feel safe to share ideas or concerns. Leaders can create this environment by listening, not blaming, and encouraging open conversations. This way, the team knows they're in a place where they can grow and learn.#

Look at Patagonia, a company known for caring about the environment. Its founder, Yvon Chouinard, didn't just talk about being eco-friendly; he showed it in the company's actions. This made the team believe in the value of sustainability. Or take Mary Barra from General Motors. She believed in being open and taking responsibility. So, when things went wrong, she faced them head-on. This taught her team the importance of accountability and learning from mistakes.

In short, leaders are the heart of an organization's culture. They set the example, and the team follows. So, for a strong, positive culture, leaders need to lead with purpose, clarity, and heart.

SUSTAINED REINFORCEMENT

Why Continuous Reinforcement is Essential

Embedding a strong culture isn't a one-time task. Think of it as tending to a garden. You can't just plant seeds and expect them to grow without care. Similarly, to ensure a culture flourishes, leaders need to consistently nurture and reinforce it. Without this regular attention, the essence of the culture might fade or be overshadowed.

Stories That Make an Impact

Stories have a unique power to resonate and stick in our minds. When leaders share tales of the company's values in action, it paints a vivid picture of what's expected. For instance, if a company prides itself on exceptional customer service, narrating an incident where an employee went above and beyond can inspire others to emulate such behavior.

The Value of Anti-Stories

But it's not just about celebrating successes. Sometimes, sharing stories of missteps or "anti-stories" can be equally impactful. These tales highlight what happens when cultural values are overlooked. For example, if a company emphasizes honesty, discussing an instance where transparency was compromised can underscore the importance of always being truthful.

Consistent Conversations about Culture

Keeping culture at the forefront requires continuous dialogue. This means integrating cultural discussions into regular team meetings, performance reviews, and training sessions. For instance, if teamwork is a core value, leaders can kick off meetings by spotlighting a team that collaborated exceptionally well.

Recognizing and Rewarding Cultural Champions

One of the most effective ways to encourage adherence to cultural norms is through recognition and rewards. When employees see their peers being celebrated for embodying cultural values, it motivates them to act similarly. For example, if innovation is a cherished value, recognizing someone who introduced a groundbreaking idea can inspire a culture of continuous creativity.

In essence, to deeply embed a culture, it's crucial to consistently talk about it, share both positive and "anti-stories," and reward those who exemplify the desired behaviors. With persistent effort, these practices can make the culture an intrinsic part of the company's identity.

NEW KNOWLEDGE AND BEHAVIORS

Acknowledging the Cultural Aspiration

While leaders and employees might recognize and appreciate the importance of a desired culture, there's often a gap between this acknowledgment and its practical implementation. This gap isn't necessarily due to resistance or disagreement but can arise from a lack of understanding or capability to manifest these cultural values in daily operations.

The Learning Gap in Cultural Transformation

Let's take the concept of 'radical candor' as an example. A company might identify radical candor as a pivotal value to foster open communication and drive growth. However, while managers might understand the concept in theory, they may struggle to practice it in their day-to-day interactions. They might either be too direct, bordering on rudeness, or too soft, avoiding critical feedback. This is where the learning gap becomes evident. Recognizing the value of radical candor and effectively practicing it are two different things.

Formal and Informal Learning: Filling the Gap

To bridge this gap, organizations need to align their formal and informal learning and development efforts with their desired cultural values.

- *Formal Learning:* Structured training sessions can be designed to teach managers the nuances of radical candor. Through role-playing, case studies, and interactive workshops, managers can learn how to give honest feedback without being hurtful and how to encourage their teams to do the same.

- *Informal Learning:* On the other hand, informal learning opportunities, like mentorship programs or peer discussions, can provide managers with platforms to share their experiences, challenges, and learnings around practicing radical candor. These platforms can offer invaluable insights, tips, and real-life examples that can guide managers in their journey.

Aligning Development Efforts with Cultural Values

For a desired culture to truly take root, learning and development initiatives must be in sync with it. Every training program, workshop, or informal learning session should be seen as an opportunity to reinforce and bring to life the cultural values the organization aspires to. When employees, especially leaders, are equipped with the right knowledge and behaviors, they not only embody the desired culture but also inspire others to do the same.

In essence, while recognizing a desired culture is the first step, equipping the workforce with the tools, knowledge, and behaviors to live it out is crucial. Only then can an organization truly transform its culture from a mere aspiration to a lived reality.

CLOSING NOTE

Dear Reader,

As we wrap up "Hope is not a strategy," we want to emphasize the deep influence of culture and alignment in any organization's success. We started this book to spotlight the often-missed elements that make companies thrive.

In our Author's note, we talked about the common misunderstandings around culture and alignment. Through this book, we've tried to clear up these misconceptions, stressing that just hoping isn't enough. Real success comes from deliberate actions, regular reminders, and a solid commitment to culture.

Think of culture as the backbone of an organization. It's what guides and connects everyone, influencing their choices and actions. Just as the smell of fresh bread can bring back memories, a strong culture can drive an organization to achieve great things.

However, understanding culture's importance and actually making it a part of daily operations are two different things. This is where leaders and teams need to come together, aligning their goals and values to succeed.

We've shared real-life examples and practical advice to show how to build and maintain a strong organizational culture. Whether they're stories of companies that have thrived or examples from sports, we've given a complete picture of what it takes.

To be honest, we have high hopes for this book. We want you to finish it not just with new knowledge, but with a drive to make changes. To be proactive. To question the usual ways. And to understand that while hope is essential, it's the deliberate steps, rooted in a strong culture, that truly make a difference.

We recognize that our exploration of culture and alignment is just the beginning. While this book has delved deeply into these critical aspects, we acknowledge there's more to be written, particularly on Steps 4, 5, and 6.

We chose to release this framework first because getting the foundation right is crucial. Implementation matters, but without a solid understanding of what needs to be implemented, efforts can fall short. Consider this book as your groundwork for building a culture that not only exists but thrives.

But then, we can't just 'hope' to write the next book, can we?

So here's our public commitment - we will finish the draft of the next book focusing on Steps 4, 5 and 6 in 2024 and you can hold us accountable!

In closing, we ask you to think, reflect, and take action. Culture isn't just an idea; it's the heart of your organization. And just like our hearts need care to keep us going, culture needs regular attention to keep an organization on the right track.

Remember - you will find additional resources on our website https://www.alignbydesign.in/hopeisnotastrategy and you can write to us at harish@alignbydesign.in or sirisha@alignbydesign.in if you have any additional queries.

Thank you for being with us on this journey. Here's to creating organizations that don't just hope for the best but actively work towards it.

Best wishes,
Harish & Sirisha

REFERENCES

- Ghoshal, S. (2005). Bad Management Theories are Destroying Good Management Practices. Academy of Management Learning & Education, 4(1), 75–91.
- Chatman, J. A., & O'Reilly, C. A. (2016). Paradigm lost: Reinvigorating the study
- Ferguson, A., & Moritz, M. (2015). Leading: Learning from Life and My Years at Manchester United. Hachette Books.
- Choudary, S. P. (2015). Housing.com: What went wrong? Harvard Business Review. https://hbr.org/2015/07/housing-com-what-went-wrong
- Isaac, M. (2019). Super Pumped: The Battle for Uber. W. W. Norton & Company.
- Chesky, B. (2016). Airbnb's Work to Fight Discrimination and Bias. Airbnb Newsroom.
- Nadella, S., & Nichols, G. (2017). Hit Refresh: The Quest to Rediscover Microsoft's Soul and Imagine a Better Future for Everyone. HarperBusiness.
- Agarwal, R. (2020). OYO's Response to COVID-19: A Message from our Founder & Group CEO. OYO Rooms Blog.
- Choudhury, S. (2019). OYO's Ritesh Agarwal Sets Up Culture Advisory Board. LiveMint.
- Maheshwari, S. (2019). Oyo Bet Everything on China and India. Now It's Paying the Price. The New York Times.
- Sharma, M. (2020). Inside OYO's Culture Overhaul. People Matters.
- Sull, D., Homkes, R., & Sull, C. (2015). Why Strategy Execution Unravels—and What to Do About It. Harvard Business Review.
- Chatman, J. A., & Cha, S. E. (2003). Leading by Leveraging Culture. California Management Review, 45(4), 20-34.
- Berson, Y., Oreg, S., & Dvir, T. (2008). CEO values, organizational culture and firm outcomes. Journal of Organizational Behavior
- Schein, E. H. (2010). Organizational culture and leadership (Vol. 2). John Wiley & Sons.
- Kotter, J. P., & Heskett, J. L. (1992). Corporate Culture and Performance. Free Press.
- Denison, D. R. (1990). Corporate culture and organizational effectiveness. John Wiley & Sons.

- Cameron, K. S., & Quinn, R. E. (2011). Diagnosing and changing organizational culture: Based on the competing values framework. John Wiley & Sons.
- Hsieh, Tony. (2010). Delivering Happiness: A Path to Profits, Passion, and Purpose. Business Plus.
- Schein, E. H. (2010). Organizational culture and leadership (Vol. 2). John Wiley & Sons.
- Isaac, Mike. (2019). Super Pumped: The Battle for Uber. W. W. Norton & Company.
- Sinek, Simon. (2014). Leaders Eat Last: Why Some Teams Pull Together and Others Don't.
- Schein, E. H. (2010). Organizational culture and leadership (Vol. 2). John Wiley & Sons.
- Kotter, J. P., & Heskett, J. L. (1992). Corporate Culture and Performance. Free Press.
- Denison, D. R. (1990). Corporate culture and organizational effectiveness. John Wiley & Sons.
- Cameron, K. S., & Quinn, R. E. (2011). Diagnosing and changing organizational culture: Based on the competing values framework.
- Sinek, Simon. (2009). Start with Why: How Great Leaders Inspire Everyone to Take Action.
- Sinek, S. (2009). Start with why: How great leaders inspire everyone to take action. Penguin.
- Dyer, J. H., Gregersen, H. B., & Christensen, C. (2011). The innovator's DNA: Mastering the five skills of disruptive innovators. Harvard Business Press.
- Brown, P. C., & Tedlow, R. S. (2003). The rise and fall of WeWork. Harvard Business Review.
- "Patagonia's Mission Statement." Patagonia.
- "The Zappos Family Mission Statement." Zappos. https://about.zappos.com/our-unique-culture/zappos-core-values
- "About Us." Swiggy. https://www.swiggy.com/about-us
- "Apple Mission Statement 2020." Mission Statement Academy. https://mission-statement.com/apple/
- "The Culture Code: The Secrets of Highly Successful Groups" by Daniel Coyle.
- "Why Apple Is a Great Marketer." Forbes.
- "Find Your Why: A Practical Guide for Discovering Purpose for

You and Your Team" by Simon Sinek, David Mead, and Peter Docker.
- "The Dream Manager" by Matthew Kelly.
- "Playing to Win: How Strategy Really Works" by A.G. Lafley and Roger L. Martin.
- "Playing to Win: How Strategy Really Works" by A.G. Lafley and Roger L. Martin.
- "The Dream Manager" by Matthew Kelly.
- "The Lean Startup: How Today's Entrepreneurs Use Continuous Innovation to Create Radically Successful Businesses" by Eric Ries.
- Harvard Business Review article, "A Look Back at Why Blockbuster Really Failed and Why It Didn't Have To" by Michael Schrage, provides an in-depth analysis of Blockbuster's missteps.
- "WeWork's Failed IPO Changed Everything for the Company" by Eliot Brown.
- "The Everything Store: Jeff Bezos and the Age of Amazon" by Brad Stone.
- Johnson & Johnson: Johnson & Johnson's recall of Tylenol in the Harvard Business Review case study, "The Tylenol Murders" by Richard A. D'Aveni.
- "BP's Deepwater Horizon Bill Tops $65bn," The Guardian, 2018
- "Patagonia's Anti-Growth Strategy," The New Yorker, 2015
- "Survey: 72% of Americans Say This Is the No. 1 Reason to Work," Motley Fool, 2020
- "Connecting People to Purpose," Gallup, 2017
- "Unilever's Sustainable Living Brands Deliver Superior Performance," Unilever Global Company Website, 2018
- "Volkswagen's Emissions Cheating Scandal: Five Years Later," Autoweek, 2020
- "B Corp Directory," B Corporation Official Website
- "Best Buy's Overseas Strategy Is Failing In Europe," Forbes
- "How Domino's Pizza Came to Be a Success Story in India," Business Today, 2018.
- "How Netflix Expanded to 190 Countries in 7 Years," Harvard Business Review, 2019.
- "Why In-N-Out Burger won't expand to the East Coast," CNBC
- "How Kodak Failed," Forbes, 2012.
- "The Tata way: Blending corporate strategy with a social

- conscience," World Finance, 2018.
- "IKEA's Innovation Strategy," Medium, 2020.
- "Nokia's fall from grace," The Telegraph, 2013
- "Google's 'Cultural Fit' Test Is as Cultish and Pseudoscientific as It Sounds," Quartz, 2017.
- "Infosys: The IT Crown Jewel," Forbes India, 2019.
- "How Diverse Leadership Teams Boost Innovation," BCG, 2018.
- "Zappos Family Core Values," Zappos Insights, 2020.
- "WeWork's Implosion Shows the Danger of Much-Hyped Leadership Styles," Quartz at Work, 2019.
- "The Google Way: Give Engineers Room," New York Times
- "BMW's Efficient Dynamic strategy: Less emissions with more driving pleasure," BMW Group, 2010.
- "Jack: Straight from the Gut," by Jack Welch, 2001.
- "From Command to Empowerment: An Indian Case Study," Human Resource Management International Digest, 1997.
- "Netflix: The 'Culture Deck' That Helped Shape Company's High-Performance Culture," Forbes, 2018
- "Flipkart's Valuation: Mark Down Blues," Forbes India, 2016.
- "Inside Apple's Culture of Secrecy," The New York Times, 2012.
- "The Responsible Company," by Yvon Chouinard and Vincent Stanley, 2012.
- "Amazon's Twitter Army Was Handpicked For 'Great Sense Of Humor,' Leaked Document Reveals," The Intercept, 2021.
- "Japan's 'karoshi' culture: Death by overwork," Aljazeera, 2019.
- "Novo Nordisk's 'Aspirational Working Hours' Program," 2018.
- "Infosys Well-being Framework," 2020.
- "Dotcom Bubble," Investopedia, 2020.
- "The Last Kodak Moment?," The Economist, 2012.
- "Reliance's Journey: From Textiles To Digital Services," Economic Times, 2019.
- "Unilever's Sustainable Living Plan," Unilever, 2020.
- "How Tesla's Strategy of Long-term Sustainability Has Paid Off," TechHQ, 2020.
- "Amazon's Customer Obsession," Forbes, 2019.
- "The Secret of Apple's Success: Product-centric Thinking," Medium, 2018.
- "How Flipkart Won India's E-commerce Market," Business Today, 2018.

- "The Rise and Fall of Nokia," BBC, 2018.
- "The Last Kodak Moment?," The Economist, 2012.
- "Samsung's Balancing Act Between Customer-centricity and Product Innovation," Marketing Interactive, 2020.
- "How Valve Stays Innovative with a Flat Organizational Structure," HBR, 2021.
- "Toyota Production System," Toyota Motor Corporation, 2020.
- "Netflix's Unique Culture and Organizational Structure," Forbes
- "Nokia's downfall: Blame its hierarchical structure," The Conversation, 2015.
- Rosenberg, A. (2015). 'The Cupcake Model: How Dropbox Scaled Up to Serve 400 Million Users', Medium. Retrieved from medium.com.
- Atlassian. (2023). 'Our Culture'.
- Isaac, M. (2019). 'Super Pumped: The Battle for Uber', W. W. Norton & Company.
- ByteDance. (2023). 'ByteDance Culture'.
- Wiedeman, R. (2020). 'Billion Dollar Loser: The Epic Rise and Spectacular Fall of Adam Neumann and WeWork', Little, Brown and Company.
- Ghemawat, P., & Nueno, J. L. (2006). Zara: Fast Fashion. Harvard Business School Case 703-497.
- Siemens AG. (2023). History.
- Zoho Corporation Pvt. Ltd. (2023). Culture.
- Kotter, J. P. (2012). Accelerate! Harvard Business Review, November 2012 Issue.
- Tesla, Inc. (2023). Tesla Culture.
- IBM Corporation. (2023). IBM Culture. Retrieved from IBM Careers page.
- Song, J. (2015). 'Samsung's Attempt To Transform
- Fan, Lixiong. (2018). 'How ByteDance Became the World's Most Valuable Startup.' Sixth Tone.
- Spotify Engineering Culture. (2014). Part 1 & Part 2.
- Isaacson, W. (2011). Steve Jobs. Simon & Schuster.
- Carlson, Nicholas. (2015). 'What Happened When Marissa Mayer Tried to Be Steve Jobs.' The New York Times.
- Clark, Pilita. (2019). 'The art of leadership, according to Ryanair's Michael O'Leary.' Financial Times.
- Gascoigne, J. (2013). 'Buffer's Salary Transparency Experiment: What We've Learned So Far.' Open.Buffer.com.

- Isaacson, W. (2011). Steve Jobs. Simon & Schuster.
- SAP SE. (2023). 'Our Company Culture.' Life at SAP.
- Newcomer, E. (2014). 'God View: Uber Allegedly Stalked Users For Party-Goers' Viewing Pleasure.' Buzzfeed News.
- Yuan, E. (2020). 'A Message to Our Users.' Zoom Blog.
- Spotify Engineering Culture https://vimeo.com/85490944
- "OYO in Full Expansion Mode in India After Raising $1 billion in Funding," Business Today, 2018
- "Open Company, No Bullsh*t: Atlassian's 5 Values," Atlassian Blog, 2017
- "Bad Blood: Secrets and Lies in a Silicon Valley Startup," John Carreyrou, 2018 -
- "Netflix Culture: Freedom & Responsibility," SlideShare, 2009"Toyota Culture: The Heart and Soul of the Toyota Way," McGraw-Hill, 2008
- "GitHub: How we got here," GitHub Blog, 2018
- "The rise and fall of Fab.com," The New York Times, 2015
- Atlassian Company Culture
- DBS Bank Annual Report 2019
- The Smartest Guys in the Room: The Amazing Rise and Scandalous Fall of Enron by Bethany McLean and Peter Elkind.
- "Leading: Learning from Life and My Years at Manchester United."
- TechCrunch, The Verge, or even in the book "Spotify Teardown: Inside the Black Box of Streaming Music."
- Apple's commitment to quality can be traced in various biographies of Steve Jobs, such as Walter Isaacson's "Steve Jobs,"
- Swiggy's balance of speed and quality
- Aristotle's concept of the 'Golden Mean' can be found in Aristotle's work "Nicomachean Ethics."
- "The Art of War" by Sun Tzu, "Leading" by Alex Ferguson,
- "The Hard Thing About Hard Things" by Ben Horowitz
- "The Evolution of Cricket: From Test to T20." The Roar, www.theroar.com.au/cricket/.
- "The Inside Story of How Spotify Transitioned to Remote Work." HRM Asia, www.hrmasia.com/spotify-remote-work-transition/.
- "The Rise and Fall of Blockbuster." Investopedia, www.investopedia.com/blockbuster-rise-and-fall/.
- "How Lego Became The Apple Of Toys." Fast Company,

- www.fastcompany.com/3040223/when-it-clicks-it-clicks.
- "The Bayern Code." DW, www.dw.com/bayern-munich-mia-san-mia/.
- "2018 Letter to Shareholders." Amazon,
- "The Evolution of Roles in Football: From Total Football to Tiki-Taka." Sportskeeda, www.sportskeeda.com/football/.
- "How Does a F1 Pit Crew Work?" Motorsport Week, www.motorsportweek.com/.
- "The Rise and Fall of Kodak." Forbes, www.forbes.com/kodak/.
- "Inside Zoho University's Unique Initiative." The Hindu BusinessLine, www.thehindubusinessline.com/zoho-university/.
- "T-Shaped Skills and Agile Organisations." Scrum.org, www.scrum.org/t-shaped-skills-agile-organisations.
- Drucker, Peter. "The Effective Executive: The Definitive Guide to Getting the Right Things Done." Harperbusiness Essentials, 2006.
- "IKEA: How the Swedish Retailer Became a Global Cult Brand." Business Case Studies, www.businesscasestudies.co.uk.
- "How Netflix's Customer Obsession Created a Customer Obsession." Harvard Business Review, www.hbr.org.
- "Nike's Mass Customization Model." Business Model Navigator, www.bmi-lab.ch/nike-id.
- "Kodak and the Brutal Difficulty of Transformation." Strategy+Business, www.strategy-business.com.
- "How Zoho Balances Standardization and Customization." ZDNet, www.zdnet.com/zoho.
- Drucker, Peter. "The Practice of Management." Harper & Row, 1954.
- Lewis, M. (2004). Moneyball: The art of winning an unfair game. W. W. Norton & Company.
- Byju's success story: How Byju Raveendran built a multibillion-dollar edtech firm. (2021, July 23). Business Today.
- NoBroker's journey to a $1 billion valuation. (2022, January 17). The Economic Times.
- Chandrasekaran, R. (2019, October 14). How Zoho aims to put Tenkasi on the map with 'swadeshi software'. The Economic Times.
- How Big Data Is Changing The Nature Of Sports. (2018, December 17). Forbes.
- Davenport, T. H., & Kirby, J. (2015). Beyond Automation.

- Harvard Business Review.
- "Leading at Scale: Spotify's Matrix Mission" - Harvard Business Review, 2020
- "How Zoho Built a Billion-Dollar Business" - Forbes India, 2020
- "Inside the Revolution at Etsy" - The New York Times, 2017
- "Manchester United: The Commercialisation of a Global Football Brand" - Sports Pro Media, 2010
- "Monzo's Radical Approach to Management" -Sifted, 2020.
- "Spotify's Agile Organizational Structure" - Corporate Finance Institute, 2021
- "Finnish EdTech Company Claned Uses AI to Personalize Learning" - eLearningInside, 2018
- "Zappos is struggling with Holacracy because humans aren't designed to operate like software" - Quartz, 2016
- "How Real Estate Start-up, NoBroker, Achieved Profitability" - Economic Times, 2020
- "The Pit Wall: The Nerve Centre of a Formula 1 Team" - F1 Chronicle, 2021
- "The Rise of Paytm: India's Leading Fintech Innovator" - Forbes, 2021.
- "BharatPe: Revolutionizing Digital Payments for Merchants in India" - Economic Times, 2021.
- "Leeds United: A cautionary tale" - Guardian, 2007.
- "Culture Eats Strategy for Breakfast" - Peter Drucker, Management Challenges for the 21st Century, 1999.
- "Netflixed: The Epic Battle for America's Eyeballs" by Gina Keating
- "How NoBroker turned a controversial idea into a successful business" by Anu Hariharan, Y Combinator Blog
- "Leadership Lessons from the T20 World Cup 2007" by Anil Kumble in Economic Times.
- "Zoho: From Humble Beginnings to Global Market Leader," TechRadar, 2021.
- "PropertyGuru's Collaboration Story," PropertyReport, 2022.
- "Byju's: A Case Study on Growth through Balance," HBR
- "Phil Jackson Quotes," BrainyQuote, 2021.
- "The Downfall of a Competitive Startup," European Business Review, 2023.
- "How Zoho Fosters Innovation," Business Today, 2022.
- "The Strategy of Byju's," Economic Times, 2022.

- "PropertyGuru's Path to Success," Southeast Asian Business Review, 2022.
- Hsieh, T. (2010). Delivering Happiness: A Path to Profits, Passion, and Purpose. New York, NY: Business Plus.
- Gino, F. (2019). The Business Case for Curiosity. Harvard Business Review.
- Sullivan, J. (2016). Netflix's Approach To Talent And Culture. Gartner.
- Dumitrescu, L. (2016). How Spotify Balances Employee Autonomy and Accountability. Harvard Business Review.
- Tindall, I. (2016). "BHS: How did it happen?" Retail Gazette.
- Scorsese, M. (2011). A Personal Journey with Martin Scorsese Through American Movies. The Criterion Collection.
- McChrystal, G. S., Collins, T., Silverman, D., & Fussell, C. (2015). Team of teams: New rules of engagement for a complex world. Penguin.
- Swisher, K. (2014). "Yahoo's Mayer on the Talent Hunt for Tech Stars Like News Digest's Nick D'Aloisio". Re/Code.
- Ek, Daniel. "How Spotify Saved the Music Industry (But Not Necessarily Musicians)." Freakonomics. 2021. https://freakonomics.com/podcast/daniel-ek-rebroadcast/
- Liker, Jeffrey K. The Toyota Way: 14 Management Principles from the World's Greatest Manufacturer. McGraw-Hill, 2004.
- "Why T20 is a different ball game for cricket." The Economist. 2010. https://www.economist.com/game-theory/2010/05/14/why-t20-is-a-different-ball-game
- Choudary, Sangeet Paul. "Zomato's Rough Ride in the Global Food Delivery Market." INSEAD Knowledge. 2017. https://knowledge.insead.edu/entrepreneurship/zomatos-rough-ride-in-the-global-food-delivery-market-6066
- Aaker, David A. Strategic Market Management. Wiley, 2001.
- Greenwald, Bruce C. N., and Judd Kahn. "Competition Demystified: A Radically Simplified Approach to Business Strategy." Penguin, 2005.
- Muñoz, George. "Kodak's Downfall Wasn't About Technology." Harvard Business Review. 2016. https://hbr.org/2016/07/kodaks-downfall-wasnt-about-technology
- https://mastersofscale.com/daniel-ek-how-to-build-trust-fast/
- Drucker, P. (1967). The Effective Executive. Harper & Row.
- Employee testimonial: www.glassdoor.com/Reviews/Go-Jek-

Reviews
- Zara's Business Model: www.forbes.com/zara's-fast-fashion
- Atlassian's Open Work Culture: www.atlassian.com/company/values/open-company-no-bullshit
- WeWork's Downfall: www.businessinsider.com/weworks-failed-ipo-explained
- Mercedes F1's Double-Stack Pit Stop: www.formula1.com/en
- Employee review: www.glassdoor.com/Reviews/Revolut-Reviews
- Toyota's Kaizen Approach: www.toyota-global.com/company/toyota_traditions/quality/mar_apr_2006
- Netflix's Culture: www.jobs.netflix.com/culture
- Theranos' Downfall
- Australian Cricket Team's Strategy: www.espncricinfo.com/australia/content/story/analysis.html
- Employee review: www.glassdoor.com/Reviews/Aldi-Reviews
- OYO's Disruptive Model: www.forbes.com
- Microsoft's Balance: www.cnbc.com/microsoft's-transformation-under-satya-nadella
- Kodak's Downfall: www.businessinsider.com/the-rise-and-fall-of-kodak
- Aldi's customer review: www.localnewspaper.com/aldi-review
- Gojek's success: www.techcrunch.com/gojek-success-story
- Arsenal's style of play: www.arsenal.com/style-of-play
- SpaceX's innovative approach: www.spacex.com/about-us
- Kodak's downfall: www.nytimes.com/kodak-fall
- IKEA culture: www.ikea.com/about-us
- Slack's diversity initiative: www.slack.com/diversity-and-inclusion
- Barcelona's Tiki-taka: www.bbc.com/tiki-taka
- English cricket team's diversity: www.ecb.co.uk/diversity-in-cricket
- Zomato's cultural balance: www.zomato.com/culture
- Abercrombie & Fitch's downfall: www.nytimes.com/abercrombie-fitch-downfall
- Blackberry's downfall: www.forbes.com/blackberry-downfall
- Salesforce's culture: www.salesforce.com/ohana-culture
- Jose Mourinho's management style: www.bbc.com/jose-mourinho-style

- Arsene Wenger's nurturing approach: www.arsenal.com/wenger-legacy
- Flipkart's culture: www.flipkart.com/culture
- Nokia's downfall: www.theguardian.com/nokia-downfall
- All Blacks Culture: https://www.rnz.co.nz
- Buffer's focus on employee happiness
- Amazon's work culture: https://www.nytimes.com
- Zappos' employee-centric approach: https://hbr.org/2010/07/how-zappos-infuses-culture-using-core-values
- Grab's people-centric culture: https://www.businesstimes.com.sg/hub/ceos-of-the-year-2019/grabbing-the-opportunity-to-make-a-difference
- Google's hiring strategy: https://www.inc.com/business-insider
- Yahoo's downfall: https://www.forbes.com/what-caused-yahoos-downfall/
- Mercedes and Red Bull Racing: https://www.autosport.com/red-bull-mercedes-f1-row-over-engin
- Zappos' customer service strategy: https://www.forbes.com/sites/micahsolomon/2018/09/15/the-secret-sauce-to-zappos-customer-service-success-recipe-included/
- Tesla's focus on internal operations: https://www.cnbc.com/2020/10/02/tesla-q3-2020-deliveries.html
- Reliance Industries' balanced approach: https://www.relianceindustries.com/about-us
- The downfall of Nokia: https://www.bbc.co.uk/news/technology-20095753
- Spotify's customer acquisition strategy: https://www.cbinsights.com/research/report/spotify-teardown/
- Adobe's focus on customer retention: https://www.forbes.com
- Grab's balanced approach: https://www.techinasia.com
- The downfall of MoviePass: https://www.vox.com
- Mailchimp's focus on user experience: https://www.userzoom.com/blog/mailchimp-and-the-importance-of-user-experience/
- Ryanair's bottom-line focus:

https://www.economist.com/gulliver/2019/09/06/ryanairs-ceo-on-the-secret-of-his-success
- Flipkart's balancing act: https://inc42.com/startups/flipkart-startup-story/
- The downfall of Kodak: https://www.bbc.com/news/business-16441930
- Liverpool FC's Brand Identity: https://www.liverpoolfc.com/corporate/brand-values
- Nykaa's Adaptability: https://www.forbesindia.com/article/real-issue/how-nykaa-has-changed-the-way-indian-women-buy-beauty-products/51791/1
- BlackBerry's Decline: https://www.bbc.com/news/business-24182067
- D-Mart's Employee-Centric Approach: https://www.moneycontrol.com/news/business/companies/d-mart-q2-profit-seen-up-40-employees-to-get-rs-279-cr-esop-benefit-5978351.html
- Better.com Layoff Incident: https://www.cnn.com/2021/12/05/tech/bettercom-ceo-apology/index.html
- Richard Branson Quote: https://www.virgin.com/richard-branson/my-philosophy-putting-your-employees-first-branson-centre-blog
- Formula 1's commitment to carbon neutrality: www.formula1.com/en/latest/features/2019/11/formula-1s-2030-carbon-neutral-plan-explained.html
- Zomato's "Feeding India" initiative: www.feedingindia.org
- Zomato's IPO: www.businesstoday.in/markets/ipo-corner/zomato-ipo-opens-today-issue-price-band-gmp-other-details/story/442696.html
- Volkswagen's 'Dieselgate' scandal: www.bbc.com/news/business-34324772
- Moneyball's approach to building a winning team: www.hbr.org/2004/09/moneyball
- SoundCloud's early focus on R&D: https://www.billboard.com/articles/business/8521538/soundcloud-200-million-users-ceo-interview/
- The fall of Nokia: https://www.investopedia.com/articles/markets/090215/story-behind-nokias-fall-grace.asp
- Tesla's R&D commitment: https://www.cnbc.com/elon-musk-

says-tesla-will-spend-billions-on-gigafactories-in-2020.html
- Adyen's balanced approach: https://www.adyen.com
- D-Mart's approach to ethics: https://economictimes.indiatimes.com
- Uber's growth-at-all-costs strategy: https://www.npr.org/ubers-tumultuous-year-in-5
- Buffer's radical transparency: https://buffer.com/transparency
- The downfall of Theranos: https://www.wsj.com
- Gravity Payments: https://www.inc.com
- WeWork: https://www.forbes.com
- Lemonade: https://www.forbes.com/sites/steveandriole/2020/07/16/lemonades-ipo-what-can-we-learn-from-it/
- Kodak: https://www.forbes.com/sites/chunkamui/2012/01/18/how-kodak-failed/
- Freshworks Culture: https://www.freshworks.com/company/careers/culture/
- Grab vs. Uber: https://www.reuters.com/article/us-uber-grab-idUSKBN1H30B9
- WeWork Crisis: https://www.bbc.com/news/business-50036819
- Salesforce: The Ohana Culture [Salesforce, 2021]
- Zoho Corporation: A Unique Management Approach [Forbes, 2022]
- Ferguson's Formula [Harvard Business Review, 2013]
- Bad Blood: Secrets and Lies in a Silicon Valley Startup [John Carreyrou, 2018]
- Screw It, Let's Do It: Lessons In Life [Richard Branson, 2006]
- Basecamp's Four-Day Work Week [Inc, 2020]
- Zomato's Work-Life Integration Approach [Economic Times, 2022]
- Klarna's Hybrid Work Model [TechCrunch, 2022]
- The Downfall of Yahoo [Business Insider, 2015]
- Alex Ferguson's Leadership Style [Harvard Business Review, 2013]
- Apple's Leadership-Centric Approach [Forbes, 2011]
- IKEA's Teamwork-Driven Model [Harvard Business Review, 2019]
- Zara's Emphasis on Teamwork [Business Insider, 2015]

- Salesforce's Balanced Model [Business Insider, 2020]
- WeWork's Failure [The New York Times, 2019]
- Phil Jackson's quote [ESPN, 2014]
- ByteDance's Learning Culture [HBR, 2021]
- Kodak's Downfall [Forbes, 2012]
- Spotify's Culture of Innovation [Business Insider, 2019]
- Leicester City's Complacency [BBC, 2017]
- Mahindra & Mahindra's Balanced Approach [Economic Times, 2021]
- Blockbuster's Failure [The Guardian, 2013]
- Zomato's Innovative Approach [Forbes India, 2022]
- Hermès's Emphasis on Experience [NY Times, 2019]
- The Decline of Sears [Business Insider, 2018]

ABOUT THE AUTHORS

Sirisha Bhamidipati

Sirisha is a highly accomplished professional with a diverse consulting, program management, and leadership development background. She completed her MBA from IIM A and a Fellowship in Leadership in Management from Carnegie Mellon University, where she was awarded the prestigious Nehru Fulbright scholarship. She is also a certified Design Thinking practitioner from d-school, Stanford University. With over a decade of experience working with Cognizant Technology Solutions, she managed complex domain-intensive engagements, ramping teams from 5 to 560 in less than six months. In 2015, Sirisha was recognized as a "Global Emerging Transformation Leader" by Training Magazine in the US.

Since 2017, Sirisha has been working on culture building, organization design, and people strategy consulting, focusing on driving 10X growth for her clients. She specializes in business leadership, strategic alignment, culture building, organization design, driving strategy to execution, leadership development, and driving innovation. Her expertise and experience have helped me become Align By Design, a sought-after partner for leaders who want to empower their companies through strategic alignment.

B V Harish Kumar

Harish is a seasoned entrepreneur and consultant with a background in engineering, innovation, and culture building. He has studied at the College of Engineering, Pune, and MDI Gurgaon. He has worked with several top companies, including Infosys, Cognizant, and BMC Software, in consulting, marketing, and project management roles.

In 2014, Harish co-founded Choose To Thinq, a boutique agency that helps individuals and teams build future relevance.

He has been instrumental in helping companies like VMware and IDeaS - an SAS company build a culture of intrapreneurship and pursuit of excellence.

In addition to his work with Global Captive Centres, Harish has also worked extensively with leadership teams in SMEs. He brings a wealth of experience from his own entrepreneurial journey, having started Tender Leaves - an innovative online book library service in 2010.

With his expertise in leadership advisory, change management, and habit building, Harish, co-founder at Align By Design, is committed to helping leaders empower their companies through strategic alignment and unlock their potential.

www.ingramcontent.com/pod-product-compliance
Lightning Source LLC
Chambersburg PA
CBHW030131170426
43199CB00008B/34